NETWORKS OF POWER IN MODERN GREECE

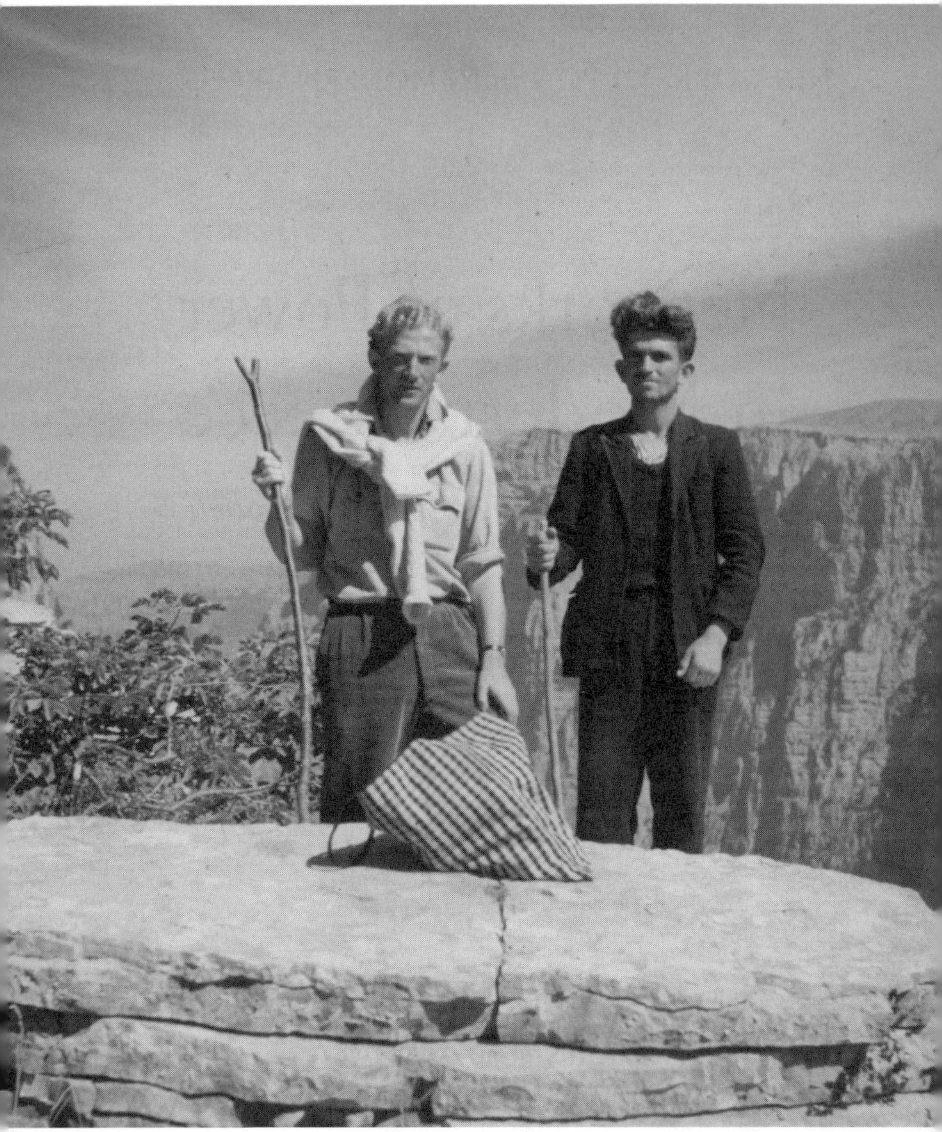

MARK MAZOWER
editor

Networks of Power in Modern Greece
Essays in Honour of John Campbell

HURST & COMPANY, LONDON

First published in the United Kingdom by
HURST Publishers Ltd,
41 Great Russell Street, London, WC1B 3PL
© Mark Mazower and the Contributors, 2008
All rights reserved.
Printed in India

The right of Mark Mazower and the Contributors
to be identified as the authors of this volume
has been asserted by them in accordance with
the Copyright, Designs and Patents Act, 1988.

A catalogue data record for this volume is available
from the British Library.

ISBN 978-1-85065-922-8

www.hurstpub.co.uk

CONTENTS

The Contributors — vii

1. Ottoman State Policy in Mediterranean Trade and Shipping, c.1780-c.1820: The Rise of the Greek-Owned Ottoman Merchant Fleet — 1
   Gelina Harlaftis and Sophia Laiou

2. Women in the Greek War of Independence — 45
   Helen Angelomatis-Tsougarakis

3. Villagers, Notables and Imperial Collapse: the Virgin Mary on Tinos in the 1820s — 69
   Mark Mazower

4. Dreaming of Buried Icons in the Kingdom of Greece — 89
   Charles Stewart

5. Bonds Made Power: Clientelism, Nationalism and Party Strategies in Greek Macedonia (1900-1950) — 109
   Basil C. Gounaris

6. 'Modern Greece': An Old Debate — 129
   John Koliopoulos

7. Andreas Papandreou: Radical without a Cause — 137
   Thanos Veremis

8. The Ethnographer as Theorist: John Campbell and the Power of Detail — 147
   Michael Herzfeld

9. Marital Failures: Glimpsing the Margins of Marriage
   in Greece   169
   Roger Just

10. Presents, Promises and Punctuality: Accountability and
    Obligation in Greek Social Life   189
    Renée Hirschon

11. Bread and Sheep: A Comparative Study of Sacred
    Meanings among the Ambeliots and the Sarakatsani   209
    Juliet Du Boulay

12. Sarakatsani Reflections on the Brazilian Devil   231
    João de Pina Cabral

13. John Campbell   255
    Michael Llewellyn Smith

Autumnal Refrain   269
    Haris Vlavianos

Index   271

THE CONTRIBUTORS

HELEN ANGELOMATIS-TSOUGARAKIS is Professor of Modern History at the Department of History, Ionian University. She defended her doctorate at the University of Oxford in 1986 and is the author of, among other works, *The Eve of the Greek Revival: British Travellers' Perceptions of Early Nineteenth-Century Greece* (Routledge, 1990); *Hē Ionios Akadēmia : to chroniko tēs hidrysēs tou prōtou Hellēnikou panepistēmiou, 1811-1824* (Athens, 1997), and *Ta taxidia tou Lordou Guilford stin Anitoliki Mesogeio* (Athens, 2000).

JULIET DU BOULAY is author of *Portrait of a Greek Mountain Village* (OUP 1974), of articles in anthropological journals, and of *Cosmos, Life, and Liturgy in a Greek Orthodox Village* (forthcoming, Denise Harvey).

BASIL C. GOUNARIS is Associate Professor of Modern History at the Department of History and Archaeology, Aristotle University of Thessaloniki. He is the author and editor of several works, including *Steam over Macedonia, 1870-1912: Socio-Economic Change and the Railway Factor* (Boulder, Co. 1993); *Stis ochthes tou Hydragora: oikogeneia, oikonomia kai astiki koinonia sto Monasteri, 1897-1911* (Athens, 2000), and *Egnosmenon Koinonikon Fronimaton*. His most recent work is *Ta Valkania ton Ellinon. Apo to Diafotismo eos ton A' Pankosmio Polemo* (Thessaloniki, 2007).

GELINA HARLAFTIS has graduated from the University of Athens in 1981 and has completed her graduate studies in the Universities of Cambridge (M.Phil.) at Newnham College (1981-1982) and Oxford (D.Phil.) at St Antony's College (1983-1988). She has taught at the University of Piraeus from 1991 to 2002 and since 2003 is Assoc. Professor at the Ionian University in Corfu. She is also President of the International Association of Maritime Economic History (2004-2008). Among her publications are *Greek Shipowners and Greece 1945-1975*, (Athlone Press, 1993), *History of Greek-owned Shipping* (Routledge, 1996), *Diaspora Entrepreneurial Networks: Five Centuries of History*, (Berg, 2005) with I. Baghdiantz McCabe and I. Minoglou. Her last book is with Maria Christina Chatziioannou, *Following the Nereids: Sea Routes and Maritime Business, 16th-20th Centuries*, (Athens, 2006).

MICHAEL HERZFELD, Professor of Anthropology at Harvard University since 1991, is the author of, among other works, *The Body Impolitic: Artisans and Artifice in the Global Hierarchy of Value* (Chicago, 2004), *Cultural Intimacy: Social Poetics in the Nation-State* (2nd edition, New York, 2005), and *Evicted from Eternity: The Restructuring of Modern Rome* (forthcoming 2009). He also filmed and produced *Monti Moments: Men's Memories in the Heart of Rome* (2007). Among the honours he has received are the Rivers Memorial Medal of the Royal Anthropological Institute (1994), the J.I. Staley Prize of the School of American Research (1994), and an honorary doctorate of the Université Libre de Bruxelles (2005). He is currently working on research on both Italian and Thai ethnography.

RENÉE HIRSCHON was educated at the universities of Cape Town, Chicago, and Oxford. The author of *Heirs of the Greek Catastrophe: the Social Life of Asia Minor Refugees in Piraeus* (Oxford, 1989), and editor of *Crossing the Aegean: An Appraisal of the 1923 Compulsory Population Exchange between Greece and Turkey* (New York, 2003), she is a Senior Research Fellow and College Lecturer, St Peter's College, University of Oxford. She is also a Senior Member of St Antony's College, and a Research Associate of the Refugee Studies Centre, Oxford University.

ROGER JUST studied Classics at the University of Melbourne. He came to Oxford in 1973 and completed his DPhil in Social Anthropology under the supervision of John Campbell in 1981. From 1982 to 1984 he was Assistant Director of the British School at Athens; from 1985 to 1989 Lecturer in Modern Greek Studies at the University of Melbourne; and from 1990 to 2001 Senior Lecturer in Anthropology at the University of Melbourne. Since 2002 he has been Professor of Social Anthropology at the University of Kent. He is the author of *Athenian Women in Law and Life*, and *A Greek Island Cosmos: Kinship and Community on Meganisi*.

JOHN S. KOLIOPOULOS is Professor of Modern History, Aristotle University of Thessaloniki. He is the author of many books including *Brigands with a Cause* (Oxford, 1987) and *Plundered Loyalties* (London, 1999). His latest work (with Thanos Veremis) is *Greece: the Modern Sequel* (London, 2002).

THE CONTRIBUTORS

SOPHIA LAIOU is lecturer in Ottoman History at the History Department, Ionian University. Her principal area of interest is the social and economic life of the islands of the Aegean Sea and the Greek mainland during the Ottoman period. She is the author of *I Samos kata tin Othomaniki periodo* (Thessaloniki, 2002), and is a member of the Turkish Studies Association and the Society of Mediterranean Maritime Historians.

MICHAEL LLEWELLYN SMITH was British Ambassador in Poland and Greece. He has written *Ionian Vision: Greece in Asia Minor, 1919-1922* (revised ed. London, 1998), *Athens: A Cultural and Literary History* (Oxford, 2004), *The Great Island: A Study of Crete* (1965) and *Olympics in Athens 1896: the Invention of the Modern Olympic Games* (London, 2005). He is now writing about the life and times of Eleftherios Venizelos.

MARK MAZOWER studied at St Antony's College, Oxford between 1983 and 1988 and taught at Princeton, Sussex and Birkbeck College London. Since 2003 he has been Professor of History at Columbia University. Among his publications are *Inside Hitler's Greece: the Experience of Occupation, 1941-44* (Yale UP, 1993), *Dark Continent: Europe's Twentieth Century* (London, 1998) and *Salonica, City of Ghosts: Christians, Muslims and Jews, 1430-1950* (London, 2004). His most recent book is *Hitler's Empire: Nazi Rule in Occupied Europe* (London, 2008).

JOÃO DE PINA-CABRAL is Research Coordinator at the Institute of Social Sciences of the University of Lisbon. He was President of the Portuguese Association of Anthropology (1989-1991) and President of the European Association of Social Anthropologists (2003-5). His books include *Sons of Adam, Daughters of Eve: the Peasant Worldview of the Alto Minho* (Oxford, 1986), *Between China and Europe: Person, Culture and Emotio in Macao* (London/New York, 2002), and as joint editor (with John Campbell), *Europe Observed* (Basingstoke, 1992) and (with Frances Pine), *On the Margins of Religion* (New York, 2007). He has published extensively and carried out fieldwork in the Alto Minho (Portugal), Macau (China) and Bahia (Brazil).

CHARLES STEWART is Reader in Anthropology at University College London and author of *Demons and the Devil: Moral Imagination in Modern Greek Culture* (Princeton, 1991) and editor of *Creolization: History, Ethnography and Theory* (Walnut Creek, CA., 2007).

THANOS VEREMIS is Professor of Political Science at the University of Athens and President of National Council of Education. He is the author of numerous works including *The Military in Greek Politics* (London, 1997) and (with John S. Koliopoulos) *Greece: the Modern Sequel* (London, 2002).

HARIS VLAVIANOS studied at Bristol and Oxford and is Professor of History and Politics at the American College of Greece (Deree). In addition to *Greece 1941-1949: From Resistance to Civil War* (London, 1992), he has published eight collections of poetry—the most recent being *After the End of Beauty* (2003) —and two books of essays, and has translated into Greek the works of such well-known poets as Whitman, Pound, Blake, Ashbery, cummings, Stevens, Longley and Pessoa. His own work has been translated into numerous languages.

1

OTTOMAN STATE POLICY IN MEDITERRANEAN TRADE AND SHIPPING, c.1780-c.1820: THE RISE OF THE GREEK-OWNED OTTOMAN MERCHANT FLEET[1]

Gelina Harlaftis and Sophia Laiou

"What indeed was an Ottoman ship? Few local mariners knew any rules of the sea, their papers were often incomprehensible, their crews resisted investigation with spirit. An honest Greek or Muslim was ordinarily armed to the teeth to defend himself; he might fly the red-white-blue of an Ottoman infidel, the green-white-red of a good Muslim, a Union Jack if he came from the Ionian Islands, or a blue and white striped flag if he was in Greek waters. The only true test was to see his cargo and his ship's papers. So unless a pirate were actually caught at his trade, naval captains risked a diplomatic row every time they sent a boarding-party to search a suspect vessel."[2]

Written by a British historian, this account of Ottoman ships implies that there were no rules or regulations, that the Ottoman vessels owned by either Christians or Muslims were under no jurisdiction and that they were synonymous with piracy and fraud. It is a view shared by many historians. Mainstream Greek historiography in particular has ignored the Ottoman political and economic framework within which the Ottoman Greek shipowners and captains were active. Behind this attitude, justified perhaps by the fact that

---

1   A first version of this article was presented at the XIVth International Economic History Congress in Helsinki, August 2006 under the title "Ottoman State, Finance and Maritime Trade: the Emergence of an Ottoman-Greek Fleet, 1780-1820".

2   Allan Cunningham, *Anglo-Ottoman Encounters in the Age of Revolution. Collected Essays*, vol. 1, edited by Edward Ingram, London: Frank Cass, 1993, p. 166.

until recently access to the Ottoman sources was difficult, there was the belief that the Ottoman state did not show any special interest in shipping and trade, since the latter did not coincide with the military, religious and bureaucratic structure of "Ottoman feudalism".[3]

The Ottoman alienation from the sea is "an age-old trademark" based on "civilizational terms", writes Edhem Eldem.[4] "The Ottomans were perceived and/or imagined as Turks and, as such, bore all the cultural traits of a nomadic people whose links with the sea were, by definition, tenuous, remote and, at best, accidental." Greek national historiography follows this line, interpreting the reliance of the Ottoman imperial navy on Greek seamen as a reflection of the "negligence and inability" of the "Turks" in trade and shipping. "It was only natural for the Greeks to develop commerce due to their ancient commercial tradition, Byzantine heritage, the sea environment and the backwardness of the conqueror."[5] Biological explanations are also used to support the view that "Turks have a natural aversion for the sea".[6] The fact that the Ottoman state had no merchant fleet of any significance and that not only its international but also its domestic trade during the 18th century was in the hands of the French is an argument frequently encountered in the French-language literature in particular.[7]

---

[3] Vassilis Kremmydas, "I Othomaniki autokratoria kai i anankastiki autonomisi tou emporiou" (The Ottoman Empire and the forced independence of commerce), *O Politis* 40 (1997), p. 33 and generally, pp. 30-3. For a similar view, expressed however in more direct terms, see Konstantinos Alexantris, *I anaviosis tis thalassias mas dynameos kata tin Tourkokratian* (The Revival of our Maritime Strength during Turkish rule), Athens: Ekdosis Istorikis Ypiresias B.N., 1960, pp. 27, 35.

[4] Edhem Eldem, "Strangers in their Own Seas? The Ottomans in the Eastern Mediterranean Basin in the Second Half of the Eighteenth Century", unpublished paper. We wish to thank Professor Eldem for making this paper available to us. It has recently been published in Turkish under the title "Kontrolü Kaybetmek: 18 Yüzyılın İkinci Yarısında Doğu Akdeniz'de Osmanlı Varlığı", Ö.Kumrular (ed.), *Türkler ve Deniz*, İstanbul: Kitap Yayınevi, 2007, pp. 63-78.

[5] Lazaros Houmanidis, "Peri tis oikonomias kai nautilias ton trion nison Ydras, Spetson kai Psaron kata tin Tourkokratian" (About the economy and shipping of the three islands of Hydra, Spetses and Psara during the period of Turkish rule), *Epistimoniki Epetiris tis Panteiou Anotatis Sholis Politikon Epistimon*, Athens 1972, p. 180.

[6] Michael Lambrinides, *Istorikai selides (1320-1821). Oi Alvanoi kata tin kyrios Ellada kai tin Peloponnison. Ydra-Spetsai* (The Albanians in the Greek Mainland and Peloponnese. Hydra and Spetses), Athens 1907, reprint, Athens: Notis Karavias Bookshop: 1987, p. 38.

[7] Daniel Panzac, "International and Domestic Maritime Trade in the Ottoman Empire during the 18th century", *International Journal of Middle East Studies*,

It is certainly true that during the period under examination Greeks in the eastern Mediterranean developed an important fleet based on the islands and port towns of the Aegean and Ionian seas. They did so as Ottoman or Venetian subjects, and under various flags, but mainly under the Ottoman. But thanks to the results of a major research project that has provided the archival evidence for this paper, many of the older assumptions described above look questionable.[8] The aim of this paper is twofold. The first is to demonstrate the importance of an Ottoman fleet involved in Ottoman external and domestic trade with deep-sea going vessels that were fully armed and owned by Ottoman Greeks. Ottoman-flag vessels traded in all the main Italian port cities and Malta from the beginning of the 18th century, and showed an extraordinary growth after the 1780s. Moreover, the records provide evidence of the existence of a large coastal shipping fleet that ensured a large portion of the short-distance trade of the Empire. The second aim is to examine the policy of the Ottoman state towards the merchant marine and commerce. Evidence from the Istanbul archives reveals that systematic records were kept of all Ottoman flag-vessels, following a policy, initiated by Selim III (1789-1807), of protecting Ottoman-flag ships and their captains, with the specific aim of limiting foreign competition. It seems that the Levantine mariners and their Ottoman rulers understood very well "the rules of the sea."

Ottoman ships in Mediterranean shipping

In the 1780s the main local merchant shipping fleets of the Mediterranean were on the western side the French and those of the Italian states, the Spanish and the Austrians, and on the eastern side the Ragusans and the Ottoman fleets. Not all fleets were involved in the long-routes of the Mediterranean trade, that is the trade between the Eastern and Western Mediterranean and beyond Gibraltar. The French, according to the statistics of Ruggiero Romano

---

24, 2 (1992), pp. 189-206. See also Eldem, "Strangers in their Own Seas?"

[8] The research project entitled "Greek Maritime History in the Eighteenth Century" was funded by the EU and the Greek Ministry of Education. Its aim was to identify, chart and interpret the path of the fleet of Ottoman and Venetian Greek subjects in the trade and shipping of the Mediterranean Sea during the 18th century. The project was led by Gelina Harlaftis and Katerina Papakonstantinou, who was the post-doctorate researcher; in charge of the research in the Istanbul Archives was Sophia Laiou. The team consisted of 20 individuals including Greek, Turkish, Italian, Maltese and Dutch researchers who worked in the Archives of Venice, Istanbul, Trieste, Malta, Messina, Naples, Livorno, Genoa, Marseillse, London and Amsterdam, along with those of Athens, Corfu, Cephalonia, Hydra and Spetses. More than 15,000 ships were registered for the period 1700-1821.

for the European merchant fleets in 1786-87, owned 5,268 ships of 729,340 tons; however, only a portion of these ships were involved in the Mediterranean trade, the others trading in the Atlantic and northern Europe.[9] The French ships trading between the Western and Eastern Mediterranean belonged almost entirely to Marseilles, which had the monopoly of trade with the Levant.[10] According to the above mentioned statistics, the five Italian regional states (which despite the various changes of power in the 1780s had remained as they were divided more or less since the 15th century) owned altogether the second biggest fleet in the Mediterranean with 2,350 ships (253,815 tons). But it was only the fleets of the Kingdom of the Two Sicilies (Naples) with 1,047 vessels (132,222 tons) and that of the Republic of Venice with 418 vessels (60,332 tons) that owned ships of an average size of 130-140 tons trading on the long routes of the Mediterranean. The rest, Genoa (and Piedmont), the Vatican State and Tuscany, owned small vessels that carried the local trade of the Italian peninsula and the regional trade within the Western Mediterranean, particularly with the French and Spanish coasts.

The third shipping fleet in the Mediterranean was that of Spain with 1,202 ships (149,460 tons). Almost all big Spanish ships were involved in the colonial trade; the Mediterranean Spanish fleet consisted of small vessels engaged entirely in the western Mediterranean trade, very rarely trading beyond Sicily and Malta. The fourth power that rose in the Adriatic—centred in Trieste—was that of the Hapsburg Empire, which in the late 1780s owned a fleet of 1,142 ships (84,090 tons). This fleet was composed of small and medium-sized vessels with an average size of 74 tons, equipped with crews from the Dalmatian coastline, and it was involved mostly in the trade between the Adriatic and the ports of the Italian peninsula.[11]

The two key local fleets of the Eastern Mediterranean were those of the Ragusans and the Ottomans. The Ragusans, whose state was affiliated to the Ottoman Empire, were among the traditional local seafarers of the Balkans, trading with big vessels in the Mediterranean. It seems that there was an upsurge of their shipping activities in the second half of the 18th century, and although they also carried cargoes from Salonica and Smyrna, they were heavily involved in the Alexandria-Livorno route.[12] In 1786 they owned 163 vessels of 40,479

---

9   For shipping statistics of all European fleets for 1786-1787, see Ruggiero Romano, "Per una valutazione della flotta mercantile europea alla fine del secolo XVIII", in *Studi in onore di Amintore Fanfani, V*, Milan 1962.

10 Paul Masson, *Histoire du commerce français dans le Levant au XVIIIe siècle*, Paris: Hachette, 1911, p. 97.

11 See fn. 9.

12 Jean Filippini, "Raguza e l'attività commerciale livornese nel Settecento" in Jean

tons, which means vessels of an average of 250 tons.[13] Ruggiero Romano in his statistics does not include the Ottoman fleet as there were barely any available statistics of Ottoman-flag vessels involved in the long routes of the Mediterranean, trading within the eastern Mediterranean and between the western and eastern Mediterranean. For the 1780s there is an estimate of about 400 vessels (48,000 tons); the fleet was composed of vessels of an average of 120 tons.[14] It seems then that in the 1780s, the Ottoman fleet was comparable to or even bigger than those of the once omnipotent sea powers of Genoa and Venice.

The Ottoman fleet was involved in the long routes of the Mediterranean and the Greeks were the traditional local seafarers of the Ottoman Empire who worked as merchant captains and seamen in Istanbul, the Black Sea and the Aegean ports, as shipwrights in the Ottoman shipyards, as crews in the Imperial Ottoman fleet, or as crews and captains in the fleets of the Barbary corsairs.[15] They owned small craft for the coastal trade between the islands and the main coasts of Greece and Asia Minor. In the late 18th century they emerged as the most dynamic neutral fleet in the Mediterranean and took advantage of European rivalry for the economic and political control of the Levant. They

---

Pierre Filippini, *Il porto di Livorno e la Toscana (1676-1814)*, vol. 2, Edizioni Scientifiche Italiane, 1998, p. 84.

13   Romano, op. cit.

14   The number of 400 Ottoman ships is an estimate based on French sources, given by Traian Stoianovich, "L'Economie balkanique aux XVIIe et XVIIIe siècles principalement d'après les archives consulaires françaises)", thesis, doctorat d'université, Université de Paris, 1952, p. 114, cited in Georgios B. Leon (Leontaritis), "Elliniki emporiki nautilia (1453-1850)" (Greek merchant shipping) in Stelios A. Papadopoulos, *Elliniki emporini nautilia* (Greek merchant shipping), Athens: National Bank of Greece, 1972, p. 42. The average tonnage of 120 tons for the Ottoman Greek vessels is based on evidence from *Amphitrete*. An estimate of the size of the Ottoman flag fleet is a work under process and will be published in Gelina Harlaftis and Katerina Papakonstantinou (eds), *The Rise of Greek Shipping in the Mediterranean Trade of the 18th Century*, forthcoming. Michel Fontenay, on the basis of the above evidence, has made an estimate of about 500 Ottoman Greek ships of 100 tons in his "The Mediterranean World, 1500-1800: Social and Economic Perspectives" in V. Mallia Milanes (ed.), *Hospitaller Malta, 1530-1798, Studies on the Early Modern Malta and the Order of St. John of Jerusalem*, Malta: 1993, pp. 41-110.

15   Vassilis Sfyroeras, *Ta ellinika pliromata tou tourkikou stolou* (The Greek Crews of the Turkish Fleet), Athens 1968; Aikaterini Bekiaroglou-Exadaktylou, *Othomanika naupigeia ston paradosiako elliniko choro* (Ottoman Shipyards in the Traditional Greek Area), Athens: Politistiko Technologiko Idryma ETVA, 1994, pp. 138-49; Halil İnalcık and Donald Quataert (eds), *An Economic History of the Ottoman Empire, 1300-1914*, Cambridge University Press, 1994, p. 181; Nikos Svoronos, *To emporio tis Thessalonikis ton 18o aiona* (The commerce of Thessaloniki in the 18th century), Athens: Themelio, 1996, p. 157.

competed with the other important northern European fleets that traded in the Mediterranean, such as the British, the Dutch, the Swedish and the Danish.¹⁶ By the end of the Napoleonic wars, under the Ottoman flag, they had more than doubled their fleet. After the 1820s, Greeks under the flag of the Greek state, along with the British, became the main carriers in the Eastern Mediterranean and the Black Sea during the rest of the 19th century.¹⁷

Results

We traced Ottoman Greek vessels and other Greek-owned vessels under various flags in Venice, Trieste, Malta, Livorno, Genoa, Marseilles, Barcelona, Malaga and Cadiz. In all ports, apart from Venice, Sanità Archives have survived for most or all the 18th century and up to the mid-19th century. These include detailed and valuable information, as they were registered by the quarantine officials, according to the declaration of their captains, concerning the name of the ship, the type of ship, name of captain, place of origin, nationality of vessel, number of seamen, port(s) where cargoes where loaded, kind of cargo and weight, length of journey, ports approached, merchants to which cargoes were destined (for sources see Appendix I).

The processed data as shown in Table 1, showing the annual average for every five year period of the arrival of Greek-owned ships under Ottoman and other flags, clearly indicate the impressive growth of Greek-owned vessels in Italian, Maltese, French and Spanish ports. Between 1773 and 1787 the number of Greek-owned vessels entering these ports rose fivefold, from 36 vessels to 166; the slight decline during the years 1788-92 is due to the second Russo-Ottoman war. During the first five years of the Napoleonic wars the annual number of Greek-owned ships entering the above-mentioned ports almost tripled in comparison with the previous five-year period: from 128 ships arriving annually during 1788-92 to 312 ships during 1793-97. Owing to the French conquests and Napoleon's Egyptian expedition there were some problems in the sea trade particularly during the period 1798-1802; the annual number of Greek-owned ships dropped to 290. In the next

---

16   According to the shipping statistics by R. Romano, the British in 1786 had the biggest European fleet with 881,963 tons, followed by the Dutch with 1,871 ships of 397,709 tons, by the Swedish with 1,224 ships of 169,279 tons. The Hanseatic towns owned the fourth biggest northern European fleet with 567 ships of 101,347 tons and the Portuguese the fifth one with 300 tons of 84,843 tons. Romano, "Per una valutazione".

17   Gelina Harlaftis, *A History of Greek-owned Shipping: The Making of an International Tramp Fleet, 1830 to the Present Day*, London: Routledge, 1996, tables 3.5-3.13.

five year period that included the beginning of the continental blockade in 1806, the Greek-owned vessels trading in the western Mediterranean ports reached their peak with the impressive annual average of 349 vessels.

Table 1: *Annual average for every five-year period of number of Greek-owned ships arriving at the ports Venice, Trieste, Malta, Livorno, Genoa, Marseilles, Barcelona, Malaga and Cadiz*

Year	Venice	Trieste	Malta	Livorno	Genoa	Marseille	Barcelona	Malaga	Cadiz	Total
1768-1772	8	11	9	10						38
1773-1777	11	6	5	14						36
1778-1782	13	26	25	18						82
1783-1787	11	40	73	30	12					166
1788-1792	13	14	55	39	7					128
1793-1797	10	25	39	71	134	33				312
1798-1802	7	3	63	71	110		15	12	9	290
1803-1807	17	1	147	91	13		22	35	23	349

Source: Appendix II

As is evident from Table 1, the importance of the Adriatic ports of Venice and Trieste shrank in comparison to those of the Italian western coast. Greek-owned ships, mainly under Ottoman flag, arrived in increasing numbers at Malta, Livorno and Genoa, reaching the unprecedented number of 250-300 on average annually during the Napoleonic wars (in contrast with the 20-30 ships that arrived in Venice and Trieste). Livorno and Genoa became the main centres of transit trade, with depots for grain that fed not only the northern Italian peninsula but also France, through Marseilles, and the Iberian peninsula, through Barcelona, Malaga and Cadiz.[18] At the time of

---

[18] For the Livorno grain trade see Jean Pierre Filippini, "Il commercio del grano a Livorno nel Settecento" in Jean Pierre Filippini, *Il porto di Livorno e la Toscana (1676-1814)*,vol. 2, pp. 318-71. For Marseilles see Charles Carrière, *Négociants marseillais au XVIIIe siècle,* Marseille: Institut Historique de Provence, 1973, vol. 2, pp. 57-67 and Ruggiero Romano, *Commerce et prix du blé à Marseille au XVIIIe siècle*, Paris 1956. For Genoa see Laura Calosci, "Génova y la transformación del comercio Mediterráneo de Cataluña (1815-1840)", Departament d'Història i Institucions Econòmiques, Divisio de Ciencies Juridiques, Economiques i Sociales, Universitat de Barcelona, 2002-2003, pp. 34-44. For Malaga, Cadiz and Barcelona see Eloy Martín Corrales, "Cereales y capitanes greco-otomanos en la Málaga de fines del siglo XVIII", in *Estudis d'Història Econòmica,*

the Napoleonic wars the Ottoman flag was a neutral flag and Ottoman ships replaced those of France which disappeared from the Levant trade after the 1780s[19]. The Ottoman vessels competed successfully with those of Ragusa and of other European powers to establish themselves as the main carriers of the Levant and the opening Black Sea grain market.

In the 1790s the Italian peninsula came under French control.[20] Grain was very much in demand and the sea trade continued on neutral vessels, since off the entrances of the main ports, the English navy and privateers of all nations were waiting to attack. In 1796 the Greek-owned vessels mainly under Ottoman flag (at least in Livorno, see Figure 7) followed an upward trend and in 1796 reached their peak; more than 500 vessels entered all main ports of the Italian, French and Spanish coast (Figure 1). It is mainly arrivals at the ports of Genoa (347 ships) and Marseilles (65) that shoot up. The victories of the French in the entire Italian peninsula, however, brought a wave of reaction. That same year commerce shrank, but it soon recovered and stabilized for the next six years (Figure 1). In June 1800 Napoleon struck again to reconquer Italy; the victory at Marengo over the armies of the Second Coalition marked the beginning of Italy's Napoleonic period. Between 1800 and 1808 all Italian territories of Italy fell directly under his control. In November 1806 Bonaparte imposed the Continental System to destroy British trade. But everywhere in Europe, merchants whose business was endangered by the blockade were able to penetrate the system, and the British turned Malta into their main transit trade point. Thus the next peak of Greek-owned vessels in the west was in Malta in 1809 with 347 ships (Figure 1) most under the flag of Jerusalem (see Figure 8).

	vol. 1989/2, pp. 87-114 and Eloy Martin Corrales, "La flota greco-otomana en Cádiz a fines del siglo XVIII" in *Actas del II Congreso de Historia de Andalucía, Andalucía Moderna (II)*, Cordoba 1995, pp. 389-400.
19	For an insightful analysis of the relations of the French Levant trade with Malta and the increasing competition from the Greeks and their eventual predominance in the Levant trade of the island see Xavier Labat Saint Vincent, *Malte, une escale du commerce français en Méditerranée au XVIII siècle*, Presses Universitaires de Paris Sorbonne, forthcoming, Part I, chapter III, section II.
20	Giulano Procacci, *History of the Italian People*, London: Penguin Books 1991, pp. 255-71; Girolamo Arnaldi, *Italy and its Invaders*, Cambridge, MA: Harvard University Press 2005, pp. 168-86.

Figure 1: *Greek-owned vessels under Ottoman and other flags in the ports of Venice, Trieste, Malta, Livorno, Genoa, Marseilles, Barcelona, Malaga and Cadiz, 1780-1815*

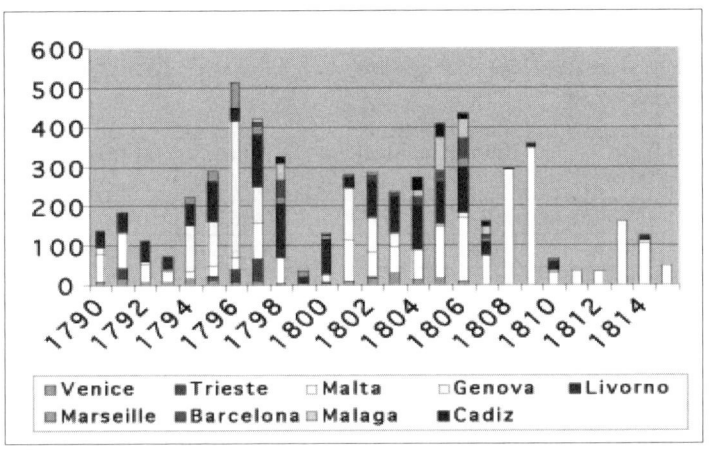

Source: as Appendix II

It is clear from the above analysis that the expanding Greek-owned fleet was a neutral fleet for most of the period under examination, using mainly the Ottoman flag, but also other flags if the political circumstances dictated. It thereby became highly important for the Levant trade, and particularly in grain for the main Western Mediterranean port cities. In the 1780s it carried almost 30% and in the 1790s almost 45% of the entire Levant trade of Livorno (Table 2). During the 1790s it carried one third of the grain from Levant and the Barbary States to Marseille (Table 3), while in 1796 Ottoman vessels were the only grain carriers to that city. But beyond grain and the Levant trade, the archival evidence indicates that Greek-owned vessels remained in the Western Mediterranean and carried the regional trade among Genoa, France, Spain and Portugal before returning to the Levant.[21] The presence of Greek-Ottoman ships in the Spanish ports of Barcelona, Malaga and Cadiz indicates their importance for the long distance trade and cabotage of these ports (Figure 1 and Appendix II).[22] In this way they became important not only in the grain trade from the Levant but in the total trade of these ports. The percentage of Greek-owned vessels in the total ship movements of Genoa and Livorno from 1792 to 1805 is indicated in Figure 2. During the years 1796-98 they comprised up to 30%

---

21 See Table 4 in this paper and Gelina Harlaftis, "Greek Shipping in the 18th Century" in Gelina Harlaftis and Katerina Papakonstantinou (eds), *The Rise of Greek Shipping in the Mediterranean Trade of the 18th Century*, forthcoming.

22 Eloy Martín Corrales, "Cereales y capitanes greco-otomanos en la Málaga de fines del siglo XVIII", in *Estudis d'Història Econòmica*, vol. 1989/2, pp. 87-114.

9

of Genoa's entire ship movements and 25% of Livorno's; in 1801 the Greek vessels comprised up to 25% of Genoese ship movements. In the years between they represented 5-10% of the total number of ships entering these two ports.

Table 2: *Ottoman Greek ships entering at the port of Livorno from Levant (annual average for a five-year period)*

Years	Ottoman Greek (a)	Total (b)	(a)/(b)
1768-72	6.6	65.8	10%
1773-77	10.6	82.8	13%
1778-82	9.2	78.8	12%
1783-87	24.6	94.4	26%
1788-92	30.2	103.2	29.3%
1793-97	61.8	142.2	43.5%

Source: Jean Pierre Filippini, *Il porto di Livorno e la Toscana (1676-1814)*, vol. 2, Edizioni Scientifiche Italiane, 1998, table XVIII, p. 145

Table 3: *Entries of ships to the port of Marseilles from the Levant and Barbary states*

Year	(a) All ships	(b) Greek-owned ships	(b)/(a)
1789	341		
1790	286	2	1%
1791	393	3	1%
1792	366		
1793	80		
1794	34	4	12%
1795	124	28	22%
1796	69	65	94%
1797	85	21	25%
1798	64	18	28%

Sources: a) see Charles Carrière, *Négociants marseillais au XVIIIe siècle,* volume 2, Marseilles, Institut Historique de Provence, 1973, p. 1043. b) Processed data from the data base *Amphitrete, 1700-1821,* Pythagoras Research Project, Ionian University/Greek Ministry of Education, 2006

Figure 2: *Percentage of Greek-owned vessels under Ottoman and other flags in the ports of Livorno and Genoa*

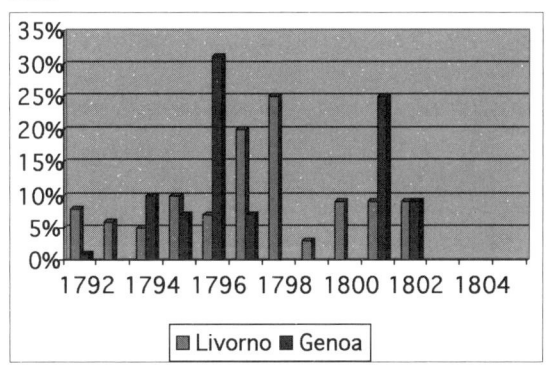

[Bar chart showing percentages from 1792 to 1804 for Livorno and Genoa]

Source: Appendix V

Naturally, Greek-owned vessels were not only significant in the main western Mediterranean ports, but also in the eastern Mediterranean and the Black Sea. The French consuls provide us with important information on the Greek-owned vessels in Alexandria and Odessa. Up to almost 400 Greek-owned vessels arrived in Alexandria in the 1780s, representing an average of 50% of the total arrivals at that port (Figures 3 and 4). These data stop abruptly with the French Revolution and restart in 1810, when almost 300 Greek-owned vessels are recorded in the following years (Figure 3), representing 70% of the total arrivals at that port. This is the period where the Russian grain started conquering the Mediterranean markets, when the Russian steppes began to be extensively cultivated, ultimately becoming the most important granary of Europe in the rest of the 19th century. Odessa, a new port city founded in 1794 by the Russians, as well as the port cities of the Azov, particularly Taganrog, witnessed an impressive and ever-increasing rate of grain exports.[23] Greek-owned vessels under the Ottoman and Russian flags from 1800 to 1821 constituted an average of 60% of Odessa's total departures and some times became the exclusive carriers of the Odessa exports (Figure 4).

---

23 For the increase in Russian grain trade and shipping from the Black Sea ports see Gelina Harlaftis, *A History of Greek-owned Shipping: The Making of an International Tramp Fleet, 1830 to the Present Day,* London: Routledge, 1996, table 1.2, pp. 18-19. For Odessa see Patricia Herlihy, *Odessa: A History, 1794-1914,* Cambridge, MA: Harvard University Press 1986.

Figure 3: *Greek-owned vessels under Ottoman and other flags at the ports of Alexandria and Odessa*

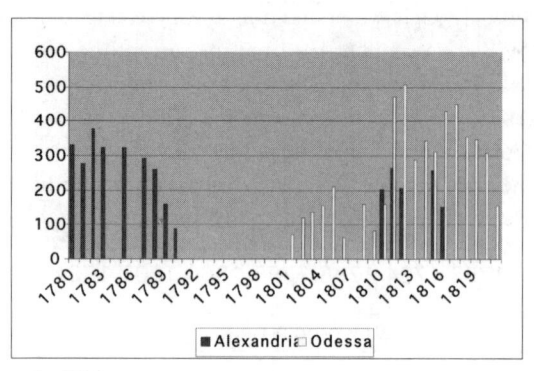

Source: Appendix VI

Figure 4: *Percentage of Greek-owned vessels under Ottoman and other flags of the total arrivals of the ports of Alexandria and Odessa*

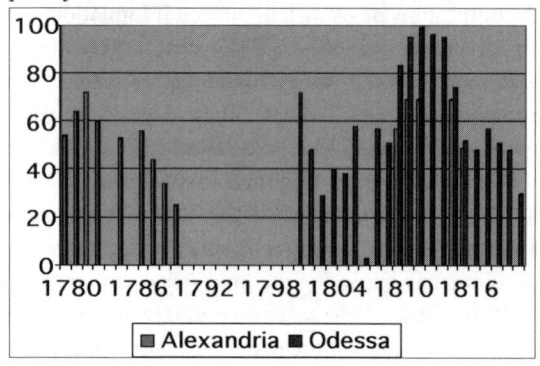

Source: Appendix VI

The Ottoman archives provide mainly information regarding trade between Istanbul and the Black Sea. This information consists of permits for Russian Black Sea ports like Hacabey or Odessa and Taganrog in the Azov, along with the ports of the south Black sea coast like Kerassund. As Figure 5 indicates, there was an upward trend in the 1790s in numbers of ships trading in the Black Sea. The gap in the issuing of permits as documented in the Istanbul archives after 1787 is the result of the second Russo-Ottoman war—a war really for the control of the Black Sea—waged between 1787 and 1792. Although the Greek-owned vessels in the ports of Genoa and Livorno especially flourished in the 1790s (see Figure 1), the low numbers we have from Istanbul include only permits to sail in the Black Sea ports, and the amount of cargoes of grain from the Black Sea was still low; grain still came from the Aegean coasts and southeastern Mediterranean. The rise in the number of permits to 40-60 ships during the period 1799-1802, however, indicates the increasing trade and the new dynamism of the Black Sea grain that from the turn of the century onwards conquered the Mediterranean and northern European markets(see Figure 5). Figures from 1804 to 1821 include mainly the evidence from Register no.3, which will be explained in detail in the next section (Table 5). This information indicates the large number of vessels involved in the Mediterranean and the opportunities they were able to seize during the Continental Blockade.

Figure 5: *Number of Ottoman Greek ships getting permits/documents from Istanbul for navigation in the Black Sea, 1780-1803*

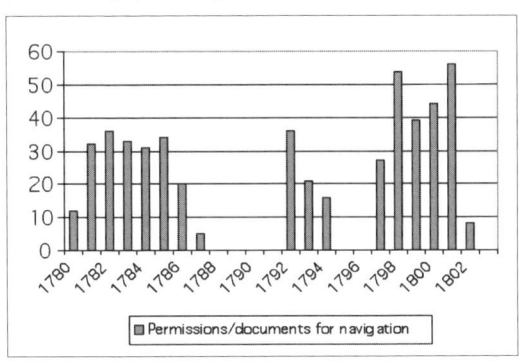

Source: *Amphitrete, 1700-1821,* Pythagoras Research Project, Ionian University/Greek Ministry of Education, 2006

Table 4: *Arrivals of Greek-owned ships at Genoa, 1784-1811*

Arrivals from	Number of ships	%
Eastern Mediterranean	612	60%
Aegean Sea	428	70%
South-eastern Mediterranean	158	26%
Ionian Sea	17	3%
Black Sea	9	1%
Western Mediterranean	400	40%
Total	1012	

Sources: Avvisi, 1784-1797; Archivio di Stato di Genova, Pandetta 12, Ufficio di Sanità, Arrivi di Capitani e Padroni, 1682-1694, (1801-1811)

In order to give a picture as to the origin of grain bound for western Mediterranean ports, we have chosen to analyze the origin of the grain cargoes to Genoa as indicated in Table 4. It seems that of the 612 ships that arrived at the port of Genoa from the 1780s to the 1790s from the Levant, a large part remained in the western Mediterranean to trade regionally before returning to the eastern Mediterranean. From the ships that arrived from the Levant, 70% came from places bordering the Aegean Sea, 26% from the south-eastern Mediterranean, 1% came directly from the Black Sea to Genoa and only 3% from the Ionian islands. Although Black Sea ports' trade significantly increased after the turn of the century, we assume that the importance of the Black Sea grain is under-represented and that it was transported in the Aegean islands to be re-exported to the western Mediterranean.

More than one-third of the grain came from northwestern Aegean, mainly from the Gulf of Volos, the main export area for grain from the plains of Thessaly, as is evident from the arrivals to Malta and Genoa. The other two-thirds of the cargoes of grain came from the northeastern and southwestern Aegean, mainly from the islands of Psara and Lesbos, Hydra and Spetses. Apart from Lesbos the other three islands, Psara, Hydra and Spetses, are barren islands, merely rocks in the sea, definitely without any production of grain. What happened was that all four islands had become transit points, where grain was deposited until it was trans-shipped on board vessels to take it to the west. This trans-shipment from ship to ship is recorded many times in the archival material. Psara and Lesbos most likely received grain from the Black Sea or Thessaly, whereas Hydra and Spetses were depots for grain from the Peloponnese and the Black Sea. Storage on ships or in deserted areas of islands that were notorious for lack of rain and moisture meant less damage to the cargo. In this way, the need for grain in the west formed this chain of transit nodes on the islands of the Aegean.

Needless to say, the transit points became also the maritime centres of the Aegean as they developed in the last third of the 18th century: Hydra, Spetses and Psara. Under the impact of the dramatic increase in demand for grain during the Napoleonic wars these latter three islands built large merchant ships as grain carriers, and the Aegean islanders developed a special trade and shipping system. The evidence from the Ottoman archives reveals that the ships from islands of the northern and central Aegean like Skopelos, Mykonos, Santorini, Tinos and Kasos (31% of the total permits received, as shown in Figure 6) were small to medium size ships with an average crew of 12. These carried grain from the Black Sea, Thessaly or Asia Minor to the island depots of the Aegean from where the captains of big deep-sea going vessels of Hydra, Psara and Spetses (a total of 51% of the permits received) carried it to the western Mediterranean ports. The sailing shipowners of Messolongi and Galaxidi, who received a total of 18% of the permits granted, carried the grain and other cargoes from the Gulf of Corinth and the coast of western Greece in the Ionian Sea to Malta and Livorno.

Figure 6: *Percentage of Ottoman Greek ships according to places of origin, 1780-1820*

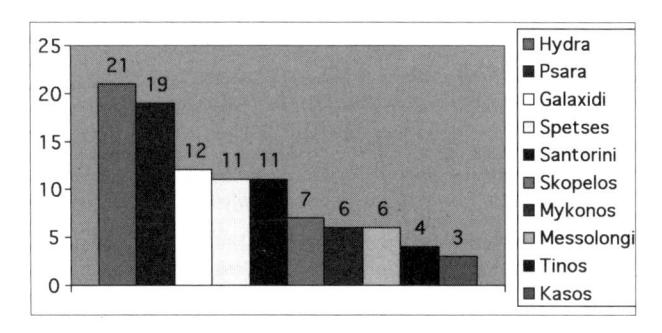

Place	%
Hydra	21
Psara	19
Galaxidi	12
Spetses	11
Santorini	11
Skopelos	7
Mykonos	6
Messolongi	6
Tinos	4
Kasos	3

Source: A.DVNS. IZN 1-5, *Ottoman Archives of the Prime Ministry, Istanbul*

Map 1: The main maritime centres of the Ottoman Greek fleet, 1780-1820

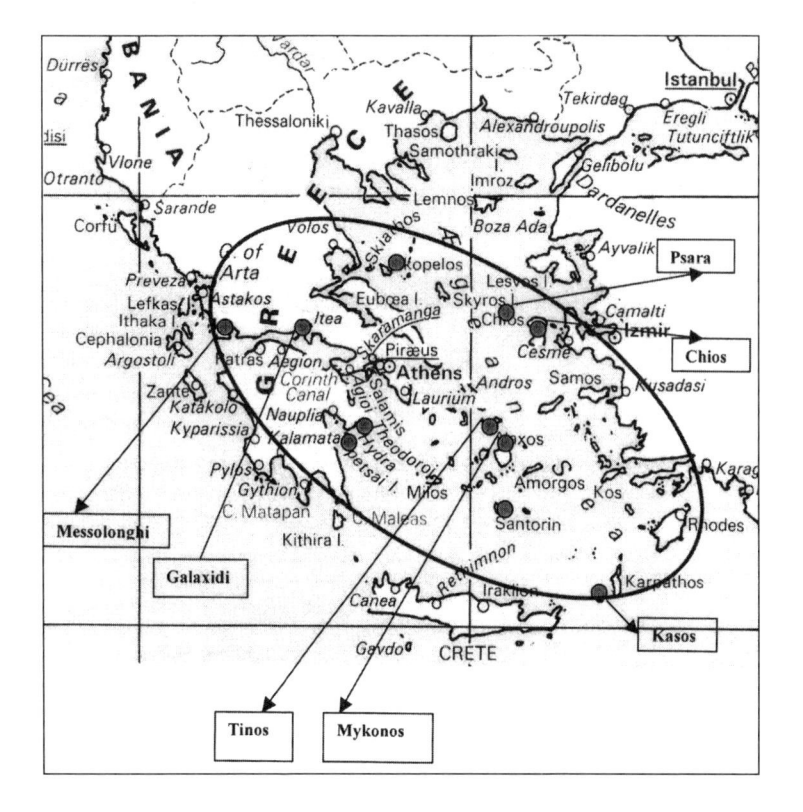

It was from the Ionian Sea that the rise of the Ottoman fleet first started. The increase in maritime trade was linked with the impressive increase in land trade that was connected with the development of entrepreneurial networks of Ottoman Greeks in the Balkans and western European cities from the early 18th century, and particularly after the Treaty of Belgrade (1739), when with the achievement of peace in the area there was a great stimulus to trade in southeastern Europe. Apart from becoming the main land carriers of the Balkans, the Ottoman Greeks in the last third of the 18th century developed combined land and sea transport between western Balkans and the Italian cities of Trieste, Ancona, Messina, Livorno and Genoa, as well as Malta.[24] In relation to this latter trade, an important Greek-owned fleet developed, belonging to Ottoman and Venetian Greeks. The main maritime centres of the Ionian Sea were Cephalonia and Ithaca, on the Venetian side, and Messolongi, Aetoliko and Galaxidi, on the Ottoman side (see Map 1). This fleet served the hinterland of Epirus, Aitoloakarnania and western Peloponnese, and sailed mostly under the Ottoman flag, even if the vessels were owned by Cephalonians or Ithacans.

It was in parallel to this development on the western frontier of the Ottoman Empire, in the second half of the 18th century, that the Greek-owned fleet grew in the Aegean Sea as we have indicated above. By the 1820s, an international entrepreneurial network, commercial and maritime, of diaspora Ottoman Greeks had been formed and expanded on two axes: the first one was the formation of networks within the Ottoman Empire, and the second the formation of land and maritime trade networks of Greek entrepreneurial networks from the Black Sea to northern Europe.[25]

24 See Olga Katsiardi-Hering, *I elliniki paroikia tis Tergestis, 1751-1830* (The Greek Community in Trieste, 1751-1830), 2 vols., Athens: University of Athens, Department of Philosophy, 1986; Katerina Papakonstantinou, "Ellinikes emporikes epicheiriseis stin Kentriki Europi to deuteron miso tou 18ou aiona. I oikogeneia Pontika" (Greek Mercantile Enterprises in Central Europe in the Second Half of the Eighteenth Century: the Case of the Pondikas Family), unpublished PhD thesis, University of Athens 2002; Angeliki Inglesi, *Voreioelladites emporoi sto telos tis tourkokratias. Stauros Ioannou (1790-1820)* (Traders from Northern Greece at the end of Ottoman rule. Stavros Ioannou), Athens: Istoriko Arheio-Politistiki symvoli tis Emporikis Trapezas tis Ellados, 2004.

25 Olga Katsiardi-Hering, "I elliniki diaspora: i geographia kai i typologia tis" (The Greek Diaspora: Geography and Typology), in Spyros I. Asdrachas (ed.), *Elliniki Oikonomiki Istoria 15os-19os aionas* (Greek economic history 15th-19th centuries), Athens: Politistio Idryma Omilou Peiraios, 2003, pp. 237-47; Gelina Harlaftis, *History of Greek-owned Shipping*, pp. 6-9, 40-51, 70-89; Gelina Harlaftis, "Mapping the Greek Maritime Diaspora from the early 18th to the Late 20th Century", in Ina Baghdiantz McCabe, Gelina Harlaftis and Ioanna Minoglou (eds), *Diaspora Entrepreneurial Networks. Five Centuries of History*, Oxford: Berg 2005, pp. 147-71.

Ottoman policy towards maritime commerce: protection and the flag

A major issue for all who sailed on the Mediterranean sea was the safe transfer of commodities, that is, protection from the attacks of the Barbary corsairs, pirates, and European privateers. Risk at sea and continuous danger of attacks meant that there could be no safe conduct in the Mediterranean without an armed merchant vessel of a certain substantial size. This was certainly acknowledged by the Ottoman officials, and the Ottoman Greek vessels were well armed as the Ottoman archival evidence indicates. For example, all 239 ships of 1805 and 367 ships of 1809 of the islands or port towns of Hydra, Psara, Spetses, Trikeri, Mykonos, Sifnos, Kasos, Patmos, Tinos, Limnos, Poros and Messolongi (as per DVNS.İZN.d. 3) were armed. On 1 February 1805, for instance, the ship of Gika Gianni from Hydra carried 35 men and 8 cannon, 35 rifles, 25 carbines, 35 knives and 35 pistols.[26] The largest ship of that year must have been the ship of Yorgi Dimitri, also from Hydra, that carried 60 men with 16 cannon, 60 rifles, 40 carbines, 60 knives, and 60 pistols.[27] These were large ships between 100 and 200 tons, and it is with this kind of ships that they traded in the West. Although between 1805 and 1821 the average crew was 30 men, large crews of 50 and 60 men were not unusual, all armed and ready to fight.

The arming of ships was only one of the measures taken by the Ottoman state to protect maritime commerce in the Ottoman seas.[28] The second step was the effort to restrict the foreign protection system, which allowed the *beratlı* Ottoman subjects not only to enjoy the privileges offered to the foreign merchants as stipulated in the Capitulations, but also to avoid the payment of the

---

26   DVNS.İZN.3, p. 33
27   DVNS. İZN. d.3, p. 27.
28   Nevertheless, attacks against Ottoman Greek ships were quite frequent. Numerous references in Antonios Lignos (ed.), *Archeion tis koinotitas Ydras, 1778-1832* (Archive of the Community of Hydra, 1778-1832), Peiraias: typois ephim. Sfairas, 1921 (henceforth: AKY), (vol. 1, pp. 36, 45, 48, 50-2, 55-56, 65, 69, 77, 82, 85-86, 77, 163, 233, 235, 264-65, 267-301, vol. 2, pp. 33-4, 176, vol. 3, pp. 112-49, 97-101, 110) show that the Barbary and Maltese corsairs and pirates, as well as some Ottoman subjects from the Mani peninsula, constituted a major threat. According to Daniel Panzac, *Les Corsaires Barbaresques. La fin d'une épopée, 1800-1820*, Paris: CNRS, 1999, pp. 63-4, between 1798 and 1803 there was an upsurge of attacks from the Barbary corsairs as a result of the sudden decrease in the Maghreb's resources due to the end of its long-established commercial relations with France. Moreover, the destruction of the Order of St John in Malta by Napoleon in 1798 left the way open to the traditional profession of the Barbary states, that of plundering.

capitation tax (*cizye*) and to pay reduced rates on other taxes.[29] This new attitude towards commercial policy was initiated in August 1802, during the reign of Selim III, when it was declared that select non-Muslim *reaya* who were engaged with international trade would be renamed "merchants of Europe" (*Avrupa tüccarları*), who would get their *berats* from the Sublime Porte and would have the same privileges as the other "protégés", without entering, however, under a foreign protection.[30] In the same period the Ottoman state for the first time opened Ottoman embassies and consulates in the European countries, which would also promote the economic interests of the Ottoman subjects active abroad. Between 1802 and 1807 Ottoman consulates were established in Messina, Palermo, Naples, Livorno, Genoa, Venice, Trieste, Marseilles and Lisbon.[31] Thus, from the Messina Archives we are informed that Antonino Genzardi was in 1792 the Ottoman consul in Palermo;[32] the Archives of Corfu tell us that Lambros Varvessis was the Ottoman consul in Messina at the beginning of the 19th century;[33] from the Archives of the Community of Hydra

---

[29] The secondary bibliography on the foreign protection system is extensive. See mainly Halil İnalcık, "İmtiyazat", *Encyclopaedia of Islam*, 2nd ed., v. III, pp. 1179-89; Maurits H. Van den Boogert, *The Capitulations and the Ottoman Legal System. Qadis, Consuls and Beratlis in the 18th Century*, Leiden-Boston: Brill, 2005, pp. 34-6, 42-5 for a reconsideration of the view that the foreign merchants (*müstemin*) enjoyed full legal autonomy; Ali İhsan .Bağış, *Osmanlı Ticaretinde Gayrî Müslimler*, 2 baskı, Ankara 1998, pp. 19-41; P. Kondoayannis, "Oi prostateuomenoi" (The protégés), *Athina* 29 (1917), pp. 1-160; Christine Philliou, "Mischief in the Old Regime: Provincial Dragomans at the Turn of the 19th Century", *New Perspectives on Turkey* 25 (fall 2001), pp. 103-21.

[30] M.Çadırcı, "II Mahmut devrinde (1808-1839) Avrupa ve Hayriye Tüccarları", *Türkiye'nin Sosyal ve Ekonomik Tarihi*, ed. Osman Okyar and Halil İnalcık, Ankara: Meteksan 1980, pp. 237-241; Bruce Masters, "The Sultan's Enterpreneurs: The Avrupa tüccaris and the Hayriye tüccaris in Syria", *International Journal of Middle East Studies* 24/4 (1992), pp. 579-97. Bağış, *Osmanlı Ticaretinde*, pp. 68-74; Edhem Eldem, *French Trade in Istanbul in the 18th Century*, Leiden: Brill 1996, p. 292; Mouradgea D'Ohsson, *Tableau général de l'empire ottoman*, v.7, re-edition, İstanbul: Isis, 2001, p. 368.

[31] Bağış, *Osmanlı Ticaretinde*, pp. 63-4. See also Eldem, *French Trade*, p. 293, where it is mentioned that in 1806 a high Ottoman official asked the French ambassador Sebastiani to implement the principle of reciprocity included in the Capitulations text.

[32] Fabio di Vita, "Greek Ships in Sicily during the 18th Century: Health Practices and Commercial Relationships" in Gelina Harlaftis and Katerina Papakonstantinou (eds), *The Rise of Greek Shipping in the Mediterranean Trade of the 18th Century*, forthcoming.

[33] Gerasimos Pagratis, "I Consolati della Repubblica Settinsulare (1800-1807) in Sicilia", in the 2nd Mediterranean Maritime History Network Conference, Messina/Taormina, 3-7 May 2006, unpublished paper.

we learn that Enrico Popie Geltemestri (*sic*) was the Ottoman consul in Lisbon during the same period;[34] and from the Genoa Archives we are informed that the Chiot Nicolas Petrocochino was the Ottoman consul in Genoa in 1813.[35]

One aspect of the above-mentioned policy is clearly revealed in the Ottoman register DVNS. İZN.D. 3, located in the Prime Ministerial Archive of Istanbul. The register contains 179 pages and covers the period 1804-1821.[36] The register has the general title *Reaya İzn-i Sefine Defteri,* written on the cover, but on page 6 a whole section begins, going up to page 163, with the title "Reaya-i devlet-i aliyeden Bahr-i Sefid'de ticaret edenlerin yedlerine verilecek evamirin defteridir" (Register of the orders which will be given to the subjects of the exalted state who practice commerce in the Aegean Sea). There are 1,423 entries from 1804-21 referring to Christian *reaya*;[37] each of them includes the name of the captain and his origin, the type and sometimes the name of the ship, the number of the seamen, the armament and sometimes a résumé of three decrees, which are given to the captain.[38] The first decree was addressed to the captains of the three *ocaks* of North Africa (Algeria, Tripoli and Tunisia), who were asked not to harass the captain and his ship during the voyage in the Aegean. The second one was addressed to the Ottoman judges and customs officials in the Aegean islands as well as in the coastal areas of Anatolia and Rumelia, demanding that they should not harass the captain if the latter had paid the custom dues "according to custom" and the "other taxes". The third decree was addressed again to the Ottoman judges and the collectors of the capitation tax in the Aegean islands and the above-mentioned coastal areas, asking them not to demand the capitation tax from the captain. These decrees were issued according to a report submitted by the chief admiral (*kapudan paşa*) or the head of the imperial navy yard (*tersane emini*) or even by the supervisor of the naval affairs (*umur-i bahriye nâzırı,* bearing also the title of the third *defterdar*). Occasionally the orders are given *in extenso,* particularly in the first pages of the register.[39]

---

34   *AKY*, vol. 2, pp. 339-41.

35   *Almanaco di Genova per l'anno 1813*, p. 7.

36   The last entry is dated in 12-21/4/1821 (evahir-i Receb 1236), a little after the Greek revolution had begun. Pages 165-72 are blank and pages 173-9 include orders regarding various issues of the maritime commerce.

37   There is only one reference to a Muslim Ottoman, one İbrahim son of İbrahim from Cyprus. A.DVNS.İZN 3, p. 147.

38   Sometimes the captains were also the shipowners.

39   See DVNS.İZN.3, pp.6-10. Also see pp. 18-19, where there are the three orders, titled as *temin emri* (safety order), *ticaret emri* (commerce order) and *muafiyet emri* (tax exemption order), given to a certain Lazari Yorgi from the island of Hydra.

The register is divided into sections in accordance with the office of the Grand Vezir and the *Reisülküttab* (Minister of Foreign Affairs, responsible for the issuing of the berats), and the length of the entries varies. Besides the type of entry described above there are shorter entries, where it is stated that three decrees were granted to the captain regarding safe conditions for trade and exemption from the capitation tax (*temin ve ticaret ve muafiyeti*), issued in accordance with a report of one of the above-mentioned officials.

In the first pages of the register there is a request submitted to Selim III in September 1804, most probably by the then chief admiral of the Ottoman fleet or by the dragoman of the imperial fleet, referring to the increased use of the Russian flag or flags of other states by the Ottoman subjects of the islands of the Aegean Sea, who were under foreign protection. It was also stated that, although according to the 17th article of the treaty of Küçük Kaynarca (1774) those of the *reaya* who wished to abandon the country (and settle in Russia) had a time-limit of one year to remove their movable property, their profession should be asked, since they declared that they belonged to the protégés (of Russia). Because of the financial loss to the state caused by the extensive use of the protection system and the use of foreign flags, it was proposed to offer certain privileges (*imtiyazlar*) to the *reaya* ship-owners and captains in order to "attract and gather" them (*celb ve telifleriyle*). Indeed, those who abandoned the foreign protection and "returned to the Ottoman state" would pay the "usual" custom dues and should not be pressured to pay more.[40] They would travel in safety and no Ottoman official could disturb them. They would be exempt from the payment of the customary dues (*tekalif*), while those of the captains who also owned the ships they commanded would be exempt from the capitation tax. Finally, it was proposed that they should be free to dress themselves as they wished. The official requested the issuance of the necessary sultanic orders for the implementation of these privileges.[41]

---

40 The official refers to the arbitrary levies, *avanias*, which the Ottoman officials in the ports usually demanded from the merchants. See İnalcık and Quataert (eds), *An Economic and Social History of the Ottoman Empire*, vol. 2, p. 695.

41 DVNS. İZN 3, p.2. The grant of "privileges" to the islanders at the beginning of the 19th century is also referred in the Greek secondary sources. According to them, the "privileges" aimed to eliminate Russian influence and included among others the "more effective protection on behalf of the Ottoman state". See Anastasios Orlandos, *Peri tis nisou Petsas i Spetson* (Regarding the island of Petsa or Spetses), Peiraias 1877, pp. 37-8; Alexandris, *Anaviosis*, p. 279; Konstantinos Svolopoulos, "O ellinikos emporikos stolos kata tas paramonas tou agonos tis anexartisias. Anekdotos pinax tou F. Pouqueville" (The Greek merchant marine on the eve of the struggle for independence. The unpublished table of F. Pouqueville), *Eranistis* I/59 (1973), pp. 200-1.

The request was accepted and the new "system" regarding the merchant marine was applied. In this context, a letter written again in September 1804 by the then dragoman of the imperial fleet, Panayotis Mourouzis,[42] and addressed to the inhabitants of the island of Hydra presented the "new system". The inhabitants of the island would have to send a list with the names of the *reaya* captains in order to receive a certain number of *berat*s and firmans. The local notables would distribute the official documents, under the proviso that those who were interested would provide letters of guarantee.[43]

These measures demonstrate the new policy of Selim III, aiming at the support of Ottoman maritime commerce against the "foreigner", that is ships owned by Ottoman subjects but flying a foreign flag. This new policy can certainly be combined with the above-mentioned policy of the "merchants of Europe" (*Avrupa tüccarları*); the latter, however, was initially not very successful and the year 1806 was crucial for these "protégés". In May, a Hydriot sent a letter from Istanbul to the notables of his island, referring to the forced sale of the "protégés'" shops and the fact that the state treasury would get 10% of the price. The rich *beratlı* would have to move to the state by which they were protected, without however having the right to take their families with them. This new policy concerned the *beratlı* of all the foreign states.[44] Five months earlier a memorandum had been sent to the ambassadors of Great Britain, France, Austria and Russia, which restricted the privileges of the *beratlı* (prohibition of movement and restrictions on occupation), while in May it was established that the "merchants of Europe" would receive their *berat*s from the Sublime Porte by paying 1,500 ğuruş. The protégés of Russia were threatened with the seizure of their ships.[45] In July 1806, a mandate issued by the treasurer of the imperial naval yard was addressed to the local notables of the island of Hydra, instructing them to send a list of the captains who used the Russian flag on their ships, declaring also the reasons why they did so. It was also stated

---

42   Panayotis Mourouzis was dragoman of the imperial fleet from December 1803 until December 1806. Vassilis Sfyroeras, *Oi dragomanoi tou stolou, o thesmos kai oi phoreis* (The Dragomans of the Fleet. The institution and the personnel), Athens 1965, pp. 148-53.

43   *AKY*, vol. 2, pp. 177-8.

44   *AKY*, vol. 2, p. 372.

45   For the events of 1806 see Bağış, *Osmanlı Ticaretinde*, pp. 85-93; Van den Boogert, *The Capitulations*, pp. 29, 109-11. Also W.M. Leake mentioned the request of the *reaya* of the islands of Spetses and Hydra to the Sublime Porte in 1806; they were "envious of the lower duties and other commercial advantages which their protected countrymen partake with Frank traders and provoked at their insolence", and protested at the unequal conditions of trade. William Martin Leake, *Travels in the Morea*, vol. II, Amsterdam: Hakkert 1968, pp. 344-5.

that because many ships of Ottoman subjects used the Russian flag, it seemed necessary to "change the flags".[46] In the same month a list of the "*reaya* ships" as well as of the consuls and vice-consuls in Hydra was requested, since the appointment of *reaya* in these positions was against the agreements (*ahdname*) between the Ottoman Empire and the foreign governments.[47] At the same time, those of the captains who wished to abandon the foreign flags and use the Ottoman one would not face any negative consequences.[48]

A number of warranty letters presented by the captains are mentioned in the register.[49] The need for presenting a warranty letter is referred in the above-mentioned letter of Mourouzis. Those of the captains who acquired the official documents by themselves in Istanbul had to present a warranty letter issued by the local notables of their places of origin. There are cases where the guarantors of the captains were the local notables (*kocabaşılar*) of the islands of Hydra and Spetses, and the port town of Galaxidi, who guaranteed the exclusive use of the Ottoman flag. If, however, the Ottoman flag was not raised or the captain possessed patents from other states, or even if his actions turned against the "official system", the guarantors would have to remit 5.000 ğuruş into the treasury of the imperial naval yard.[50] If the captain did not present such a warranty letter and the lapse was established, the ship and the merchandise would be seized by the state and the captain would be punished.[51]

In the Ottoman register under study only the 6.5% of the entries mention the existence of warrantors (93 entries). The vast majority of the 6.5% are entries from 1806, a very crucial year as stated above. The others are from the years 1807-8 and 1812-16. It seems that the policy of providing warranty letters was gradually abandoned or the mechanisms of control became lax over time. However, what is important is the study of the persons who acted as warrantors. Besides the local notables of the island from which the captain and/or shipowner came, the majority of them were Greek inhabitants of Istanbul or merchants staying in one of the *han* of the capital. In most cases the war-

---

46   *AKY*, vol. 2, p. 398.
47   *AKY*, vol. 2, pp. 392-5, 399-400.
48   *AKY*, vol.2, p. 402.
49   The practice of presenting guarantors (*kefil*) was extensively used by the Ottoman state as a means to ensure that certain obligations would be fulfilled on behalf of the Ottoman subjects. For example the non-Muslim Ottoman subjects who applied for permission to travel to the Black Sea they had to provide similar warranty letters, stating that they would not stay in Russia. Bostan, "İzn-i Sefine Defterleri", p. 29.
50   See for example DVNS.IZN.3, p. 77. *AKY*, vol. 2, pp. 392, 393.
51   DVNS. IZN.3, pp. 64, 68, 74, 76.

rantors were of the same local origin as the captains or they came from a near place of origin, while some of them must have been relatives. When the occupation of the warrantor is mentioned, they were merchants (*tacir*, *bazirgân*), shop-owners in Istanbul, and in two cases the warrantors are characterized as "merchants of Europe".[52] Also, the *vekil* of the island of Syros in the capital is mentioned,[53] along with Greek artisans working in the imperial naval yard,[54] owners of coffee-shops[55] and certain local notables from the place of origin of the captain or from nearby.[56] In nine cases the warrantors were Ottoman Muslim officials, merchants or other professionals. For example, Kostas son of Panayotis from Messolongi presented as warrantor a certain Hüseyin ağa, official in the *sancak* (district) of Yanya (Yannena), and Andronis from Sfakia (Crete) presented three Muslim merchants.[57] Also, Kostantis son of Yorgi from Çeşme presented as warrantor Hacı Halil, a *kapan* merchant[58].

It seems that the warrantors and the captains/ship-owners were partners in a common enterprise. Although we do not know the exact legal framework of their partnership or if there were other partners in it, it seems that the investment of capital in enterprises was a common practice not only for people who possessed and circulated capital (merchants, notables, officials) but also for other professionals such as artisans. Also, it must be stressed that the common interest led to intra-communal and intra-confessional co-operation, revealing how Ottoman officials wished to take advantage of external trade.[59]

---

52   Dimitrakis Ralli, warrantor for Panayotis son of Andoni from Izmir, and Yannis son of Vitali, warrantor of Stathis son of Yorgis, from Istanbul are characterized as "merchants of Europe". DVNS. İZN 3, p. 146.

53   DVNS.İZN 3, pp. 63, 67.

54   DVNS.İZN 3, pp. 63, 149.

55   DVNS.İZN 3, pp. 71, 77.

56   DVNS.İZN 3, p. 63, 65, 67.

57   DVNS.İZN 3, p. 134, 143 respectively. See also DVNS.İZN 3, 71, 73

58   DVNS.İZN 3, p. 144. The *kapan* merchants were responsible for the importation of foodstuffs to Istanbul and quite often they were also shipowners. According to Çizakça, these merchants were acting as investors, who formed partnerships with other merchants. Çizakça, *A Comparative Evolution*, pp. 117-22. See also Halil İnalcık, "Capital Formation in the Ottoman Empire", *The Ottoman Empire: Conquest, Organization and Economy*, London: Variorum Reprints, 1978, pp. 120, 136 for the involvement of Ottoman officials in trade and investment of capital in partnerships.

59   See also Suraiya Faroqhi, *The Ottoman Empire and the World Around It*, London: I.B. Tauris 2006, pp. 159-60 on how the Ottoman state and some officials profited from foreign trade despite the low customs dues because of the Capitulations.

The dragoman of the imperial fleet was involved in the procedure of submitting the warranty letters to the imperial naval yard, or even in the issuing of such letters, in the case of captains who did not possess such documents from the local notables. It is also probable that for each letter of guarantee which came to the attention of the dragoman of the fleet, the latter would receive a certain sum of money, as was the case with the issuing of permits for voyages to the Black Sea.[60]

At the same time Selim III was trying to reorganize the Ottoman navy by employing educated personnel and constructing modern ships with the help of foreign experts and Greek shipbuilders. In 1806 a Ministry of the Navy was established for the first time, and also there was a reorganization of the navy's administration.[61] The Sultan's efforts to Ottomanize the merchant marine can thus be set within the broader scope of the reforms that he tried to impose.[62] In this context, the answer of Selim III to the above-mentioned request of his high official, as revealed in a copy of his "imperial script" (*hatt-i hümayun*), is illuminating for his way of thinking. Not only does he give his consent to the proposed measures, he urges that official to try his utmost to increase the number of merchants and ships, since no one has ever tried this before. Indeed, he stresses that the only business of the foreign states is commerce. He adds that there are no Ottoman commercial ships left and he does not know what to do about this.[63] The Sultan seemed to be very much concerned about the severe impoverishment of the Ottoman merchant marine, comparing it with the foreign ones active in the eastern Mediterranean. His goal was economic: improving the international competitiveness of its subjects in Mediterranean trade and shipping would help the Ottoman empire's economy.

On the other hand, his policy also had a socio-political aspect. His aim was to strengthen the state against social groups which could threaten it, such as the janissaries and the *ulema*. The *reaya*-protégés formed another such group, since they could not be fully controlled by the state. Hence reverting to the

---

60 According to Sfyroeras, in 1803 the dragoman received 100 ğuruş for each ship authorized to enter the Black Sea. Sfyroeras, *Oi dragomanoi*, p. 45.

61 Stanford Shaw, "Selim III and the Ottoman Navy", *Turcica* 1 (1969), pp. 222-3, 229-30. The author has characterized these naval reforms as "the most successful aspect of Selim III's efforts to restore the empire", op. cit., p. 240.

62 Stanford Shaw, *Between Old and New. The Ottoman Empire under Sultan Selim III, 1789-1807*, Cambridge, MA: Harvard University Press, 1971.

63 "Benim vezirim bu makule hususa daima vakit olunub takrir mücebince nizam verile ve daima üzerine olunub teksir-i tüccara ve sefaine sarf-ı makdur olunsun zira ticareti ve teksir-i sefaini hiç kimesne iltizam eylemiyor ma heza düvel-i sairenin ancak maslahatı emr-i ticaretdir. Bizim ise, ticaret sefaini kalmadı. Bilmem tedarikin tariki nedir.", DVNS.İZN 3, p. 2.

idea that social mobility should be restricted or under the strict control of the state in order to maintain social integrity did not have only financial motives (such as loss of revenue from the capitation tax, or frustration at the state's inability to confiscate the property of a protégé), but political ones too: it aimed at extending the state's control over all strata of Ottoman society.[64] Besides, a special characteristic of the state's attitude towards the economy was the maintenance of the political-economic "traditional order" and the division of labour that this entailed. This meant that the Ottoman state felt uncomfortable about methods of capital accumulation which did not belong to this "order", especially by people who did not belong to the political-military elite.[65] As Quataert has shown, Selim III also tried to restore the clothing laws, which were first imposed in the 16th century, in order to distinguish Muslims and non-Muslims, *reaya* and Ottoman officials. It is indicative that the Sultan invoked the need not only to preserve the moral order, but also to strengthen the local cloth industry.[66] In this respect it is certainly not by chance that in 1806 the clothing laws for the non-Muslim *reaya* became stricter.[67] Thus Selim III allowed certain "privileged" non-Muslim *reaya* to dress themselves as they wished, because the state interests so dictated, and on the same time he followed stricter sartorial regulations for the rest of the non-Muslim *reaya*. The broader scope of his policy allowed this ambiguity, which also helped to appease the conservatives and opponents of his reformation in Istanbul.

These measures for control of external trade and limitation of the protection system were taken in a period of turbulent international relations, characterized by the expansionist foreign policy of Napoleon Bonaparte and the efforts of Britain and Russia to stop it. Both sides needed the alliance of the Ottoman Empire, while at the same time they were trying to control it in political terms and also to establish their economic interests in the eastern Mediterranean. The above-mentioned measures coincided with the victory of France in the battle of Austerlitz in December 1805 and the reorientation of Ottoman foreign policy towards an alliance with France, followed by the declaration of war against Russia in December 1806. The imposition of the new policy against

---

64 Van den Boogert, *The Capitulations*, p. 111; Masters, "The Sultan's Entrepreneurs", pp. 579, 585; Philliou, "Mischief in the Old Regime", pp. 115-20.

65 Şevket Pamuk, *A Monetary History of the Ottoman Empire*, Cambridge University Press 2000, pp. 12-13; İnalcık, "Capital Formation", p. 97; Eldem, *French Trade*, p. 270.

66 Donald Quataert, "Clothing Laws, State, and Society in the Ottoman Empire, 1720-1829", *International Journal of Middle East Studies* 29 (1997), pp. 410, 412.

67 Kontoyannis, "Oi prostateuomenoi", p. 32 fn. 2

the protégés has thus naturally been explained as the result of France's strong influence in the Sublime Porte and an effort to limit Russian influence over the non-Muslim Ottoman *reaya*. It is thought that the Phanariote Dimitrios Mourouzis, a well known "friend" of Russia, played an important role, because he tried to appease the Sultan's pro-Russian political positions by suggesting the limitation of the protection system.[68] On the other hand, there is the explanation that Mourouzis tried to protect Greek protégés from the arbitrary reactions of the Ottoman government, whenever relations between the Ottoman state and the foreign state that granted the protection worsened. He also wanted to favour the Greek protégés, because the issuing of a *berat* by the Sublime Porte in order to become a "merchant of Europe" cost much less than getting a *berat* from a foreign ambassador or consul and thereby becoming a *beratlı*/protégé.[69]

Without intending to underestimate the international conditions, however, we believe that Selim III's commercial policy was driven by more than merely the deterioration of Russian-Ottoman relations. It also had a much broader scope, aiming at the improvement of the Ottoman economy as a whole.

Certainly the attempt to limit the protection system and also to restore the clothing laws predated Selim III.[70] But how successful was he, in comparison with his predecessors? In the register DVNS.IZN.3, for the period 1804-8 there are 479 entries for non-Muslim Ottoman subjects who requested and received sultanic decrees which ensured for them freedom for trade, protection from piratical attacks, exemption from the capitation tax and the payment of the custom dues only "according to the custom" (*ber mutad*) and not more. There are only two entries for 1807 and six for 1808, as is evident from Table 5. This disparity can be explained by the war against Russia, during which the inhabitants of Hydra, and possibly other islanders too, were asked to demobilize their ships by burning the steering and other basic ship's equipment, in order to prevent their use by the Russians,[71] and also by the dethronement

---

68 Bağış, *Osmanlı Ticaretinde*, pp. 77-8; Shaw, *Between Old and New*, p. 341. Demetrios Mourouzis was appointed dragoman of the Sublime Porte in 1808, Sfyroeras, *Oi dragomanoi*, pp. 143, 152-3.

69 David Urquhart, *La Turquie; ses resources, son organization municipale, son commerce*, Paris: Arthus Bertrand, 1836, vol. III, pp. 162-3 fn.1; Georg G. Gervinus, *History of the Greek Revolution and Resurrection*, Athens: Ch.N. Philadelpheus 1864, pp. 87-8.

70 Van den Boogert, *The Capitulations*, pp. 105-9. According to Bağış, *Osmanlı Ticaretinde*, pp. 36-7, before the initiative of Selim III, whenever the Ottoman state tried to limit the number of the protégés, the foreign ambassadors managed to prevent any such effort.

71 *AKY*, vol. 3, pp. 43-6.

Years	Number of vessels
1804	42
1805	239
1806	190
1807	2
1808	6
1809	367
1810	106
1811	55
1812	153
1813	51
1814	14
1815	36
1816	40
1817	18
1818	36
1819	23
1820	34
1821	11
Total	1.423

Table 5: Number of Ottoman Greek vessels registered in Istanbul between 1804-1821 as revealed in DVNS.İZN 3

Source: Başbakanlık Osmanlı Arşivi, *DVNS. İZN. 3*

of Selim III and the political turbulence that followed. For the period 1809-20 there are 960 entries, with uneven distribution. However, in the year 1809, 367 non-Muslim Ottoman subjects applied for the grant of the above-mentioned decrees, much more than in any other year.

The register does not mention any special status of the applicants, that is, whether they were "merchants of Europe". The only criterion that can help is the payment or not of the capitation tax. According to Masters, who consulted registers from 1815 and 1839-61, the "merchants of Europe" in Aleppo paid the capitation tax but much less than normally, while the payment of the specific tax meant to "remind" them their *reaya* status.[72] However, in the above-mentioned letter of 1804 written by the then dragoman of the imperial fleet, the captains who followed the "new system" would not pay the capitation tax.[73] Also, Urquhart mentions that the "merchants of Europe" would be exempted.[74] It is probable, however, that in the course of the time the exemption from the capitation tax was abolished.

Nevertheless, the answer to the question whether the applicants belonged to the "merchants of Europe" or shared special privileges as Ottoman subjects does not alter the reality: from the above-mentioned evidence, we have the picture of a social-professional group, which followed the regulations of the "new system" in relation to the merchant marine, shared the same privileges with the protégés of the foreign states and at the same time remained *reaya*. The fact that the register is divided into sections according to who was the current *Reisülküttab* strengthens the argument that the applicants shared a special status.

The effectiveness of the Ottoman effort to control external trade and to "regain" the *reaya* can be ascertained only if we have a clear picture of the *beratlı*. In fact, both Ottoman and Western sources show extensive use of the Ottoman flag even before the implementation of this new policy. Table 6 in-

---

72   Masters, "The Sultan's Enterpreneurs", p. 582.
73   Urquhart, *La Turquie*, p. 162-3 fn.1.
74   Urquhart, *La Turquie*, p. 163.

dicates the proportionate use of the Ottoman flag during the period 1780 to 1810 as recorded in almost 5,000 Greek-owned ships. More than 80% of the Greek-owned ships that traded to Malta, Livorno and Genoa, that is on the long routes of the Mediterranean, flew the Ottoman flag. As far as the Russian flag is concerned, for which there is an extensive Greek bibliography stressing the impetus due to the treaty of Küçük Kaynarca in 1774,[75] in the 1767-1815 period use of the Russian flag by Greek-owned vessels trading in western Europe was indeed very limited, as the archival evidence on which Table 6 is based indicates. In Genoa it was almost nil, in Malta 6% of the Greek-owned vessels carried the Russian flag, and in Livorno 9%. For the whole period and for the three ports only 6% of the vessels that traded west flew the Russian flag. The use of the Russian flag was minimal before 1800s and there were just a few vessels that flew it during the two Russo-Ottoman wars of 1768-74 and 1787-92. There was more use of the Russian flag between 1800 and 1808 but never exceeding 30 ships, or 20% of the Greek-owned vessels trading with Livorno or Malta. Moreover, according to Kremmydas' calculations between 1810 and 1821 half of the ships which passed from the port of Patras had the Ottoman flag and belonged to *reaya* of Greek origin.[76] And according to Pouqueville, in 1816 63.6% of the Greek merchantmen flew the Ottoman flag and 36.3% the Russian[77].

Table 6: *Greek-owned ships under various flags, 1780-1810*

Port	Ottoman flag	Venetian flag	Russian flag	Ionian	Other*	Total number Of ships
Malta	64%	3%	6%	4%	23%*	2,352
Livorno	83%	6%	9%	2%	0%	1,604
Genoa	98%	1%	0.2%	0	0,8%**	1,024
	83%	3%	6%	2%	8%	4,980

* Jerusalem, Prussian, Austrian, British, French
Source: Processed data from the data base *Amphitrete, 1700-1821*, Pythagoras Research Project, Ionian University/Greek Ministry of Education, 2006

---

75   "After 1776 the majority of ships of 'Greek ownership' carried the Russian flag", Georgios Dertilis *et al.*, *Istoria tou ellinikou kratous, 1830-1920* (History of the Greek state, 1830-1920), Athens: Estia, 2005, p. 196. On the other hand, Vassilis Kremmydas is rather sceptical of this argument: "what is generally believed, that the Russian flag acted as a panacea for Greek shipping, or as a catalyst for its development is a non-academic exaggeration. It seems that its use took a long time to spread...". Vassilis Kremmydas, *Elliniki nautilia*, vol. 1, p. 22 fn. 2.

76   Vassilis Kremmydas, *Synkyria kai emporio stin proepanastatiki Peloponniso (1793-1821)* (Conjuncture and trade in the pre-revolutionary Peloponnese 1793-1821), Athens: Themelio, 1980, pp. 189, 209-10.

77   Svolopoulos, "O ellinikos emporikos stolos", p. 201.

OTTOMAN STATE POLICY

During the Russo-Ottoman war of 1806-12 the use of the Russian flag disappears, and only for the Greek-owned ships trading in Malta do we have the use of the flag of Jerusalem for only two years, 1808 and 1809, as is evident from Figure 8. The Jerusalem flag used as one of convenience by a number of states of the time was the flag of the Order of St John of Malta.[78] Its use by the Greeks was temporary, as very few Greek-owned ships traded under the Jerusalem flag after 1810.

The Venetian flag was also very little used, probably even by Venetian Greeks of the so-called "Venetian Levant", and it disappeared with the extinction of the Republic in 1797. The use of the Ionian flag appears with the short-lived establishment of Septinsular Republic on the Ionian islands. The "other" flags comprise the short-term use of various flags, Prussian, Austrian, British or French.

Figure 7: *Greek-owned vessels arriving at the port of Livorno under Ottoman and other flags, 1767-1815*

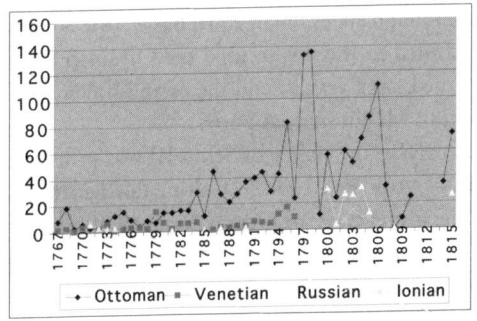

Source: Appendix III

Figure 8: *Greek-owned vessels arriving at Malta under Ottoman and other flags, 1780-1810*

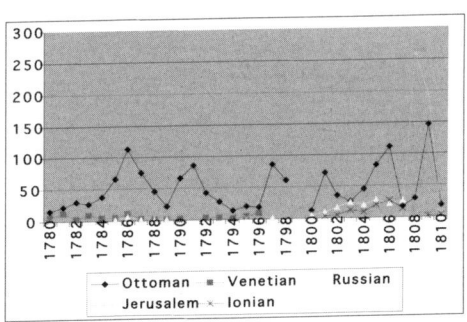

Source: Appendix IV

---

78   Jean Pierre Filippini, *Il porto di Livorno e la Toscana (1676-1814)*, 2nd volume, Edizioni Scientifiche Italiane, 1998, p. 64.

From the above it is evident that the international situation, together with the Ottoman protection of Greek ship-owners and merchants, gave an important boost to the Ottoman merchant fleet that now developed as the main carrier of the Levant trade. However, how can this rise be combined with Selim's dramatic statement that there were no Ottoman merchantmen in 1804? It seems that the slight increase in the use of the Russian flag in the first years of the 19th century alerted the Ottoman officials. Moreover, this increase must have been higher as far as the regional trade in the Aegean and Black Sea was concerned, more so when the trade with the Black Sea was very important for the provisioning of Istanbul.[79] Thus, the insistence on the question of the flag and the limitation of the *beratlı* were due to the need to control political and economic developments within the Ottoman society, and were not intended to be directed against commercial activity. At the beginning of the 19th century the Ottoman state developed a specific commercial and maritime policy, which aimed at limitation of the protection system in order to have its merchants compete with the foreign states on an equal basis. This policy was expressed by the privileges accorded to those who used the Ottoman flag, authorization to construct well-armed large vessels, and the establishment of Ottoman consuls in western European Mediterranean ports.

In the final analysis, the policy of Selim III was prophetic and the formation of a powerful Ottoman Greek fleet ultimately backfired: at least some of the *beratlı*s and the protégés of the Ottoman state with their armed vessels contributed to the formation of a Greek revolutionary navy that joined the Greek War of Independence in 1821.

---

79   See also Kremmydas, *Elliniki nautilia*, vol. 1, p. 22 fn. 2.

APPENDIX I : SOURCES

In Malta the Sanità archives were found for the whole of the 18th century up to 1816 in the National Library of Malta in Valletta, under the title "Archives of the Order of St. John, Commissarii di Sanità, 639, Registri arrivi di quarantena, 818 volumes 1-14". For the port of Livorno most researchers, apart from Jean Pierre Filippini, have looked for the Ufficiali di Sanità in the Archivio di Stato di Firenze, as the Livorno officials would send such documentation to the central government. The documents of the Ufficiali di Sanità archives after 1778 in the Archivio di Stato di Firenze were destroyed in the Florence flood of 1877, and it is more than once stated that the documentation of the Livorno Sanità archives does not exist after 1778.[80] In the Archivio di Stato di Livorno, however, all the Sanità books for the port are found intact in the series 33, "Magistrato poi Dipartimento di Sanità marittima (1606-1860)", volumes 621-626 and 696-706, where complete evidence of the daily arrival of ships from Levant and the Barbary States are registered in the port with all their details from 1767 to 1860.[81] In Genoa, evidence of arrivals of ships from suspected areas are found in the Archivio di Stato di Genova, "Ufficio di Sanità. Arrivi di Capitani e Padroni" and in the "Registro di Spedizioni dei Capitani e Patenti" for the years 1780-1819. Furthermore, daily arrivals at the port of Genoa from all destinations are published in the valuable weekly maritime and commercial Journal of Genoa named *Avvisi* that ran from 1778 to 1797; we found this journal in microfilms in the Biblioteca Universitaria of the University of Genoa.[82] All the Italian archives of Sanità include arrivals of foreign vessels, excluding their own national coastal craft. In Marseilles the evidence derives from the Archives Départementales des Bouches du Rhône, Serie 200 E 474-604, "Dépositions et Arrivages. Déclarations faites par les capitaines de bâtiments à leur arrivée". The problem with these French archives is that those enormous volumes include all arrivals including small coastal craft of even five tons. Data for Trieste were found in the Archivio di Stato di Venezia, in the series "Cinque Savi alla Mercanzia". In Venice no Sanità documentation has survived, but we were able to draw valuable data of Greek-owned ships under

---

80   See Despoina Vlami, *To fiorini, to stari kai i odos tou kipou. Ellines emporoi sto Livorno, 1750-1868* (The *fiorini*, the grain and the Garden street. Greek merchants in Livorno, 1750-1868), Athens: Themelio 2000, p. 77.

81   Jean Pierre Filippini in his opus on Livorno trade and shipping clearly refers to these archives which he has extensively used. See Jean Pierre Filippini, *Il porto di* Livorno, vol. 2, pp. 100-1.

82   We would like to thank Dr Elisabetta Tonizzi for making it possible to access this valuable Journal.

the Venetian flag from the Archivio di Stato di Venezia, in the series "Scuole piccole e suffragi, san Nicolo dei marineri", which is the guild of the Venetian seamen. This series is complete for the whole of the 18th century and contains details of all the crews of Venetian flag vessels.

As far as the Ottoman sources are concerned, we have drawn evidence from five register books catalogued as "*İzn-i Sefine Defterleri*" (DVNS.İZN.d. 1, 2 4, 5), located in the Prime Minister's Office Archive of Istanbul (Başbakanlık Osmanlı Arşivi, BOA), which include permits for the ships sailing to and from the Black Sea during the period 1780-1821.[83] Register no. 3 (DVNS.IZN. d3) includes registration of all vessels that sailed in the Aegean Sea and the Mediterranean from 1804 to 1821, following the new "system" (*nizam*) which was applied by the Ottoman State during the reign of Selim III. Moreover, information on Greek-owned vessels was drawn from *Cevdet-i Maliye* 3893, 4311 and 4870 (BOA) and from court registers located in the State Archives of Macedonia, in Thessaloniki. Archival research in this valuable material gave us a harvest of 2,104 registrations of Ottoman Greek vessels. These registrations do not reveal the actual number of vessels but the number of voyages for which permissions or documents were granted.

We have not visited the Spanish archives but we have drawn evidence from the processed data, drawn partly from the Suprema Junta de Sanidad del Reino and published in the periodical *Diario de Barcelona, 1792-1801,* in Eloy Martin Corrales, "La flota greco-otomana en Cádiz a fines del siglo XVIII" in *Actas del II Congreso de Historia de Andalusia, Andalusia Moderna (II),* Cordoba 1995, pp. 389-400 and in Eloy Martín Corrales, "Cereales y capitanes greco-otomanos en la Málaga de fines del siglo XVIII", *Estudis d'Història Econòmica,* vol. 1989/2, pp. 87-114.

Greek-owned vessels were selected according to the names of the captain and the ship; as evidence from the local archives has shown, our working hypothesis is that most captains were also owners of their vessels or co-owners with other local entrepreneurs.[84] So, for example, when we find in the ar-

---

83 We would like to thank the stuff of the BOA archive for facilitating our research there as well as Dr Phokion Kotzageorgis. For these registers see İdris Bostan, "İzn-i Sefine Defterleri ve Karadeniz de Rusya ile Ticaret Yapan Devlet-i Aliyye Tüccarları 1780-1846", *Türklük Araştırmaları Dergisi* 6 (1990), pp. 21-41. According to Dr Hacı Veli Aydın, a member of the research group as described in footnote 8, more than 80% of these vessels belonged to Ottoman Greeks. Hacı Veli Aydin, "Greek merchants and seafarers in the Black Sea, 1780-1820", in Gelina Harlaftis and Katerina Papakonstantinou (eds), *The Rise of Greek Shipping in the Mediterranean Trade of the 18th Century,* forthcoming.

84 The main financier of the shipowners of Spetses, for example, was the Peloponnesian Hadjipanayiotis Politis, also a merchant and shipowner, established in

chives Yiorgi Burbachi from Messolongi with the pollaca *Madonna di Broso,* or Andrea di Dimitri with the pollaca *Madonna di Hydra* or Andrea Lucheri from Galaxidi with the *Madonna di Megaspileo*, we register the ships as Greek-owned. And we have to note that we met no Muslim names of Ottoman vessels trading in the Italian and French ports. Moreover, the employees of the Sanità of Malta wrote down the captains of the Ottoman flag vessels owned by Greeks as "Greci" and the Genoese officials distinguished them according to their island of origin, as "*ottomano idriotto*" or "*ottomano ipsariotto*", while the French consuls referred to the Ottoman vessels as "*grecs*" or "*turcs*". A question that arises is why vessels and captains would be described as "Greek" in the western Mediterranean European ports. A preliminary remark could be that we have an ethnic-religious self-determination on behalf of Ottoman Greeks, but further research is necessary especially for the periods in which this term appears. Also, it seems that this ethno-religious connotation was accepted or applied by the port authorities of Malta or the French consuls. Finally, could this specific characterization, apart from being an ethno-religious determination, also denote a sort of "brand name" in the Mediterranean entrepreneurship that reflected "trustworthy service"? That is, was an Ottoman Greek captain from Messolongi or Hydra or Psara who traded regularly to the west considered reliable? Whatever the case, we presuppose that a "Greek" or "Greek-flag" ship can be considered as an "Ottoman" one. It should also be emphasized that our statistics rely on arrivals of ships, and count under what flag they were registered upon arrival. It is very probable that the captains changed the flags of their ship during the voyage[85].

Leonidion, opposite the island of Spetses on the Peloponnesian coast. Hadjipanayiotis-Politis was a relative of the equally wealthy Peloponnesian merchant Trouchanis or Trochanis, as well as of the leading Spetsiot Mexis family, which in turn was related through intermarriage to most of the important Spetsiot shipping families. From the archives of his business that were found and studied by Vassilis Kremmydas, it has been calculated that between 1783 and 1821 he was the co-owner of 26 deep-sea going sailing ships, together with the Spetsiots Hadjiyannis and Tehodarakis Mexis, Demetrakis Yannouzas, Lazarou-Orloff, Dimigionis (Ginis), Zakithinaios, Klissas, Panos, Santos, Sklias, Gikas Tzioupas (Tsoupas) and Spyridonos. Apart from being a co-owner of sailing ships, he collaborated with over fifty Spetsiot shipowners and provided the capital required, *sermagia*, for the purchase of cargo. During the forty-year course of his commercial and maritime enterprises he provided capital for cargoes on over 300 ships, over and above the cargoes transported by his own vessels. See Vassilis Kremmydas, *Archeio Chatzipanagioti* (Hadjipanagiotis Archive), Athens 1973, pp. 149-51.

85 See also Vassilis Kremmydas, *Elliniki nautilia, 1776-1835* (Greek shipping, 1776-1835), Athens: Istoriko Archeio. Emporiki Trapeza tis Ellados, 1985, vol. 1, pp. 36-8.

On the other hand, there were certainly vessels owned by Ottoman Muslims, or co-owned by them and Greeks.[86] But it seems that these were mostly engaged in the regional trade of the eastern Mediterranean and the Black Sea and that the Ottoman Muslims preferred to act mainly as investors in maritime commerce, which could mean part-ownership of vessels, and not necessarily as shipowners/captains and/or merchants.

The combined data from the above archives were fed into the *Amphitrete* database from where we were able to form the statistics as shown in Appendices that form the basis of the quantitative analysis that has been presented. We have followed the usual method adopted by maritime historians dealing with shipping statistics. The number of ships arriving at a certain port at a particularly year really means the total number of voyages that a certain number of vessels made. If, for example, 54 ships arrived at the port of Livorno in the year 1794, this does not mean that 54 different ships arrived at the port of Livorno that year. There might be one ship that arrived four times at Livorno (or made four voyages that year to Livorno) and there might be another 25 ships that made only one trip that year to Livorno. What is important here for the general picture and for the analysis of shipping statistics is the total number of arrivals at a port and not the number of individual ships trading in the port.

---

86   See Vassilis Kremmydas, "Katagrapfi ton emporikon ploion tou Irakleiou to 1751" (Register of the merchant ships of Herakleion in 1751), *Mnimon* 7 (1978-79), pp. 12-17; Murat Çizakça, *A Comparative Evolution of Business Partnerships, The Islamic World and Europe, with Specific Reference to the Ottoman Archives*, Leiden: Brill 1996, pp. 86-130; Edhem Eldem, "Strangers in their Own Seas?"

APPENDIX II

Arrivals of Greek-owned ships in the ports of Western Mediterranean

Year	Venice	Trieste	Malta	Genoa	Livorno	Marseilles	Barcelona	Malaga	Cadiz
1780	5	23	24		21				
1781	9	12	35		17				
1782	21	38	33		22				
1783	20	21	35	20	22				
1784	14	66	43	2	36				
1785	8	68	73	5	12				
1786	5	22	132	20	46				
1787	8	25	81	12	33				
1788	22	16	49	8	24				
1789	8		24	1	32				
1790	11		68	15	43	2			
1791	18	25	87	5	47	3			
1792	6	2	46	6	50				
1793	6		31	1	34				
1794	16	1	15	120	55	17			
1795	14	8	28	112	99	28			
1796	5	33	30	347	34	65			
1797	10	56	91	91	133	21	12	5	
1798	1	3	66		135	18	41	44	16
1799	4	4			11	17			
1800	4	2	21		88	11	2	2	
1801	10	1	103	132	28		3	3	
1802	17	4	61	87	94		15	6	2
1803	29	1	65	37	91		10	3	
1804	13	1	76		110		22	18	33
1805	15		131	8	107	7	21	84	34
1806	9		161	15	112	25	49	50	11
1807	0		72	4	33	9	9	20	15
1808	0		293		2				
1809	0		347	2	8	1			
1810	0		31	4	25	5			
1811	0		35		0				
1812			33		0				
1813			35		0				
1814			43	4	13				
1815									
1816					120				
1817		1							
1818					122				
1819					112				
1820					91				
1821									

Sources: For Venice, Trieste, Malta, Genoa, Livorno and Marseilles see *Amphitrete, 1700-1821,* Pythagoras Research Project, Ionian University/Greek Ministry of Education, 2004-2006. For Barcelona, Malaga and Cadiz data are derived from the *Diario de Barcelona, 1792-1801,* in Eloy Martin Corrales, "La flota greco-otomana en Cádiz a fines del siglo XVIII" in *Actas del II Congreso de Historia de Andalusia, Andalusia Moderna (II),* Cordoba 1995, pp. 389-400.

APPENDIX III

Greek-owned ships at the port of Livorno 1767-1815 according to their flags

Year	Ottoman	% Ottoman/total	Venetian	% Venetian/total	Russian	% Russian/total	Ionian	% Ionian/total	Total
1767	8	80	2	20					10
1768	19	90	3	10					22
1769	3	75	1	25					4
1770	6	60	4	40					10
1771	3	33			6	67			9
1772	3	37	2	25	3	38			8
1773	8	50	6	38	2	12			16
1774	12	75	1	6	3	19			16
1775	15	88	2	12					17
1776	9	75	3	25					12
1777	4	57	3	43					7
1778	8	80	2	20					10
1779	7	32	15	68					22
1780	14	67	7	23					21
1781	14	82	2	12	1	6			17
1782	16	73	6	27					22
1783	16	73	6	27					22
1784	29	81	7	19					36
1785	11	92			1	8			12
1786	45	98	1	2					46
1787	28	85	3	9	2	6			33
1788	22	92	2	8					24
1789	28	87	4	13					32
1790	37	86	4	9	2	5			43
1791	40	85	7						47
1792	44	88	6						50
1793	29	85	5						34
1794	43	78	12						55
1795	82	83	17						99
1796	24	71	10						34
1797	133	100							133
1798	135	100							135
1799	11	100							11
1800	57	65			31	35%			88
1801	24	86			4	14%			28
1802	60	64			27	29%	7	7%	94
1803	51	56			26	29%	14	15%	91
1804	69	63			32	29%	8	8%	110
1805	86	80			13	12%	8	8%	107
1806	110	98					2	2%	112
1807	33	100							33
1808	1	50			1	50%			2
1809	8	100							8
1810	25	100							25
1811									
1812									
1813									
1814	35								35
1815	73	73			26	27%			99

Source: *Amphitrete, 1700-1821,* Pythagoras Research Project, Ionian University/Greek Ministry of Education, 2004-6

APPENDIX IV

Arrivals at the port of Malta, 1780-1810

Year	Ottoman	Venetian	Russian	Jerusalem	Ionian	Other	Total
1780	15	7		2			24
1781	22	13					35
1782	30	3					33
1783	26	9					35
1784	38	5					43
1785	66	5	2				73
1786	113	11	7			1	132
1787	75	3	2			1	81
1788	46	1	2				49
1789	22	1	1				24
1790	66	2					68
1791	87						87
1792	43	3					46
1793	28	3					31
1794	14	1					15
1795	21	4		2		1	28
1796	19	9				2	30
1797	87		2			2	91
1798	62					4	66
1799	0						0
1800	12		5			4	21
1801	73		10		3	16	103
1802	36		18		5	2	61
1803	27		25		13		65
1804	46		21		9		76
1805	83		28		21		132
1806	112		22		26		160
1807	18		26	9	14	5	72
1808	30			259		4	293
1809	146			192	1	8	347
1810	19			7	3	1	31
Total	1482	80	171	471	95	49	2352

Source: Pythagoras Research Project, Ionian University/Greek Ministry of Education, 2004-6

APPENDIX V

Participation of Greek-owned ships in the total arrivals of the ports of Livorno and Genoa, 1792-1805

Year	Livorno Total arrivals	Greek-owned Arrivals	%	Genoa Total arrivals	Greek-owned arrivals	%
	(a)	(b)	(b)/(a)	(c)	(d)	(d)/(c)
1792	646	50	8%	992	6	1%
1793	547	34	6%	1229	1	
1794	1135	55	5%	1155	120	10%
1795	1048	99	10%	1549	112	7%
1796	457	34	7%	1114	347	31%
1797	683	133	20%	1.256	91	7%
1798	575	135	25%	828		
1799	405	11	3%	181		
1800	945	88	9%	251		
1801	316	28	9%	517	132	25%
1802	1003	94	9%	953	87	9%
1803	633	91	14%	566	37	6%
1804	943	110	12%	136		
1805	713	107	15%	140	8	6%

Sources: For Livorno, ASL, Governo civile e militare di Livorno, F. 61, 664-665, F. 82, 129-131, F. 89 274. For Genoa, see Luigi Bulferetti e Claudio Constantini, *Industrie e commerci in Liguria nell'eta del Risorgimento*, Milano 1965, p.161, data from A.N.P., F20 191, Etat général des navires. For Greek-owned vessels, Pythagoras Research Project, Ionian University/Greek Ministry of Education, 2006.

APPENDIX VI

Participation of Greek-owned vessels in Alexandria and Odessa, 1780-1821

	Alexandria Total arrivals	Greek Arrivals	%	Odessa Total departures	Greek Departures	%
1780	618	332	54			
1781	432	277	64			
1782	527	379	72			
1783	541	324	60			
1784						
1785	614	325	53			
1786						
1787	527	293	56			
1788	589	260	44			
1789	467	158	34			
1790	364	90	25			
1791						
1792						
1793						
1794						
1795						
1796						
1797						
1798						
1799						
1800						
1801				99	71	72
1802				256	121	48
1803				473	136	29
1804				382	154	40
1805				552	209	38
1806				106	61	58
1807				29	1	3
1808				276	158	57
1809				158	81	51
1810	356	204	57	190	158	83
1811	383	266	69	498	472	95
1812	299	205	69	514	507	99
1813				300	287	96
1814				360	343	95
1815	372	256	69	422	313	74
1816	311	153	49	826	430	52
1817				933	450	48
1818				621	356	57
1819				675	345	51
1820				635	306	48
1821				532	157	30

Sources: Vassilis Kremmydas, *Elliniki nautilia*, vol. 1, pp. 39, 73. His data for Alexandria derive from Archives du Ministère des Affaires Étrangères, Correspondence Consulaire et Commerciale, Alexandrie, vol. 16-26 (1732-1835) and from Archives Nationales de France (ANF), série Affaires Étrangères, sous-série BI (Correspondence Consulaire), 112-114, Alexandrie, vol. 13-15 (1777-1790), and sous- série BIII (Mémoire et Tableaux Statistiques), 272-280 (1780-1826). For Odessa, General Archives (Public Record Office), Foreign Office, 359/1, Odessa (1801-1835).

BIBLIOGRAPHY

Alexantris, Konstantinos (1960) *I anaviosis tis thalassias mas dynameos kata tin Tourkokratian* (*The Revival of our Maritime Strength during the Tourkokratia*), Athens: Ekdosis Istorikis Ypiresias B.N.

Arnaldi, Girolamo (2005) *Italy and its Invaders,* Cambridge, MA: Harvard University Press.

Baggiani, D. (1994) "Appunti per lo studio del movimento di navi e merci a Livorno tra XVIII e XIX secolo", *Ricerche Storiche,* a XXIV, 3, pp. 701-17.

Bağış, Ali İhsan (1998) *Osmanlı Ticaretinde Gayrî Müslimler,* 2 baskı, Ankara.

Bekiaroglou-Exadaktylou, Aikaterini (1994) *Othomanika naupigeia ston paradosiako elliniko choro* (Ottoman Shipyards in the Traditional Greek Area), Athens: Politistiko Technologiko Idryma ETVA.

Bostan, İdris (1990) "İzn-i Sefine Defterleri ve Karadeniz de Rusya ile Ticaret Yapan Devlet-i Aliyye Tüccarları 1780-1846", *Türklük Araştırmaları Dergisi* 6, pp. 21-41.

Bulferetti, Luigi and Claudio Constantini (1965) *Industrie e commerci in Liguria nell' eta del Risorgimento,* Milan.

Çadırcı, M. (1980) "II Mahmut devrinde (1808-1839) Avrupa ve Hayriye Tüccarları", *Türkiye'nin Sosyal ve Ekonomik Tarihi,* Osman Okyar-Halil İnalcık (eds), Ankara: Meteksan, pp. 237-41.

Calosci, Laura (2002-3) "Génova y la transformación del comercio Mediterránneo de Cataluña (1815-1840)", Departament d'Història i Instituciones Econòmiques, Divisio de Ciencies Juridiques, Economiques i Sociales, Univcrsitat de Barcelona.

Carrière, Charles (1973) *Négociants marseillais au XVIIIe siècle,* Marseilles: Institut Historique de Provence, vol. 2, pp. 57-67.

Çizakça, Murat (1996) *A Comparative Evolution of Business Partnerships, The Islamic World and Europe, with Specific Reference to the Ottoman Archives,* Leiden: Brill.

Cunningham, Allan (1993) *Anglo-Ottoman Encounters in the Age of Revolution. Collected Essays,* vol. 1, edited by Edward Ingram, London: Frank Cass.

D'Ohsson, Mouradgea (2001) *Tableau général de l'empire ottoman,* v.7, re-edition, İstanbul: Isis.

Dertilis. Georgios *et al.* (2005) *Istoria tou ellinikou kratous, 1830-1920* (History of the Greek state, 1830-1920), Athens: Estia.

Eldem, Edhem (2007) "Kontrolü Kaybetmek: 18 Yüzyılın İkinci Yarısında Doğu Akdeniz'de Osmanlı Varlığı", Ö.Kumrular (ed.), *Türkler ve Deniz*, İstanbul: Kitap Yayınevi, pp. 63-78.
—— "Strangers in their Own Seas? The Ottomans in the Eastern Mediterranean Basin in the Second Half of the Eighteenth Century", unpublished paper.
—— (1996) *French Trade in Istanbul in the 18th Century*, Leiden: Brill.
Fabio di Vita, "Greek Ships in Sicily during the 18th Century: Health Practices and Commercial Relationships" in Gelina Harlaftis and Katerina Papakonstantinou (eds), *The Rise of Greek Shipping in the Mediterranean trade of the 18th century*, forthcoming.
Faroqhi, Suraiya (2006) *The Ottoman Empire and the World around it*, London: I.B. Tauris.
Filippini, Jean Pierre (1998a) "Il commercio del grano a Livorno nel Settecento" in Jean Pierre Filippini, *Il porto di Livorno e la Toscana (1676-1814)*, vol. 2, pp. 318-71.
—— (1998b) "Raguza e l'attività commerciale livornese nel Settecento" in Jean Pierre Filippini, *Il porto di Livorno e la Toscana (1676-1814)*, vol. 2, Edizioni Scientifiche Italiane.
Gervinus, Georg G. (1864) *History of the Greek Revolution and Resurrection*, Athens: Ch.N. Philadelpheus.
Harlaftis, Gelina (1996) *A History of Greek-owned Shipping: The Making of an International Tramp Fleet, 1830 to the Present Day*, London: Routledge
—— (2005) "Mapping the Greek Maritime Diaspora from the Early 18th to the late 20th Century", in Ina Baghdiantz McCabe, Gelina Harlaftis and Ioanna Minoglou (eds), *Diaspora Entrepreneurial Networks. Five Centuries of History*, Oxford: Berg.
—— and Katerina Papakonstantinou (eds), *The Rise of Greek Shipping in the Mediterranean Trade of the 18th Century*, forthcoming.
Herlihy, Patricia (1986) *Odessa: A History, 1794-1914*, Cambridge, MA: Harvard University Press.
Houmanidis, Lazaros (1972) "Peri tis oikonomias kai nautilias ton trion nison Ydras, Spetson kai Psaron kata tin Tourkokratian" (About the economy and shipping of the three islands of Hydra, Spetses and Psara during the period of Turkish rule), *Epistimoniki Epetiris tis Panteiou Anotatis Sholis Politikon Epistimon*, Athens, pp. 177-244.
İnalcık, Halil (1978) "Capital Formation in the Ottoman Empire", *The Ottoman Empire: Conquest, Organization and Economy*, London: Variorum Reprints, 1978, XII, pp. 97-140.
—— "İmtiyazat", *Encyclopaedia of Islam*, 2nd ed., v. III, pp. 1179-89.

—— and Donald Quataert (eds) (1994) *An Economic History of the Ottoman Empire, 1300-1914*, Cambridge University Press.

Inglesi, Angeliki, *Voreioelladites emporoi sto telos tis tourkokratias. Stauros Ioannou (1790-1820)* (2004) (Traders from Northern Greece at the End of the Ottoman Rule. Stavros Ioannou), Athens: Istoriko Arheio-Politistiki symvoli tis Emporikis Trapezas tis Ellados.

Katsiardi-Hering, Olga (2003) "I elliniki diaspora: i geographia kai i typologia tis" (The Greek Diaspora: Geography and Typology), in Spyros I. Asdrachas (ed.), *Ellimiki Oikonomiki Istoria 15os-19os aionas* (Greek Economic History 15th-19th Centuries), Athens: Politistio Idryma Omilou Peiraios.

—— (1986) *I elliniki paroikia tis Tergestis, 1751-1830* (The Greek Community in Trieste, 1751-1830), 2 vols., Athens: University of Athens, Department of Philosophy.

Kondoayannis, P. (1917) "Oi prostateuomenoi" (The protégés), *Athina* 29, pp. 1-160.

Kremmydas, Vassilis (1997) "I Othomaniki autokratoria kai i anankastiki autonomisi tou emporiou" (The Ottoman Empire and the forced independence of commerce), *O Politis* 40, pp. 30-3.

—— (1978-79) "Katagrapfi ton emporikon ploion tou Irakleiou to 1751" (Register of the merchant ships of Herakleion in 1751), *Mnimon* 7, pp. 12-17.

—— (1973) *Archeio Chatzipanagioti* (Hadjipanagiotis Archive), Athens.

—— (1985) *Elliniki nautilia, 1776-1835* (Greek Shipping, 1776-1835), Athens: Istoriko Archeio. Emporiki Trapeza tis Ellados, vol. 1.

—— (1980) *Synkyria kai emporio stin proepanastatiki Peloponniso (1793-1821)* (Conjuncture and Trade in the Pre-revolutionary Peloponnisos 1793-1821), Athens: Themelio.

Lambrinides, Michael (19o7, reprint 1987) *Istorikai selides (1320-1821). Oi Alvanoi kata tin kyrios Ellada kai tin Peloponnison. Ydra-Spetsai* (The Albanians in the Greek Mainland and Peloponnese, Hydra and Spetses), reprint Athens: Notis Karavias bookshop: 1987, p. 38.

Leake, William Martin (1968) *Travels in the Morea*, v.II, Amsterdam: Hakkert.

Leon (Leontaritis), Georgios B. (1972) "Elliniki emporiki nautilia (1453-1850)" (Greek Merchant Shipping) in Stelios A. Papadopoulos, *Elliniki emporini nautilia* (Greek Merchant Shipping), Athens: National Bank of Greece, pp. 13-48.Lignos, Antonios (ed.) (1921) *Archeion tis koinotitas Ydras, 1778-1832* (Archive of the Community of Hydra, 1778-1832), Peiraias: typois ephim. Sfairas, vols. 1-3

Masson, Paul (1911) *Histoire du commerce français dans le Levant au XVIIIe siècle,* Paris: Hachette.

Masters, Bruce (1992) "The Sultan's Enterpreneurs: The Avrupa tüccaris and the Hayriye tüccaris in Syria", *International Journal of Middle East Studies* 24/4, pp. 579-97.

Orlandos, Anastasios, *Peri tis nisou Petsas i Spetson* (Regarding the island of Petsa or Spetses), Peiraias 1877.

Pagratis, Gerasimos (2006) "I Consolati della Repubblica Settinsulare (1800-1807) in Sicilia", in the 2nd Mediterranean Maritime History Network Conference, Messina/Taormina, 3-7 May, unpublished paper.

Pamuk, Şevket (2000) *A Monetary History of the Ottoman Empire,* Cambridge University Press.

Panzac, Daniel (1992) "International and Domestic Maritime Trade in the Ottoman Empire during the 18th century", *International Journal of Middle East Studies,* 24, 2, pp. 189-206.

—— (1999) *Les Corsaires Barbaresques. La fin d'une epopee, 1800-1820,* Paris: CNRS.

Papakonstantinou, Katerina (2002) "Ellinikes emporikes epicheiriseis stin Kentriki Europi to deuteron miso tou 18ou aiona. I oikogeneia Pontika" (Greek Mercantile Enterprises in Central Europe in the Second Half of the Eighteenth Century: the Case of the Pondikas Family), unpublished PhD thesis, University of Athens.

Philliou, Christine (2001) "Mischief in the Old Regime: Provincial Dragomans at the Turn of the 19th Century", *New Perspectives on Turkey* 25 (fall 2001), pp. 103-21.

Procacci, Giulano (1991) *History of the Italian People,* London: Penguin Books.

Quataert, Donald (1997) "Clothing Laws, State, and Society in the Ottoman Empire, 1720-1829", *International Journal of Middle East Studies* 29, 3, 403-25.

Romano, Ruggiero (1956) *Commerce et prix du blé à Marseille au XVIIIe siècle,* Paris.

—— (1962) "Per una valutazione della flotta mercantile europea alla fine del secolo XVIII", in *Studi in onore di Amintore Fanfani, V,* Milan.

Sfyroeras, Vassilis (1965) *Oi dragomanoi tou stolou, o thesmos kai oi phoreis* (The Dragomans of the Fleet. The Institution and the Personnel), Athens.

—— (1968) *Ta ellinika pliromata tou tourkikou stolou* (The Greek Crews of the Turkish Fleet), Athens.

Shaw Stanford (1971) *Between Old and New. The Ottoman Empire under Sultan Selim III, 1789-1807,* Cambridge, MA: Harvard University Press

―― (1969) "Selim III and the Ottoman Navy", *Turcica* 1.

Stoianovich, Traian (1952) "L'Economie balkanique aux XVIIe et XVIIIe siècles (principalement d'après les archives consulaires françaises)", thesis, doctorat d'université, Université de Paris.

Svolopoulos, Konstantinos (1973) "O ellinikos emporikos stolos kata tas paramonas tou agonos tis anexartisias. Anekdotos pinax tou F. Pouqueville" (The Greek merchant marine in the eve of the struggle for independence. The unpublished table of F. Pouqueville), *Eranistis* I/59.

Svoronos, Nikos (1996) *To emporio tis Thessalonikis ton 18o aiona* (The Commerce of Thessaloniki in the 18th Century), Athens: Themelio.

Urquhart, David (1836) *La Turquie; ses resources, son organization municipale, son commerce*, Paris: Arthus Bertrand, vol. III.

Van den Boogert, Maurits H. (2005) *The Capitulations and the Ottoman Legal System. Qadis, Consuls and Beratlis in the 18th Century*, Leiden-Boston: Brill.

Vlami, Despoina (2000) *To fiorini, to stari kai i odos tou kipou. Ellines emporoi sto Livorno, 1750-1868* (The fiorini, the grain and the Garden street. Greek merchants in Livorno, 1750-1868), Athens: Themelio.

2

WOMEN IN THE GREEK WAR OF INDEPENDENCE

Helen Angelomatis-Tsougarakis

The history of women during the Greek War of Independence (1821-30) has attracted comparatively more attention than their role in the periods of Venetian and Ottoman domination. Contemporary official documents usually refer rather cursorily to the hardships, the sacrifices and the often tragic fate of the civilian population during those years. Additional evidence exists in sources such as memoirs or histories written by those who actually participated in the war, or who lived soon after. There are also several books written by Philhellenes who took part in these events; such sources, however, are fragmentary, often subjective and partial, or second-hand. And their accounts are usually embellished so as to add a romantic or exotic interest.

In Greece, women's lives and their contribution to the War of Independence stimulated considerable interest early on, initially among other women, but also among others, including amateur historians. In these books and articles we find individual stories and accounts of tragic or extraordinary events in which women usually figure prominently. However, their documentation is poor, or not easily verifiable, and occasionally there is no documentation at all. Some accounts may be based on oral family tradition, but the emphasis on the heroism of these women often obscures their genuine historical value.[1]

Most of this literature is already dated and often of dubious academic merit, mixing documented facts with romantic assumptions, improbable claims and patriotic rhetoric intended to appeal perhaps to a wide national readership.[2]

---

1 Several of the earliest articles were published in the first feminist newspaper in Greece, *Ephimeris ton Kyrion*, in the last years of the 19th century.

2 Sotiria Alimperti, *Ai Iroides tis Ellinikis Epanastaseos*, Athens 1933; Sotiria

Two well-known women whose life and role in the Revolution defied the usual constraints of generally accepted female activities have attracted more attention: Laskarina Bouboulina, the widow of a ship owner on the island of Spetses, who fought during the War with her own ship and participated in various other important war events and Manto Mavrogenous, a maiden of a distinguished family whose members had held important offices in the Ottoman Empire. Manto contributed to the war effort financially: with her own funds she fitted out a ship and paid soldiers to fight in the War, becoming a pauper herself in the process.

However, even these two women are usually presented in a romantic and idealized way which obscures rather than clarifies their role. The existing bibliography offers a wealth of information in need of closer and scholarly examination. This paper attempts to contribute to this by presenting an overview of the existing sources as well as by identifying the continuities and discontinuities in women's lives during this crucial period.

The lives of the Christian population under Ottoman rule were affected over centuries by diverse geographical, administrative, and economic factors. There were obvious differences between the rural and urban populations and in social stratification, differences that were decisive in women's lives. There was a gulf between the women of affluent levels of society and those in the lower and poorer ranks, who comprised the majority of the Christian population regardless of ethnic origin, whether Greek, Albanian or Vlach. The women of more affluent families led a comfortable and sheltered, redundant life. They were also strictly confined. Young girls lived in complete seclusion until they married and only as married women, mainly as widows, and thus heads of their own families, were they able to become involved in financial and other economic activities.

By all accounts, the women of the lower classes led a very hard life. In rural areas, more often than not, they worked as unpaid labourers along with the other members of their families, either as sharecroppers or on their own land. Particularly in mountainous areas and on the islands, the men were away most of the time working as carriers, artisans, traders or sailors. Thus, the cultivation of the land was almost exclusively in the hands of women, along with all other everyday necessary tasks such as carrying wood, stones and water. It is difficult to distinguish between those who worked for their families without any wages

---

Alimperti, *Manto Mavrogenous*, Athens 1931. Koula Xiradaki, *Gynaikes tou '21. Prosphores, Iroismoi kai Thysies*, Dodoni, Athens-Giannina 1995. Manouil Tasoulas, *Manto Mavrogenous. Istoriko Archeio*, 2nd ed. Athens: The Municipality of Mykonos and "Perivolaki", 1997.

and others who were paid for their labour. There is no doubt, however, that a great number of women worked as hired labourers.

The most important aspect of a woman's life was marriage. Her whole life was centred on her family. Marriages were arranged by the families and they were totally dependent on the future bride being endowed with an adequate dowry measured according to the family's financial status. Girls were given in marriage by their parents and their preference or personal consent was of no consequence. Later in the marriage they could ask for a divorce on the grounds that they were either coerced or were below the age of consent, and since the Church was strict about this, it was nearly always granted. Early marriages and even earlier betrothals were the norm, as was the considerable age difference between the groom and bride, who could be as young as 12 years old or even younger.

Public or community affairs of any kind were for the vast majority of women quite beyond their interest or possible involvement. There were, however, cases of women belonging to high-ranking families such as the Phanariots who were actively though secretly involved in the affairs of the Ecumenical Patriarchate, lending money and trying to influence the election or the fall of a patriarch. Women's education was non-existent, or minimal. Only families of scholars or those with a high rank in society cared enough to provide privately some basic education for their daughters.[3]

As might be expected, the outbreak of the Greek War of Independence brought about important changes in women's lives, but neither everywhere, nor at the same time, nor in the same degree. In most of the small Aegean islands life went on as before usually without dramatic changes. Some islands, however, suffered destructions and massacres. Life as it was known before was totally extinguished. In Chios in 1822 and in Psara in 1824 a great number of women were killed, many more were sold as slaves, and the surviving population was obliged to move to other places. Other islands, Crete and Cyprus in particular, also went through very difficult times. The consequences of the fighting were tragic for the civilian population of continental Greece: Thrace, Macedonia and Thessaly suffered the most initially, until the revolt was suppressed in those regions. The rest of Greece also suffered, but more gradually.

Nevertheless, some aspects of traditional life continued unchanged regardless of circumstances. Wherever possible, young girls and even married women

---

3 For an overview of Greek women's life and social status see Helen Angelomatis-Tsougarakis, "Greek Women (16th-19th century): the Travellers' View", *Mesaionika kai Nea Ellinika* (Akadimia Athinon, Kentron Ereunis tou Mesaionikou kai Neou Ellinismou), 4 (1992), pp. 321-403.

were kept strictly secluded by their families.[4] Women still laboured in the fields, while the men sat smoking their pipes, and drinking coffee, waiting for the news of the battles.[5] Philhellenes noted that the women were carrying out all the agricultural labour and they also cultivated silkworms to make silk, and wove for long hours. Indeed, one of them describes a refugee family from Livadia living in a hut near Epidavros (Piada) whose young daughter wove almost 12 hours a day, often commencing weaving as early as three o'clock in the morning[6]. When circumstances allowed, they were also employed in jobs such as wet nurses for orphans, or abandoned babies, or as cooks paid with public funds.[7] On certain occasions women were also used as couriers, carrying letters back and forth, and were paid a small sum for their services.[8] None of this is very surprising or unexpected since women of the lower classes worked just as hard before the War and often did jobs which might have been considered unfit for women.

Upper class women who lived in some safety also went on with their everyday life, providing their husbands, who lived elsewhere, with necessary clothes, taking care of the affairs of the household, receiving visits and offering hospitality to travelling officials or Philhellenes. Housewives continued to worry about household matters as the wife of G. Kountouriotis did for the special arrangements needed in order to receive Ioannis Kapodistrias, the Governor of Greece, at her house in Hydra.[9]

---

[4] Julius Millingen, *Memoirs of the Affairs of Greece; Containing an Account of the Military and Political Events, which Occurred in 1823 and Following Years with Various Anecdotes Relating to Lord Byron and an Account of his Last Illness and Death*, London 1831, pp. 107-9. K. Simopoulos, *Pos eidan oi xenoi tin Ellada tou '21*, 1: 1821-1822, Athens 1979, p. 427; 2: 1822-1823, Athens 1980, pp. 62, 284, 311. Olivier Voutier, *Mémoires du colonel Voutier sur la guerre actuelle de la Grèce*, Paris 1823, p. 56. Jean Philippe Paul Jourdain, *Mémoires historiques et militaires sur les événements de la Grèce: depuis 1822, jusqu'au combat de Navarin ...*, Paris 1828, 1, p. 46.

[5] K. Simopoulos, *Pos eidan oi xenoi tin Ellada* 2, p. 314, and 4: 1824-1826, Athens 1982, pp. 81-2.

[6] Edward Blaquiere, *Letters from Greece: with Remarks on the Treaty of Intervention*, London 1828, pp. 48-50.

[7] K.A. Diamantis, *Athinaikon Archeion, Archeia ek tis Neoteris Ellinikis Istorias ek ton Syllogon Gianni Vlachogianni*, Athens 1971, pp. 106, 125, 157, 181, 182, 192, 205, 219, 224, 229, 237.

[8] Alexandros D. Kriezis, *Apomnimoneumata (Giornale dia tin Anexartisian tou Genous)*, ed. Emm. G. Protopsaltis, Athens: Vivliothiki G. Tsoukalas and Son, 1956, p. 34.

[9] K.A. Diamantis (ed.), *Archeia Lazarou and Georgiou Kountouriotou*, tomos enatos (Apo 30 Septemvriou eos 21 Dekemvriou 1827, 1828 kai 1829), Athens

Other aspects of women's lives also continued as before. Thus, arranged marriages continued to be the norm, and betrothals, weddings, childbirths, love affairs, and adulteries occurred. Indeed they took on new dimensions.

Marriages had always been used as a means of securing political, diplomatic or financial alliances between states as well as between individuals. During the period of Ottoman domination the social and financial status of families dictated the choice of the future spouse both for men and women. However, in the Greek War of Independence traditional arranged marriages acquired a particular importance as they established steady alliances and confirmed trust among the leading figures of the Greek fighters and politicians. According to Photakos[10] "marriages were then respected, and a relation by marriage was considered like that of a relation by blood." The women were expected to consent to their families' decisions and they did.

Thus, there are several known cases of matches linking the families of some of the more powerful chieftains. We also know of attempts to secure betrothals that would bridge a gap between members of opposing parties. The best known match is perhaps the one Theodoros Kolokotronis arranged for his son Panos, who married Bouboulina's daughter Eleni. This marriage, in addition to the considerable dowry it brought to Kolokotronis's family,[11] secured a bond between one of the leading figures of the Morea with one of the influential ship-owning families fighting at sea, a family that would ensure the support of the whole island of Spetses for Kolokotronis's faction. As for Bouboulina, with this marriage she greatly extended her own influence in the Morea.

When Panos Kolokotronis was killed in one of the civil wars, his father Theodoros hoped to keep his son's widow in the family, intending to give her in marriage to another family later on. Bouboulina, however, secretly took her daughter back, leaving behind her dowry, even though she was entitled to keep it. Two explanations regarding this unusual event have been offered by contemporary sources. One states that Bouboulina had already talked previously with General Theodorakis Grivas from northern Greece, and intended to give her daughter to him, linking her with the party of northern Greek fighters.[12]

        1968, p. 210.

10   Photakos, Photios Ch., (pen name of Photios Chrysanthopoulos), *Apomnimoneumata peri tis Ellinikis Epanastaseos,* Athens, 1898, 2, p. 72.

11   Maxime Raybaud, *Mémoires sur la Grèce, pour servir à l'histoire de la guerre de l'Indépendence accompagnés des plans topographiques ... avec une introduction par Alph. Rabbe,* Paris 1825, 2, p. 31.

12   Nikolaos Kasomoulis, *Apomnimoneumata Stratiotika peri tis Epanastaseos ton Ellinon 1821-1833. Protassetai Istoria tou Armatolismou,* Introduction and notes by Giannis Vlachogiannis, Athens 1939-1942, 2, p. 80. Kanellos Deligiannis,

The second version is that Panos's widow Eleni had a love affair with Grivas[13] and her mother intervened to get her the husband she wanted, making sure at the same time that she would not be exposed as an immoral and wanton woman who had had an extramarital affair.

Theodoros Kolokotronis also arranged the marriage of his other son Gennaios to Photeini, daughter of the Souliote chieftain Kitsos Tzavelas, succeeding where the most important of northern Greece fighters, Georgios Karaiskakis, had failed. This match resulted in Tzavelas terminating his alliance with Zaimis and other members of the Government and joining Kolokotronis's party.[14] Moreover, Kolokotronis engaged his younger son Kollinos, roughly about 12 years old at the time, to Kanellos Deligiannis's daughter Mariori, who was eight years old.[15] This engagement caused many complaints among Kolokotronis's followers and supporters and resulted only in problems.[16] In the end, the marriage never took place and Kolokotronis subsequently married his son to the granddaughter of the Phanariot Ioannis Karatzas, former Grand Dragoman of the Sublime Porte.[17] This unsuccessful betrothal has been considered as either an attempt by Kolokotronis to reconcile the existing hatred between himself, a former *klepht,* and the *koçabaşi* Kanellos Deligiannis and his family, or as means to secure with the help of Deligiannis a position as commander of the garrison at the fort of Nauplio for his son Panos.

There are several other examples that demonstrate how the principal figures of the Revolution sought to consolidate their alliances by marrying themselves, or by betrothing their children or one of their close relatives, to spouses of equally important families. Thus, Papaflessas managed to betroth his niece to Konstantinos Mavromihalis of the great Maniote family.[18] Alexandros Mavrokordatos gave his accomplished sister Aikaterini in marriage to Spyridion

---

Apomnimoneumata, notes by G. Tsoukalas, ed. Emm. G. Protopsaltis, Athens: Vivliothiki G. Tsoukalas and Son, 1957, 2, p. 207.

13   Photakos, op. cit., 2, p. 451.

14   Gennaios Kolokotronis, *Apomnimoneumata,* ed. Emm. G. Protopsaltis, Athens: Vivliothiki G. Tsoukalas and Son [1955], p. 154. Photakos, op. cit., 2, p. 451. Nikolaos Kasomoulis, op. cit., 2, p. 348.

15   Mihail Oikonomou, *Istorika tis Ellinikis Paliggenesias i, o Ieros ton Ellinon Agon,* ed. Emm. G. Protopsaltis, Athens: Vivliothiki G. Tsoukalas and Son, 1957, 1, p. 192. Kanellos Deligiannis, op. cit., 1, pp. 128-9. Amvrosios Phrantzis, *Epitomi tis Istorias tis Anagennithisis Ellados, Archomeni apo tou Etous 1715 kai Ligousa to 1835,* Athens 1839-1841, 2, pp. 272 ff.

16   T.A. Stamatopoulos, *O Esoterikos Agonas prin kai meta tin Epanastasi,* Athens 1971, 1, pp. 309 ff.

17   Mihail Oikonomou, op. cit., 2, p. 47.

18   Photakos, op. cit., 2, p. 72.

Trikoupis, and General Dimitrios Makris wedded Eupraxia, daughter of the city notable Samos Razi-Kotsikas, during the siege of Mesolongi by the Turks.[19]

Love and financial considerations sometimes brought about major conflicts between the leaders and even between relatives. Gennaios Kolokotronis, for example, was in love with the sister of Ioannis Notaras, the rich *koçabaşi* of Corinth, and was ready to invade her village (Trikkala, in the Corinth area) with his soldiers to claim her. He was dissuaded at the last moment by Ioannis Makrygiannis, who stated that if such a violent abduction occurred, Gennaios would never receive her dowry from her brother. Eventually the lady in question was wedded to Georgios Mavromichalis.[20] Thus, in the end Gennaios married the wife his father chose for him.

Ioannis Notaras himself was involved in a conflict with his relative Panagiotis Notaras for the hand of Sophia, the rich and beautiful daughter of another *koçabaşi* of Corinth, Theocharis Rentis. This rivalry ended in some serious fighting between their troops, but it had also another, perhaps more important motive: the revenue from the local Corinthian currant production. As a result of this conflict the small town of Sofiko and its inhabitants suffered seriously. In the end, Sophia married neither of these men, but after Notaras's death she was given in marriage to General Dimitrios Kallergis.[21] There are other recorded attempts to arrange marriages between various chieftains' female relatives.[22] There is no mention, however, of these girls' reactions to these arrangements. In this respect there were no changes in Greek society.[23]

There was, however, an unconventional betrothal, that of Manto Mavrogenous to prince Demetrios Ypsilantis, General of the Greek army and brother of the official leader of the Greek War of Independence, which as an exceptional case attracted considerable attention. Manto, a girl of a distinguished family, arranged her own marriage without the involvement of her mother, brother and other relatives. Moreover, she made provisions to safeguard her interests

---

19 Nikolaos D. Makris, *Istoria tou Mesolongiou*, ed. Emm. G. Protopsaltis, Athens: Vivliothiki G. Tsoukalas and Son, 1957, pp. 44-5.

20 Photakos, op. cit. 1, p. 524. Ioannis Makrygiannis, *Stratigou Makrygianni Apomnimoneumata*, ed. Giannis Vlachogiannis, 2ⁿᵈ ed. Athens 1947, 1, pp. 197, 200-1.

21 Christos Vyzantios, *Istoria ton kata tin Ellinikin Epanastasin Ekstrateion kai Machon on Meteschen o Taktikos Stratos apo tou 1821 mechri tou 1833*, ed. Emm. G. Protopsaltis, Athens: Vivliothiki G. Tsoukalas and Son, 1957, p. 141. T.A. Stamatopoulos, op. cit., 3, p. 414.

22 Photakos, op. cit., 2, p. 426. Nikolaos Kasomoulis, op. cit., 2, pp. 9-10, 160, 166, 184.

23 Millingen, op. cit., pp. 109-10.

and the good name of her family, requiring Ypsilantis to sign a document guaranteeing financial compensation if a breach of promise occurred and the wedding did not take place. When the prince did not keep his promise, she was determined to pursue her legal rights and present her case to the authorities of the country, the Ministry of Religion first (in 1825) and later the Governor of Greece, Ioannis Capodistrias (in 1830). However, she never received compensation, as the signed paper which proved her case had been torn by a friend of Ypsilantis, to whom it had been given as a third party for safekeeping.

Marriages arranged for political purposes were just some of many unions which continued to occur despite the hardships and the danger. Even special trips were made in order to celebrate a wedding. The family of an elder named Papadopoulos or Mourtogiannis, for example, went to Poros to wed his daughter to Christodoulos Mexis or Poriotis.[24] We also know of a man who was captured by the Turks as he climbed the mountains of Alonistaina in order to meet families there, find a girl to marry, and reach an agreement with her family. It is interesting to note the comment of Photakos[25] on this occasion. The Greeks, he writes, despite the presence of the enemy in their fatherland, and regardless of their burnt villages which they were obliged to desert, thus residing on the rocks here and there, wanted to increase their numbers and took care to marry. Fighters continued to think about their eventual marriages to girls they secretly loved, and mothers, or even the girls themselves, may have made similar plans. One might assume this from what N. Kasomoulis writes about his desire to marry a daughter of his former leader, Nikolaos Stornaris, who had been killed in Mesolongi.[26]

However, a new phenomenon emerged as a result of the War: men began to marry Turkish women who were first converted and baptized. Others simply kept Turkish women as concubines.[27] It was also not unknown for foreign Philhellenes and soldiers of fortune to be engaged or married to Greek girls. Johan Jacob Meyer, the editor of the Mesolongi newspaper *Ellinika Chronika*, who died in the siege, was married to a local girl Altana Grylinou Inglezou, the Prussian artillery officer Al. Kolbe was engaged to another.[28] We are also

---

24   Photakos, op. cit., 2, 426.
25   Ibid. 2, p. 324.
26   Nikolaos Kasomoulis, op. cit., 1, pp. 339, note 1, 349 note 5.
27   Georg Ludw. von Maurer, *Das Griechische Volk in öffentlicher, kirchlischer und privat-rechtlicher Beziehung vor und nach dem Freiheitskampfe bis zum 31 Juli 1834*, Heidelberg 1835, 1, p. 133. Ioannis Makrygiannis, op. cit., 1, p. 24. Olivier Voutier, *Lettres sur la Grèce, notes et chants populaires extraits du portefeuille du colonel Voutier*, Paris 1826, pp. 60-1, 104.
28   Nikolaos Kasomoulis, op. cit., 2, p. 283 note 2. Samuel Howe, *An Historical*

informed of three Greek women, prisoners from Tripolitsa, who were said to have willingly followed a renegade French officer in the army of Ibrahim, who kept them as his harem, when he returned to Egypt.[29]

Divorces were also granted during the revolution. Previously they were granted by the Church, the local bishop, or the Patriarch, according to Byzantine laws. In the period of the Ottoman rule, there had been considerable relaxation of the strict Byzantine law regarding divorces, which were often permitted "*kat' oikonomian*", as a kind of special dispensation in order to avert those seeking an easy divorce from turning to Islamic law.[30] During the war, the Church remained the authority for granting a divorce, but the whole procedure was the responsibility of the Ministry of Religion, whose Minister was normally a prelate and its officials clergymen. Finally, the members of the Court granting the divorce were all clergymen with a presiding bishop, much as it was in the past.[31]

Adultery had been and was still at that time the most common and acceptable reason for divorce. Indirect evidence indicates that despite the hard and dangerous circumstances of everyday life, or because of them, adultery might have become more common than before. Some local communities following their traditional laws inflicted hard punishments on the adulterers. We are told, for example, of the lover of a young married woman who was put in the stocks, and of her own public ridicule and subsequent exile from her island, Mykonos.[32]

There appears to have been a relaxation of the otherwise very strict moral rules that had earlier prevailed among the Greeks.[33] We are told of loves, passions, secret meetings, and even elopements, which were quite rare in the

---

Sketch of the Greek Revolution, New York 1828, p. 310. K. Simopoulos, op. cit., 5: 1826-1829, Athens 1984, p. 470.

29 K. Simopoulos, ibid., pp. 105, 106, 108, 109.

30 Dimitrios S. Ginis, " Oi Logoi Diazygiou epi Tourkokratias", *Epistimoniki Epetiris tis Scholis Nomikon kai Oikonomikon Spoudon Panepistimiou Thessalonikis*, 8 (1960), pp. 239-83. K.I. Dyovouniotis, *Nomokanonikai Meletai*, 1, Athens 1917. For further bibliography see Helen Angelomatis-Tsougarakis, op.cit., *Mesaionika kai Nea Ellinika*, 4 (1992), p. 395 note 353.

31 Georg Ludw. von Maurer, op. cit., 1, pp. 131-2. *Archeia tis Ellinikis Paliggenesias 1821-1832*, "*Lyta Engrapha*" *A' kai B' Vouleutikis Periodou, tomos ektos, Ypourgeia B'*, Athens: Vouli ton Ellinon, 1981, 14, pp. 261-2. N.P. Papadopoulos, *Katakaimenou Moria Selides tou 1821*, Athens 1974, 1, pp. 235-44.

32 Maxime Raybaud, op. cit., 2, pp. 117-18.

33 Nikolaos Kasomoulis, op. cit., 1, p. 170, note 2, felt obliged to comment on that subject since there was a noticeable difference later on. Changes in the local customs were initially introduced by young men returning from long stays in European cities, but they were frowned upon by the rest of the Greeks and these young men were considered dissolute.

past, although we cannot say with any certainty how widespread these were.³⁴ The fact that many such incidents were narrated by Europeans who fought in Greece does not add much to their validity since they might have been an exaggeration for purposes of romantic interest.

Nevertheless, it is well documented that concubinage, formerly rare and encountered mainly in the Ionian Islands, became common among the chieftains. They were sometimes followed, even in their expeditions, by young women dressed in men's clothes. Occasionally, these men married the girls in question. Prominent military and political leaders such as Theodoros Kolokotronis, Georgios Karaiskakis and Ioannis Kolettis were among those said to have concubines.³⁵ Karaiskakis indeed remembered in his will Mario, the Ottoman girl he kept always with him in the camps.³⁶ Kolettis was notorious for his affairs not only with the widow of the chieftain Christos Palaskas, but also with a couple of Ottoman girls. He is said to have been the subject of jokes, because he travelled accompanied with these girls dressed in European attire on horseback.³⁷ Kolettis was blamed by his contemporaries not only as responsible for the death of Palaskas but also for taking his widow as a mistress, a fact that was perhaps more offensive than his role in the death of her husband.³⁸ The controversial chieftain of Western Greece Varnakiotis also had three concubines, the most influential of whom, Rina Koutzoubaboula, marched ahead of Varnakiotis's lieutenant carrying a gun.³⁹

---

34   P. Monastiriotis, D. Christidis, M. Poulos and N. Karoris, *Apomnimoneumata Athinaion Agoniston,* ed. Emm. G. Protopsaltis, Athens: Vivliothiki G. Tsoukalas and Son, 1957, pp. 22, 34, 37, 38, 40. T.A. Stamatopoulos, op. cit., 1, pp. 453-4. K. Simopoulos, op. cit., 5, pp. 470-1. Kalliroi Parren, "Eleni Vasou", *Ephimeris ton Kyrion,* no. 296, 6 March 1893, pp. 2-3; no. 298, 21 March 1893, pp. 1-2.

35   K. Simopoulos, op. cit., 5: 1826-1829, pp. 471-2.

36   Gennaios Kolokotronis, op. cit., pp. 163-4. D. Ainian, *Apomnimoneumata,* ed. Emm. Protopsaltis ed., Athens: Vivliothiki G. Tsoukalas and Son, 1957, p. 136.

37   Georg Ludw. von Maurer, op. cit., 1, pp. 132-3. Nikolaos Kasomoulis, op. cit., I, pp. 321-2. D. Petrakakos, *Koinovouleutiki Istoria tis Ellados: Istoriki, dogmatiki kai Kritiki Ereuna epi ti Vasei ton Anekdoton tou Ethnous Archeion. Tomos Protos, Agones Tessaron Aionon yper tis Politikis Eleutherias apo tis Aloseos mechri tis 3is Septemvriou 1843 (1453-1843),* Athens 1935, p. 307, note 2. K. Simopoulos, op. cit., 2, p. 308, note 2; 5, pp. 470-3.

38   Ioannis Makrygiannis, op. cit., 1, pp. 158, 242. Nikolaos Spiliadis, *Apomnimoneumata dia na Chrisimeusosin eis tin Nean Ellinikin Istorian (1821-1843),* ed. Ch. N. Philadelpheus, Athens 1851, 1, p. 346.

39   Emm. G. Protopsaltis (ed.), *Istorikon Archeion Maurokordatou, Mnimeia tis Ellinikis Istorias 5, Engrapha tou 1824,* Athens: Akadimia Athinon, 1971, band

Many girls and women were raped when taken prisoners by the enemy. Among the many known cases an exceptional one was narrated to General Makrygiannis[40] by a woman who had been raped successively by 38 Turks. The sources are contradictory about rapes committed by Greeks. Some claim that rapes were seldom, if ever, committed by Greek soldiers and *klephts*, particularly those of the Morea, since they respected women and avoided this foul deed. The superstition that a bullet would be the just punishment of those engaged in sins of the flesh was believed to be a powerful deterrent.[41] However, there are indeed reported rapes of Greek women during the civil wars, usually by men from northern Greece who fought in the Morea, or even by local men under circumstances unrelated to the War. We know for example of a girl in Athens, eventually freed by General Makrygiannis,[42] who was held hidden against her will by some young Athenians.

A novelty, as far as we know, was the appearance of female dancers and musicians who performed more or less professionally in the Morea. The spectacular dance of a certain Anastasia is described in detail by one of the Philhellenes present during her performance, which included dancing with a sword.[43] A woman with a tambourine, accompanied by a male violinist, was taken along as his entertainer by Papaflessas on his way to fight Ibrahim Pasha.[44]

As we have seen, the sheltered life of upper class women continued as long as they resided in places away from the areas under attack, although hardships were unavoidable. When the war events neared their homes, male family members moved them permanently or for brief periods to safer places. Similar operations were occasionally organized by various towns or villages whenever there was imminent danger to the civilian population.[45] The Ionian Islands, close both to the Morea and to western Greece, were a common place to send women and children, though occasional obstacles were presented by the British. Some of the fortresses, like Chlomoutsi in Ileia, or large, fortified monasteries like Mega Spilaion at Kalavryta were also the temporary abode of women and children.[46]

IV, p. 585.

40   Op. cit., 2, p. 19.

41   Ioannis Philimon, *Dokimion Istorikon peri tis Ellinikis Epanastaseos*, Athens 1860, 3, p.

42   Kanellos Deligiannis, op. cit., II, p. 114. Ioannis Makrygiannis, op. cit., 1, pp. 144, 182-3, 190. T. Stamatopoulos, op. cit., 1, p. 457; IV, pp. 153-4.

43   K. Simopoulos, op.cit., 4, pp. 108-9.

44   Ioannis Makrygiannis, op. cit., 1, p. 214.

45   Ioannis Philimon, op. cit., 3, p. 147.

46   Ibid., 3, p. 151. Kanellos Deligiannis, op. cit., 3, p. 79. Nikolaos Spiliadis, op. cit., 3, p. 87.

When these movements were made as a well-organized preventive measure, they might have caused discomfort and concern for women and children, but they were certainly not dramatic. More often than not, however, the subsequent events were disastrous and tragic. At that point, any class distinction among the unfortunate women and their children who fled for their lives vanished. There were instances in which pregnant women delivered their babies on board the Greek ships that saved them from a massacre, as happened with those fleeing Kydonies (Ayavalik).[47] As would be expected, refugees had to live in new locations in various degrees of hardship, a dearth of food being often one of the serious problems faced.[48] The suffering of civilians in besieged towns, like Mesolongi or Athens, was understandably great. Thus an effort was made to send women and children away for their own sake and for the defenders themselves, who would save food and not have to worry. Women from the besieged Mesolongi remained for some time on the small island of Kalamos in the Ionian Islands, but then most returned to their town and suffered the dire consequences of its eventual fall.[49] On another occasion women from Macedonia found shelter in the islands of the Northern Sporades. Those who survived the total destruction of the island of Psara were taken initially to Nauplio and later to the island of Syros. Athenian women were moved to the island of Salamina to avoid the siege.

There was much worse. In the existing sources there is an endless succession of horrific descriptions, narrating in a vivid and disturbing way the disorderly and panic-stricken flight of women and children, of every rank and from many regions, in a frequently vain search for shelter in the mountains, in caves and at dangerous heights, when the Ottoman or Egyptian forces approached. It was quite usual for young girls and women with children to commit suicide rather than be captured. They chose to fall from the cliffs alone or took with them their children, or even the enemy soldiers who held them. They often drowned themselves in lakes, rivers, wells or the sea rather than surrender. Sometimes terrified mothers deserted their babies in order to escape.[50] It was also not unusual for

---

47 Nikolaos D. Patras (ed.), *Istorika Imerologia ton Ellinikon Naumachion tou 1821. Ek ton Imerologion tou Naumachou An. Tsamadou*, Athens 1886, p. 46.

48 Samuel Howe, op. cit., p. 373.

49 Spyromilios, *Apomnimoneumata tis Deuteras Poliorkias tou Mesolongiou 1825-6, Eisagogi Io. Vlachogianni*, Athens: Vivliothiki G. Tsoukalas and Son, 1957, p. 217.

50 Nikolaos Spiliadis, op. cit., 3, pp. 14-15, 21. Kanellos Deligiannis, op. cit., 3, pp. 78, 112. Mihail Oikonomou, op. cit., 2, pp. 34, 77. Photakos, op. cit., 2, pp. 256, 307-8, 319-20, 353. Spyridon Trikoupis, *Istoria tis Ellinikis Epanastaseos*, 2nd ed. Athens 1860, 1, p. 243. Artemios Michos, *Apomnimoneumata*, ed. Emm. G. Protopsaltis, Athens: Vivliothiki G. Tsoukalas and Son, 1957, p.

Greek husbands and fathers to kill their own wives and children rather than have them fall into enemy hands. The women themselves, after fighting off the Turks, killed each other to avoid capture, or asked their menfolk to kill them as did the women of the island of Psara and Mesolongi.[51] Occasionally, women tried to fight the enemy, throwing rocks at them or using any available means.[52]

Similar desperate acts occurred in order to avoid not the Turks, but opposing factions of the Greeks. The Greeks on opposite sides often treated women with cruelty. Such accusations were usually brought against the men from Roumeli, who had been called in to assist the government in Nauplio against the followers of Kolokotronis, and only rarely against the Moraites themselves.[53]

Women preferred death to capture because if they did not convert to Islam those who were taken prisoners by the Turks might suffer a torturous death. Alternatively, they might end up as slaves. There are frequent accounts of women and children prisoners suffering this. We shall mention here only those captured outside the town of Mesolongi, who were impaled in order to terrorize the besieged population observing them from the walls,[54] and the wives of some leaders of the revolution in Naousa,[55] who submitted to unbelievable tortures. Besides individual cases of torture and horrible death at the hands of the enemy, large-scale massacres occurred at Kydonies, Psara, Chios and Mesolongi, to mention the most notorious.

It was common for women and young boys to be sold as slaves in the markets of the Levant. Girls distinguished for their beauty ended up in the harem of the Pasha who had won a battle or taken a besieged town, and others were dispatched to the brothels of Constantinople. Often, when a beautiful girl or woman was noticed by the Turks, she was singled out in the treaty of surrender and before a safe passage was agreed upon with the defenders of a town.[56] We do not have accurate numbers about the women captured and subsequently

---

60. Edward Blaquiere, op. cit., pp. 6-7.

51   *Ellinika Chronika: Ephimeris Ektaktos,* no 54 (1824), p. 2. Nikolaos Kasomoulis, op. cit., 2, pp. 252-3. Samuel Howe, op. cit., p. 308.

52   Nikolaos Spiliadis, op. cit., 3, p. 21.

53   Ibid. 3, p. 80. Ioannis Makrygiannis, op. cit., 2, p. 46. T. Stamatopoulos, op. cit., 3, p. 428; 4, pp. 153-4.

54   *Ellinika Chronika,* no. 99, 9 December 1825, p. 4. Nikolaos Kasomoulis, op. cit., 2, pp. 252-3.

55   Spyridon Trikoupis, op.cit., 2, pp. 173-4. F.C.H.L. Pouqueville, *Histoire de la régénération de la Grèce: comprenant le précis des évènements depuis 1740 jusqu'en 1824. Avec cartes et portraits,* Paris 1824, 1, pp. 534, 537, 538.

56   Photakos, op. cit., 2, p. 442. Spyromilios, op. cit., p. 235. Nikolaos D. Makris, op. cit., p. 57. Spyridon Trikoupis, op. cit., 3, p. 328. Samuel Howe, op. cit., p. 37.

sold as slaves, but rather estimates for some of the most striking cases. A considerable number of the women of Chios in 1822 (10,000 of them according to Samuel Howe)[57] and many of the women of Mesolongi in 1825 suffered this fate. Captured women and children after the fall of Mesolongi were estimated at 3,000 and those killed along with old men at 2,000.[58] Only seven or thirteen women were said to have survived the exodus from the town.[59] We do not have precise numbers for the young women and boys taken prisoners at Psara or killed there.[60]

Some accounts of slavery are quite shocking: one girl was sold forty times within the same day;[61] another girl from Chios killed herself to avoid marriage to the Turk who had bought her, while her mutilated sister, whose hand had been cut off, was ransomed.[62] Mothers were separated from their children under tragic circumstances, and older women were killed since they were not easily sold as slaves. The massacres of the women and children and the selling of others as slaves became widely known narratives at the time and moved the peoples of Europe and the United States, thus boosting the Philhellenic movement. The tragic events during the fall of Mesolongi became also widely known. There was initially a collective decision of the Guards of Mesolongi to kill each other's womenfolk and children before their secret exodus from the besieged town. They were dissuaded from this plan by the bishop Iosif of Rogai, and they finally agreed to take their families with them.[63] The women, who participated in the exodus, were dressed in men's clothes since they preferred to be taken for men during the battle and to be killed rather than taken alive.[64]

Dressing as men appears to have been rather common for women who, for whatever reason, were in the camps with the Greek troops, or were travelling alone. This novel and daring action did not cause comment, and indeed it must have seemed appropriate. The women were also proud of having dressed as men. We are told, for example, of a very old woman, a survivor of the exodus, who, many years later in liberated Greece, asked to be buried in the carefully

---

[57] Samuel Howe, op. cit., pp. 101-2, 103 note. Philip Argenti (ed.), *The Massacres of Chios Described in Contemporary Diplomatic Reports*, London 1932, *passim*.
[58] Samuel Howe, op. cit., p. 310. Kanellos Deligiannis, op. cit., 3, pp. 113-14.
[59] Nikolaos Kasomoulis, op. cit., 2, p. 283. Spyridon Trikoupis, op. cit., 3, p. 339.
[60] Samuel Howe, op. cit., p. 202.
[61] Photakos, op. cit., 2, p. 334. K. Simopoulos, op. cit., 5, pp. 35-6, 100-1.
[62] Olivier Voutier, op.cit., pp. 252-7.
[63] Nikolaos Kasomoulis, op. cit., 2, pp. 252-3.
[64] Nikolaos D. Makris, op. cit., p. 67-8. D. Ainian, op. cit., p. 186.

preserved men's clothes she had been wearing at the time.[65] It is also noteworthy that in 1840 Manto Mavrogenous was buried in a lieutenant-general's uniform, although she herself never dressed as a man, but rather wore European clothing.[66]

Many of the women who survived these misfortunes lived afterwards at Nauplio and faced a life of total poverty. Deaths of women and children from starvation were not unknown.[67] The women and children of those killed in action, or those who had been freed from slavery, were often obliged to beg in order to secure their livelihood.[68] Many of these women submitted applications to the authorities describing their desperate situation, or the services rendered either by their dead relatives or themselves to the War, and asking for a small pension. The Greek government made some efforts to take care of those destitute women and children,[69] but the problem was far too great and the means were so meagre that very little was actually done to alleviate their misery.

Women, however, were not just victims; they also participated actively in the War. There have been claims, often based on circumstantial evidence, that some women became members of the Philiki Etaireia, the secret society that had organized the revolution, and that they had helped its cause in various ways, but no woman's name is included in the existing lists of its members. Ioannis Philimon[70] mentions one Kyriaki, wife of Michail Nautis in Smyrna, who had supposedly been initiated after discovering that her husband was a member of the Philiki Etaireia, to which she subsequently contributed a considerable amount of money. Indeed, she continued to offer funds during the War. There are also several women who assisted as spies and messengers, but there is no conclusive evidence that they were actually members of the Society.[71] In any case, it seems rather improbable that the Society initiated any woman into its secret membership.

Women, even children, helped in the warfare in various tasks. For example, they carried food and other supplies to the camps,[72] and carried water to fill

---

65   Nikolaos D. Makris, op. cit., p. 68-9.
66   Manouil Tasoulas, op.cit., p. 290.
67   Nikolaos Dragoumis, *Istorikai Anamniseis,* ed. Alkis Angelou, *Nea Elliniki Vivliothiki,* Athens: Ermis, 1973, 1, 91.
68   Ioannis Makrygiannis, op. cit., 1, pp. 162-3, 2, 11.
69   *Archeia Ellinikis Palingenesias 1821-1832,* 14, pp. 257-8.
70   Op. cit., 1, p. 170.
71   Koula Xiradaki, op.cit., pp. 316-39, and *Oi Gynaikes sti Philiki Etairia – Phanariotisses,* Athens 1971, where one can find collected bibliography but not a very strict academic approach on the subject.
72   Photakos, op. cit., 1, p. 85.

the reservoirs of the fortress of Nauplio, which was expecting a siege. On many occasions they carried big rocks in order to have a ready supply to cast down upon the approaching enemy.[73] Several women voluntarily spied on the Turks, collected information for the Greeks, or were used as couriers or messengers as noted above.[74] During the siege of Mesolongi, women were actively involved in building and reinforcing its walls and the mines, a labour they usually carried out at night. In this effort, the wives and daughters of the leaders also participated and encouraged the rest.[75] Athenian women helped in the preparation of ammunition and weapons in Athens.[76]

Often, women collected money for the War and, if they did not have any, they offered their jewels instead.[77] Those who were wealthy financed various projects to such a degree that they themselves were ruined financially. Manto Mavrogenous is the best known example. Those who were educated wrote letters to the women of Europe and the USA for the Greek cause and seeking the support of women abroad, or wrote poems which were sometimes printed as pamphlets in Greece and elsewhere.[78] Finally, they actually participated in battles.

Two women have dominated the collective Greek consciousness for their distinguished participation in the revolution: Laskarina Bouboulina and Manto Mavrogenous. The bibliography on them is extensive and there is no reason to dwell on it here. Less known is another widow who helped with her husband's ship in the war after his death, Domna Visvizis from Ainos in Thrace.[79] We

---

73 Ibid. II, pp. 114-15, 184-5.

74 *Apomnimoneumata Athinaion Agoniston*, pp. 68, 75. Koula Xiradaki, *Gynaikes tou '21*, p. 326.

75 *Ellinika Chronika*, no. 42 (27-5-1825), p. 8; no. 46 (10-6-1825), p. 2. D. Urquhart, *The Spirit of the East*, London 1838, 1, pp. 53-4. Samuel Howe, op. cit., p. 263.

76 Dionysios Sourmelis, *Istoria ton Athinon kata ton yper Eleutherias Agona Archomeni apo tis Epanastaseos mechri tis Apokatastaseos ton Pragmaton. Diirimeni eis Tria Vivlia*, Aigina, 1834, p. 3.

77 Samuel Howe, op. cit., p. 330.

78 [Evanthia Kairi], *Epistoli Ellinidon tinon pros tas Philellinidas Syntetheisa para tinos ton Spoudaioteron Ellinidon*, Ydra 1825. Edward Blaquiere, *Narrative of a Second Visit to Greece, Including Facts Connected with the Last Days of Lord Byron Extracted from Correspondence, Official Documents etc*, London 1825, pp. 118-19, 132-4. Theodore Blancard, *Les Mauroyéni. Essai d'étude additionelle à l'histoire moderne de la Grèce, de la Turquie et de la Roumanie*, Paris: Ernest Flammarion, 1909, pp. 651 ff. Angeliki Palli, *Odi eis Psara*, Paris 1825.

79 Ioannis Philimon, op. cit., 3, p. 433. K.A. Diamantis, "Oi Thrakes eis tin Ypiresian tis Patridos", *Archeion tou Thrakikou Laographikou kai Glossikou Thisavrou*, 25 (1960), pp. 71, 73; and "Thrakes Agonistai kata tin Epanastasin tou 1821",

have vague evidence only for a woman said to have been captain of her own small company of men. Konstantina Zacharia, daughter of a notorious *klepht* of the Morea killed in the early years of the 19th century, was very young, but she had been fighting in the first years of the revolution and was twice seriously wounded in battle. Greek sources do not mention her, but E. Blaquiere met her and her accounts to him were confirmed by Sisinis, the primate of Gastouni. Pouqueville's reference to Konstantina on the other hand seems mostly inaccurate.[80] Another woman who participated as a soldier in various battles was Staurianna Savvaina, a middle aged widow with five children from Mani. She had joined the troops of Kyriakoulis Mauromichalis and fought in the battle of Valtetsi, in Sterea Ellada, in Trikorpha and elsewhere. In 1829, she petitioned for a small pension describing her services in the War, as attested in certificates from the Maniote leaders with whom she had fought, and she was granted the pension with a commendation for her bravery.[81]

We also know of a great number of other women who are reported to have taken part in battles, or in defending themselves against the enemy. Some names are preserved, but their individual roles are often not clearly documented. We must assume that there is some segment of truth in their participation in the War.[82]

There is no doubt that many women fought along with men on several occasions. They very seldom carried guns, and they usually fought with improvized weapons such as wooden clubs and iron bars, sickles or scythes, and stones. Women experienced in warfare such as those of Mani and Souli figure more prominently in the records. The Souliote women's sudden attack, for example, was decisive in the victory of the Souliote troops at the battle of Navariko.[83] Maniote women also followed the troops in the siege of Tripolitsa,

---

ibid. 29 (1963), pp. 122-42; 30 (1964), pp. 33-40.

80 Edward Blaquiere, op. cit., pp. 22-8. *A Picture of Greece in 1825; as exhibited in the personal narrative of James Emerson, Esq., Count Pecchio, and William Humphreys, Esq. comprising a detailed account of the events of the late campaign, and sketches of the principal military, naval and political chiefs*, London 1826, II, p. 240 note. F.C.H.L. Pouqueville, op. cit., 2, pp. 351-2.

81 Kallirroi Parren, "Agnostoi Iroides tou 1821. Stauriana, Modena kai Mesolongitides", *Ephimeris ton Kyrion*, no. 158, 25 March 1890, pp. 2-3. Andreas Mamoukas, *Ta kata tin Anagennisin tis Ellados, itoi Sylloji ton peri tin Anagenomenin Ellada Syntachthenton Politeumaton, Nomon kai allon Episimon Praxeon, apo tou 1821 mechri Telous tou 1832*, Piraeus 1852, 11, p. 119. Dionysios Kokkinos, *I Elliniki Epanastasis*, 3rd ed., Athens 1957, 2, p. 175.

82 Kallirroi Parren, " I Alephanto", op. cit., no. 171, 24 June, p. 3 and "Adamantia Grigoriadou", *ibid.* no 184, 21 October 1890, pp. 5-6.

83 Christoforos Perraivos, *Apomnimoneumata Polemika*, ed. Emm. G. Protopsaltis,

subsequently participating in the looting.[84] They fought very bravely in various locations, either along with a small number of men or by themselves, when Ibrahim Pasha's Egyptian troops invaded Mani. They resisted the siege successfully, barricaded in the family towers, and fought in the battles of Verga and Polyaravos. Some of these Maniote women are known by name and there are several songs that commemorate their bravery.[85] Women of various regions of Greece often helped men in battles by throwing rocks and stones.[86]

It was quite exceptional for a woman to be involved in political intrigues, or at least in decision making. Bouboulina was one of these, but it is doubtful if Manto Mavrogenous was able to exert any political influence on public matters outside her island of Mykonos. However, Blaquiere claims that "her labours as a mediatrix have indeed often proved very successful".[87] Indirectly, we may assume that a very small number of women might have played some minor part, possibly through influencing their husbands or via their own personal connections, but we do not have understanding of their role—whether they actually had a real effect on important events. General Gouras's wife Asimina, the proud and powerful daughter of a rich primate, is believed to have influenced her husband to sign the resolution asking for British Protection, despite the fact that he belonged to the French Party.[88] Nikitaras's wife Angelina, daughter of the *klepht* Zacharias and half-sister to the aforementioned Konstantina, seems to have played some part in the beginning of the second civil war, acting as an intermediary between the two factions. She corresponded in 1824 with the Greek government, which was trying to persuade her to secretly assist its troops to enter Nauplio. In her case, existing documents show that she was actually involved in the events and that she had used her status as a housewife to avoid complying with requests of the government.[89] There is also an uncorroborated reference to Eleni, the wife of General Vasos, as his counsellor and trusted secretary who handled all of

---

Athens: Vivliothiki G. Tsoukalas and Son [1956], p. 112. Cf. Spyridon Trikoupis, op. cit., 2, p. 250.

84   N.A. Veis, "Engrapha Aphoronta eis tin Poliorkian tis Tripoleos (1821), *Armonia*, vol. 5 (1901), p. 232. Kanellos Deligiannis, op. cit., 1, p. 271.

85   Nikolaos Spiliadis, op. cit., 3, pp. 61-2. Mihail Oikonomou, op. cit., 2, p. 150, 155. Photakos, op. cit., 2, p. 309, Spyridon Trikoupis, op. cit., 4, p. 26-7, 32. Kanellos Deligiannis, op. cit., 3, p. 72. D. Vagiakakos, *Maniatika. A' O Ibraim enantion tis Manis*, Athens 1961, pp. 48, 86, 97.

86   Photakos, op. cit., 2, 354-5. Dionysios A. Kokkinos, op. cit., 4, pp. 364-5.

87   Op. cit., p. 118.

88   T. Stamatopoulos, op. cit., 1, p. 326.

89   Koula Xiradaki, op. cit., pp. 221-6.

his correspondence with Kioutachi Pasha.[90] Finally, we know of an unusual public demonstration held by Athenian women refugees on the island of Salamina. The women demonstrated under the balcony of the residence of General Fabvier, the commander of the regular army, demanding that he should not desert Athens as he was planning, but remain and assist the besieged Athenians on the Acropolis of Athens. It is also said, however, that this demonstration was instigated by the Athenian primate Zacharitsas.[91]

The great changes brought about by the War are clearly manifested in two novel phenomena which affected women's traditional way of life and, indeed, the entire Greek population. The first is the operation of one and then of several brothels in Patras, and the second is the establishment of a school for girls in Athens and Syros.

Prostitution was nearly unknown in Greece before the War, brothels were non-existent, and women of irregular life and suspicious morals were punished by both Greeks and Ottomans, usually by exile.[92] In the early years of the revolution prostitution was still quite rare and foreigners, who wrote about Greek women, tended to praise their character and their morals.[93] In 1828, however, when the French Expedition arrived in the Morea, we have accounts of Greek prostitutes in Patras, who were said to have been led to this condition by men. Most of the details are given in a book written by J. Mangeart,[94] who participated in the Expedition. His whole account does not seem quite plausible, and he may have exaggerated a great deal in order to render his books more stimulating, but it is also hard to believe that he fabricated everything. It seems probable that under the trying circumstances and with foreign troops stationed in the Morea, prostitution made its appearance among the destitute female population.

Schools for girls were non-existent before the revolution, and those few women who were literate were taught by their mothers, close relatives, or priests. Exceptional, of course, were, the Phanariot women who had private

---

90 Kallirroi Parren, "Eleni Vasou", *Ephimeris ton Kyrion*, no 298, 21 March 1893, pp. 1-2.

91 Georgios Psyllas, *Apomnimoneumata tou Viou mou*, Eisagogi: Nikolaos Louros, ed. Eleutherios G. Prevelakis, *Mnimeia Ellinikis Istorias 8*, Athens: Akadimia Athinon, 1974, pp. 123-4.

92 Helen Angelomatis-Tsougarakis, op. cit., *Mesaionika kai Nea Ellinika*, 4 (1992), pp. 348-50.

93 Samuel Howe, op. cit., pp. 373-4 note.

94 *Souvenirs de la Morée recueillis pendant le séjour des Français dans le Péloponèse*, Paris 1830; the references here are to its Greek translation by G. Tsoukalas, *Anamniseis apo ton Moria*, ed. Emm. Protopsaltis, Athens: Vivliothiki G. Tsoukalas and Son, 1957, pp. 120-7.

tutors. Some were not only fluent in foreign languages but also quite learned. A few female relatives of Greek scholars were also properly educated. Some females published their own scholarly works and translations in the years preceding the revolution.[95] The establishment of schools for girls under the conditions prevailing in Greece during the war years was an enormous and novel step for Greek society, bringing it forward to modern times and westernized ideas. Moreover, it required not only willingness but also the means to support such institutions. Thus a *parthenagogeion,* a girls' school, was established by the Philomousos Etaireia in Athens as soon as the town was liberated from the Turks in 1824. The school, called "Parthenon", was on the Acropolis itself, and the word's meaning in Greek was appropriate since it was a school for young virgins, *parthenes*. This school used the Lancasterian method and was attended by 52 girls of the best Athenian families. Although its head was a man, the scholar Nikolaos Nikitopoulos, the teachers and supervisors were women. The school was obliged to close down a couple of years later when Athens was again besieged by the Turks.[96] There was also a school for girls established at the same time as a boys' school by the municipality of the island of Syros. The head was a woman this time although at first a missionary, Cork, supervised both new schools. The Syros school was attended by 161 girls. In 1828, one more girls' school was established by the scholar Evanthia Kairi.[97]

Thus, the revolution, acting as a violent catalyst combined with new spiritual, political and social orientations, stimulated the painful passage of women from the traditional life and values of the Greeks under Ottoman domination to a life of greater freedom, incorporating new values and addressing new challenges on the road to fulfilment in the independent Greek State.

---

95 Helen Angelomatis-Tsougarakis, op. cit., *Mesaionika kai Nea Ellinika,* 4 (1992), pp. 350-64.

96 Tryfon E. Evangelidis, *I Paideia epi Tourkokratias: Ellinika Scholeia apo tis Aloseos mechri Kapodistriou,* Athens 1936, 1, pp. 244-7.

97 *Ibid.*, 2, pp. 81-2.

BIBLIOGRAPHY

Ainian, D. (1957) *Apomnimoneumata,* ed. Emm. Protopsaltis, Athens: Vivliothiki G. Tsoukalas and Son.
Alimperti, Sotiria (1933) *Ai Iroides tis Ellinikis Epanastaseos,* Athens.
—— (1931) *Manto Mavrogenous* Athens.
Angelomatis-Tsougarakis, Helen (1992) "Greek Women (16th-19th century): the Travellers' View", *Mesaionika kai Nea Ellinika* (Akadimia Athinon, Kentron Ereunis tou Mesaionikou kai Neou Ellinismou), 4, pp. 321-403.
Archeia tis Ellinikis Palingenesias 1821-1832, "Lyta Engrapha" A' kai B' Vouleutikis Periodou, tomos ektos, Ypourgeia B', vol. 14, Athens: Vouli ton Ellinon, 1981.
Argenti, Philip (ed.) (1932) *The Massacres of Chios Described in Contemporary Diplomatic Reports,* London.
Blancard, Theodore (1909) *Les Mauroyéni. Essai d'étude additionelle à l'histoire moderne de la Grèce, de la Turquie et de la Roumanie,* Paris: Ernest Flammarion.
Blaquiere, Edward (1825) *Narrative of a Second Visit to Greece, Including Facts Connected with the Last Days of Lord Byron Extracted from Correspondence, Official Documents etc,* London.
—— (1828) *Letters from Greece: with Remarks on the Treaty of Intervention,* London.
Deligiannis, Kanellos (1957) *Apomnimoneumata,* notes by G. Tsoukalas, ed. Emm. G. Protopsaltis, 1-2, Athens: Vivliothiki G. Tsoukalas and Son.
Diamantis, K.A. (1971) *Athinaikon Archeion, Archeia ek tis Neoteris Ellinikis Istorias ek ton Syllogon Gianni Vlachogianni,* Athens.
—— (1968) *Archeia Lazarou and Georgiou Kountouriotou,* tomos enatos (Apo 30 Septemvriou eos 21 Dekemvriou 1827, 1828 kai 1829), ed. K.A. Diamantis, Athens.
—— (1970) "Oi Thrakes eis tin Ypiresian tis Patridos", *Archeion tou Thrakikou Laographikou kai Glossikou Thisaurou,* 25 (1960), 69-87.
—— (1963) "Thrakes Agonistai kata tin Epanastasin tou 1821", *Archeion tou Thrakikou Laographikou kai Glossikou Thisaurou,* 29, 5-176.
Dragoumis, Nikolaos (1973) *Istorikai Anamniseis,* ed. Alkis Angelou, 1-2, *Nea Elliniki Vivliothiki,* Athens: Ermis.
Dyovouniotis, K.I. (1917) *Nomokanonikai Meletai,* Athens.
Ellinika Chronika, Ephimeris Ektaktos.
Emerson, James, Count Pecchio and William Humphreys (1826) *A Picture of Greece in 1825; as exhibited in the personal narrative of James Emerson,*

Esq., Count Pecchio, and William Humphreys, Esq. comprising a detailed account of the events of the late campaign, and sketches of the principal military, naval and political chiefs, I-II, London.

Evangelidis, Tryphon (1936) *I Paideia epi Tourkokratias: Ellinika Scholeia apo tis Aloseos mechri Kapodistriou,* 1-2, Athens.

Ginis, Dimitrios (1960) "Oi Logoi Diazygiou epi Tourkokratias", *Epistimoniki Epetiris tis Scholis Nomikon kai Oikonomikon Spoudon Panepistimiou Thessalonikis,* 8, 239-83.

Howe, Samuel (1828) *An Historical Sketch of the Greek Revolution,* New York.

Jourdain, Jean Philippe Paul (1828) *Mémoires historiques et militaires sur les événements de la Grèce: depuis 1822, jusqu'au combat de Navarin ...,* Paris.

[Kairi, Evanthia] (1825) *Epistoli Ellinidon tinon pros tas Philellinidas Syntetheisa para tinos ton Spoudaioteron Ellinidon,* Ydra.

Kasomoulis, Nikolaos (1939-1942) *Apomnimoneumata Stratiotika peri tis Epanastaseos ton Ellinon 1821-1833. Protassetai Istoria tou Armatolismou,* Introduction and notes by Giannis Vlachogiannis, 1-4, Athens.

Kokkinos, Dionysios (1956-1960) *I Elliniki Epanastasis,* 3rd ed., 1-12, Athens: Melissa.

Kolokotronis, Gennaios (1955) *Apomnimoneumata,* ed. Emm. G. Protopsaltis, Athens: Vivliothiki G. Tsoukalas and Son.

Kriezis, Alexandros (1956) *Apomnimoneumata (Giornale dia tin Anexartisian tou Genous),* ed. Emm. G. Protopsaltis, Athens: Vivliothiki G. Tsoukalas and Son.

Makris, Nikolaos (1957) *Istoria tou Mesolongiou,* ed. Emm. G. Protopsaltis, Athens: Vivliothiki G. Tsoukalas and Son.

Makrygiannis Ioannis (1947) *Stratigou Makrygianni Apomnimoneumata,* ed. Giannis Vlachogiannis, 2nd ed., 1-2, Athens.

Mamoukas, Andreas (1839-1852) *Ta kata tin Anagennisin tis Ellados, itoi Syllogi ton peri tin Anagenomenin Ellada Syntachthenton Politeumaton, Nomon kai allon Episimon Praxeon, apo tou 1821 mechri Telous tou 1832,* 1-11, Piraeus.

Mangeart, J. (1830) *Souvenirs de la Morée recueillis pendant le séjour des Français dans la Péloponèse,* Paris. Greek translation by G. Tsoukalas in *Anamniseis apo ton Moria,* ed. Emm. Protopsaltis, Athens: Vivliothiki G. Tsoukalas and Son, 1957.

Maurer, Georg Ludw. Von (1835) *Das Griechische Volk in öffentlicher, kirchlischer und privat-rechtlicher Beziehung vor und nach dem Freiheitskampfe bis zum 31 Juli 1834,* Heidelberg.

Michos, Artemios (1957) *Apomnimoneumata,* ed. Emm. Protopsaltis, Athens:

Vivliothiki G. Tsoukalas and Son.

Millingen, Julius (1831) *Memoirs of the Affairs of Greece; Containing an Account of the Military and Political Events, which Occurred in 1823 and Following Years with Various Anecdotes Relating to Lord Byron and an Account of his Last Illness and Death,* London.

Monastiriotis, P., D. Christidis, M. Poulos and N. Karoris (1957) *Apomnimoneumata Athinaion Agoniston,* ed. Emm G. Protopsaltis, Athens: Vivliothiki G. Tsoukalas and Son.

Oikonomou, Mihail (1957) *Istorika tis Ellinikis Paliggenesias, i, o Ieros ton Ellinon Agon,* ed. Emm. G. Protopsaltis, 1-2, Athens: Vivliothiki G. Tsoukalas and Son.

Papadopoulos, N.P. (1974) *Katakaimenou Moria Selides tou 1821,* Athens.

Parren, Kallirroi (1890a) "Agnostoi Iroides tou 1821. Stauriana, Modena kai Mesolongitides", *Ephimeris ton Kyrion,* no. 158, 25 March 1890, pp. 2-3.

―― (1890b) "I Alephanto", *Ephimeris ton Kyrion,* no. 171, 24 June 1890, p. 3.

―― (1890c) "Adamantia Grigoriadou", *Ephimeris ton Kyrion,* no. 184, p. 21, October 1890, pp 5-6.

―― (1893) "Eleni Vasou", *Ephimeris ton Kyrion,* no. 296, 6 March 1893, pp. 2-3, and no. 298, 21 March 1893, pp. 1-2.

Patras, Nikolaos (ed.) (1886) *Istorika Imerologia ton Ellinikon Naumachion tou 1821. Ek ton Imerologion tou Naumachou An. Tsamadou,* Athens.

Perraivos, Christoforos (1956) *Apomnimoneumata Polemika,* ed. Emm. Protopsaltis, Athens: Vivliothiki G. Tsoukalas and Son.

Petrakakos, D. (1935) *Koinovouleutiki Istoria tis Ellados: Istoriki, dogmatiki kai Kritiki Ereuna epi ti Vasei ton Anekdoton tou Ethnous Archeion. Tomos Protos, Agones Tessaron Aionon yper tis Politikis Eleutherias apo tis Aloseos mechri tis 3is Septemvriou 1843 (1453-1843),* Athens.

Philimon, Ioannis (1859-1861) *Dokimion Istorikon peri tis Ellinikis Epanastaseos,* 1-4, Athens.

Photakos, Photios Ch. (pen name of Photios Chrysanthopoulos) (1898) *Apomnimoneumata peri tis Ellinikis Epanastaseos,*1-2, Athens.

Phrantzis, Amvrosios (1839-1841) *Epitomi tis Istorias tis Anagennithisis Ellados, Archomeni apo tou Etous 1715 kai Ligousa to 1835,* 1-2, Athens.

Pouqueville, F.C.H.L. (1824) *Histoire de la regénération de la Grèce: comprenant le précis des évènements depuis 1740 jusqu'en 1824. Avec cartes et portraits,* Paris.

Protopsaltis, Emm. (ed.) (1871) *Istorikon Archeion Maurokordatou, Mnimeia tis Ellinikis Istorias,* 5, band IV *Engrapha tou 1824,* Athens: Akadimia

Athinon.

Psyllas, Georgios (1974) *Apomnimoneumata tou Viou mou,* Eisagogi: Nikolaos Louros, ed. Eleutherios G. Prevelakis, *Mnimeia Ellinikis Istorias 8,* Athens: Akadimia Athinon.

Raybaud, Maxime (1825) *Mémoires sur la Grèce, pour servir à l histoire de la guerre de l'Indépendence accompagnés des plans topographiques ... avec une introduction par Alph. Rabbe,* I-II, Paris.

Simopoulos, K. (1979-1984) *Pos eidan oi xenoi tin Ellada tou '21,* 1-5, Athens.

Sourmelis, Dionysios (1834) *Istoria ton Athinon kata ton yper Eleutherias Agona Archomeni apo tis Epanastaseos mechri tis Apokatastaseos ton Pragmaton. Diirimeni eis Tria Vivlia,* Aigina.

Spiliadis, Nikolaos (1851-1857) *Apomnimoneumata dia na Chrisimeusosin eis tin Nean Ellinikin Istorian (1821-1843),* ed. Ch. N. Philadelpheus, 1-5, Athens.

Spyromilios (1957) *Apomnimoneumata tis Deuteras Poliorkias tou Mesolongiou 1825-6, Eisagogi Io. Vlachogianni,* Athens: Vivliothiki G. Tsoukalas and Son.

Stamatopoulos, T.A. (1971-1975) *O Esoterikos Agonas prin kai meta tin Epanastasi,* 1-4, Athens: Kalvos.

Tasoulas, Manouil (1997) *Manto Mavrogenous. Istoriko Archeio,* 2nd ed. Athens: The Municipality of Mykonos and "Perivolaki".

Trikoupis, Spyridon (1860-1862) *Istoria tis Ellinikis Epanastaseos,* 2nd ed. 1-4, Athens.

Urquhart, D. (1838) *The Spirit of the East,* London.

Vagiakakos, D. (1961) *Maniatika. A' O Ibraim enantion tis Manis,* Athens.

Veis, N.A. (1901) "Engrapha Aphoronta eis tin Poliorkian tis Tripoleos (1821), *Armonia,* teuchos 5, pp. 227-33.

Voutier, Olivier (1823) *Mémoires du colonel Voutier sur la guerre actuelle de la Grèce,* Paris.

Vyzantios, Christos (1957) *Istoria ton kata tin Ellinikin Epanastasin Ekstrateion kai Machon on Meteschen o Taktikos Stratos apo tou 1821 mechri tou 1833,* ed. Emm. G. Protopsaltis, Athens: Vivliothiki G. Tsoukalas and Son.

Xiradaki, Koula (1995) *Gynaikes tou '21. Prosphores, Iroismoi kai Thysies,* Athens-Giannina: Dodoni.

—— (1971) *Oi Gynaikes sti Philiki Etairia* – Phanariotisses, Athens.

3

VILLAGERS, NOTABLES AND IMPERIAL COLLAPSE: THE VIRGIN MARY ON TINOS

Mark Mazower

We see that while the organization of administration stretches down, as it were, from the central Government towards the village community, but loses power and the ability to take decisions the further it extends from its point of origin, the structure of the system of patronage, which is based on social relationships between clients seeking for a man with the ability and friendship connections to protect them and a patron who accepts those duties in return for political allegiance, grows upwards....[1]

In the summer of 1824—it was the middle of August, two days after the Orthodox *dekapentavgousto*—the Catholic bishop of Tinos wrote to his superior in Smyrna about a shocking episode that had just taken place in one of the island's upland villages:

My *coloni* from the village of Livadha tell me that this morning about 20 armed villagers from Falatadhos went to my church and opening it with great anger, tore away the picture which hangs above the altar and threw it, together with everything else they found, outside on the ground, before setting fire to [them in] a nearby store. [Having destroyed the crops in the field there,] They then closed up the church and took the key with them... They said too that if of us, whether priest or layman, went to open it, they would kill him. Then with shouts of happiness they passed off through the [entirely Catholic] village of Muzzulù, and that poor people were forced to shut themselves in their houses.... Such insults we did not even receive from the Turks themselves and I cannot conceive through what fault we have deserved to be thus abandoned, in these wretched and dangerous times, by those in whose protection—after God—we have always trusted to find a solid assistance.[2]

---

1   J.K. Campbell, *Honour, Family and Patronage: A Study of Institutions and Moral Values in a Greek Mountain Community* (Oxford, 1964), p. 260.

2   [Archives of the Catholic Archbishopic on Tinos [AKT] Blue Box, "Corrispon-

This was certainly not the first time that there had been trouble between Catholic and Orthodox villagers on Tinos, nor the first time that Bishop Collaro had been drawn into the fray. But the timing was striking—in the midst of the Greek war of independence, and at the very moment that the new Orthodox Cult of the Virgin was being established on the island. This conjuncture of events raises the question of the impact that the War of Independence was having on relations between Catholics and Orthodox on Tinos at this time. It draws our attention to what the war itself brought to the Cyclades, formerly at the centre of the Ottoman commercial system in the Aegean, well away from the main mainland centres of hostilities. And it suggests ways of understanding the local and regional background to the emergence of what would—with astonishing speed—become the new Kingdom of Greece's main pilgrimage site. This paper is a preliminary attempt to explore these issues, to gauge the importance of the somewhat neglected religious factor in the Greek war of independence, and to show how applicable John Campbell's insights into the nature of Greek politics remain for the historian.

In the course of 1821 and 1822, as insurrections against the Ottomans erupted in various parts of the mainland, the Virgin appeared to several islanders on Tinos in a sequence of dreams. She told one of them where to dig, though when he failed to find anything, the Orthodox Bishop, Gavriil, wrote this dream off as "the devi's work". She then came to the nun Pelagia, more than once, repeating instructions to dig "in Doxara's field" above the port of Ayios Nikolaos and to build a church there "just as it was before".[3] Pelagia's piety was respected and Gavriil now accepted this was not a visitation of the devil. But Doxaras's wife—he was away—did not grant permission for the digging to begin until an angry *foustanella*-clad soldier came to *her* in a dream, with drawn sword. Hard work still revealed nothing, and plague swept the island in the winter of 1822. But when the diggers stopped, Pelagia was again warned by the Virgin; the plague was interpreted by Gavriil as punishment for the islanders' lack of commitment and despite not finding anything, the diggers erected a small chapel on the site of an ancient spring. Then, at the end of January 1823, a workman's shovel split a piece of wood in two. It was an icon, recognized by the islanders as the work of St Luke and hailed as one of the most ancient icons in existence. Placed initially in the house of a local notable, the Virgin demanded a proper church, worthy of the icon, and this was consecrated in 1824, though it was not completed until 1831. By then, it had already become

---

denza col console Francese di Sira]

3   Doxaras appears to have been the uncle of Konstantinos Georgantopoulos, who will be referred to below, G.L.Dorizas, *I Tinos epi Tourkokratias kai kata ton Agona tou 1821* (Athens, 1978), p. 393.

the site of a major pilgrimage. Charles Swan records the building of the new site in 1825. Three years later, an agent of the New York Greek Committee passed by and was struck by the church's size, opulence and popularity; a few years later, it was visited by the newly arrived King Otto. By 1840 it was—in the words of a French traveller—attracting visitors from "all the islands of the Archipelago, all corners of Greece and Asia Minor". Towards the end of the century, approximately 45,000 pilgrims were arriving each year.[4]

The same booklets which recount this story for visiting pilgrims today have less to say about another notable feature of Tinos—its long-standing Catholic population. Who lives here? I once asked a farmer as I entered a mixed village on the uplands above the main town: "Us Christians and those Catholics" (*emeis oi christianoi kai avtoi oi katholikoi*), he replied. In fact the Catholic presence goes back many centuries, to the period of Venetian rule and even before. Vatican emissaries visited Tinos in the 17th century and their reports show how widely the Catholic population was dispersed through the villages of the centre and south-east of the island: only the northern "Outer Parts" (*exomeria*) remained entirely Orthodox. There were many mixed villages, and the lack of priests on both sides contributed to an atmosphere in which chapels—and often priests—were shared.[5]

Under the Venetians the island's elite was Catholic, but the Ottoman conquest in 1715 —this was the last part of the Eastern Mediterranean to fall under the sultans—started to changed this. The confessional balance of power swung towards the Orthodox, their numbers grew, their prosperity increased, and by the late 18th century communal boundaries themselves appear to have become more sharply defined. The Orthodox Bishop Gavriil, who arrived in 1810, appears to have enjoyed good relations with the Ottoman *agha* and to have perhaps encouraged him in a more anti-Catholic stand. When war broke out in 1821, and imperial Ottoman authority was overthrown, what ensued was a kind of vacuum of power. The islanders had in fact always largely governed and policed themselves; apart from the *agha* stationed there to collect taxes there were no other Turkish officials on the island. Now other political forces intervened and in the ensuing anarchy, relations between the Catholic and Orthodox communities became filled with tension.[6]

---

4 H.A. Post, *A Visit to Greece and Constantinople in the Year 1827-8* (New York, 1830), pp. 223-6; A. de Valon, *Une année dans le Levant* (Paris, 1846), I; "R", "A Panhellenic Festival of Today", *Macmillan's Magazine*, 48 (1883-4), pp. 474-7.

5 See G.Hofmann, *Vescovadi cattolici della Grecia*, vol. 2 Tinos (Rome, 1937), passim.

6 The best guide to the background to 1821 is D. Drosos, *Istoria tis nisou Tinou* (Athens, 1870).

From the start of the war, there was confusion and rumour. In the spring of 1821, news arrived of the uprisings on the mainland, and several hundred Orthodox islanders volunteered to join the Greek forces. At about the same time the Ottoman *agha* of the island sought refuge in the home of the French consul, Michel Spadaro, before being spirited away to Istanbul on a French boat. The French consul himself was anxious about Turkish reprisals if the *agha* was harmed, and warned that "local anarchy" was only being held in check by the arrival of French or British naval vessels: crowds of angry Greeks, armed, had besieged his house for some days, hoping to get him to hand the *agha* over. The "anarchy" was heightened by the arrival of what he called "pirates"—the pro-revolutionary Spetsiote corsair-captains who arrived in their ships off Tinos in April. One of them abducted the Muslim passengers found on an Austrian boat they had illegally stopped, and brought them to the island as prisoners: several escaped and were sheltered by Catholic notables, but others were held as slaves, and one was caught and killed in the fields outside the village of Mesi (by the church now known as Ay.Ioannis tou Tourkou).

In the capital, Spadaro appealed to one of the island's main notables to have the Muslim passengers released, but despite his role as a member of the island assembly, those notables either could not or would not get involved: "You understand we are more obeyed than obeying; as "Chiefs of Police" our authority does not extend outside the city—in the countryside other villages take no account of us, and govern themselves. We have no force at our disposal." Outside the city lurked the potential anarchy of every village for itself. And across the seas were the twin threats of violence. One came from the Ottoman fleet, the other from the leaders of the revolution. On Tinos, the Spetsiot sea-captains—arresting Turks in the Greek cause—were the first forceful signs of a new centre of authority, the Revolution, bidding to fill the resultant vacuum of power.[7]

I think it is very likely that the incident with the Muslim captives formed the basis for the remarkable story which Konstantinos Metaxas, the first commissioner of the Provisional Government to the Archipelago, tells in his memoirs about the lengths to which he was willing to go to bring the islands round to the Greek side. According to Metaxas—who only arrived in 1822—he was on Tinos when a Psara captain told him he had captured some thirty Turkish pilgrims on an Austrian boat bound for Syria (and the *hajj*). Metaxas took

---

[7] M.C.D. Raffenel, *Histoire des evénéments de la Grèce* (Paris, 1822), pp. 94-5; was it another Austrian vessel that was seized, according to the French consul in Smyrna on 29 July 1821 (carrying "wealthy Armenian pilgrims, rich in gold and silver")? See N. Mavris, ed., *Istorikon Archeion Kasou*, I (Athens, 1937), p. 204.

charge of them—or so he says—and decided to distribute them around those islands whose commitment was suspect. He then plotted to send groups of pro-revolutionary "freedom-lovers" to each place who would force the notables to hand over the Turkish hostages; the desire for revenge would take its bloody course and the island notables would be implicated and forced onto the side of the Revolution. This "harsh decision" —as Metaxas describes it—is probably an elaboration after the event of what had really happened, before his arrival, the previous year. Whether or not it can be taken at face value, his telling of the story amply testifies not only to the nature of the war and to the self-image of the revolutionary, but also to the real resistance he and the pro-independence side in general encountered from the unconvinced notables of the Cyclades.[8]

In April 1821, the 57-year-old Bishop Gavriil was elected head of the *dimogerontia* of Tinos. There is general agreement that he was not really up to the task and lacked political sensitivity. Yet the challenges would have taxed the most sophisticated operator. Jubilation at the revolution quickly soured. There was bad blood between the Teniots and the Hydra-Spetsiot fleet—brawls and even murders as the sailors came ashore. The islanders saw the latter as unruly free-loaders and thieves, while the latter criticized their unwillingness to commit more substantially to the struggle. Between these two groups of islands— the one [Hydra and Spetses] barren but well-armed, the other (Syros, Paros, Tinos and Naxos) wealthy but poor in arms—there was bound to be conflict, and so it happened.[9]

The island was constantly being visited by "freedom-lovers" urging a more belligerent stand against the Turks. In early 1822, for instance, islanders from neighbouring Mykonos came and showed off a grisly trophy of war— "two dozen rotting heads" —following their victory over a Tunisian frigate which had stopped at the island for water.[10] But in the war's early months, and despite the first indications of plague, many on Tinos appeared to be more concerned about amusing themselves and getting on with business than with fighting. When the French Philhellene Maxime Raybaud stopped off in early 1822, he described the Tiniots as "extremely given over to pleasure". A theatre was

---

[8] K. Metaxas, *Istorika Apomnimonevmata ek tis Ellinikis Epanastaseos* (Athens, 2002 ed.), pp. 73-5. For a dispassionate view of Metaxas' methods, see J.P. Jourdain, *Mémoires historiques et militaires sur les événements de la Grèce depuis 1822* (Paris, 1828), pp. 228-34.

[9] F. Vitali, "O Tinou Gavriil Sylivos kai I symvoli tou eis tin ethnegersian tou 1821", *Epetiris Etaireia Kykladikon Meleton* [*EEKM*] (1971-73), pp. 137 ff.

[10] On Syros, see Raybaud, *Mémoires sur la Grèce pour servir à l'histoire de la guerre de l'indépendence*, ii, pp. 445-6; for a matter-of-fact account of seizing a Turkish ship and the aftermath, see G. Saktouri, *Istorika imerologia tou navtikou agonos tou 1821* (Athens, 1890), p. 12.

showing ancient tragedy, and there was much dancing at night. During Carnival, anti-Ottoman feelings took a humorous form: "masked people strolled through the streets, grotesque imitators of the religious ceremonies and official usages of the Turks, these cadis, imams, dervishes, formed on the spur of the moment, excited the gaity of the crowd."[11]

But as the key commercial centre in the Cyclades, Tinos was certainly aware of the war and the suffering it brought. It was a natural stopping-off point for refugees from the Asia Minor mainland or the eastern islands, and they poured into the island, especially after the massacres on Chios in the spring of 1822. More than three hundred desperate and terrified survivors were rescued in the harbour in Smyrna by HMS *Cambrian* alone, which disembarked them at Tinos in September.[12] With them came goods, bargaining and a crowded market in the main town. But they also brought disease, anger and instability, and although most eventually moved on, if only to Syros—where they entirely altered the complexion of the island—there were several years of serious strain. The plague of 1822-23 in particular was for a time a major threat, leading villages to bar entry to strangers and further hastening the fragmentation of authority on the island. By 1825 Tinos was home to some 16,000 refugees and the roads in the town by the port were "impassable" because of the throng.[13]

For the leaders of the Revolution, capturing Turks and killing them or holding them for ransom was small beer. Much more important was to establish their political and fiscal authority over the island and its riches. Eventually taxes and customs duties from the Cyclades became one of the insurgents' most important sources of income. Yet this took time.[14]

The first commissioner, sent by Ypsilantis in June 1821, quickly left. It was not until May 1822 that Emmanuel Spiridon was appointed Eparch, and a five-man committee was set up to administer the Aegean islands in the name of the Provisional Government. When Spiridon arrived on Tinos, he was armed with copies of a proclamation laying out the aims of the revolution and lauding the rights of man. He combated defeatist rumours—many of them spread, he alleged, by the Catholics from Paros and elsewhere—with more favour-

---

11 Raybaud, op. cit., ii, p. 131; According to Greek records from the end of the 1820s, the prewar population of Tinos—28,000—outstripped those of both Samos (25,000) and Andros (16,000) as well as Syros (4,500). *Archeia tis Ellinikis Palingenesias, 1821-1832: Anthologio* (Athens, 2002), p. 294.

12 FO 78/112/404 seq., Moore 19 Sept. 1822.

13 On the crowds, see Raybaud, op. cit., ii, pp. 113-30.

14 Revenue charges for 1823 indicate the enormous importance of Tinos, Naxos and Santorini for the revolutionary treasury. See N. Mavris, ed., *Istorikon Archeion Kaou*, I (Athens, 1937), pp. 48-9.

able stories of his own: an Austrian ship-captain from Odessa had reportedly told him, for instance, that 150,000 Russian and 50,000 Austrian troops were massed on the Ottoman borders. More concretely, he was ordering new elections for the island assembly and the appointment of new *kapetanei* of police, and levying taxes on the harvest and trade. He could not have made such sweeping demands without local support. In 1822, Raybaud had singled out the "numerous family of the Paximades" as "the most influential on the island by its wealth, its clients, its credit and its alliances". The youthful Fransiskos Paximades had returned from the Morea as a man of the Provisional Government. He had formed his own armed unit—defying the orders of the old local council headed by Gavriil—and having attached himself to the Eparch, he was "provisionally" appointed delegate of the Government for civil and criminal matters, in other words, the island's chief of police. In the middle of June, the first tax instalment of 60,000 *grosia* was sent to Hydra.[15]

Not surprisingly, many islanders resented this. In the first place, they feared that such levies might be construed by the Turks as support for the Revolution and could lead them to be attacked by the Kapudan Pasha. News of the tragic events on Chios had already reached them. Although the Provisional Government ordered the island's fortifications to be improved, everyone knew they could not prevent an attack or massacre of the kind that the revolutionaries' attacks had triggered off on Chios.[16] The Sultan and his government had certainly not lost hope of keeping the Cyclades on the Ottoman side. Patriarch Evgenios II—successor to the ill-fated Gregorios—was issuing encyclicals calling on the islanders to demonstrate their loyalty. Communication between the Aegean islands and Constantinople had not ceased: the Kapudan Pasha's fleet made its annual rounds, shipping continued between the capital and Syros in particular, and the Ottomans were sending secret agents and confidential letters in order to contact Gavriil and others. From as early as August 1821 they were conveying offers of an amnesty via a Greek-speaking Turk, Halil Bey, travelling on English papers. Hedging his bets, Gavriil was reported to be still sending the annual tax to the Patriarch in 1822. Perhaps reflecting doubts over his allegiances—was this why Gavriil had written off the first apparition of the Virgin as the "devil's work"? —the Archbishop of Crete actually sent men from Crete to abduct him; though they failed, the action showed that prominent men on Tinos faced dangers from more than one side.[17]

15　*Archeia tis Ellinikis Palingenesias,* 1 (Athens, 1971), doc. 176; *Archeia tis Ellinikis Palingenesias, 1821-1832,* 15 [*"Lyta Engrafa": VII:A-B*] (Athens, 1994), pp. 89-90, 95-6; Raybaud, op. cit., ii, 131

16　Ibid. p. 96.

17　D. Sofianos, "Enkyklioi [Aug. 1821-Jan. 1822] tou Oikoumenikou Patriarchi

In fact many were leaving, for they could see the threat for themselves every time the Ottoman fleet passed by. On neighbouring Syros, when the fleet moored off the town in 1822, the Catholic notables came out and professed their loyalty to the Kapudan Pasha. All this was in plain view of Tinos. On 8 October 1822 the fleet passed between Mykonos and Tinos, having failed to relieve the garrison at Nafplion; the following summer it returned through the same channel, chasing boats from Psara which docked on Tinos stocking up with fruit and vegetables. In short, it was only Ottoman policy that prevented Tinos being laid waste. When a "Greek" called "Yiankos" threatened he would go back to Constantinople and tell the Ottomans that the islanders were supporting the revolution, he was arrested as a spy and sent to Hydra.

To make matters worse in the eyes of the Tiniots, the revolution offered the island heavier rather than lighter taxes. "We took up arms against the Turkish tyranny to free ourselves from our own profiteering co-nationals," wrote the villagers of Hadzirados. "But the Provisional Government has appointed men over us who will quickly make us lose our enthusiasm for the revolution." Similar complaints were pouring in from other islands, and there was unrest on Andros, Santorini, Samos and Naxos in particular. On the last-named island the Revolutionary commissioners issued a proclamation reminding the inhabitants that "if deceitful men told you that independence means not paying a tithe to the Race, this is a lie, like saying you are not at war with the Turks, you are not members of the Greek Race."[18]

Rumours that the revolt was going badly in the Morea made it even harder for the new Eparch, Spiridon, to bring in the tithe. In fact, he had to tour the villages to explain things. But the opposition would not be allayed. In February 1823, as the plague began slowly to subside—cases were still reported in March—the inhabitants of the main town, Ayios Nikolaos, denounced him to the Provisional Government: he had abused his power and shown himself to be "autocratic" and "tyrannical"; he had contributed to unrest and "anarchy" rather than allaying them, and he had lorded it over the poor refugees; he called patriots "Turk-lovers" and his incessant demands had caused many wealthy islanders to flee abroad. The Government knew it could not defy local opinion

---

Evgenikou B" peri doulikis ypotagis ton Ellinon ston Othomano kataktiti", *Deltio tou Kentrou Erevnas tis Istorias tou Neoterou Ellinismou*, 2 (2000), pp. 19-41; A. Drakaki, "Angloi proxenoi eis tas Kykladas kata tin epanastasin tou 1821", *EEKM*, 4 (1964), pp. 115-42. On the Catholics sending taxes to the Sultan, M. Raybaud, op. cit., ii, p. 125.

18   AKT 9/42, 5 April, Collaro-Smyrna; *Archeia tis Ellinikis Palingenesias, 1821-1832*, 15 [*"Lyta Engrafa": VII:A-B*] (Athens, 1994), p. 164 [16 Sept. 1822].

indefinitely and in May 1823 Spiridon was replaced by Evangelos Mantzarakis who had previously been representing it on Santorini.

For the Catholics of the islands, matters were simple. The uprising was purely an affair between Orthodox and Muslims. They wanted no part in it, and they wanted no trouble. The local leaders on Hydra had called on the Catholics of Tinos as early as April 1821 to support their "Christian brothers", but their lukewarm response had led to bad feeling. Accusations flew that they were not proper patriots, and worse—that perhaps they were in league with the Turks and spying, a kind of fifth column. (For their part, of course, the "Latins" regarded these "Greeks" as no more than pirates, covering their extortions beneath the veil of revolution.) By January 1822 Bishop Collaro, the Catholic bishop of Tinos, lamented how "in the dominant anarchy there take place all the disorders imaginable, and all the Catholics groan and suffer."

It looked therefore as though the fault line on Tinos was one of religion. When Spiridon proclaimed himself Eparch in the spring of 1822 and demanded tribute, the Catholics refused to recognize his authority or to pay up. Soon there were threats: "If you don't pay, we'll make you pay three times as much." They flew the French flag as protection and sought the help of the consul on the island, Spadaro, who was a hot-blooded man, keen to sniff out insults to his dignity, and happy to help. His superior, the French consul in Smyrna, weighed in too, advising Spiridon not to persecute the Catholics. But it was not just the new Eparch they had to worry about. Men from the northern *Exomeria*—"our enemies" wrote one Catholic priest—were attacking Catholics and at least one was stabbed to death. Meanwhile, Orthodox village leaders alleged that the Catholics insulted them and the Greek flag, stole their animals and crops and threatened to surrender to the Turks "when they take Tinos". Worst of all, they alleged, they were protected by the French.[19]

Thanks perhaps to Spadaro, French protection had indeed been invoked to cover the Catholics en masse, Catholic churches and houses flew French flags and in 1822 Catholics on Tinos loudly celebrated St Louis' Day, in this way demonstrating their allegiance to the King of France, Louis XVIII. Had they not had the French to hide behind, many Orthodox islanders alleged, the Catholics could not have afforded to take such an aloof stance. In the eyes of supporters of the Provisional Government, they were simply not behaving like members of the Greek nation. When the forceful new Eparch, Mantzarakis, arrived on Tinos in May 1823, this issue soon surfaced once more. Having gone into a Catholic church in the village of Loutra to read out his orders, and having been criticized for this by the priest, he responded angrily: "You are not

---

19   AKT 9/348-349, Priest of Kellia-Collaro, 20 March 1823.

Hellenes, that is Greeks; yes, you are born in Greece but right now you are live under the French flag." (On neighbouring Syros, the language was harsher: the Greeks called the Catholics *"skylofrangoi* [Dog-Franks], *Turcolatini* and they ask them if they are Christians or Franks... If they reply that they are Latins, then they are subjected to more opprobrious insults.") In the countryside, often only a few hundred yards separated a Catholic from an Orthodox village, and the fields were studded with chapels and churches of both persuasions. We begin to read—in the weekly bulletins of events compiled by the French consul—of robbers plundering Catholic churches; on 22 September some "Greeks" kill the brother of a Catholic priest but fail to pay the blood money; four days later, a Catholic villager knifes a Greek to death.

But was it all really about religion? After all, Spiridon's critics down in Ayios Nikolaos also alleged he had been whipping up the ill-feeling between the two faiths. Many Orthodox echoed the Catholic Bishop Collaro when he hailed the withdrawal of Spiridon's "tyrannical government" and like him saw "the present government as provisional and pretty weak". In fact, from the point of view of the Revolution, Catholic lack of support was not the main problem. After some strong words to the Bishop and the villagers, the Catholics paid up and the new Eparch was congratulated by his superiors for his pursuit of "holy unity". By the summer of 1823, the real opposition came from within the Orthodox fold.[20]

The island's politics had, since the last quarter of the preceding century, revolved around the feud between two merchant families, the Georgantopouloi and the Paximades (who had built up an important banking business between Trieste and Alexandria). The historian Drosos, who himself belonged to the Georgantopoulos faction, has helpfully analyzed the impact of their conflict. Sparked off by a dispute over a woman—Ioannis Georgantopoulos had abducted a girl as she was about to wed his rival—this soon took on wider dimensions. Based in and around the port, the Paximades party was always dependent on the support of several notable Catholic families, and by the early nineteenth century, this had given the clash a religious colour. Both had amassed fortunes in the commercial upswing of the time, and were tied to prominent Phanariot and Ottoman officials in Constantinople itself.

In 1821 both clans also had members supporting the revolutionaries. Fransiskos Georgantopoulos, whose business interests kept him in Constantinople, was a member of the Filiki Etaireia and was executed by the Ottoman authorities there in April 1821 as a sympathizer; his nephew, Antonios, then a sea-captain in Odessa, joined Ypsilantis in Moldavia. The Paximades, despite their

---

20   AKT 9/42, 5 April 1823.

close Phanariot links, also had at least one family member in the Filiki Etaireia. They also boasted one of the revolution's earliest supporters on the island, Fransiskos Paximades. Son and grandson of the leaders of the family party, this Paximades had taken a group of ninety men and fought in the siege of Tripolis and Nafplion before returning as provisional chief of police with Spiridon in 1822. His police force, financed at his own expense, was to keep order on behalf of the revolution and the *dimogerontia*; but one wonders whether, in the eyes of the Paximades' traditional opponents, it did not look rather as though the national cause was merely being used by Fransiskos Paximades as cover for party hegemony.[21]

Paximades kept his position when Spiridon was replaced as Eparch by Mantzarakis—he represented the Revolution's real local power-base—and he was a key figure in suppressing the dissent that greeted Mantzarakis' demands. In the summer of 1823, ringing bells signalled the start of an anti-government tax revolt which aimed at dissolving the local administration of the revolution, raiding its coffers and attacking its "ministers"; it was Paximades—*taxiarchos kai archigos ton oplon*—who managed to suppress it, killing its leader. Even so, opposition to him and his men remained strong among other Orthodox islanders, just as much as among the Catholics. In September of that year, Mantzarakis reported to Hydra that glorious Greek victories had made no impression on "the miserable souls of Tinos"; with the exception of the "Latins", they had not paid "an obol", citing their fear of the Turks. No one, he complained, obeyed him. Even as his letter arrived, a crowd of armed men was descending on his residence, hurling insults and firing shots. These "rural revolutionaries" (*toioutous agroikous epanastatas*) refused to pay up "like the Catholics and town-dwellers did". It took a visit by Admiral Miaoulis to restore order and warn the Tiniots to obey the Eparch.

Three weeks later, however, Miaoulis changed tactics: while still criticizing the islanders for not doing more to help, he now he blamed the Eparch himself for squandering and misusing funds and proposed taking the entire administration of the island out of his hands. This should be organized instead—he told local notables—according "to your locally established practice". But who were these notables upon whom he now even called to expel Mantzarakis, by force if necessary? Certainly not his local strong-man, the fiery revolutionary Paximades. Rather, they were the very men who had led the old *dimogerontia* that Spiridon and Mantzarakis had swept aside, and who were now currently building up the new Evangelistria church. Konstantinos Georgantopoulos, one of Gavriil's backers, was appointed temporary Eparch in late 1823. In the faint

---

21 In some accounts, this number swells to 3,000, Dorizas, *Tinos epi Tourkokratias*, p. 408.

trace left behind by the scattered and insufficient documents, one thus catches glimpses of the way the discovery of the icon, and the building of the church, was becoming a form of political capital for one side to use against the other in the struggle for local power.

It had, after all, been in the immediately preceding months, as the island was falling into chaos, ravaged by the plague on the one hand and the new Eparch on the other, that the Virgin had encouraged the diggers, that they had built the first chapel by the spring in the main town of Ayios Nikolaos, and stumbled upon the icon itself. While the rest of the island fell apart amid a welter of murders, abductions and other crimes, Bishop Gavriil had established the committee of notables to administer the digging. There was perhaps a kind of bargain here. He agreed to their having a role in guiding the emergence of the new shrine; they protected him against accusations of being inadequately committed to the Revolution. When he was accused before the Provisional Government of politicking, Gavriil was defended by these same men.

The key movers on the committee for the new church were the Kagkadis brothers, wardens of the Orthodox nunnery to which Pelagia belonged, members of a family long known as backers of the Georgantopoulos faction. Among Gavriil's other protectors was none other than Konstantinos Georgantopoulos himself. This was a coalition of notables around the Georgantopoulos family, rooting themselves in local power—and what could symbolize their rootedness better than the commitment to the earth of Tinos that had given birth to such a sacred object? They were now being preferred by Admiral Miaoulis to Fransiskos Paximades, who had bet on the national cause and the support of the mainland. The struggle between the two great island clans, in other words, did not end with the war of 1821; it merely took another form.

And at the end of 1823 it exploded into violence. Miaoulis's intervention in favour of the Georgantopoulos faction led to stalemate because the former Eparch refused to leave or to hand over the account books, while Georgantopoulos, his replacement, insisted he was now carrying out Miaoulis' orders in the name of the Provisional Government. Miaoulis himself had meantime left the island. In early December 1823 Georgantopoulos was assassinated, and Mantzarakis' secretary was killed in revenge. Bishop Gavriil testified that Georgantopoulos' murderer had told him, in a deathbed confession, that he was acting for others. and the Government's own enquiries confirmed this: the former Eparch, Mantzarakis, had been the instigator; Fransiskos Paximades had also been involved. The alleged conspirators, some five men in all, were ordered to present themselves to the government on the mainland for interrogation. But Mantzarakis did not go without scattering accusations of his own. Lingering on Santorini, he accused his accusers of ill-treating him and murdering "patriots". The very members of the executive committee of the new church were accused of involvement in the murders which had followed Georgantopoulos's death. The Kagkadis brothers, in many ways the real founders of the Evangelistria cult, were accused of keeping back money which should have been given to the Struggle, and still worse of unpatriotic behaviour.

One can understand the fury of men like Paximades and Mantzarakis, outmanouevred by men who had risked much less than they had in the national cause. Indeed Stamatelos' brother, Iakovos Kagkadis, yet another of those Tiniot merchants with extensive Ottoman connections, did admit receiving a letter from a Turkish acquaintance, warning him that Mehmet Ali's Egyptian fleet was sailing to crush the rebels of Hydra and Spetses, and offering to negotiate if the islanders wanted to make submission to the Sultan. (Later he would be described as a *tourkolatro* who had targeted his opponents for their extreme *filopatria*.)[22]

Such men were far less committed to the revolution than those they had replaced, and much more concerned about the well-being of the island as a whole. And they had good reason to be cautious. In the early summer of 1824, in an invasion spearheaded by a huge Egyptian fleet, the island of Psara was devastated, Kasos was retaken, Sfakia was crushed, and with the ship-owning islands refusing to provide protection for the Cyclades, the prestige of the Provisional Government plumbed a new low. Leros, Kalymnos and the other Dodecanese islands now submitted to the majesty of the Sultan. Advised by the local consuls, who had always been less than enthusiastic about the revolutionary cause, the Tinos assembly considered following suit, and it drew up a letter to be presented to the Kapudan Pasha. The new Eparch, Drosos Mansolas, who had thoroughly investigated the previous year's killings and tried to restore calm, now reported that the island was "extremely disturbed". He had tried in vain to get them to fortify it once he learned of the fall of Kasos, but was so unconfident of his own position that he left, urging a Greek fleet to be sent to "forestall the plans of the Western powers who are hostile to the Greek revolution." On Naxos, there were similar problems: a pro-Turkish party emerged there also, led by bishops and consuls, and the Eparch there was also obliged to flee back to Hydra.[23]

It was at this precise moment, when the authority of the Provisional Government had collapsed and a Turkish reconquest seemed likely, when tensions between the Paximades and Georgantopoulos factions were at their height,

---

22   A. Lignou, ed., *Archeion tis Koinotitos Ydras, 1778-1832*, 10 (1824) (Piraeus, 1928), p. 168; G.L. Dorizas, *I Tinos epi Tourkokratias kai kata ton Agona tou 1821* (Athens, 1978), p. 317.

23   N. Mavris, ed., *Istorikon Archeion Kasou*, 1, p. 282.

that the shocking events in the church at Livadha with which this paper opened took place. The precipitating cause was the decision of the French ministry of Marine that its flag could not be flown except on French vessels or above consular establishments. French consuls in the Levant immediately foresaw problems. On 20 August 1824 the consul in Smyrna reported: "My Tinos agent writes me that this disappearance of the white flag from all the churches has been taken by the Greeks as a sign that the Latins are at their mercy." Armed men were going around the island, whipping up feeling against the Catholics. Back in Smyrna, the Catholic archbishop—who was getting his own alarming reports from Bishop Collaro on Tinos—discussed the matter with the French consul there, Pierre David, and warned him that if French protection counted for so little, the island's Catholics (and behind them, of course, Rome) might be forced to look elsewhere, perhaps to Austria, for *une protection plus efficace*.

These words, of course, were a sign of the great game being played out in the eastern Mediterranean, and in the short term they changed little: the Catholic church near Falatadhos was sacked, the perpetrators were never punished and other similar episodes continued throughout the summer. In the longer term, however, Austrian naval commanders started indeed to play a more interventionist role alongside the French: in 1826, the Austrian admiral Paulucci, moored off Tinos as part of an anti-pirate sweep of the notorious channels there, seized two Greek warships and distributed a proclamation, warning he would protect the Catholics from harm and threatening revenge if they suffered. With French anti-piracy efforts, the Catholics were again caught in the middle. There was a tense stand-off at Syros where French efforts to catch the *Thrasyvouli*— "the most renowned and least scrupulous of the Hydra corsairs"—led several thousand men to come down to the seafront and threaten to burn the Catholic part of town if the French fired on the corsair.[24]

Tinos remained a deeply disturbed and riven island for several years to come. In 1827 Navarino removed the threat of the Ottoman fleet. But the Provisional Government did not re-establish its authority properly until the advent of Kapodistrias. Meanwhile its emissaries levied taxes as best they could and on occasions also conscripted men by none too gentle means. The islanders continued to bear the burden of feeding several thousand refugees, and to suffer from the disruption when irregulars landed and began looting. In the summer of 1826 arguments between the islanders and the new representatives of the Provisional Government led to ships loyal to the latter actually firing on the town. Piracy got worse before it got better, and the regular troop unit on the island was so badly provisioned and paid that in August 1826 it was

---

24   J. de la Graviere, *La station du Levant*, ii (Paris, 1876), pp. 13-14.

on the verge of dissolution. Even into the early years of Greek independence, "armed vagabonds", brigands and pirates continued to play a prominent role in the island economy. A battalion of Bavarian soldiers had to be sent there after islanders refused to pay taxes on their crops: Bishop Gavriil was regarded as responsible for encouraging them. A known opponent of the government on religious grounds—he had, like many clerics, staunchly opposed the idea of by-passing the Patriarchate and establishing a National Church of Greece—he was tried, acquitted and reassigned to Naxos as archbishop there.[25]

And the Evangelistria? It seems to have been during Easter in 1825 that its fame spread beyond the island. That was the time of the first great miracle, when the Virgin gave sight back to the blind four-year old child of a local family. But this was not just any family; the child concerned was Stefanos, the only son of Georgios Mavroyeni, scion of the great Phanariot clan and one of the island's leading personalities. Shortly after this, the family wet-nurse was similarly cured. Alongside the Mavroyenis' powerful national and international presence, they played a critical role in the inter-married society of upper class Tinos. On the one hand, they were related to Stamatelos Kagkades, warden of the monastery to which the nun Pelagia was attached, and perhaps *the* key figure in the establishment of the new cult of the Virgin. And on the other, they were also connected to the Paximades and to the revolution. Through the figure of Georgios Mavroyeni, the old tensions between the Paximades and Georgantopoulos clans, which had threatened to tear the island apart in 1823 and 1824, were not only overcome but replaced by unity through support for the Virgin and her miracles.[26]

The astonishingly rapid rise of the new shrine might suggest at first sight that its emergence had been part of a nationalist strategy to assert the Greek and Orthodox character of Tinos, and to associate an island whose actual role during the War of Independence had been deeply ambiguous and uncertain with the cause of the new Greece. After all, the last lingering memories of Catholic ascendancy had finally been vanquished along with the ending of Ottoman rule. Men from Falatadhos had triumphantly vandalized the church of the Virgin in Livadha; it was men from the same village whose shovels had uncovered her icon down in Ayios Nikolaos 18 months before. Yet behind faith lay local interests and above all the interests of Tinos itself and the men who ran it. The emergence of the Evangelistria reflected first and foremost the sudden vacuum of power—political but above all ecclesiastical—which the War of Independence created in the Cyclades. Between 1821 and 1833 there had been an inter-

---

25 FO 352/12B, Vitalis-Canning, 17 July 1826.
26 T. Blancard, *Les Mavroyéni: Histoire d'Orient (de 1700 à nos jours)* ii (Paris, 1909), pp. 656-7.

regnum in which the power of the Sultan and the Patriarch in Constantinople had vanished but the new political forces of the national state had not yet fully asserted themselves. By the time the Regency and the new National Church had been established, the Evangelistria cult had already emerged.

For this, neither Bishop Gavriil nor the church was really responsible. On the contrary, the Orthodox Church was in the throes of a profound crisis at both the regional and the local level. Gavriil's traditional attachment to the Patriarchate, which eventually led him to oppose the formation of the Greek national church, must have been deeply tested by the uncertainties of the 1820s. But it was not only a matter of the fractured authority of the Patriarchate; the church's crisis ran deeper still. According to Gavriil himself, when he came to survey the island's ecclesiastical holdings in 1828, although its dozens of churches and hundreds of chapels survived intact, plague, the war and starvation had decimated its personnel: of the prewar strength of 128 priests, only 65 remained.[27] In fact, the men chiefly responsible for the pilgrimage site were not Gavriil but Kagkadis, Georgantopoulos, Mavroyeni and other members of the old notable class in Tinos itself. Orthodox themselves, they had hedged their bets between Turks and Greeks, seeking at all costs to preserve stability on the island. Gavriil had acknowledged the genuineness of the icon, and in return they had protected him from accusations of failing to support the revolution. At the same time, they had also forced him to accept lay, local control of the church and its foundation. On the inscription which may be found within the church to this day, it is their names—Kagkadis first—which precede that of the archbishop.

The Virgin's fame spread rapidly: even in April 1825, Admiral Sachtouris had shown his respects to the *Panayia* in the town with a gun salute. Her rise, and her miracles, burnished with their incomparable allure the reputations of wily and sophisticated men whose political opponents had often during the war itself accused them, perhaps not without justice, of being accomodationists, lacking in patriotic fervour. The island's first *dimarchos*, appointed at the end of 1833, was none other than Stamatios Kagkadis, the man who for the entire previous decade had been treasurer and leading figure in the excavations to find the icon. It is not surprising, therefore, that when a few years later peasants on Naxos started to have visions and claimed to have discovered another

---

27 G. Dorizas, *Oi ekklisies kai ta proskynimata tis; Tinou* (Athens, nd), p. 22; cf. AKT 28/136-7, "Numerazione delle anime dei nostri cattolici di Tine fatta nel 1835" estimates the total number of Catholics on the island at 5,546 as well as roughly thirty priests.

holy icon, Bishop Gavriil—who was now the Archbishop there—put his foot down, took charge of the alleged icon, and refused to bless the proceedings.[28]

This perhaps helps us to appreciate why the rise of the Orthodox Virgin did not mean quite such a disaster for the Catholic Mary as had seemed likely in the dark days of 1824. It was certainly true that the new political arrangements introduced under Kapodistrias, with the abolition of the old Ottoman system of Catholic self-administration, made Catholics newly vulnerable to the Orthodox majority; despite their protests, communal self-government was not resurrected. And of course King Otto paid his respects to the new church on Tinos when he came in 1833. But as a good Bavarian Catholic, he was not going to allow the Catholic Church to suffer. Indeed he visited the Catholic cathedral in Tinos on the same trip and pledged his support for the island's Catholics quite openly.[29]

Within a decade, both Syros and Tinos had put behind them the ambivalent past and emerged from the war transformed. Thousands of Orthodox refugees, mostly from Chios, turned Syros into a flourishing centre of commerce and founded an entirely new town which they named after the patron of trade, Hermes. Tinos could not quite match this but it did not lag far behind. It never regained the commercial preeminence it had enjoyed under the Ottomans. Nevertheless, the establishment of the Evangelistria church brought tens of thousands of pilgrims annually, paid for what were probably at the time the best schools in Greece, and allowed the port to expand rapidly, even as the old capital on the mountain above it, Exoburgo, gradually fell into ruins. When the German Prince Puckler-Muskau visited Tinos at the end of the 1830s, he was struck by the wealth of the church— "without doubt the most beautiful and one of the largest I have yet seen in the Kingdom of Greece", the "throng of pilgrims" who came from "all over the world", and the six exemplary public schools supported by its foundation. Compared with halting, even non-existent recovery in the Peloponnese and Roumeli, devastated by years of war, this was an unexpectedly rosy outcome. Tinos had, after all, been protected by the Virgin, and its continued prosperity was not the least of her miracles.[30]

---

28 See Stewart, this volume.

29 AKT, Blue Box: Gabinelli correspondence, 5 July 1829 contains Catholic complaints to the bishop regarding the Orthodox domination of local politics. For Otto's visit, see P. Gaetano Romano, *Cenni Storici della Missione della Compagnia di Gesù in Grecia* (Palermo, 1912).

30 H. Puckler Muskau (translated by Jean Cohen), *Entre l'Europe et l'Asie: Voyage dans l'Archipel* (Brussels, 1840), ii, pp. 41-2.

BIBLIOGRAPHY

Anon., "A Panhellenic Festival of Today", *Macmillan's Magazine*, 48 (1883-4), 474-7.

Archives of the Catholic Archbishopric on Tinos [AKT].

Archeia tis Ellinikis Palingenesias, 1, Athens, 1971.

Archeia tis Ellinikis Palingenesias, 1821-1832, 15 [*"Lyta Engrafa"*: *VII:A-B*], Athens, 1994.

Archeia tis Ellinikis Palingenesias, 1821-1832: *Anthologio* (Athens, 2002).

Blancard, T. (1909) *Les Mavroyéni: Histoire d'Orient (de 1700 à nos jours)* ii, Paris.

Campbell, J.K. (1964) *Honour, Family and Patronage: A Study of Institutions and Moral Values in a Greek Mountain Community*, Oxford.

de la Graviere, J. (1876) *La station du Levant*, 2 vols., Paris.

de Valon, A. (1846) *Une année dans le Levant*, Paris.

Dorizas, G.L. (1978) *I Tinos epi Tourkokratias kai kata ton Agona tou 1821*, Athens.

—— (nd) *Oi ekklisies kai ta proskynimata tis Tinou*, Athens, nd.

Drakaki, A. (1964) "Angloi proxenoi eis tas Kykladas kata tin epanastasin tou 1821", *Epetiris Etaireia Kykadikon Meleton* [*EEKM*], 4, 115-42.

Drosos, D. (1870) *Istoria tis nisou Tinou*, Athens.

Foreign Office files, National Archives, London [FO].

Gaetano Romano, P. (1912) *Cenni Storici della Missione della Compagnia di Gesù in Grecia*, Palermo.

Hofmann, G. (1937) *Vescovadi cattolici della Grecia*, vol. 2 Tinos, Rome.

Jourdain, J.P. (1828) *Mémoires historiques et militaires sur les événements de la Grece depuis 1822*, Paris.

Lignou, A. (ed.) (1928) *Archeion tis Koinotitos Ydras, 1778-1832*, x, Piraeus.

Mavris, N. (ed.) (1937) *Istorikon Archeion Kasou*, 3 vols., Athens.

Metaxas, K. (ed.) (2002) *Istorika Apomnimonevmata ek tis Ellinikis Epanastaseos*, Athens, 2002.

Post, H.A. (1830) *A Visit to Greece and Constantinople in the Year 1827-8*, New York.

Puckler Muskau, H. (translated by Jean Cohen) (1840) *Entre l'Europe et l'Asie: Voyage dans l'archipel.* 2 vols., Brussels.

Raffenel, M.C.D. (1822) *Histoire des evénéments de la Grèce*, Paris.

Raybaud, M. (1824-25) *Mémoires sur la Grèce pour servir à l'histoire de la guerre de l'indépendence,* 2 vols., Paris.

Sachtouri, G. (1890) *Istorika imerologia tou navtikou agonos tou 1821*, Athens.

Sofianos, D. (2000) "Enkyklioi [Aug. 1821-Jan. 1822] tou Oikoumenikou Patriarchi Evgenikou B" peri doulikis ypotagis ton Ellinon ston Othomano kataktiti", *Deltio tou Kentrou Erevnas tis Istorias tou Neoterou Ellinismou*, 2, 19-41.

Vitali, F. (1971-73) "O Tinou Gavriil Sylivos kai I symvoli tou eis tin ethnegersian tou 1821", *Epetiris Etaireia Kykadikon Meleton* [*EEKM*], 137-55.

4

DREAMING OF BURIED ICONS IN THE KINGDOM OF GREECE

Charles Stewart[1]

On the day of the Annunciation in 1836 a group of villagers unearthed three icons at a spot in mountain Naxos called Argokoíli. They had been directed to this discovery by a series of dreams and visions in which the Panagía[2] appeared telling them to dig up her icon and build her a "house". These events sparked a pilgrimage to the church of the Panagía Argokoiliótissa that continues to this day, attracting approximately 5,000 visitors on the Friday after Easter Sunday, the feast day of the Panagía of the Live-Giving Spring.

On Tinos, the progression from dreams to icon discovery, to church construction, to successful pilgrimage site, proceeded relatively directly and successfully (Mazower, this volume). This was not the case on Naxos. The Greek Church and state began to repress the movement to venerate the Panagía Argokoiliótissa before the icon was even found. The present study of Naxiote dreams of icons, state opposition, and local reactions against the state offers a

---

[1] I am grateful to Robin Cormack, Veronica della Dora, Yannis Hamilakis, Ioannis Koubourlis, Evangelos Livieratos, Mark Mazower and Eleana Yalouri for generously sharing ideas and valuable research materials. An earlier version of this chapter was presented at the conference 'The Making of Modern Greece: Nationalism, Romanticism and the Uses of the Past (1797-1896), King's College London, Spetember 2006.

[2] Panagía means "All-Holy [Mother of God]". I use this name rather than Virgin Mary to remind readers that this study concerns the Greek Orthodox, not the Catholic Church. Panagía is the most common name for Mary in Greece, and the Orthodox Church differs from the Catholic in not recognizing the Immaculate Conception of Mary. For Greek Orthodox the primary association with Mary is as mother, not virgin (Dubisch 1995: 236).

NETWORKS OF POWER IN GREECE

revealing look into what the making of modern Greece involved at the local level. This episode shows that the Naxiotes embraced Orthodoxy as a faith involving mystery and revelation. Their Orthodoxy, furthermore, mediated their understanding of the past and of their land. Independence placed new bureaucratic structures and expectations upon them. At the moment under examination here Greece had been created, but the formation of Greek citizens obedient to the laws of the state, sharing a national consciousness and a historical consciousness, would take yet more time and effort.[3] This transformation could not be effected once and for all by simple instructions. New laws and programmes were set in place by successive governments including that of Capodistrias (1828-31), the Bavarian Regency (1833-35), and during King Otto's independent rule, first without a constitution (1835-44) and then with one (1844-62). The people of Naxos confronted legislation that had the effect of converting them from a self-understanding as firstly Christian—whether denominated as *Romii, Khristianoi* or even as *Éllines*[4]—to an identification as Hellenes in the sense of citizens of a European-oriented state with a genealogy extending directly, and with as little mediation as possible, back to Ancient Greece. The case of Argokoíli in the 1830s allows us to see how difficult this transition could be. This study reveals the high price that local communities sometimes paid for sovereign nationalization.

The events of interest for the present study commence in 1831 when the Panagía began to appear to three shepherds from Kóronos, siblings named María, Geórgios and Nikólaos. She instructed them to dig for an icon depicting her. These events are described in two different accounts written by a village priest of the time, Father Korrés (1962: 4, 2002a: 23), who states that these early apparitions occurred during waking visions (*phótisi, orámata*).[5] The

---

3   This formulation paraphrases the remark attributed to the Italian statesman Massimo d'Azeglio after the unification of Italy: "We have created Italy, now we must create the Italians".

4   Among other meanings, the term "*Ellinas*" (Hellene) was sporadically used before Independence to refer to someone who followed the Greek rite in Church, and obeyed the Partriarch of Constantinople—a more Christian-centred sense for that word than the post-independence meaning. Vlach-, Albanian- and Slav-speakers could all consider themselves and be considered "Hellenes" (Livanios 2008).

5   I am grateful to Iánnis Khouzoúris for providing me with photocopies of Korrés' and other reports. The events at Argokoíli have been greatly illuminated by the release of archival documents from the Holy Synod of Greece in the mid-1990s. Khouzoúris has published these in his quarterly *Argokoiliótissa*, and I cite them as "Documents". Seraïdari (2007: 184 ff) offers a good account of the 1836 discovery at Argokoíli on the basis of Korrés and a lengthy didactic poem by Khouzoúris (1996).

DREAMING OF BURIED ICONS IN THE KINGDOM OF GREECE

surrounding community debated whether these might be cases of demonic possession and this remained a speculation on all sides over the years to come. Co-villagers and officials could dismiss the visionaries with this charge. The visionaries' defenders, on the other hand, contended that everyone in the village was already currently tyrannized by the devil. With opinions split in this way, the Bishop of Naxos and Paros came to Argokoíli and blessed the excavation site with holy water (Korrés 2002a: 23).

A new sequence of events commenced in 1835 when the Panagía began appearing to two new visionaries. The first of them, Christódoulos Manolás, a young farmer, owned a plot of land at Argokoíli. At first Christódoulos was sceptical of the enterprise, especially since the faithful wanted to dig on his land. They asked him not to plant crops that season. He declared that unless the Panagía manifested herself directly, he would go ahead and plant. On 13 November 1835 Christódoulos went to bed at midnight, and while still awake he felt two heavy blows to his knees. He shouted for mercy, at which point a voice asked, "Are you convinced now that my home is at Argokoíli?" (Korrés 2002a: 23)

Through further visions, Christódoulos learned that the icon had belonged to an Egyptian family that fled persecution during the period of iconoclasm (8th and 9th centuries AD). Rather than face further persecution they prayed for the earth to swallow them up. The Panagía added that if people dug faithfully the first thing they found would be the bones of this couple and their child, which should be preserved as holy.

Hearing this, a crowd of people went to Argokoíli and began digging. Over the course of a long day, they found nothing. As they were gathering up their implements, Christódoulos saw a vision (*ephotísthi*) indicating where to strike with his pickaxe. With one blow he opened the way into a cavern. Digging inside, people quickly found some bones. Reports circulated that the bones and surrounding earth had a pleasant smell, were warm to the touch, and could cure illness. Christódoulos asked the Panagía to reveal herself there and then on top of the dirt and bones. She replied, "How can I possibly come out since you have not prepared my place. There is no throne for me should I come out now. Do not neglect the building of my house (*oíkos*), but keep working with solid faith..." (Korrés 1962: 5 and Korrés 2002a: 24).

On another occasion Christódoulos had an ecstatic vision (*ílthe eis ékstasin*) inside the parish church of Kóronos, St Marina. A divine power invisibly bound his hands in a position of supplication across his chest, and he stared skyward. Coming at him he saw a fiery wheel with the Panagía in the middle accompanied by numerous saints all dressed in white like snow and singing. Christ appeared as well and those villagers possessed by the devil began to scream and shout. One demon-possessed girl cried out: "The [Panagía] Argokoiliótissa and St Marina have arrived along with a great number of angels and they are tormenting us." A demon-possessed man named Iánnis began to foam at the mouth (Korrés 1962: 6-7).

The Bishop of Naxos, according to Father Korrés, permitted a 35-year-old itinerant monk named Gerásimos Mavromátis to travel to Kóronos ostensibly to take confessions, impose regimes of prayer and fasting and, granted the state of affairs in Kóronos, to perform exorcisms. Once arrived in Vóthroi,[6] Gerásimos began to have his own dreams, in which the Panagía confirmed what she had told Christódoulos.[7] In one dream the Panagía appeared to Gerásimos and told him that she would give a pledge (*arravóna*) to appear. He went to Argokoíli the following day and discovered a silver coin with Constantine the Great on it. Gerásimos took this coin with him and left Vóthroi to spread the word to other villages on Naxos.[8]

Soon thereafter the Panagía spoke via a new visionary, Manouíl Sakhás, like Christódoulos a farmer/shepherd from Vóthroi, married with children. She gave instructions for building her "monastery", which would be "large enough to hold all the inhabitants of the island" (Korrés 2002b: 21). In a separate vision around the same time the Panagía told Christódoulos to tell everyone "that they should build me a dwelling, a spacious hotel (*evrýchoron xenodocheíon*), a special (*xechóriston*, "separate") place to set me where those coming to visit may rest".[9]

A third phase of the story began in February 1836 when yet another visionary appeared on the scene, a man named Ioánnis Maggióros (nicknamed Doumbrogiánnis). Like Christódoulos and Manouíl, he was a poor, unlettered shepherd from Kóronos. After his first day digging for the icon he went home and during his afternoon nap he saw a vision (*vlépei eis to oramá tou*) of the Panagía. She told him that there were three icons in the cavern: one each of the Panagía, the Lament for Christ, and St John the Baptist.

6	Before the 20th century, Kóronos was known as Vóthroi. At that time the word *vóthros* meant "ravine", and the village is, indeed, built in a nexus of ravines. Over time *vóthros* came to mean "cess pit". Embarrassed by this semantic shift, the villagers changed the name to Kóronos after the nearby mountain.
7	According to the report of Canon Marmarás to the Holy Synod, 18 June 1836 (Documents 2000a: 21). Theodóritos Marmarás, a Canon of the Church (*Protosýnkelos*), was sent to Kóronos to investigate events on behalf of the Holy Synod in the late spring of 1836.
8	Canon Marmarás to Holy Synod, 18 June 1836 (Documents 2000a: 22).
9	Korrés 2002b: 21. In his account written several months later, Korrés attributed this vision to Manouíl (1962: 10).

DREAMING OF BURIED ICONS IN THE KINGDOM OF GREECE

Ioánnis saw a vision instructing him that all three icons would be found on 25 March 1836. On that day a crowd numbering in the thousands assembled. Doumbrogiánnis descended into the cavern and found the three icons.[10] These were passed among the priests and placed in a "cell" (*kellí*) that had already been built. That very day, on the crest of these wondrous events, Ioánnis had a further vision—that on 23 April, St George's day, one further icon of the Panagía would be discovered. This fourth icon was duly found. It was claimed as a work of St Luke; observers described it as being one-eighth the size of a sheet of paper, and executed as an impression (*anáglypho*) in the unusual medium of wax and mastich (*kiromastíkha*). This icon would appear to be the focus of the pilgrimage to Argokoíli today (Fig. 1).

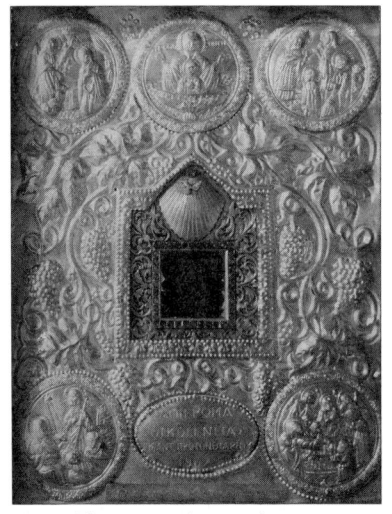

Fig 1. The wax and mastich icon venerated today at the pilgrimage to Argokoíli.

These events on Naxos overlapped with the birth of the Greek state. King Otto (Othon)[11] arrived in Greece early in 1833 along with three Bavarian regents who would serve until his 20th birthday in June 1835. Othon was a Catholic, while the regent in charge of the ministries of Justice and Ecclesiastical affairs, Professor Georg von Maurer, was a Protestant. They lost little time in establishing an autocephalous Greek national church no longer under the authority of the Patriarch of Constantinople, but under the direction of a Holy Synod of bishops elected and overseen by the King (Frazee 1969: 113).

Sections of the Orthodox population of the Kingdom of Greece felt concern that the country was getting Protestantized or Catholicized.[12] Such a fear would have been keenly felt on islands such as Naxos or Tinos (Mazower, this volume), which the Venetians

---

10   According to contemporary oral traditions he descended wearing only a robe so that no one could say that he planted the icons.

11   Frederick Otto von Wittelsbach, second son of King Ludwig of Bavaria, known as Othon in Greece.

12   As Frazee (1969: 114) has noted, Maurer's blueprint for the separation of Church and state in Greece paralleled closely the 1818 Constitution of the Bavarian Protestant Church.

had governed for centuries, and which still had Catholic populations.[13] After the Ottoman takeover in 1566 the Naxos Catholics continued to own most of the land. Furthermore, under the Capitulations Catholic clergy throughout the Ottoman Empire came under French protection. A Capitulation of 1673 permitted Catholics to fly the French flag to avoid getting caught up in the crossfire during conflicts between Muslim and Orthodox populations, such as the War of Candia (Frazee 2002: 31). When the War of Independence broke out Catholics on Naxos flew the French flag over the *kástro* and, as on Tinos, continued to pay the Turkish annual tax, and baulked at paying levies placed on them by the revolutionary government.[14] From the Catholic perspective, continuing French protection and Ottoman religious tolerance probably seemed like a better prospect than absorption into a majority Orthodox Christian state. The historian Charles Frazee characterized the relations between Catholics and Orthodox at this time as one of "simmering resentment and hatred" (1979: 319).

Among the first ecclesiastical reforms pursued by the regency government was the closure of all monasteries with less than six monks, with all property nationalized. An exception was made for Catholic monasteries and Church properties since, at the Conference of London, France had extracted the promise that Catholic lands and freedom to worship would be protected in the new state (Frazee 1979: 324). This preference must have irritated the local Naxos population, by puncturing their sense of equal entitlement as co-citizens, and members of the dominant religion of the country.[15] In addition, the Synod placed restrictions on the movement of monks outside their home monasteries. Previously, itinerant monks had been prominent spiritual reference points in the countryside, often carrying with them sacred icons and relics. The new Synod curtailed such activities along with the practice of allowing weddings and baptisms to be celebrated at monasteries (Frazee 1969: 126).

---

13   On Naxos the Catholic population at independence numbered around three or four hundred, mainly residing at Chóra, in the Venetian-built *kástro* (fortified citadel). This was the seat of the Catholic Archbishop of Greece and the site of an Ursuline convent. See Frazee 1978.

14   The Catholic resistance to Greek revolutionary taxation appears in diplomatic reports such as those of the British consul, N. Frangopulos, sent to the British Ambassador in Constantinople in 1826 (Foreign Office Archives: FO 352/12B 273669).

15   Beginning with the earliest provisional constitution drawn up by the revolutionaries in 1822, and as confirmed in the official constitution of the Greek state in 1844, the "Eastern Orthodox Church" was recognized as the dominant religion of Greece.

DREAMING OF BURIED ICONS IN THE KINGDOM OF GREECE

In addition to closing down monasteries the new government imposed restrictions on the building of private chapels and new monasteries. The erection of any such structures would henceforth require the King's permission. Furthermore, new laws aimed at protecting archaeological remains on Greek soil placed the very activity of digging under increased scrutiny. As Maurer wrote:

Beyond the fact that they hold great interest for archaeologists and historians, Greek antiquities have enormous significance, most of all, for the Kingdom of Greece. This is because it was the idea of ancient Greece that inspired general European interest in the heroic battle for modern Greece...This spirit of Greek antiquity must be maintained into the future as a magnetic bond between contemporary Greece and European civilization. (Maurer 1976[1835]: 544)

With this aim in mind, Maurer oversaw the passage of laws in May 1834 aimed at safeguarding the Greek cultural heritage. The first article in the section on antiquities (Article 61) stated that: "All antiquities inside Greece, as works of the ancestors of the Greek people, are considered the national property (*ktíma ethnikón*) of all Greeks in general" (Petrákos 1982: 132). Article 65 clarified the issue of ownership:

As regards objects discovered on privately owned land, whether beneath it, inside walls, below piles of rubble, or however else hidden: After the date on which the present law comes into force, whether these antiquities are found by chance, or intentional excavation, the State shall own half of their value… (Petrákos 1982: 133)

And Article 100 decreed that no one would be allowed to dig for antiquities without first obtaining an official permit.[16] A fine of between 25 and 200 drachmas, and confiscation of any antiquities discovered, were to be imposed on offenders.

These laws redefined many of the activities then in process deep in the interior mountains of Naxos. What had begun as a local instance of a type of visionary practice familiar throughout the Orthodox world, suddenly stood in a different light. The voice of the Panagía instructing people to unearth her icon and build her a "spacious hotel" could now be construed as an incitement to break the law on several counts.

During the period of visionary activity in the 1830s, amidst the flux in state government and legislation, Naxos received a new bishop. The Cretan Gavriíl Sylivós arrived in late 1833 from nearby Tinos, where he had played a central

---

16 Petrákos 1982: 139. In an encyclical issued under Capodistrias on 23 June 1830 the government had already taken steps to require permits to dig for antiquities (Petrákos 1982:116). In September 1833 officials on Naxos (notably customs officials) had been informed that all trading in, or excavation of, antiquities was forbidden (Documents 2000b:21).

role in validating the dreams of the nun Pelagía. Gavriíl was no stranger to charismatic visionary phenomena such as were occurring in Kóronos at the time of his arrival (Vitális 1973).

Gavriíl at first seemed sympathetic to the highland visionaries, but by early 1836 he came under pressure to close their activities down. In a letter dated 6 February 1836, he exhorted local priests in Vóthroi to persuade people to "desist from these fantasies (*phantasías*) and from disturbing the peace". If they did not, he continued, "they will be punished by the government".[17] He enclosed with that letter a warning notice from the local police to be read aloud in the villages. The Holy Synod matched the pressure from secular authorities by ordering Gavriíl to send Gerásimos and another monk back to their monastery on Paros. This action upheld the new legislation on itinerant monks discussed above.

After the discovery of the icons in early 1836, the beleaguered Bishop of Paronaxía no doubt hoped that the inhabitants of Vóthroi would return to their normal lives. The Holy Synod sent an investigator who prevailed upon two local priests to sign a document promising, "upon pain of being defrocked" (*poiní kathairéseos*), not to celebrate offices using the new icons, and not to take the icons back to the discovery site (Documents 2000c: 23). These measures did not succeed in defusing the movement. Shortly after the departure of the investigator, two men from Kóronos, who had recently been released from a five-month prison term on Syros for theft, returned to the village where they dreamed (*oneirévontai en orámati*) about further icons still buried at Argokoíli. And over the summer the original visionaries, Manouíl and Ioánnis, instigated new excavations. They claimed that on 14 September 1836, the day of the Holy Cross, people would find more icons, a gold cross and a font of holy water at Argokoíli. When word of this reached Bishop Gavriíl he wrote to the civil authorities denouncing the activities of these two "scoundrels" (*atheóphovoi*; Documents 2001a: 22), and calling for their activities to be halted.

During the ensuing year a certain amount of digging and prophesying undoubtedly continued, and on 25 March 1838 another icon was discovered. The ecclesiastical and civil authorities reached exasperation point upon learning of these events and they brought a court case against the main actors involved, on charges of fraudulent deception and profiting from this deception by pocketing donations.

The trial was held on Syros, but after some fifty character witnesses testified on behalf of the accused they were acquitted. Unable to jail the ringleaders the authorities decided to confiscate the icons. Eventually the Naxos Police Chief

---

17   Bishop of Naxos to parish priests of Vóthroi, 6 Feb. 1836 (Documents 2000b: 22).

DREAMING OF BURIED ICONS IN THE KINGDOM OF GREECE

gave the order in late 1838 and the icons were placed in two boxes and sent to the Metropolitan Church in Chóra for safekeeping. In one box they placed the icon of the Panagía Argokoiliótissa, mounted in a plating of gold and silver. The other box contained "the various fragments of old icons, including a small relief".[18] Sceptics at the time did not think that these objects were icons at all. The police chief commented that the main icon, "which does not have the least appearance of an icon, is actually an oblong rectangle of utterly rotted wood".[19] And according to the Synod's investigator the icons "[were] rotted, and worm eaten. One could not discern upon them the resemblance to any prototype."[20] The people, however, he went on to note, did not hesitate to revere them straightaway the moment they were unearthed.

The confiscation of the Naxos icons may be compared with the Bishop of Serres' confiscation in 1971 of the holy icons used by the Anastenárides in their annual firewalking ritual in northern Greece (Danforth 1989: 135, 205). Placing the Argokoíli icons into a box plunged them into darkness in an attempt at neutralization. Instead of being displayed on an icon stand illuminated by a steady train of candles lit by faithful pilgrims, the icons were sealed shut, an action analogous to reburying them in the earth from which they had been retrieved a few years earlier. Finally, the authorities placed the icons inside a cabinet (doulápi) situated in the space behind the icon screen of the Metropolitan church in Chóra. This cupboard was nailed shut and sealed with a special tamper-proof Episcopal seal.[21] The power of the icons, and along with them the charismatic appeal of the cult of the Panagía Argokoiliótissa, were now, supposedly, contained.

During this period the Naxiote dreamers had been articulating scenarios consistent with perennial Orthodox Christian traditions that wonder-working

---

18   Naxos Police Chief to Church Committee of Naxos, 2 November 1838 (Documents 2001b: 16). Note that the small wax mastich relief icon (found on 23 April 1836) was not at this time recognized as *the* icon of the Panagía Argokoiliótissa.

19   I. Ambrosiádis, Police Chief of Naxos, to the Royal Secretariat for Internal Affairs, 20 Feb. 1839 (Documents 2001c: 20): *"[i] eikón, i opoía alithós den ékhei oudemían morphín eikónos, allá tetragónou epimíki sesathroménou xýlou,..."*

20   Canon T. Marmarás to Holy Synod of Greece, 18 June 1836 (Documents 2000a: 22):*"[s]esathroménas skolikovrótous, khorís na diakrínetai ep'aftón omoíoma prototýpou..."*

21   "The Committee having pondered the matter, reached a decision, and promptly nailed shut (*ekárphose*) the cabinet containing the icons behind the icon screen and having secured this with the seal of the Bishop (*dia tis sphragídos tis Episkopís*), the holy icons thus remained safe." Church Committee of Naxos to Holy Synod, 14 July 1839 (Documents 2001c: 21).

icons could be found via visions. This theme had been standard since iconoclasm, and it had been reinvigorated after the fall of Constantinople (1453) when once again icons were cast into the sea or hidden. In the course of this long tradition relatively few icons were reported as found on land. One such exception would be the foundational icon for Néa Moní on Chios, discovered in a bush by two monks in the 11th century. In one of the earliest reported cases of large-scale environmental arson the monks torched a whole wood in order to find the icon, which remained unburnt among the ashes of the forest like the unconsumed burning bush of the Old Testament (Bouras 1982: 22). The vast majority of earlier icon discoveries, however, involved finding icons at sea, floating on the water. The famous icon of the Panagía Khrisopigís on Siphnos is said to have been found by fisherman at sea in the 18th century (Seraïdari 2005: 59), and numerous village icons on Naxos likewise emerged from the sea (Stewart 1991: 84).

Perhaps the very best example of a water-borne icon would be the icon of the Panagía Portaïtissa, which was said to have appeared in 1004 in a column of fire in the sea near Mount Athos. A monk from Iviron monastery was instructed in a dream to walk on the water and retrieve it. This icon and its story are celebrated in a cartographic icon depicting the Panagía Portaïtissa superimposed on the Aegean Sea (Fig.2). This portable icon, executed in the mid-18th century by an Athonite monk, follows the conventions of Cosmas Indicopleustes and Arabic cartography (Pazarlí and Livierátos 2002, Pazarás 1998) by placing cardinal north at the bottom rather than at the top of the map. To give the more familiar contemporary standard cardinal orientation, Fig. 3 presents a schematic rendition of the icon flipped both vertically and horizontally. In this picture, then, the dome of St Sophia in Constantinople may be seen at the upper right (northeast), the town of Nicaea, where a pious widow committed the icon to the sea to avert its destruction by iconoclasts, is pictured on the right in the centre (east), and above the icon slightly to the left (north, northwest) is Mount Athos where

Fig. 2. Cartographic icon of the Panagía Portaïtissa (18th century).

DREAMING OF BURIED ICONS IN THE KINGDOM OF GREECE

the monk Gavriíl found the icon. Just below the icon at the bottom of the map (south) is the island of Crete. The icon of the Panagía in this picture thus completely obscures the Cycladic islands; they are literally under the sign of the floating icon. Perhaps this occlusion of the Catholic-dominated Cyclades symbolically expressed the political wish to displace Catholicism (Pazarlí and Livierátos 2002: 187). The reason I have considered it in some detail here, however, has been to highlight the cultural salience of the floating icon motif in the period leading up to independence.

The icon discoveries on Tinos and Naxos broke from this tradi-

Fig. 3. Line drawing of Fig 2, inverted to give standard north–south orientation.

tion, and established a compelling new motif of buried icons requiring excavation. This creative departure reflected imaginative mental processing—some of which occurred in the unconscious during dreaming—that explored ideas of independent ownership, autochthony and locality as the new state came into being. Unlike an icon at sea, an icon buried in the ground lies fixed in place as an index of Christian presence in one's own place. At the end of the 19th century the English folklorist and classicist Lawson (1910: 301ff.) collected stories of buried icons throughout Greece, an indication that within a few generations the Tinos theme had captured the national imagination and now proliferated in multiple local versions.

A cross-cultural comparison may illuminate the situation. The indigenous religion of the Maya of highland Guatemala is prominently focused on establishing beneficial communication with spirits of the earth, which often appear to people in dreams. The Catholic Church has long inveighed against this nature-focused aspect of local religion and instructed that only dreams of the celestial God are good. The Church deemed dreams of landscape features and immanent gods to be satanic. When the Maya cultural revival got underway in the 1980s, stimulated in part by government repression, people turned back from Catholicism to Mayan religion and consequently dreams of the "sacred earth" again became prominent (Tedlock 1992). In the face of vicious army at-

99

tacks entire communities were sometimes forced to abandon their villages further, leading them to turn again to the power of their old religion. As one man put it: "The mountains collaborated with us. The mountains and the elders will never leave you. One [mountain spirit] told me in a dream: 'You go away from here because the dogs are coming.'" So we left that place and five days later the army was there" (Tedlock 1992: 461).

Something similar seems to have been involved around the time of Greek independence. People came to believe that the land was now their own, and indeed it was. The enactment of the Law for the Dotation of Greek Families in June of 1835 meant that all native-born Greeks could receive up to 2,000 drachmas worth of national property (McGrew 1985: 162). Unlike the Mayans, whose indigenous religion had been interrupted by conversion to Catholicism, which demonized the gods of the land, the Naxiotes imagined their land and their saints in ways broadly continuous with past traditions, but with new intensity. Envisioning and then finding icons buried underground symbolically undermined the Catholics, the former feudal lords and still majority landowners. The French Catholic priest Pègues, resident on Santorini during this period, commented on the pervasive mistrust between Orthodox and Catholics and then exemplified it by registering his strong conviction that both the Tinos and Naxos icon discoveries were fraudulent manipulations of the local people.[22]

As in the case of the icon discovery on Tinos (Mazower, this volume), although for different reasons, it would be too simplistic to interpret events as arising solely out of a contest between Orthodox and Catholics for political/spiritual supremacy. Orthodox villagers in mountain Naxos no doubt had their complaints against absentee Catholic landowners, the nearest of whom lived about 35 kilometres away in Chóra. As emery miners, however, they had other concerns about ownership of the land and mineral resources.

Prized for its hardness (9 out of 10 on the Mohs scale), Naxiote emery has been used since antiquity for the grinding of metals and stone. During the

---

22 Pègues (1842: 499, 549), quoted in Stewart (1991: 267). Pègues witnessed a similar icon discovery on Santorini in 1836 (1842: 552 ff). The Panagía appeared in the dreams of a man in the village of Veríssa and showed him where to dig to find her icon. First he unearthed a cross and then, eventually, the icon was discovered (and immediately stolen; Kephalliniádis 1990: 195 ff). Pègues viewed these events as he did those on Tinos and Naxos, cynically: "*[q]ue si j'ai pri un ton railleur dans l'histoire de Périssa, c'est que, en peignant des faits si comiques et l'esprit qui y présidait, il était impossible d'être sérieux*" (1842: 566). The Santorini case puts Argokoíli into perspective as but one example of a wave of visionary icon discoveries occurring throughout the Kingdom during this period, products of what Matálas (2003: 54) has termed "Lumpen" Orthodoxy.

Venetian and Turkish periods emery mining was a small industry, but one that, nonetheless, provided valuable income to the mountain villages of Kóronos and Apeíranthos. The Venetian feudal lords continued to assert ownership of all emery mined in their fiefs even after Naxos fell to the Ottomans. The mountain villages protested to the Catholic *kastrinoí* (i.e. Venetian-descended residents of the *kástro* in Chóra) that emery production and sale should be "free for the workers".[23] When the *kastrinoí* reasserted their rights over the emery,[24] the villagers appealed over their heads to the Sultan, who ordered the Catholics to "stop treating the villagers like slaves."[25] A subsequent internal agreement reached on Naxos between the *kastrinoí* and the Orthodox merchant community of Chóra known as *boúrgos* stated that they would "leave the villagers with everlasting power and control over emery and sheep" (Zevgólis 1989: 64).[26] Feudal abuses continued, however, and after further complaints from the villagers, the Ottoman Kapudan Pasha instructed the *kastrinoí* in 1780 "to allow the poor rayahs [Orthodox peasants] to sell [emery] freely"; anyone violating this freedom was to be punished by beheading (Arkhontákis and Giannoúlis 2001: 81). Gradually, then, during the Ottoman period the mountain villagers gained autonomy and control over the production and sale of emery.

In 1812, as emery became more profitable and began to be exported in larger quantities, the villagers leased the export rights to a merchant named Vassílis Láskaris for a period of 12 years. Láskaris paid 500 *grósia* annually to the local mountain communities. In addition, he paid local workers by weight for the emery they mined, and for loading it onto boats (Arkhontákis and Giannoúlis 2001: 81). The villagers renewed Láskaris' contract in 1821, before it was due, apparently to assure themselves of a good payday just as the Greek War of Independence broke out.

In 1824 the revolutionary government cancelled Láskaris' contract to export emery and gave the rights to another entrepreneur, who paid the much needed rental money directly and entirely to the government. Under Capodistrias the emery of Naxos, along with the mineral deposits on Milos and the currants of

---

23 *Eléfthero ton kopiastádon*, as they expressed it in a letter from 14 Naxos villages to the *kastrinoí* on 31 May 1719 (Zerléntis 1925: 24-5; Arkhontákis and Giannoúlis 2001: 80). The emery demand was just one item in a lengthy list of economic matters the villagers sought to resolve regarding their use of the land. Another was their assertion of the free right to collect firewood.

24 "*[D]ia to smyrígli phanerón prámma eíne apó palaióthes pos eíne dikaíoma ton aphentótopo*" (Zerléntis 1925: 25; Arkhontákis and Giannoúlis 2001: 80).

25 Firman of 1721 sent to the Franks of Naxos (Zerléntis 1925: 26; Arkhontákis and Giannoúlis 2001: 80).

26 "*Aphínousin eis tin pantoteinín exousían kai kyriótita ton chorianón próvata kai smyrígli.*" Document dated 4 Janury 1736, cited by Zevgólis (1989:64).

Corinth, were declared "national property" (*ethniká ktímata*; Arkhontákis and Giannoúlis 2001: 82). And in 1835 the government solicited bids for a ten-year contract for the mining and exportation of Naxiote emery. At this point, the villages of mountain Naxos sent two representatives to Athens to petition King Otto, who had just reached his majority and acceded to full rulership over Greece. The representatives contended that they should hold full rights over emery production because:

> The emery, which is exported from the island of Naxos, is the property of the inhabitants themselves of the two villages Apeíranthos and Vóthroi. Since it comes out of the fields, and they are owners of these fields, the necessary conclusion is that they must also be the owners of any products that are extracted from this land. Emery, the product of their fields, must belong exclusively to them.

Their statement continued toward the end:

> We beseech Your Majesty, with the tears of our eyes and the sighs of our hearts: That you deign to revoke those actions taken by the Administration against our ownership; and that you leave us the free and unfettered right, which we enjoy by natural and political law in relation to the products of our land (Arkhontákis and Giannoúlis 2001: 83).

The cold reply from the Secretariat of the Economy of the Kingdom refused to return the rights to the villagers, but assured them that they were only auctioning off the right to export emery. The villagers would remain free to regulate production, with the help of a state overseer. The poor independent state clearly needed revenue and this motivated them to dispossess the mountain villagers of Naxos. It must have been doubly distressing to the Naxiotes to learn that the winner of the 1835 export contract was an Englishman named Rothfel (Protopapadákis 1903: 16). The fear that Greek Orthodoxy was becoming alien through Western Christian influences was now matched in the industrial sphere by foreign exploitation of natural resources. Rothfel trebled the price of emery on the international market, a strategy that backfired against Naxiote interests by forcing the market to look for cheaper sources (Glézos 1989: 92). Emery deposits (of lesser quality) were located in Asia Minor and new mines opened in the Smyrna region in competition with Naxos.

When Rothfel's contract ended the villagers brought a court case to regain full rights over emery production. The High Court ruled against them in 1846. The final nail in the coffin of local autonomy over emery resources came in 1852 when a non-Naxiote man named Korgialénios bought some emery-rich land in eastern Naxos and began to export it on his own account. After the government overseer reported him the state issued a new law clarifying that emery would henceforth be mined and made available exclusively to the state.[27]

---

27   "*[T]o kath' ólin tin Náxon paragómenon oryktón Smýris exorýssetai kai diatíthetai*

DREAMING OF BURIED ICONS IN THE KINGDOM OF GREECE

From this moment onward the Naxos emery miners were consigned to become "proletarians of the state" (Glézos 1989: 84).

The period of independence was one of mixed messages for the inhabitants of mountain Naxos, and no doubt many other parts of Greece as well. The law of dotation increased private landownership at the same time as the nationalization of resources and antiquities prohibited certain uses of the land that had been customary up to that point. The land did and did not belong to the people, and this proved to be a vexing ambiguity felt deeply by the Orthodox Christian, emery mining inhabitants of Vóthroi. Independence placed the villagers in a worse position than they had been in under the Ottomans not only regarding their land, but also regarding religious practices. Under the Ottomans the villagers would easily have been allowed to build the "house", which the Panagía repeatedly requested in the early visions. Instead the villagers had to make do with building structures that they called "cells" in order not to violate the new laws of the state.

Barely two years after they sent representatives to Otto asking for their emery rights, they sent another pair of representatives to petition the King to grant them permission to construct a church to the Panagía Theotókos at Argokoíli.[28] This petition was turned down. Another petition to build a church was filed with the Holy Synod in 1840 and rejected. Finally, in 1851, a year after the Greek Orthodox Church had repaired relations with the Patriarchate, the authorities allowed the official consecration of a large cell at Argokoíli as a proper church. Naxiote assertions of religious freedom and mining rights thus tracked each other over a twenty-year period and both articulated strong connections to the land, in particular the right to own what one dug out of the ground.

Dreaming of icons, bones and other objects in the earth expressed freedom and autonomy while unintentionally challenging newly expanded state jurisdiction over the land. This ambiguity led to the escalation of events in 1830s Kóronos. State suppression and popular expression locked into a spiralling reciprocal logic of social action. Although permission to consecrate a church represented a slightly better result than the state monopoly of emery declared the following year, this outcome for the Argokoiliótissa movement, after fifteen years of struggle, was far from satisfactory. The villagers had not succeeded in building the magnificent church that the Panagía had spoken of in the dreams, and the icons remained confiscated. Indeed, at some point it emerged that the

---

apokleistikós dia logariasmón to Dimosíou" (Nómos, 17 July 1852, Zevgólis 1989: 67).

28   Petition dated 25 February 1837 (Documents 2001a: 24). Three local priests signed the petition and were later reprimanded by the Bishop for breaking their vow not to support the Argokoiliótissa movement.

icons had disappeared altogether. The sealed cupboard had been violated. All but one of the icons remain missing to this day.

The dreaming and digging in Argokoíli occurred during a period of transition in which the traditional popular imagination about the land, its past, and the nation's ancestors was rapidly superseded. The stories of buried icons, some of which were considered works of the Apostle Luke, and/or possessions of early Christians expressed a Christian historical identification that would now be marginalized as state-sponsored Hellenism took precedence. Research in Ancient History and the Classics offered a different and deeper ethnic past to contemplate. These increasingly professionalized disciplines developed highly rationalist modes of historiography, notably Ranke's historicism, which informed works on Greek history published by the German historians Zinkeisen and Droysen in the early 1830s.[29] Maurer, and other Bavarian officials were familiar with these historical works. Indeed Maurer invited Zinkeisen to take up a Chair of History at Athens University, an offer Zinkeisen declined.

Under the influence of Rankean historicism the emergent national history and archaeology insisted on basic Enlightenment research principles. These included the post-Cartesian distinction between fantasy and reality and subject and object. The historical researcher stood apart from the object of study (i.e. past events) and tried to understand them on the basis of evidence—sources of various types. Furthermore historical time was linear and progressive, which meant that the past was separated from the present. Through meticulous research the past could be understood, but historians had to be careful not to commit the sin of anachronism and assume that people in the past worked with the same suppositions and intentions as themselves. The implementation of these various tenets de-legitimized local, haptic modes of historicizing in areas like mountain Naxos (Hirsch and Stewart 2005). Dreams or visions revealing information, the smell of bones, or the warm feel of the earth could not be accepted as methodology or as reliable evidence.

To use the terminology of Marshall Sahlins, this was a conjunctural period of paradigm clash, involving—in the case of mountain Naxos— a phase of mutual misunderstanding between local people and state institutions. In the "conjuncture", which Sahlins has illustrated by reference to the 18th-century encounter between the Hawaiians and Captain Cook, misunderstandings arose because the two parties held fundamentally different assumptions about the world. They did not, however, clearly realize that they were operating at cross purposes (Sa-

---

29 Johann Wilhelm Zinkeisen, *Geschichte Griechenlands vom Anfange geschichtlicher Kunde bis auf unsere Tage*, vol. 1, Leipzig: J.A. Barth, 1832; Johann Gustav Droysen, *Geschichte Alexanders des Grossen*, Hamburg: F. Perthes, 1833. See Koubourlis (nd. a, nd. b).

DREAMING OF BURIED ICONS IN THE KINGDOM OF GREECE

hlins 1985: 125). The Hawaiians offered Cook precious objects, which they considered sacrifices because they viewed him as a god. The British interpreted these objects as trade overtures and responded in kind. The one group was operating with ideas of the sacred, the other on entirely economic assumptions.

Sahlins' example involved an early moment of cultural contact. In the case under consideration here, state Hellenism, formulated by Greek intellectuals in the diaspora with the collaboration of northern European scholars, and then imported into the new Kingdom of Greece, clashed with a village worldview. Out of such situations of creative misunderstanding culture emerged transformed. What emerged was a hybrid sense of history (and archaeology) in which modern scientific and indigenous Christian precepts mingled to form a national imagination where archaeologists could dream of imminent discoveries and statues could weep in their desire to return home (Hamilakis 2007: 139, 279).

People in mountain Naxos had, in all likelihood, long felt a strong bond with their place and their land. In the new situation, for a variety of reasons stemming from the advent of national independence, the land came to be conceived more intensively as containing powerful buried objects. Dreams and visions of buried icons opened a relationship with the past. When excavated this presence was restored to the social community. The supporters of the Argokoiliótissa movement viewed icons, bones and coins with St Constantine on them in a Christian framework of grace and redemption. The new government claimed jurisdiction over the interpretation of buried objects as evidence of a linear Greek "history", stretching back in a continuum to antiquity. Villagers in mountain Naxos came only slowly to understand, but never fully to espouse this view.

BIBLIOGRAPHY

Arkhontákis, Manólis and Giannoúlis Giannoúlis (2001) *Poíisi kharagméni stin pétra: koinonikí mními kai poiitikí me théma to smyrígli apó t' Aperáthou kai tin Kórono tis Náxou*, Athens: Atrapós.

Bouras, Charalambos (1982) *Nea Moni on Chios: History and Architecture*, Athens: Commercial Bank of Greece.

Danforth, Loring (1989) *Firewalking and Religious Healing*, Princeton: Princeton University Press.

Documents (2000a) "I istoría tis Panagías Argokoiliótissas ópos diamorphónetai vásei kai ton arkheíon tis Ierás Synódou tis Ekklisías tis Ellados", *Argokoilótissa*, 6 (19), 21–4.

—— (2000b) "I istoría tis Panagías Argokoiliótissas ópos diamorphónetai vásei kai ton arkheíon tis Ierás Synódou tis Ekklisías tis Ellados", *Argokoiliótissa*, 6 (20), 21–4.

—— (2000c) "I istoría tis Panagías Argokoiliótissas ópos diamorphónetai vásei kai ton arkheíon tis Ierás Synódou tis Ekklisías tis Ellados", *Argokoiliótissa*, 6 (21), 19–23.

—— (2001a) "I istoría tis Panagías Argokoiliótissas ópos diamorphónetai vásei kai ton arkheíon tis Ierás Synódou tis Ekklisías tis Ellados", *Argokoiliótissa*, 7 (22), 22–5.

—— (2001b) "I istoría tis Panagías Argokoiliótissas ópos diamorphónetai vásei kai ton arkheíon tis Ierás Synódou tis Ekklisías tis Ellados", *Argokoiliótissa*, 7 (24), 14–16

—— (2001c) "I istoría tis Panagías Argokoiliótissas ópos diamorphónetai vásei kai ton arkheíon tis Ierás Synódou tis Ekklisías tis Ellados", *Argokoiliótissa*, 7 (25), 19–23.

Dubisch, Jill (1995) *In a Different Place: Pilgrimage, Gender and Politics at a Greek Island Shrine*, Princeton: Princeton University Press.

Frazee, Charles A. (1969) *The Orthodox Church and Independent Greece, 1821–1852*, Cambridge : Cambridge University Press.

—— (1978) "Catholics of Naxos under Ottoman Rule", *Greek Orthodox Theological Review*, 235–42.

—— (1979) "The Greek Catholic Islanders and the Revolution of 1821", *East European Quarterly*, 13, 315–26.

—— (2002) "Catholics", in R. Clogg (ed.), *Minorities in Greece: Aspects of a Plural Society* (London: Hurst), 24-47.

Glézos, Pétros D. (1989) "I yperkekatókhroni kratikí ekmetállefsi tis Naxías smýridos", *Aperathítika*, 1, 71-106.

DREAMING OF BURIED ICONS IN THE KINGDOM OF GREECE

Hamilakis, Yannis (2007) *The Nation and its Ruins: Antiquity, Archaeology, and National Imagination in Greece*, Oxford : Oxford University Press.

Hirsch, Eric and Charles Stewart (2005) "Introduction: Ethnographies of Historicity", *History and Anthropology (Special Issue: Ethnographies of Historicity)*, 16 (3), 261-74.

Kephalliniádis, N.A. (1990) *I latreía tis Panagías sta ellinika nisiá*, Athens: Philippóti.

Khouzoúris, Ioánnis (1996) *Panagía i Argokoiliótissa: Istoría se laïkoús stíkhous*, Athens: Aprílios.

Korrés, Geórgios (1962) *Panagía i Argokoiliótissa: palaión kheirógraphon étous 1836*, Athens: Naxiakón Méllon [anátypon].

Korrés, Geórgios [19th century priest] (2002a) "I istoría tis Panagías Argokoiliótissas ópos diamorphónetai vásei kai ton arkheíon tis Ierás Synódou tis Ekklisías tis Elládos, Part I", *Argokoiliótissa*, 28.

—— (2002b) "I istoría tis Panagías Argokoiliótissas ópos diamorphónetai vásei kai ton arkheíon tis Ierás Synódou tis Ekklisías tis Elládos, Part II", *Argokoiliótissa*, 29.

Koubourlis, Ioannis (nd. a) "I epanástasi tou 1821 kai i dimiourgía tou ellinikoú ethnikoú krátous stis prótes megáles aphigíseis tis neóteris ellinikís istorías: apó tin *polyparagontikí análysi* sto skhíma tis *ethnikís teleologías*", ms.

—— (nd. b) "European Historiographical Influences Upon Young Constantinos Paparrigopoulos (1843-1853): The Testimony of 'The 1846 Lecture'", ms.

Livanios, Dimitris (2008) "The Quest for Hellenism: Religion, Nationalism and Collective Identities in Greece", in Katerina Zacharia (ed.), *Hellenisms: Culture, Identity and Ethnicity from Antiquity to Modernity*, London: Ashgate, forthcoming.

Matálas, Paraskevás (2003) *Éthnos kai Orthodoxía: Oi peripéteies mias skhésis*, Irákleio: Panepistimiakés Ekdóseis Krítis.

Maurer, Georg Ludwig von (1976), *O ellinikós laós*, trans. O. Rombáki, Athens: Tolídis.

McGrew, William (1985) *Land and Revolution in Modern Greece, 1880-1881: The Transition in the Tenure and Exploitation of Land from Ottoman Rule to Independence*, Kent, OH: Kent State University Press.

Pazarás, Theokháris (1998) "Istórisi tis thavmatourgikís élefsis tis eikónas tis Panagías Portaïtissas sti Moní Ivíron", *Deltíon tis Christianikís Archaiologikís Etairias, 9*, 385-97.

Pazarlí, Maria and Evángelos Livierátos (2002) "I Panagía ston khárti", in Evángelos Livierátos (ed.), *Órous Átho gis kai thalássis perímetron khárton metamorphóseis*, Thessaloníki: Ethnikí Khartothíki, 181-90.

Pègues, M. L'Abbé (1842) *Histoire et phénomène du volcan et des îles de Santorin*, Paris: à l'Imprimerie Royale.

Petrákos, Vasíleios (1982) *Dokímio gia tin arkhaiologikí nomothesía*, Athens: Ministry of Culture and Science.

Protopapadákis, P.E. (1903) *Monographía perí naxías smýridos kai protáseis nómon*, Athens: Estía.

Sahlins, Marshall (1985) *Islands of History*, Chicago: University of Chicago Press.

Seraïdari, Katerina (2005) *Le culte des icônes en Grèce*, Toulouse: Presses Universitaires du Mirail.

—— (2007) *"Megáli i khári tis": Latreftikés praktikés kai ideologikés syngkroúseis stis Kykládes*, Athens: Philippóti-Erínni.

Stewart, Charles (1991) *Demons and the Devil: Moral Imagination in Modern Greek Culture*, Princeton: Princeton University Press.

Tedlock, Barbara (1992) "The Role of Dreams and Visionary Narratives in Mayan Cultural Survival", *Ethos*, 20, 453-76.

Vitális, Philáretos (1973) "O Tínou Gavriíl Sylivós kai i symvolí tou eis tin ethnegersían tou 1821", *Epeterís tis Etaireías Kykladitikón Meletón*, 8.

Zerléntis, Periklís (1925) *Pheoudalikí politeía en ti níso Náxo*, Ermoupolis: Phréri [Reprinted in *Naxiaká*, 1, 3 (1985)].

Zevgólis, Tásos (1989) "Istoría tis Naxías smýridos", *Aperathítika*, 1, 63-8.

5

BONDS MADE POWER: CLIENTELISM, NATIONALISM, AND PARTY STRATEGIES IN GREEK MACEDONIA (1900-1950)

Basil C. Gounaris

As long as I can remember, military parades in Thessaloniki were headed by a platoon of *Makedonomachoi*, veterans wearing a black traditional military uniform called *doulama*, who had participated in the early 20th century Greek struggle for Macedonia.[1] The head of the parade was not only a position of honour but also of symbolic importance. The fierce fight against the Bulgarian *comitadjis* was the first relatively effective semi-brigand war that Greece had launched after independence. It was the prelude for the victorious 1912-13 campaigns which gave Greece the coastal part of Ottoman-held Macedonia. Most of all it was a war to defend a glorious and world-wide known chapter of ancient history, the heritage of Alexander the Great. Spectators were aware of the multiple symbolisms and gave them the warmest applause.

---

1   The best general account of the theme, both in English and in Greek, is still by Douglas Dakin, *The Greek Struggle in Macedonia, 1897-1913* (Thessaloniki, 1966). Extremely useful are the following papers: Dimitris Livanios, "'Conquering the Souls': Nationalism and Greek Guerrilla Warfare in Ottoman Macedonia, 1904-1908", *Journal of Byzantine and Modern Greek Studies*, 23 (1999), pp. 195-221; Iakovos D. Michailidis, "Stratiotika protypa kai klephtiki paradosi: organotika provlimata kai I kathimerini zoi sta chronia tou Makedonikou Agona", *Makedonia, istoria kai politismos*, Florina, 1997, pp. 249-80; Christos Mandatzis, "Proypologismoi, logariasmoi kai aprovleptes ethnikes dapanes: apopeires chrimatodotisis tou alytrotikou agona sti Makedonia (1904-1908)", *Thessalonikeon Polis*, 16 (2004), pp. 18-59; Christos Mandatzis, "Antartiko sto katophli mias ekchrimatizomenis oikonomias: koinoniki kai oikonomiki diastasi tou Makedonikou Agona", *Thessalonikeon Polis*, 16 (2004), pp. 60-83.

By the early 1990s it had become clear to everybody that the parading veterans were counterfeits. In the absence of surviving Makedonomachoi their next of kin, well into their 70s, dressed up twice a year and enjoyed no less honour than their fathers. What most people did not realize then was that leading the parade and mingling with the authorities soon afterwards was for most of them a way to secure petty favours for themselves and for their clientele. Indeed the counterfeit veterans as well as their fathers were members of the "National Organisation 'Pavlos Melas'", established in Thessaloniki in 1927, with branch offices all around Greek Macedonia. Its main task was to secure every possible kind of pecuniary reward for 1903-1908 fighters and their families, then stricken by interwar poverty and competition with rural settlers from Asia Minor. Apparently the second generation was serving the same cause.[2]

In 1928 "Pavlos Melas" was placed under the auspices of politicians, both liberals and royalists, who had participated themselves, mostly as army officers, in the struggle more than twenty years earlier. In late 1904, motivated by the example and the early death of Second-Lieutenant Pavlos Melas, many then junior offices and NCOs had volunteered to lead irregular bands against the Bulgarian *chetas*, already notorious after the 1903 Ilinden rising in Macedonia. Officers were no less motivated by their miserable military careers, lack of commissions, frequent transfers, and the endless search for efficient patrons.[3] Many of them were not novices in patriotic ventures. They had been active members of Ethniki Etaireia (National Society), a pressure group heavily involved in the critique of Greek parliamentary system, the disastrous Cretan campaign, and the 1897 war against Turkey.[4] Officers were not on their own in this new Macedonian campaign. Recruiting and financing were in the hands of the semi-official Greek Makedonikon Komitaton (Macedonian Committee), administered by young deputies, close relatives of leading political families, and chaired by Dimitrios Kalapothakis, the editor of daily *Embros* (Forward). Orbiting this inner circle was the Macedonian lobby of Athens. It consisted of Slav-speaking masons and other daily labourers, university students, high-school teachers and prolific history writers, few merchants and even fewer politicians, not always of

---

[2] I owe this information to Mr Charilaos Fitzios, general secretary on the board of "Pavlos Melas" in the 1990s. He was also kind enough to furnish me with a copy of the first statute.

[3] The text usually cited to describe the feelings of misery prevailing in the barracks is by Athanasios Souliotis, "O Makedonikos Agon. I Organosis Thessalonikis 1906-1908" in the volume *O Makedonikos Agonas. Apomnimonevmata*, Thessaloniki: Institute for Balkan Studies, 1984, pp. 269-73, 279-80.

[4] The most recent presentation is by Giannis N. Gianoulopoulos, '*I evgenis mas typhlosis...*'. *Exoteriki politiki kai 'ethnika themata'. Apo tin itta tou 1897 eos ti mikrasiatiki katastrophi*, Athens: Vivliorama, 2003, pp. 23-58.

Macedonian provenance. The Greek state-sponsored educational and charitable campaign in Macedonia, which involved considerable capital and human resources, had considerably strengthened this lobby. Stephanos Dragoumis, who had shared with Kalapothakis loyalty to Trikoupis and ambition for rapid change, was the undisputable head of the Macedonian circles. The death in action of his son-in-law, Pavlos Melas, made him and his own son, Ion, parts of the same legend.[5]

The effects of Greece's—and not only Greece's—four year military presence in Macedonia stretched far beyond the short-run needs of the bands. To understand the reason we must turn our attention briefly to the social and economic conditions of this land. Multiple social cleavages had developed in most Macedonian peasant communities. Mistrust between landlords and tenants, pastoralist mountaineers and lowland agriculturalists, cultivators and merchants, employers and employees, quarrels over community leadership, the different geographical origin of the local clans, the various migratory patterns, disputes over water and wood resources and pasture boundaries, clan vendettas, personal animosities deeply divided peasant communities. Such cleavages eventually shaped two factions, the bishop's friends, who formed the governing party, and the bishop's foes, the opposition. The importance of the bishop was paramount since notables in Macedonian villages had nothing in common with their influential and wealthy colleagues in the revolutionary Peloponnese a century before. Muslims were the chief owners of land throughout the 19th century and farming was far from profitable. Christian notables, outside urban centres, were hardly if at all distinguishable from their fellow villagers.[6]

The Bulgarian Exarchate benefited the most from all kinds of pre-existing cleavages, while Greeks were busy teaching classical Greek in urban and semi-urban high schools. Bulgarians managed to exploit social differences and turn them into nationalist politics. But their success is not fully understood without a reference to the reforms introduced in the *Tanzimat* era, especially to the General Regulations applied for the uniform governance of the *millet*s in the 1860s. According to the new system the notables were elected annually directly by their fellow villagers or, in towns, through electors. Such notables were expected to share and collect taxes and to administer financial affairs. They would also ap-

---

5   Basil C. Gounaris, "Social Gatherings and Macedonian Lobbying: Symbols of Irredentism and Living Legends in Early Twentieth Century Athens", Philip Carabott (ed.), *Greek Society in the Making, 1863-1913: Realities, Symbols, and Visions*, London: Variorum, Ashgate Publishing Ltd, 1997, pp. 102-4.

6   This, as well as the following paragraphs, is based on two papers of my own: "Social Cleavages and National "Awakening" in Ottoman Macedonia", *East European Quarterly*, 29,4 (1995), pp. 409-26; "Macedonian Questions", *Journal of Southeast European and Black Sea Studies*, 2, 3 (2002), pp. 63-94.

point the school committee and schoolteachers as well as the committees of any other charitable institutions. Representation was making politics far more interesting and tempting at just the right moment. In the 1890s grain crops failed too often. Marketing was not successful in spite of the construction of new railway lines. In the 1900s things did not improve either. In 1902 a substantial earthquake devastated central Macedonia. The reprisals of the Ottoman Army, after the Ilinden rising in 1903, shook the hinterland even more vigorously. Transatlantic emigration was reaching its peak, wages were high and insecurity prevailed everywhere. The frequent presence of the army and the international gendarmerie reduced the chances for illegal profits.

In this social and financial context nationalism easily became the driving force of local society. Since educated urban merchant families were proud of their Greek national feelings and bishops were increasingly supporting Greek nationalism, to some landless peasants Greek nationalism meant in effect exploitation. In some cases mistrust developed between Albanian- and Vlach-speaking mountainous semi-urbanized towns and the Slav-speaking rural communities in the vicinity, who produced the necessary food and raw materials but felt financially exploited by the former. It was unsurprising that in such cases the pro-Bulgarian sentiments of some Slav-speaking tenants and smallholders grew stronger. Conversion to the Bulgarian Church, instead of the Ecumenical Patriarchate of Constantinople, implied real financial profits as well: newcomers expected to escape from the heavy dues which were imposed upon them by the local Patriarchist Bishops, or even to get free schooling, which did not involve mostly language classes as in the Greek case. They also expected to administer church property and the local educational institutions in their own way. Eventually, the opposition was oriented towards the Bulgarian cause, while "the best and honest householders" (or, seen from a different angle, the "conservatives") sided with the Greeks.

These two sides or camps, although wrapped up in the mantle of national ideology, were not actually ethnic groups. Even the Greek Consul General in Thessaloniki was very specific about this: "As usually," he wrote, "in the villages of Macedonia antagonism of interests takes precedence but later on it is necessarily transformed into a national confrontation."[7] Evidently nationalist propaganda and armed clashes tended to forge distinctive population groups with national preferences in the non-Greek-speaking regions. But by 1912 such a partition was not complete, nor could it have been completed in the course of only one generation (1870-1900) under any circumstances. Siding with, or even fighting for, a certain camp did not necessary imply different cul-

---

7   Archives of the Greek Foreign Ministry, File 1904 Proxeneio Thessalonikis, Koromilas to Foreign Minister, Thessaloniki, 9 Aug. 1904, confidential No. 450.

ture or different genealogical and historical myths. Although the indispensable national myths had been circulated through education, no camp could boast of stability of its members or claim that belonging to a camp could sufficiently predict choices of activity.[8] All in all, Christian camps in Macedonia were not yet closed social groups with distinctive features, which would impose certain activity options. They were essentially political parties demarcated by porous and fluctuating borders, and not ethnic groups.

Such parties existed not only inside communities with divided religious loyalties but within relatively homogeneous communities as well, Patriarchist and Exarchist alike. We know more about the clashes which divided IMRO and the Supreme Committee but only a few things about the confrontations inside the Greek-speaking Patriarchist communities. In such places a new elite, properly educated, nationally-minded, and extremely unwilling to return to the fields, tempted by the salaries and other perks offered by the Greek state, joined the local national committees set up by the Greek brigand officers. Very much as IMRO had done in Macedonia, the Greek national ideology was to create a state within the state. Such committees were not simply responsible for the promotion of the national cause or for the local infrastructure deemed necessary for sustaining band operations. They also assumed judicial power, in an attempt to keep the Turks out of Christian business. Moreover they provided for various kinds of stipends, allowances, scholarships and offices—not just teaching positions—to trusted relatives and co-villagers, services paid for by the state-sponsored Committee in Athens. Salaries were not high but they were regular, and this was extremely important for a society on the threshold of monetization.

This political power of the local committees could not be exercised without the presence of armed bands. Thus the local captain, usually a second-lieutenant of the Greek Army, or a more or less trusted local chieftain with his armed following, evolved into a second pole of power in close co-operation with the Greek consulates. The national ideals of the cause and the great risks taken by both sides sanctified the nature of his special relation with the local committee. Backed up by a specific armed band, the committee was in a position to challenge the "governing party" of the Bishop or any other foe. If the local rural notables were unwilling to shift to the Exarchist camp and seek outside military

---

8   Cf. Anthony Smith, *The Ethnic Origin of Nations*, Oxford: Blackwell, 1989, pp. 22-31; Fredrik Barth, "Introduction", Fredrik Barth (ed.), *Ethnic Groups and Boundaries*, London: Allen & Unwin, 1969, pp. 9-38, and Fredrik Barth, "Enduring and Emerging Issues in the Analysis of Ethnicity", Hans Vermeulen and Cora Govers (eds), *The Anthropology of Ethnicity*, Amsterdam: Spinhuis, 1994, pp. 11-32.

support, then the balance could easily change. In the presence of so many social cleavages and far more personal antipathies the power of local committees was not only used for the national cause. Indeed their members could even name any rivals as targets of the bands, on the ground that they were leaking information or were unwilling to support the Greek cause. They were the ultimate judges of loyalties, sometimes judges and jury together. They also exploited their influence to solve in their favour any problem arising between their own communities and neighbouring villages. Needless to say, incidents of violence multiplied and made bonds with the officers even tighter.[9]

Nationalism also played an important role in urban politics of Macedonia, where numerous committees and clandestine organizations were involved. All charitable, athletic, artistic and educational associations or initiatives, in other words all the features of a rising urban bourgeois class, had to do with the promotion of Greek nationalism. Political parties were forged, modernizers and conservatives, but disputes over community authority did not escalate into open warfare. The Bulgarians, the Jews and the pro-Romanian Vlachs were a far more real threat inside towns. Naturally the Greek urban higher strata, entrepreneurs, absentee landlords, and money lenders were in a position to impose their national will upon their clients, tenants or debtors in many ways, not necessarily violent. Eventually the escalation of the band war in Macedonia integrated every single village in this network of nationalized politics, of course not always on the Greek side. Band leaders—many Cretans among them— very much like the Armatoles of previous centuries, turned into undisputed national leaders, brigands with a noble cause but also patrons, dispensing punishments and rewards, surrounded by informers and clients of various kinds. The elections of 1908 and 1912 for the Ottoman Parliament were indeed a dress rehearsal for what was to follow. The consulates mobilized their networks in an attempt to win as many seats as possible for the Greek deputies. So did all the other national parties.[10]

9   There are three detailed studies concerning different villages in eastern, central and western Greek Macedonia respectively: Hans Vermeulen, "Agrotikes syngrouseis kai koinoniki diamartyria stin istoria enos makedonikou choriou (1900-1936)" in Stathis Damianakos (ed.), *Diadikasies koinonikou metaschimatismou stin agrotiki Ellada*, Athens: Ethniko Kendro Koinonikon Erevnon, 1987, pp. 221-44; Anastasia Karakasidou, *Fields of Wheat, Hills of Blood: Passages to Nationhood in Greek Macedonia*, University of Chicago Press, 1997, pp. 108-20; Persephoni Karabati, "Koinonikes anakatataxeis sta chronia tou Makedonikou Agona: to archeio tou Stergiou Misiou", unpublished MA thesis, Aristotle University of Thessaloniki, 1996.

10 Emre Sencer, "Balkan Nationalisms in the Ottoman Parliament 1909", *East European Quarterly*, 38,1 (2004), pp. 41-64. See also the two articles by Stojian Makedonski, "La révolution jeune-turque et les premières élections parlemen-

Officers returned to Athens but not to their miserable barracks. The unprecedented success of their efforts against the Bulgarians, advertised by the Press, had had a tremendous impact on Greek politics. Who was to reap the unexpected political advantage? Surprisingly the Young Turks' revolt (July 1908) and the consequent shrinking of the band war put the reverse question: Who was to be blamed for the decay of the Greek organization in Macedonia? Officers put the blame on the Theotokis government. They said he should have shut down the Macedonian Committee of Kalapothakis and let the diplomats and the army (well acquainted after four years of close cooperation) take over the struggle; chieftains and brigands were no longer required, the army was enough. A colonel of Artillery, Panagiotis Danglis, was eventually appointed as the head of a "Panhellenic Organization", which was expected to replace the Committee and take over clandestine operation inside Turkey.[11] But Danglis could not alter the fact that Greek-Turkish relations had improved and brigand operations were no longer an option in Macedonia. The military had to stay at ease, but this was more than they could live with.

Complaints had appeared about the absence of adequate and substantial rewards for veterans as early as the spring of 1908. NCOs, who were so anxious to get promoted to warrant officers and had hoped that their bravery in action might pave their way to the officers" corps, were now bitterly disappointed. Beneficial promotion for bravery took the form of a tough competition. No similar measure was taken for officers. Claims for transfers, indemnities or moral rewards multiplied. Patrons were in a frenzy, unable to satisfy demands; tension was rising, conspiratorial clusters were formed, and memos were forwarded to Danglis, to the ultimate patron of *Makedonomachoi*, Crown Prince Constantine, even to King George himself.[12] Amidst this turmoil Kalapothakis attacked Premier Theotokis, holding him responsible for the deterioration of the situation in Macedonia and calling the "Panhellenic Organization" a state-run terrorist centre.[13] Under pressure from the Porte, in late June 1909 all Greek officers serving as undercover attachés in the Empire were withdrawn.

---

taires de 1908 en Macédoine et en Thrace orientale", *Études Balkaniques*, 10, 4 (1974), pp. 133-46; "Le régime jeune-turc et les deuxièmes élections parlementaires de 1912 en Macédoine et Thrace orientale", *Études Balkaniques*, 14, 2 (1978), pp. 258-71.

11 Ion Dragoumis was also heavily involved, see Vasilis K. Gounaris, "Apo ti Makedonia sto Goudi: drastiriotites ton makedonomachon stratiotikon (1908-1909)", *Deltion tis Istorikis kai Ethnologikis Etaireias tis Ellados*, 29 (1986), pp. 197-8.

12 Ibid, pp. 216-19.

13 *Embros*, 23-24 Feb. 1909; *Akropolis*, 24 and 26 Feb. 1909; *Neon Asty*, 24 Feb. 1909.

This was why all the veterans participated so actively and massively in the 1909 coup. If the protection of national rights had been publicized as the measure of successful governance, then veteran *Makedonomachoi* had every right to take over the state at least temporarily. Theotokis resigned and Kalapothakis himself suggested his compatriot Kyriakoulis Mavromichalis for Prime Minister, a politician well known for his criticism of the parliament. All those who had been involved in the struggle for Macedonia, officers and civilians, ran to get as many offices as they could, to make the state fit for them. Veterans even managed to have their former patron, the consul at Bitola, Dimitrios Kallergis, appointed as Foreign Minister in Dragoumis' cabinet, which was soon to follow Mavromichalis'.[14] This was not irrelevant to Mavromichalis' decision to limit, down to one fourth, the amount of money channelled secretly from the Foreign Ministry to the Athens-based and politically active clientele of the Macedonian Committee. The initial suggestion by Danglis, who had resigned in November 1909, was to shut the Committee down completely, since it was impossible, under the circumstances, to check the distribution of money.[15]

The Balkan Wars put the officers back into business—all of them got promotions—and the annexation of Macedonia's coastal part to Greece created the necessary room for everybody who had a personal or other interest in occupying a position of authority in this new province. Prefects and sub-prefects were chosen among ex-consuls, educated and trusted Macedonians, Athenians of Macedonian extraction, but also among many old-Greece low-ranking political patrons. Stephanos Dragoumis himself was appointed Governor General of (Greek) Macedonia in 1913. Soon locals, especially non-Greek-speakers and Muslims, realized that new patrons were now necessary to handle both their new and old problems, the most serious being the excesses of tax-farmers and the handling of low-ranking civil servants and gendarmes, who multiplied during the chaos created by the Great War and the division of Greek Macedonia into various zones occupied by different armies, friendly or enemy.[16]

It was just before that War, in 1915, that elections took place for the first time; in fact there were two elections, the latter without the participation of the

---

14 Periklis Al. Argyropoulos, "O Makedonikos Agon. Apomnimonevmata" in the volume *O Makedonikos Agonas. Apomnimonevmata*, Thessaloniki: Institute for Balkan Studies, 1984, pp. 56-60.

15 Georgios Aspreas, *Politiki istoria tis Neoteras Ellados*, Athens: Chrysima Vivlia, 1930, pp. 130-1.

16 For a first-hand view see Georgios Modis, *Anamniseis*, M. Pyrovetsi and I. Michailidis (eds), Thessaloniki: Ekdoseis Panepistimiou Makedonias, 2004, pp. 159-63; see also Vasilis K. Gounaris, "Sti Makedonia tou Megalou Polemou, 1914-1919", *Thessalonikeon Polis*, 1 (2000), pp. 179-92.

Venizelist Liberal Party. We do not have a complete list of the 1915 candidates but we know that every important person who had even a remote connection with Macedonia was included. Konstantinos Demertzis (who was to become Premier in 1936), for example, had a grandmother from Siatista. The lawyer Athanasios Argyros, the chairman of a Macedonian association in Athens, was elected *in absentia* deputy for Serres together with Ioannis Dellios, a high school master in Athens, also of Macedonian extraction. The Dragoumis father and son were both elected. The most prominent candidates were the deputies who had served in the Ottoman parliament, followed by numerous local patrons, entrepreneurs or landed proprietors, some of them well known for their connection with the pre-1912 patriotic networks. From the scant available evidence it looks that some ex-chieftains had already been hired to extract votes. For the time being the anti-Venizelist Laikon Komma, or the Populists, seemed to lead the political contest.[17]

The following year, 1916, Venizelos' provisional government took over the Macedonian provinces of Greece. Compulsory military service for all locals, the presence of the Armée d'Orient, the gradual influx of Asia Minor refugees, the worsening of the local economy, cut off from its vast hinterland, and the numerous mistakes of the Venizelist local administration easily pushed Macedonian voters over to the royalist camp of the Populists. Venizelos took the blame for all the misfortunes of integration, which overlapped with war and occupation by friendly or enemy forces. This disadvantage forced the Liberals to treat their supporters more generously than they should. They tried to consolidate their grip by promising landed property to those who had contributed to the national struggle. Moreover Venizelos assisted the penetration of many Cretan reservists, ex-chieftains in Macedonia, into the regular army. Reservists were more easily manipulated since they lacked tenure. But they did not manage to reverse the situation. The Cretan Premier lost the 1920 elections.

Similar measures were taken in the early 1920s, after the Asia Minor disaster. Liberals tried anew to stimulate the recruitment of former chieftains who had fought for Macedonia or Epirus or in any other place, in order to control the army as firmly as possible. But all these measures were no more than personal favours. On the other hand the settlement of the refugees, the distribution of the *chiflicks* and the introduction of the New Calendar aggravated local complaints. Pastoralists had been deprived of their pastures and peasants of their dreams to take over Muslim property, which was the most fertile land. Last but not least, the Greek Communist Party's agreement with the Communist Balkan Federation on the aim of a "United and Independent Macedonia",

---

17   Vasilis K. Gounaris, "Voulephtes kai kapetanioi: Pelateiakes scheseis sti mesopolemiki Makedonia", *Ellinika*, 41 (1990), p. 321 note 23.

in 1924, and the reappearance of *comitadjis* posed a new threat for internal security. If all the sacrifices of Macedonian Patriarchists had been in vain, then Venizelos was definitely the cause of all their misfortunes.[18]

Between 1923 and 1933 five elections took place in Greece. It was no surprise that all parties did their best to safeguard and to enlarge their clienteles. One of the measures deemed appropriate by almost all parties was the involvement of increasing numbers of veteran fighters in Macedonian politics as deputies. Laden with laurels, real or imagined, after almost twenty years of fighting, they were already familiar with politics—especially the army officers—and were still considered as local heroes in Macedonia. It is easy to guess on what grounds they started to rebuild or reinforce their local networks. In 1927 deputies of Macedonia submitted a memorandum to the government asking for material assistance for volunteer fighters. Pensions topped the list of the demands. It was the same year that the National "Pavlos Melas" Organization, mentioned above, was founded in Thessaloniki.[19]

However, it was the liberal government of Venizelos which passed in 1929 the first law to set up a committee for preparation of the veterans' official list. The pressure put upon former band leaders and former diplomats by their ex-comrades to furnish them with the indispensable reference letters must have been enormous. Some resisted, other did not. It is revealing that an officer had a standard reference letter printed leaving only a few gaps to fill in the name and origin of the recommended person. Apparently the situation was getting out of control. In 1930 the law was altered to include also the volunteers who had fought in Epirus and Samos, as well in the Balkan Wars. Venizelist deputies had now a fair chance to improve their clienteles and that is what they did, most of them without any reservation. Among those who were favoured were many Cretans. Some were clients of Venizelos' adjutant, Pavlos Gyparis, others of the Defence Minister Georgios Katechakis, both veterans of the Struggle themselves. Some of them had supported Venizelos' Provisional Government. Such staunch Venizelists were classified as "band-leaders" instead of "common fighters", which meant higher pensions. Registration for the list, however, did not cease.[20]

The Populists came back to power after the 1932 and 1933 elections with many more veteran fighters on their ballot papers. The power of this lobby was impressive and it was the right moment to exercise it. The land reclaimed from

---

18   Vasilis K. Gounaris, "Oi Slavophonoi tis Makedonias. I poreia tis ensomatosis sto elliniko ethniko kratos, 1870-1940", *Makedonika*, 29 (1993-94), pp. 220-8.

19   Genika Archeia tou Kratous, Georgios Tsondos Papers, file 12, Psiphisma No. 7517, Edessa, 10 June 1928.

20   Gounaris, "Voulephtes kai kapetanioi", pp. 329-31.

the notorious marshes in central and eastern Macedonia was ready for distribution and the quarrel between locals and refugees over Muslim property was peaking. The Venizelists had so far openly supported the refugees. Something had to be done exclusively for the locals and veterans could not be anything but local Macedonians, Slav-speakers or not. Eventually a law was passed in 1935, which secured the priority of the veterans to claim and get plots of land at the place of their permanent residence. Just before the 1935 referendum which restored the Monarchy, the lengthy appendixes to the initial register were verified by Parliament, but getting both land and pension had been judged to be incompatible. Yet there were more complaints and one more electoral campaign to go before the Metaxas dictatorship. The register was inflated out of all proportions.[21]

Free from clientelistic pressures, Ioannis Metaxas, soon after he had seized power, summoned a new committee which instantly removed the Balkan War and Samos volunteers from the register, unless they had been killed or wounded in action. The state budget was relieved but the "Pavlos Melas" organization was further aggrieved. In fact there is some evidence suggesting that a certain branch office even tried to bypass Metaxas and address a petition directly to King George II.[22] Just on the eve of the 1940 war a veteran from the Kavala region wrote a letter to his Populist patron, an ex-naval officer: "Please Sir, if it is possible, send me your visiting card, for we tobacco-growers have been ruined, and a member of our family must join the public sector." The visiting card with a hand-written note was the ultimate proof of protection.[23]

The list of veterans included some hundreds of inhabitants of Macedonia, not more than two thousand in all. Obviously they were not only these veterans who voted in favour of ex-captains. Veterans were only the backbone of a larger clientele, which was never rewarded but proved no less loyal that the old friends of the officers. This point merits further analysis. Liberals in Macedonia had invested a lot in their refugee voters. They controlled numerous border communities, which were considered as bastions of Hellenism in an allegedly ethnically alien hinterland, where the Bulgarian Committees were rumoured to be directing the locals' vote to the Royalist parties. It was a faulty but very convenient interpretation: any electoral defeat was not political but the direct result of clandestine Bulgarian operations. Their opponents, the Populist Party, maximized the political importance of the Slav-speakers' vote and the neces-

---

21 Ibid, pp. 331-3.
22 Ibid, pp. 333-4.
23 Diefthynsis Istorias Stratou, Admiral S. Mavromichalis Papers, Chatzoulas to Mavromichalis, Mesoropi, 14 May 1940.

sity to reward them for their national services. In other words they accepted, at least indirectly, that they patronized a population which required "special attention". Meanwhile the Populists did not hesitate to address the same concerns for autonomy and Bulgarophilia, to others, like the party of "Makedoniki Enosis" [Macedonian Union], a local Populist branch, which broke loose in 1935 and got considerable support in non-Greek-speaking areas.[24]

However, both Liberals and Populists agreed that national service during the Macedonian Struggle was a valid currency which could buy jobs, scholarships, exemption from military service and other benefits. More generally, invocation of the national interest came in handy whenever there was a petition for or against something or the need to make a public or private case more persuasive. For example, after the Great War the Mayor of Edessa asked the Prefect not to send any Bulgarian prisoners to his town, as they might revive local pro-Bulgarian sentiments. The Prefect passed the petition to the Governor General, stressing that the actual reason was the fear of epidemics. The Mayor thought that the national argument would be more effective that a threat to public health.[25] Such concerns and arguments were especially important for the organization of education, which had the additional task to promote the assimilation of non-Greek-speakers as smoothly as possible.

The priority of the national interest was taken for granted in Greek Macedonia. Very much as in the past, all associations and public gatherings focused on the importance of patriotism, of Hellenism, of tradition. Being nationally minded was becoming a political must in a place where domestic danger was seen as endemic. In 1920s Communism was a clear and present danger. Reservist associations, boy scouts, and various other national societies for youths and adults were determined to fight it. Prominent among them stood the association of the refugees from Bitola, Vlachs well known for their wealth, culture and ardent Greek nationalism, which had driven them out of Serbia. If Communists were indeed ready to hand Macedonia over to their Bulgarian comrades, then all those who had fought or belonged to families who had checked Slav propaganda in the past had to be mobilized anew. In the first conference of the veteran *Makedonomachoi* in 1928, among many economic

---

24   Iakovos D. Michailidis, "Politikes anazitiseis sto Mesopolemo: I periptosi tis 'Makedonikis Enosis'", in Georgios Kioutoutskas (ed.) *I Edessa kai I periochi tis. Istoria kai politismos. Praktika A Penelliniou Epistimonikou Symposiou*, Edessa: Steph. Vagourdis, 1995, pp. 355-65. See also George Th. Mavrogordatos, *Stillborn Republic. Social Coalitions and Party Strategies in Greece, 1922-1936*, Berkeley: University of California Press, 1983, pp. 280-91.

25   Istoriko Archeio Makedonias/Geniki Dioikisi Makedonias, file 103, Petsos to the Prefect of Pella, Edessa 13 Oct. 1918 and the Prefect of Pella to the Governor General, Edessa, 15 Oct. 1918.

demands they asked for guns, for the preparation of bands to protect their land from thieves, Bulgarians, and Communists. They did not ask the state to compensate them for their past deeds, they argued, but to assist their present task as vigilantes.[26] Their military patrons were unanimously encouraging them in this direction and the same trend easily became an article of faith during the Metaxas dictatorship. At least Macedonia was ready to welcome and to digest his national rhetoric; it had been practicing such views for years. In this context the Etaireia Makedonikon Spoudon (Society for Macedonian Studies) was founded in 1939 in Thessaloniki by refugees, wealthy merchants and university professors, all of them from Bitola, Kroushevo, western Greek Macedonia, and some others. Bulgarians had already set up their own "Macedonian Scientific Institute" in Sofia.

To sum up, in the inter-war period voting for veteran fighters, especially voting Conservatives, or publicly declaring anti-Communist feelings was identified as denouncing Bulgarian nationalism. A vote for the Populist pro-Royalist Party, against "Venizelo-Communists", was above all a patriotic vote. Deputies with fighting experience in Macedonia were symbols and guarantors of the national feelings of their voters, although some of them, like Georgios Tsontos, had massacred their family members just twenty years before. The local representatives of the deputies were petty local patrons: notables, teachers, and other former members of national committees, people bound to their political bosses through war experience. They had now been transformed into a party mechanism expecting a place in the register of veterans, which would subsidize their inadequate incomes or expand their landholdings. In return they scrutinized the national and political loyalties of their fellow villagers. The threat of Communism expanded their authority as guardians outside the Slav-speaking zone.[27] These local patrons offered to their own village clienteles mediation in dealings with an alien state with Cretan gendarmes and Peloponnesian public servants, who knew nothing of the local languages and habits.[28] To recall John Campbell, patronage is made necessary by the distance between the state and the nation. When citizens are excluded from the world of state agencies and

---

26 Gounaris, "Voulephtes kai kapetanioi", pp. 327-9.

27 It is now clear that Slav-speakers in Macedonia did not exceed some 120,000; see Iakovos D. Michailidis, "The War of Statistics: Traditional Recipes for the Preparation of the Macedonian Salad", *East European Quarterly*, 32,1 (1998), pp. 9-21.

28 Vasilis K. Gounaris, '*Egnosmenon koinonikon phronimaton*': *koinonikes kai alles opseis tou antikommounismou sti Makedonia tou Emphyliou Polemou*, Thessaloniki: Epikendro, 2005 2nd edn, pp. 33-55.

public mechanisms, they turn to powerful patrons to fight back their way into the state.[29] Greek Macedonia seems to have been a typical case.

But in this case political allegiance also implied national allegiance. If the party and the patrons disappointed their voters, shifting the vote was not an option, for it would be a clear sign of loose national feelings. Patronage, Campbell has written, converts impersonal and ephemeral connexions into permanent and personal relationships. Thus the initial motive, protection in exchange for political power, takes on a strong moral quality.[30] In this case it took a national quality. If patronage has always been the means through which a local community is bound to the state, then in the case of Greek Macedonia it was the way communities were bound to the nation also. It was a development extremely convenient for the patronage mechanism but also for the nation-state, which could boast of assimilation before any real measures bore fruits. It was even more important for late inter-war anti-Communist politics. The fervour and the reports of the local vigilantes confirmed that indeed a domestic enemy, be it Communist or Bulgarian or both, had to be real.

The military co-operation of the left-wing World War II resistance (ELAS) and later on of the Communist Democratic Army with the Slav-Macedonian National Front—to the extent that this front was "national"—inevitably strengthened and justified Greek anti-Communism anew. The fierce persecution of the old *Makedonomachoi* in the 1940s by both the Bulgarian occupation army and the Communist bands justified retrospectively the inter-war concerns for domestic security. It was a faulty conclusion, yet of paramount political importance. The Bulgarization of the Communist enemy connected the Civil War to the early 20th century Greek-Bulgarian conflict. Architect of this connection was Georgios Modis, a veteran fighter himself, Governor General of Macedonia in 1945, the most popular speaker in major public gatherings during the period, a prolific writer of historical novels and numerous anti-Slav articles.[31]

The equation of Slavs with Communists identified anti-Communism with nationalism, a conclusion that was particularly important for the conservative parties, especially in the post-war period. Numerous "national" and "patriotic"

---

29   John K. Campbell, *Honour, Family, and Patronage. A Study of Institutions and Moral Values in a Greek Mountain Community,* Oxford University Press, 1964, pp. 260-1.

30   Ibid, p. 259.

31   Vasilis K. Gounaris, "'EAMovoulgaroi' kai Makedonomachoi: Ideologikes kai alles vendetes sti Makedonia tou Emphyliou Polemou" in Ilias Nikolakopoulos, Alkis Rigos and Grigoris Psalidas (eds), *O Emphylios Polemos: Apo ti Varkiza sto Grammo, Fevrouarios 1945- Avgoustos 1949,* Athens: Themelio, 2002, pp. 233-5.

associations and leagues appeared in Thessaloniki as well as in other Macedonian towns. The study of their statutes revealed that the common denominator of these initiatives was to muster all the nation-minded people of Greek Macedonia (*Ethnikophrones*) and to inspire them with "traditional virtues". There is ample evidence in the newspapers that in 1945-46 electoral campaigns in various associations were launched on the basis of patriotism vs. communism. Some thirty associations addressed an open letter pressing for a coalition between the Liberal and the Populist Party, an idea which came close to succeeding in January 1946, but eventually did not work. In any case the important thing was that the refugee voters were clearly abandoning the Liberals. If Slav-speakers had identified themselves either with the Bulgarians or with the Communists (or with both), then Asia Minor refugees had to distance themselves, and this was not a political choice.[32]

Politicians were not the only group to exploit anti-Communism. Very much as in the early 20th century, nationalism was a tax-free "currency" to improve living standards. Since standards were very low in post-war Macedonia, the inflation of this currency was inevitable. By the beginning of 1947 approximately two million petitions for compensation had been submitted for damage suffered during Greece's triple occupation. The competition of various social groups for the satisfaction of economic demands intensified during the Civil War and evidence suggests that various political patrons, old and new, were illegally involved in this procedure. Among them was whoever had easy access to the UNRRA distribution mechanism: deputies, administration officials, officers of the army and the gendarmerie, and, the most notorious of all, the leaders of the militias. Pressure groups were also formed. An important category of them were the unions of war veterans, and various other reservists. Along with them marched the victims of the Civil War, people evacuated from the war front, homeless and destitute civilians. They mobilized their patron deputies to legitimize their financial demands and sought the most convincing arguments, to gain priority for their own claims. The statutes of such unions reveal that expressions of concern for the national interests of the state and anti-Communist hints were indeed indispensable. It was not only a matter of political correctness. In all their meetings with ministers and other officials, in all their petitions the members of such unions would present their urgent economic demands together with assurances of their allegiance to the army, the government, the nation, and their support for the anti-Communist struggle, then in full spate. For years this rhetoric was the standard way to approach the state mechanism, in fact an important alibi for social protest in a state under

---

32   Gounaris, *Egnosmenon koinonikon phronimaton*, pp. 71-100.

martial law. In the late 1940s this trend was followed by various population groups and associations. They had to give reassurances of their loyalty to the state and to seek the protection of their patron, who was expected to act as guarantee for their true convictions. Although in the long run few reservist organizations gained considerable advantages, the fact remains that for the rest anti-Communist rhetoric during the Civil War secured some extra food and clothing, a peddler's license, a position in the list of the state subsidized *antartopliktoi* (people stricken by the "*antartes*" or brigands), or at best a low paid job in the broader public sector.[33]

Until the end of Civil War, a discrepancy is detectable between the people's will to offer their loyalty to anti-Communism and, on the other hand, the state's ability to reward them substantially and not only symbolically for their true or alleged devotion. This financial weakness of the state, felt bitterly but not exclusively in Greek Macedonia, created the necessary ground for various networks of intermediaries and petty patrons to flourish and to multiply. The questioning of loyalty—be it national of politica—meant additional and profitable business which attracted more individuals into a game that in the inter-war years had been mastered by various local notables. More vigilantes co-operating with the police meant additional—not always justifiable—questioning of loyalties and insecurity. Insecurity, in the absence of a strong state mechanism, made the presence of networks and protectors imperative and stronger, since the latter controlled access to social welfare, the labour market, and various kinds of supplies and state services, even to justice.

In other words the structure and practices for mutually beneficial—but not always institutionalized—relations between the citizens and the state, with reference to their national and/or political allegiance, originally established in Greek Macedonia in the early 1900s, dominated society and politics in the same region by the end of the 1940s. Insecurity and shortage of sufficient resources to satisfy the financial needs of the local population perpetuated social conflicts and necessitated the presence of protectors. But it was more than that. Indeed, under such favourable circumstance clientelism took on a life of its own. In the absence of substantial alternative channels of communication between the administration in Athens and its northern provinces in Macedonia such practices have played—some still do play—an important part in political manoeuvring. They have remained the preserve of the conservative parties since the late 1980s. Then they were successfully adapted by the "patriotic PASOK" to make up for the apparent deficit of political ideology. Anti-Communism is no longer fashionable or functional but the merits and

---

33   Ibid, pp. 101-74.

politics of *ethnikophrosyni* (i.e. being nation-minded), or alternatively excessive zeal for the Macedonian Question, are still known to many and appreciated by all, not only by conservatives and not in Greek Macedonia exclusively. The politics of nationalism in Greece around 1900 were, in a way, the by-products of excessive clientelism, which made modernization impossible without expansion. Exported nationalism politicized Macedonia in every aspect; nationalized politics made Macedonia an integral part of the Greek system of patronage, where officers were active and experienced players. After World War II the fear of the Slavs assumed the proportions of a national panic and the military was reintroduced as the true saviour. The bonds between patrons and clients, forged during two real or alleged national wars against the Bulgarians and against the Communists—or was it just one war with two stages?—produced enormous political power, beyond criticism, which stretched outside the boundaries of Greek Macedonia. This easily manipulated potential has tempted many ever since. But the overdose of *ethnikophrosyni* in the long run created more political side-effects for national patrons that it solved problems for them. In a strange way Macedonia has paid its debt back to Athens by returning the surplus of nationalism to Greek politics.

BIBLIOGRAPHY

Unpublished sources
Archives of the Greek Foreign Ministry, File 1904 Proxeneio Thessalonikis.
Diefthynsis Istorias Stratou, Admiral S. Mavromichalis Papers.
Genika Archeia tou Kratous, Georgios Tsondos Papers, file 12.
Istoriko Archeio Makedonias/Geniki Dioikisi Makedonias, file 103.

Books and articles
Argyropoulos, Periklis Al. (1984) "O Makedonikos Agon. Apomnimonevmata" in the volume *O Makedonikos Agonas. Apomnimonevmata*, Thessaloniki.
Aspreas, Georgios (1930) *Politiki istoria tis Neoteras Ellados*, Athens.
Barth, Fredrik, "Introduction", Fredrik Barth (ed.), *Ethnic Groups and Boundaries* (London, 1969).
—— (1994) "Enduring and Emerging Issues in the Analysis of Ethnicity", in Hans Vermeulen & Cora Govers (ed.), *The Anthropology of Ethnicity*, Amsterdam, pp. 11-32.
Campbell, John K. (1964) *Honour, Family, and Patronage. A Study of Institutions and Moral Values in a Greek Mountain Community*, Oxford.
Douglas, Dakin (1966) *The Greek Struggle in Macedonia, 1897-1913*, Thessaloniki.
Gianoulopoulos, Giannis N. (2003) *"I evgenis mas typhlosis...". Exoteriki politiki kai 'ethnika themata'. Apo tin itta tou 1897 eos ti mikrasiatiki katastrophi*, Athens.
Gounaris, Basil C. (1986) "Apo ti Makedonia sto Goudi: drastiriotites ton makedonomachon stratiotikon (1908-1909)", *Deltion tis Istorikis kai Ethnologikis Etaireias tis Ellados*, 29, 175-256.
—— (1990) "Voulephtes kai kapetanioi: Pelateiakes scheseis sti mesopolemiki Makedonia", *Ellinika*, 41, 313-35.
—— (1993-94) "Oi Slavophonoi tis Makedonias. I poreia tis ensomatosis sto elliniko ethniko kratos, 1870-1940", *Makedonika*, 29, 209-237.
—— (1995) "Social Cleavages and National 'Awakening' in Ottoman Macedonia", *East European Quarterly*, 29:4, 409-26.
—— (1997) "Social Gatherings and Macedonian Lobbying: Symbols of Irredentism and Living Legends in Early Twentieth Century Athens", in Philip Carabott (ed.), *Greek Society in the Making, 1863-1913: Realities, Symbols, and Visions*, London, pp. 99-112.
—— (2000) "Sti Makedonia tou Megalou Polemou, 1914-1919", *Thessalonikeon Polis*, 1, 179-92.

—— (2002a) "Macedonian Questions" *Journal of Southeast European and Black Sea Studies*, 2, 3, 63-94.

—— (2002b) "'EAMovoulgaroi' kai Makedonomachoi: Ideologikes kai alles vendetes sti Makedonia tou Emphyliou Polemou", in Ilias Nikolakopoulos, Alkis Rigos and Grigoris Psalidas (eds), *O Emphylios Polemos: Apo ti Varkiza sto Grammo, Fevrouarios 1945-Avgoustos 1949*, Athens, pp. 233-45.

—— (2005) '*Egnosmenon koinonikon phronimaton*': *koinonikes kai alles opseis tou antikommounismou sti Makedonia tou Emphyliou Polemou*, Thessaloniki, 2005 2nd edn.

Karakasidou, Anastasia (1997) *Fields of Wheat, Hills of Blood: Passages to Nationhood in Greek Macedonia*, Chicago and London.

Karabati, Persephoni (1996) "Koinonikes anakatataxeis sta chronia tou Makedonikou Agona: to archeio tou Stergiou Misiou", unpublished MA thesis, Aristotle University of Thessaloniki.

Livanios, Dimitris (1999) "'Conquering the Souls': Nationalism and Greek Guerrilla Warfare in Ottoman Macedonia, 1904-1908", *Journal of Byzantine and Modern Greek Studies*, 23, 195-221.

Makedonski, Stojian (1974) "La révolution jeune-turque et les premières élections parlementaires de 1908 en Macédoine et en Thrace orientale", *Études balkaniques*, 10, 4, 133-4.

—— (1978) "Le régime jeune-turc et les deuxièmes élections parlementaires de 1912 en Macédoine et Thrace orientale", *Études Balkaniques*, 14:2, 258-71.

Mandatzis, Christos (2004a) "Proypologismoi, logarismoi kai aprovleptes ethnikes dapanes: apopeires chrimatodotisis tou alytrotikou agona sti Makedonia (1904-1908)", *Thessalonikeon Polis*, 16, 18-59.

—— (2004b) "Antartiko sto katophli mias ekchrimatizomenis oikonomias: koinoniki kai oikonomiki diastasi tou Makedonikou Agona", *Thessalonikeon Polis*, 16, 60-83.

Mavrogordatos, George Th. (1983) *Stillborn Republic. Social Coalitions and Party Strategies in Greece, 1922-1936*, Berkeley.

Michailidis, Iakovos D. (1995) "Politikes anazitiseis sto Mesopolemo: I periptosi tis 'Makedonikis Enosis'", in Georgios Kioutoutskas (ed.) *I Edessa kai I periochi tis. Istoria kai politismos. Praktika A Penelliniou Epistimonikou Symposiou* Edessa, pp. 355-65.

—— (1997) "Stratiotika protypa kai klephtiki paradosi: organotika provlimata kai I kathimerini zoi sta chronia tou Makedonikou Agona", in *Makedonia, istoria kai politismos*, Florina, pp. 249-80.

—— (1998) "The War of Statistics: Traditional Recipes for the Preparation of the Macedonian Salad", *East European Quarterly*, 32, 1, 9-21.

Modis, Georgios, *Anamniseis* (2004) M. Pyrovetsi and I. Michailidis (eds), Thessaloniki.

Sencer, Emre (2004) "Balkan Nationalisms in the Ottoman Parliament 1909", *East European Quarterly*, 38:1, 41-64.

Smith, Anthony (1989) *The Ethnic Origin of Nations*, Oxford.

Souliotis, Athanasios (1984) "O Makedonikos Agon. I Organosis Thessalonikis 1906-1908" in *O Makedonikos Agonas. Apomnimonevmata*, Thessaloniki.

Vermeulen, Hans (1987) "Agrotikes syngrouseis kai koinoniki diamartyria stin istoria enos makedonikou choriou (1900-1936)" in Stathis Damianakos (ed.), *Diadikasies koinonikou metaschimatismou stin agrotiki Ellada*, Athens, pp. 221-44.

Newspapers
Akropolis, 1909; *Embros*, 1909; *Neon Asty*, 1909.

6

'MODERN GREECE': AN OLD DEBATE

John Koliopoulos

When did the Greeks turn modern and how *Greek* have the modern Greeks actually been? These and similar questions have been asked by students of Greece at least since Shakespeare's time, if not before. The subject has been discussed by many generations of Greek and foreign scholars, particularly since the Greek war of independence, when the Greeks and the Greek Question were projected in the West as a question deserving the serious attention of Western governments, not only of Western liberals sympathizing with the Greek cause. One century later, a Western scholar, the philosopher of history Arnold Toynbee, wrote under the impact of the traumatic experiences of the 1919-22 Greco-Turkish war, of the liberal vision of a regenerated Hellas as "one of the extravagances of Western philhellenism". He added that the attraction of the West to Greece at the time of the Greek war of independence was a "curse which the West has set upon Greece", which had led to Greece's "spiritual pauperisation" and was responsible for "what Greece had lost or failed to win". The impact of Western institutions and values on Greece, according to the disenchanted student of civilizations, could not take root and produce tangible results, notwithstanding the efforts of one century to absorb these institutions and values.[1]

Greece was falling short of expectations of both the Classicists and the Medievalists or Orientalists. The Greeks, the Classicists were convinced, could not credibly claim descent from the ancient sages and the heroes that inhabited classical Greek lands. Similarly, by opting for a revival of the classical ideal and link, the Orientalists were equally convinced, the Greeks were spiritu-

---

1   Arnold Toynbee, *The Western Question in Greece and Turkey*, Boston-New York 1922, pp. 351-2.

ally "pauperised", because they were distancing themselves from their medieval moorings. The Byzantine traditions were being undermined, while the classical Greek ideal was simply unattainable.

From George Finlay to Toynbee and from Toynbee to Romily Jenkins and Cyril Mango, the Greeks have been measured up against constructs of the past and found wanting in qualities associated with either classical Greece or Byzantium. Both constructs, the Byzantine no less than the classical Greek inheritance, as fashioned in the West, have been used ever since to judge the performance and experiences of the Greeks. The appeal of these past constructs has of late been losing power, and students of Greece have settled down to the idea that the Greeks of today, notwithstanding their own identification with either or both of their cultural inheritances, need not strive to prove exclusive attachment to either, as far as their identity is concerned.[2]

Two aspects of the strictures against the Greeks of modern times, however, which appear to have been eluding disenchanted classicists as much as medievalists, are worth mentioning in order to examine the question of "modernity" in Greek history. So far as the idea of a Greek founding national myth of a continuity in space and time is concerned, we should note that: i) that founding myth did succeed in just the ways national founding myths generally operate in the formation of national identities, which are not difficult to discern, nor easy to refute; and ii) as a nation state, the Greek did perform, as nation states are concerned, well above the expectations of its disenchanted critics of earlier days.

Identities are constructs; so, to a large extent, is periodization. To examine Greek identity and performance in the context of Greek history, especially in relation to ancient Greece, it is necessary to scrutinize anew the question of Greek modernity. When did the Greeks enter modern times? Or, perhaps better: when did modern times invade the historical Greek lands? These questions have to be answered anew by students of Greece, since older periodizations of Greek history are no longer accepted without reservations.

One basic premise for any inquiry should be that there can be only one definition of modernity, i.e. the idea that modern times, irrespective of the criteria or the factors employed to identify their beginning, constituted the departure from what the Italians of the 15th century described as the *"medium aevum"*

---

2   See Richard Clogg's perceptive article "Writing the History of Greece: Forty Years on", *Cambridge Papers in Modern Greek*, 11 (2003), pp. 25-50. See also Ioannis S. Koliopoulos, *I "peran" Ellas kai oi alloi Elllines. To synchrono Elliniko Ethnos kai oi eteroglossoi synoikoi Christianoi (1800-1912)* ["Yonder" Greece and the other Greeks: The modern Greek nation and the heterolingual cohabitant Christians, 1800-1912], Thessaloniki 2003, with the relevant bibliography.

or "middle ages". Whether the profound changes in 15th-century Italian city-states, which Jakob Burkhardt proposed as the beginning of modern times, or the control of capital and violence or subtler social and economic changes on which subsequent theories focused, are accepted as the dawn of the modern age, the element of departure from a state of political and social organization towards what Lord Acton described as mentalities, affairs and organization nearer to us and recognizable as our own is a principal element of the beginning of modern times. The element of progress is the key to that departure.[3]

The notion of a "modern" Greek nation, of a "new-born" nation, was projected by the Greeks themselves and in so many words in the war of independence. "The present-day Greek", wrote the editor of a newspaper in insurgent Greece, "is not reborn, as is commonly believed, he is born." He was the child of a "famous and proud father", possessed the "constitution" and almost the same intellectual powers and was expected, with the appropriate upbringing, to grow and become like his father. The "modern" or "new-born" nation, however, was not new as the American or the Belgian nation was; it was not like a new branch springing from a tree. "Descent" from an old "stock", the ancient Greek stock, was not direct; it was a cultural descent, and language was the irrefutable link uniting the new nation to the old.

But this approach was far from being the dominant one, although it was favoured by the Westernized Greeks whose influence appeared to be far greater than their numbers. Realities in insurgent Greece favoured a more traditional approach to the definition of the Greek nation, one that had religious affili-

---

3   See *The Cambridge Modern History*, Cambridge UP, Cambridge MA 19-34 (reprint of 1902 edn), i, p.1. See also W.I. Bousma, "The Renaissance and the Drama of Western History", *American Historical Review,* 84 (1979), pp. 1-150; Robert Brenner, "Agrarian Class Structure and Economic Development in Preindustrial Europe", *Past and Present,* 70 (February 1976), pp. 30-75 and consequent discussion in subsequent numbers of the journal *Past and Present* (78 pp. 24-5, 79 pp. 55-69, 80 pp. 3-65 and 57 pp. 16-113); John Jay, "Crise du féodalisme et conjoncture de prix à la fin du Moyen Age", *Annales,* 34/2 (1979), 305-18; Guy Bois, "Sur la monnaie et les prix à la fin du Moyen Age: Réponse à John Jay", *Annales,* 34/2 (1979), 319-23. For the beginning of modernity in Greek lands see Constantine Paparrigopoulos, *Istoria tou Ellinikou Ethnous...* [History of the Greek Nation...], Athens 1874, v, p. 5 and *Prolegomena* [Prologue], 2nd edn. of vol. 5, ed. C.Th. Dimaras, Athens 1970, pp. 84-5, 90-1, 155; A.E. Vakalopoulos, *Istoria tou neou Ellinismou* [History of Modern Hellenism], i, Thessaloniki 1974, pp. 5, 46 ff. and *Nea Elliniki Istoria, 1204-1985* [Modern Greek History, 1204-1985], Thessaloniki 1996, pp. 11 ff.; Anastasios Polyzoides, *Geniki istoria apo ton archaiotaton chronon mechri ton kath' emas* [General history from the earliest times till our own times], ed. G.P. Kremos, Athens 1889, i, p. 12 and the same author's *Ta Neohellenika...* [Neohellenica], 2 vols., Athens 1874.

ation as a principal component. When it came to defining citizenship in the first charter of the insurgent country in 1822 (the constitution of Epidaurus, in January 1822), religious affiliation was given prominence: Greek citizens were those Eastern Orthodox Christians who lived in the districts of Greece and had taken up or were to take up arms against the Ottoman Sultan's rule. "Greece" and the "Greek nation" were, in view of so many uncertainties about the outcome of the war and in view of the participation in that war of numerous Christians whose mother tongue was Albanian, Vlach or Slav, left undefined. When, however, it became apparent that the new Greece would be confined to the southern tip of the Greek peninsula, a new notion was fashioned, that of "yonder" or "outer" Greece, while the non-Greek-speaking Orthodox Christians of this "yonder" Greece were to be liberated and Hellenized in speech as well as in sentiment, when they were not already.

One more element, in addition to language and religion, was added, without dropping the initial criteria for defining Greek identity: sentiment or conscience, to keep up with the requirements of Romanticism. The romantic "will" to belong to a community, irrespective of other more tangible criteria, was and continues to be an element hard to refute as a criterion for defining one's identity. But more than sentiment or religion, the Greek language and the cultural descent it has signified, since the question of Greece and the Greeks and their future was projected onto the scene, was the notion of continuity of the Greek nation.

Seen from this angle, modernity in Greek history, as was established by the Greek historian Constantine Paparrigopoulos, appears to be weak even as a construct. The Greek *medium aevum*, although its beginnings might be the same as those of the Western *medium aevum*, did not end at the time the Western did. In vain does the student of Greece search for the historic Greek lands, in the 15th century, developments and changes similar to the ones in the West which have been accepted as signifying a departure from the previous state of things.[4]

It is worth noting in this context that, before the beginning of Greek modern history was set in the 15th century, modernity in Greek history was proposed on the basis of criteria different from the ones proposed by Paparrigopoulos. "Modern Greece", which was a loan from Western historiography, was meant to signify Greece of the 19th century or post-Enlightenment Greece, or even Greece following the Roman conquest in the 2nd century BC. The loss of sovereignty and independence in the latter case, and the dawning of the "new age" in the Greek lands in the former, were the criteria used for setting the be-

---

4   See Koliopoulos, *I peran Ellas kai oi alloi Elllines...*, pp. 26 ff.

ginning of modern Greek history. In the former case, the Greek *medium aevum* was stretched by at least three centuries in comparison with the Western, while in the second the Greek *medium aevum* was identified with the long centuries of Greek lack of sovereignty.

Today, after two centuries of debate on the end of Greece's *medium aevum*, after the imagining of Greece by Koraés and other Greek Enlighteners and the reimagining of her by Paparrigopoulos and the Romantics of 19th-century Greece, after questioning of the constructs of both the Classicists and their critics, it seems to be futile to search for a Greece other than the one that emerged from the Philhellenic "extravagance" of early 19th century. It is a Greece vastly different from classical Greece and from Greece of Byzantine and post-Byzantine times, but a Greece all the same.

The laments of the Orthodox fundamentalists for the loss of the reputed Greek Eden before the Orthodox *Oecoumene* was invaded and destroyed by the nation-state, as well as the laments of the post-modernists for the equally fictional multicultural pre-national Greece,[5] should not move students of Greece more than other fashionable efforts of scholars of past days eager to fall in line with the political correctness of the day. Denying the Greek founding national myth of a continuity of the Greeks in history, from classical Greece to Byzantium and from Byzantium to post-Byzantine Greece, and rejecting the end-product of that myth—i.e. Greek speaking Greeks and Albanians, Vlachs and Slavs moulded in the Greek "melting pot" and proud all as reborn Hellenes—fly in the face of the simple truth that human communities have always changed, adjusting to the needs and the requirements of changing times. Telling young Greeks today that their family names are often reminders of their Albanian or other non-Greek descent may cause them to reply that so are the names of Seferis and Hatzikyriakos-Ghikas.

Greece of today is no less Greece than Classical Greece and its sequels, not only because the Greeks have chosen to believe that that is the case, but for one more reason which is impossible to refute: the Greek language, which has survived the cataclysmic foreign invasions of past centuries. When the French general who landed on the island of Corfu in the summer of 1797 to take possession of the island from the Venetians was presented with a copy of Homer's *Odyssey* by the local Greek priest, this was not only a grand gesture appropriate for the occasion. Texts of the Greek language in use from Byzantine times to modern times, official texts as well as non- official and common language ones, should no longer be seen as "sad relics of departed worth", but as monuments of a most resilient language surviving the onslaughts of foreign invaders and

---

5 See Christos Yannaras, *I Neoelliniki tautotita* [Modern Greek Identity], Athens 1983.

their tongues.⁶ Those inhabiting parts of the historical Greek lands and speaking that great language have the right to be called Greeks and to call their country Greece, as much as the classical Greeks had.

---

6   Koliopoulos, *I "peran" Ellas kai oi alloi Elllines...*, pp. 165 ff.

'MODERN GREECE': AN OLD DEBATE

BIBLIOGRAPHY

Bois, Guy (1979) "Sur la monnaie et les prix à la fin du Moyen Age: Réponse à John Jay", *Annales*, 34:2, 319-23.

Bousma, W.I. (1979) "The Renaissance and the Drama of Western History", *American Historical Review*, 84, 1-150.

Brenner, Robert (1976) "Agrarian Class Structure and Economic Development in Pre-industrial Europe", *Past and Present*, 70 (Feb. 1976), 30-75.

Clogg, Richard (2003) "Writing the History of Greece: Forty Years on", *Cambridge Papers in Modern Greek*, 11, 25-50.

Jay, John (1979) "Crise du féodalisme et conjoncture de prix à la fin du Moyen Age", *Annales*, 34:2, 305-18.

Koliopoulos, Ioannis S. (2003) *I "peran" Ellas kai oi alloi Elllines. To synchrono Elliniko ethnos kai oi eteroglossoi synoikoi Christianoi (1800-1912)*, Thessaloniki.

Paparrigopoulos, Constantine (1874) *Istoria tou Ellinikou Ethnous*, Athens, vol. 5.

—— (1970) *Prolegomena* (Prologue), 2nd edn. of vol. 5, ed. C.Th. Dimaras, Athens.

Polyzoides, Anastasios (1889) *Geniki istoria apo ton archaiotaton chronon mechri ton kath' emas*, ed. G.P. Kremos, Athens, vol. 1.

—— *Ta Neohellenika* (1874), Athens, vol. 1-3.

Toynbee, Arnold (1922) *The Western Question in Greece and Turkey*, Boston-New York.

Vakalopoulos, A.E. (1974) *Istoria tou neou Ellinismou* (History of Modern Hellenism), vol. I, Thessaloniki.

—— (1996) *Nea Elliniki Istoria, 1204-1985*, Thessaloniki.

Yannaras, Christos (1983) *I Neoelliniki tautotita*, Athens.

7

ANDREAS PAPANDREOU, RADICAL WITHOUT A CAUSE

Thanos Veremis

The phenomenon of Andreas Papandreou remains a riddle in Greek politics that begs to be deciphered. Eleven years after his death there has been no serious attempt to shed light on the times and actions of a man who secured the devotion of a certain public and the derision of another. Now it is only the occasional billboard with his picture issued by his declining numbers of followers that reminds the passer-by of his triumphant career.

The end of the military regime in 1974 provided the setting for a significant change in Greek political life. The regime had oppressed all political formations but was exceptionally brutal towards the left. Andreas Papandreou made it his task to castigate the right for having spawned the rebellious colonels, although the historical leader of the conservative camp, Constantine Karamanlis, legalized the Communist Party following the fall of the junta. After 1974 a wider spectrum in parliament, including a Socialist and two Communist parties, introduced unprecedented pluralism to the Greek Parliament. It was also the time when a period of sustained growth had run into an abrupt end due to the oil crises and the paralyzing stagflation they generated. Had it not been for this abrupt blight in popular expectations politics would most probably have picked off from where the colonels had frozen its development.[1] The pre-1967 liberal reform would have found its worthy successor in the Union for the Democratic Centre, a party of liberal celebrities that made their mark by resisting the dictatorship. There was certainly much promise and talent in this heir

---

1 Thanos Veremis, "The Union of the Democratic Center", in Howard R. Penniman (ed.) *Greece at the Pols. The National Elections of 1974 & 1977*, Washington DC: American Enterprise Institute, 1981.

of the old Centre Union. The new political and social circumstances, however, and especially the Papandreou factor upset all predictions. The Union for the Democratic Centre lost 48% of its constituency to Papandreou's Panhellenic Socialist Movement (PASOK) in the 1977 elections and its deputies were dispersed between New Democracy and PASOK.

Unlike Karamanlis who made the peaceful transition to democracy possible by striking a balance between the right and the liberal centre, Papandreou swept his public away by introducing an altogether new political product. It consisted of a series of radical messages transmitted by a novel medium—the leader himself. He offered the people a new narrative "based on a comprehensive worldview and the promise of radical change (*allaghi*). This construction of the social and political universe was spread in two axes. The first divided the world into "metropolis" and "periphery", the latter being dependent on the former. The second axis represented the ostensibly inherent struggle between an exploiting "establishment", both foreign and domestic, and the "people"— that is, all the "nonprivileged Greeks" opposed to the establishment."[2]

Andreas' discourse exacerbated polarization in Greek politics and created a *distinct type of strategy with important political implications.*[3] Although PASOK was perceived by part of its constituency as a party close to the centre, its leadership insisted on its polarizing strategy. Kalyvas offers the following explanation: "The Center Union, a party of the centre-left, evolved into the main opposition party in the beginning of the 1960s. It forged a collective identity based to a great extent on the republic vs monarchy cleavage, the traditional cleavage... which goes back to the 1915 "national schism".[4]" Was the new dividing line forged by Andreas between the "Right" and the "Democratic Forces" based on class analysis? One of the few party intellectuals, Costas Simitis, considered class politics as improbable in a country consisting mostly of self-employed people and small property owners.[5] Furthermore, the scant policy differences between New Democracy and PASOK did not justify the polarizing discourse initiated by Andreas. Although PASOK did embark on some redistributive policies during its first years in power by raising minimum wages and pensions, on the whole it avoided radical reforms.[6] PASOK's left-right cleavage

---

2   Takis S. Pappas, "Political Leadership and the Emergence of Radical Mass Movements in Democracy", *Comparative Political Studies*, forthcoming, p.10.
3   Stathis N. Kalyvas, "Polarization in Greek Politics: PASOK's First Four Years, 1981-1985", in *Journal of the Hellenic Diaspora*, Vol. 23,1 (1997), p.84.
4   Ibid., p.92.
5   Costas Simitis, "Introduction" in Mouzelis *et al., Laikismos kai Politiki* (Populism and Politics), Athens: Gnosi, 1984, p. 15.
6   Kalyvas, op..cit., p. 102.

referred to the victors and vanquished of the 1946-49 Civil War rather than to a Marxist class struggle. Ultimately, the main target of the conflict was the control of the state apparatus and the spoils that went with it. The major casualty of Andreas' polarization tactics was *the long-term legitimacy of democratic institutions*.[7] Unlike the Communist Party which was a veritable organisation[8] opposed to the Greek establishment PASOK, by and large, observed the rules of parliamentary democracy. In practice, however, Andreas often challenged certain principles of the constitutional regime by giving priority to the "needs" of the people over the authority of institutions.[9]

Son of a prominent politician of the liberal centre and an educated mother of Polish descent, Andreas Papandreou was enrolled at the American-sponsored Athens College, studied briefly at the University of Athens and graduated from Harvard with a PhD in economics. According to his contemporaries in American academia he was thoroughly Americanized during his career as professor in various prominent institutions of learning.[10] A product of the FDR era when New Deal economics prevailed, Papandreou combined his youthful predilection for the left, under the Metaxas dictatorship, with liberal politics of the Adlai Stevenson variety. There is even evidence that he actively took part in the Minnesota campaign for Stevenson in one of his rare political escapades.[11]

The formative years of Papandreou are the least known to the commentators who tried to explain his meteoric rise based entirely on the evidence of his Greek sojourn. His success in producing a socialist mutation where his father's centrist coalition had failed in the 1960s must be sought in his own fresh look at Greek society. Unlike both right and left, ideologies that recruited their followers by invoking exclusive principles of nationalism and internationalism, or success through personal effort as opposed to collective solidarity, Papandreou exhibited laxity instead of discipline. Above all, he invoked the flawless instinct of the common man as the sole validating principle of his policy. He therefore became the exponent of a populist view with no precedent in Greek politics. Papandreou's idea of the common people connects with Thomas Jefferson's prototype of the average citizen or even with Andrew Jackson's preference for backwoodsmen. Populism as the cult of the average person has deeper roots in the American than in the European tradition. With little opposition from an

---

7   Ibid., p. 101.
8   Ibid., p. 85.
9   Ibid., p. 96.
10 Michalis Macrakis, *Andreas Papandreou. The Formative Years (1933-43)* Athens: Katoptro, 2000, p. 160.
11 Ibid., p. 162.

ancien régime of royalists, the Lockean revolutionaries of 1776 started off in a state of nature where the individual could prosper without the impediments of rank and privilege. The young Andreas must have been impressed by a society that celebrated modest origin and rendered this an advantage in politics. Nowhere in Europe was the view of the average citizen held in higher esteem than in the United States of the forties.

Papandreou's populism appears to be American in origin with the appropriate modifications to fit the Greek case. The American "noble savage" is a self-made person, independent of societal solidarity. Andreas' public consisted of the "underprivileged" struggling against the "privileged establishment" (*katestimeno*). Making the state compliant with their needs was their ultimate goal. Andreas professed to act as a mere reflection of the popular will while providing a rhetorical mirror to please his public's narcissism.[12] Although he did establish a direct rapport with his followers in the time-honoured populist mode, he in fact manipulated public sentiments that he himself often inflamed. His so-called dialogue with the people was no more than a well-staged soliloquy. "The masses wanted to hear their own voice. And indeed it was their voice that came from Papandreou's lips unchanged – contradictory, disjointed, vague, neither more nor less refined, but enormously amplified, like the echo of a voice in a canyon... For the myth of the Savior always goes hand in hand with the myth of the People. The People are always right. They only need someone to tell them they are right. And thus the frenzied applause and cheers of the crowd muffled the contradictions and dissonances and made the flaws in PASOK's internal organization seem trivial."[13]

PASOK was founded in 1974 as a party fashioned entirely after the leadership of Papandreou. The use of the term "movement" allowed its founding father a free hand that a normal party might have checked. Andreas described the constituent elements of PASOK in his 19 January 1975 speech to the Central Committee: "Part of PASOK consists of the old youth movement of the *Centre Union party* (EDIN). Another of something called "Andreism" a group with an affinity to the leader rather than the movement. Finally the third element is based on the left, the conventional as well as the extraparliamentary."[14] In

---

12 Angelos Elephantis, "PASOK and the Elections of 1977: The Rise of the Populist Movement," in Howard R. Penniman (ed.) *Greece at the Polls. The National Elections of 1974 & 1977*, Washington DC: American Enterprise Institute for Public Research, 1981, pp. 113-16.

13 Ibid., p. 119.

14 Stelios Kouloglou, *Sta ichni tou tritou dromou. PASOK 1974-86* (In the Tracks of the Third Way. PASOK 1974-86), Odysseas, 1986, p. 30.

the July 1977 elections for the Central Committee of PASOK the "Andreists", handpicked by the leader himself, outnumbered the old guard of the party.[15]

Andreas' description of his own choice of socialism remained nebulous throughout his years in power. In an interview on 3 November 1977 he defined Socialism as not being kin to Social Democracy: "Social Democracy is capitalism with a polite mask. It is based on similar relations of production and on an identical set of values. Its purpose is not to abolish the exploitation of man but to improve class differences in order to preserve rather than do away with capitalism, imperialism and monopolies."[16] The charm Andreas exercised over his followers prevented voices of dissent being raised, even as the movement abandoned Marxism and embraced Social Democracy and finally liberal reformism.

Foreign policy was the subject of Andreas' most famous improvizations. It was also the field where he made his spectacular about-turns and his worst predictions. Thus he considered membership of NATO and the European Community a national catastrophe, he rejected the possibility of an allied attack against Iraq in 1991 and when it did result in the Gulf War predicted a long and disastrous involvement of Western forces. In 1984 he embarked on the "Peace Initiative of the Six" for a Nuclear Freeze, along with Swedish Prime Minister Olaf Palme, the Indian Prime Minister Indira Gandhi, and Presidents Miguel de la Madrid of Mexico, Julius Nyerere of Tanzania and Raul Alfonsín of Argentina. Ted Koppel, the anchorman of the ABC "Night Line" programme, put the most pertinent question to his guests from the Initiative: "…noble goals, good intentions, but what in heaven's name makes you think that either the United States or the Soviet Union will pay any attention to you?"[17] The answers were full of high principles, but a few years later the leaders of the two superpowers made the most effective deal for nuclear arms reduction in the history of the Cold War. Few of Andreas' followers noticed the futility of his many stillborn causes. Those that did also questioned the wisdom of the celebrated common man for exhibiting such unquestioned toleration of his leader's flawed judgement. In the aftermath of one of Andreas' stunts, a professor wrote a sparkling piece on collective stupidity as a factor that should not be underestimated in public affairs.[18] Papandreou

---

15   Ibid., p. 32.
16   ??, 3 November 1975, cited in Potis Paraskevopoulos, *Andreas Papandreou 1960-95* (in Greek), Synchroni Elliniki Istoria, 1995, pp.174-9.
17   *The Peace Initiative of the "Six"*, Department of Documentation, Athens News Agency, April 1985.
18   Thanassis Diamandopoulos, "I politiki chrisimotis ton vlakon" (The Political Utility of Stupid People) *Oikonomikos Tachydromos*, 2 March 1995.

abused the trust of his public so often that populism became discredited and was evicted from official parlance.

In its early phase PASOK was troubled by the struggle between the party activists and ideologues and the leader's plans for establishing absolute control over his party. After many a purge "the organization was reduced to incessant party activism and leader legitimizing purposes".[19] Since the ideological features of PASOK were entirely determined by the leader, what remained to be settled were questions of organization.[20] The internecine organizational strife between the various power groups allowed Papandreou to preside over the movement with Olympian detachment. Although a person of very high intelligence, Andreas had little inclination for cultural recreation and his major source of entertainment was popular music (Tolis Voskopoulos and Rita Sakelariou) and cowboy films. He rarely appeared at high-brow performances and no intellectual was ever included in his circle of friends. After the 1975 wholesale exclusion of Dimokratiki Amyna—an organization of liberal-leftist academics that had resisted the junta—from any cooperation with PASOK, the party was deprived of a rare source of intellectual nourishment. From then on the small intelligentsia that inhabited the Greek Parliament gathered in the miniscule Eurocommunist party.

After Contantine Karamanlis' departure from New Democracy and the party's prolonged exile in the opposition, disarray and pessimism prevailed in its ranks. The populist PASOK and its tactician leader became the pacesetter of politics. Andreas' major achievements were in maintaining power and controlling the state apparatus. The sole master of Greek politics for at least a decade, Papandreou was without a rival in keeping his opponents off balance and the excitement of his public undiminished. His genius for day-to-day improvizations was perhaps his greatest asset and shortcoming. As his friend Adamantios Pepelasis once put it,[21] his intelligence towered over that of his contemporaries but his view of the future was short-term and so was his planning. Psychological portraits drawn mainly by individuals with little sympathy for his person present him as a master of deception and the art of exploiting others.[22] Be that

---

19   Takis Pappas, "Patrons Against Partisans: The Politics of Patronage in Mass Ideological Parties", *Party Politics*, forthcoming.

20   Michalis Spourdalakis, *The Rise of the Greek Socialist Party*, London: Routledge, 1988, p. 278.

21   Interview with A. Pepelasis in 1990.

22   Manos Markoglou, *Enas symboulos tou Andrea thymatai kai apokalyptei* (An Advisor to Andreas Remembers and Reveals), Athens: Papazissis Publishers, 1989; Christina Rassia, *Theka chronia syzygos tou Andrea Papandreou* (Ten Years the Wife of Andreas Papandreou), Athens: Xenophon, 1992.

as it may, the dearth of creativity within his party was certainly his own responsibility. Political discourse was therefore impoverished throughout his years in power and his anti-intellectual heritage lives on in the Greek parliament.

The loyalty of PASOK deputies to the leader notwithstanding, Takis Pappas contends that most of them had cultivated significant clientelist bases. Despite the initial intention of the founder to create a mass organization structure that would promote internal party democracy and recruitment on an ideological, not on a patronage basis, most senior members of PASOK chose to implement laws so as to allocate state resources and services to their supporters. Papandreou did not appear to mind because he understood that any organizational strategy was expensive and time-consuming. Furthermore, "…intermediary party organizations, bolster the party institutions and formalize new rules and procedures. This meant a protracted effort full of ideological debates, intra-party disputes and factional divisions. In addition it was feared that ambitious politicians in control of crucial sections of the organization would attempt to gain autonomy vis-à-vis the party leader."[23]

When the ailing Papandreou was no longer fit to lead his party, the members of PASOK displayed a surprising instinct for survival by choosing Costas Simitis to replace the founder. Simitis, who was never Papandreou's favourite and had been on various occasions subjected to the usual humiliating treatment by the leader, not only injected PASOK with a new modernizing spirit but also attempted to wipe out the major accusation, that of populism. According to Simitis, controlling the state and the benefits it promised became the major objective of Greek populism. "Populism transfers the social problem from the plane of ideology to a level that does not disturb the status quo of social relations. The assistance of the state and the benefits derived from it is the sole objective of political struggles in Greece."[24]

The sociologist Nicos Mouzelis, an associate of Simitis, went further in the analysis of Greek populism by presenting the phenomenon as a method of vertical mass recruitment and inclusion, as well as a venue for renewal of political actors. Traditional clientelism was a much slower process for accomplishing recruitment and more conservative in preserving the status quo.[25] Nevertheless, whereas populism benefited the leader, patron-client relationships forged lasting ties between deputies and members of their constituencies. We have

---

23   Takis Pappas, "Patrons against Partisans: The Politics of Patronage in Mass Ideological Parties", *Party Politics*, forthcoming.
24   Costas Simitis, "Introduction" in N. Mouzelis *et al.*, *Laikismos kai Politiki* (Populism and Politics) Athens: Gnosi, 1989, p. 15.
25   Ibid., pp. 29-32.

already noted that populism notwithstanding, clientelism was practiced extensively by PASOK politicians.[26]

Andreas' vision of reform faltered between his Western education and the ideological creation of his own making. Had he been a modernizer he would have empowered a civil society by favouring a plurality of institutions *both opposing and balancing the state*.[27] His view of civil society however was essentially Marxist. In other words, Andreas saw civil society as a mere facade that disguised the domination of the state by the ruling class. His preference for a world free of greed and competitiveness had little impact among the prominent members of PASOK. The outcome of his half-hearted attempt to transform his flock was that the cadres he bequeathed to his successor were clientelistic and "incapable of effective enterprise".[28] During the two decades of PASOK in power, there was a resurgence of Greece's traditional "segmentary" society[29] which militated against modernization and development. In spite of Simitis' attempt to reverse this process, civil society had become a concept more alien to the average Greek than before 1981.

Civil society also suffered from Andreas' populist onslaught on trade unionism. Defining the struggle of the many non-privileged with the few privileged as the only genuine social conflict, he declared war against all elites that did not reflect the average person. He thus eradicated meritocracy from model state schools such as Varvakio and Peiramatiko in order to promote the levelling of society.

By considering parliament (under PASOK) the embodiment of popular sovereignty and therefore the blueprint of the general will, he embarked on neutralizing of those organized interests he could not control. Since PASOK did not count on a majority in the larger trade unions, it chose the atomization of their leaderships by imposing the system of proportional representation in the elections of union officials. Needless to say Andreas did not consider using proportional representation in parliamentary elections, except for barring New Democracy from power in 1989.[30] The description of the paralyzing effect

---

26 See Pappas, op.cit., *Party Politics*.

27 Ernest Gellner, *Conditions of Liberty: Civil Society and its Rivals*, London: Hamish Hamilton, 1994, p.1.

28 Ibid., p. 5.

29 "Segmentary community avoids central authority by firmly turning the individual into an integral part of the social sub-unit (the family, the clan, clientelistic networks)", op. cit., p. 8.

30 George Th. Mavrogordatos, "Civil Society Under Populism" in Richard Clogg (ed.), *Greece 1981-89. The Populist Decade*, New York: St Martin's Press, 1993, pp. 47-53.

of proportional representation on the management of trade unionism is described by George Mavrogordatos in great detail.[31] It is sufficient to note here that the ensuing system required consensual decisions that invited constant government intervention. The all-party consensus necessary for managing any outcome "resulted in the complete penetration and domination of interest associations by external party machines. Far from merely ratifying an existing state of affairs (...proportional representation) actually forced party divisions even where none existed or were relevant before, thereby destroying the cohesiveness of all associations, down to the smallest."[32] Thus, although PASOK polarized parliamentary politics, it became a champion of consensual politics in the trade unions, preserving for itself the regulatory vote of the state. A divided civil society was "passively cannibalized by the state".[33]

The transition from Andreas' unpredictable rule to Costas Simitis' orderly terms in office revealed the weakness that the movement had inherited from its maker. Once Andreas was incapacitated, the structure of his authority began to crumble. Since the question of succession remained unsettled, the rivals for the party's support were given to improvizations of transitional rule without realizing that much had changed during the leaders absense. Akis Tzochatzopoulos, who believed that his unquestioning loyalty to Andreas should be rewarded, was bitterly disappointed.

Simitis' progress from his January 1996 election by the party to replace Andreas as Prime Minister to his final triumph in the party congress of June 1996 as leader of PASOK would have been unthinkable in the heyday of the movement's populism. Populist stereotypes however proved to be ephemeral since the common voter of 1996 was not the same animal as his 1981 counterpart.[34]

An individual without a spot of corruption on his record and singularly uncharismatic, the quiet academic outfoxed the establishment of party bureaucrats. He did not however dismantle the power base of his opponents within the party, but Prime Minister he divorced his policy-making from the influence of the old guard. He was therefore free to implement his policy while they were allowed to plunder the state with impunity.

Andreas died shortly before votes for the new leader were cast in the party congress of June. George Papandreou, who replaced Simitis as leader of

---

31	Mavrogordatos, op. cit. See "Drowning in Numbers", pp. 54-61.
32	Ibid., p. 58.
33	Ibid., p. 60.
34	For the most detailed account of Simitis' transition to power, see I.K. Pretenteris, *I Defteri Metapolitefsi* (The Second Transition) Athens: Polis, 1996, pp. 211-23.

PASOK before the 2004 elections, was an unlikely person to continue his father's legacy.

Papandreou could be considered a failure in his long-term attempt to polarize politics, to inject it with his brand of populism and to maintain the cult of the leader in Greek politics. His legacy lives on in such ailing institutions as tertiary education in which his 1982 reforms implanted polarization, by introducing party politics in the university, as well as populism, by allowing teaching assistants with little qualification access to an academic career with no further competition. Be that as it may, a large segment of society has returned to the segmentary, clientelistic family-oriented practices, which they know best.

It has been argued that Andreas' major contribution to Greek politics was the empowerment of the left which had been barred from political life after the Civil War.[35] In fact, because of their youth or their intentions, none of PASOK's leading members had made their mark in socialist history before their appearance in the movement. The Liberal centre during its *tour de force* of the mid-1960s had extricated the left from its isolation and had advocated tolerance for the Communists in Greece. Andreas certainly made his own forceful advocacy of socialism and succeeded in making the concept popular with a significant part of the Greek electorate. Civil society nevertheless suffered a setback during his long term in power and the "segmentary" community had its heyday. Why did one of the most gifted Greek politicians turn his back to the role of the modernizer, for which he was well groomed, and choose to become a radical without a cause? The question lingers.

---

35 T.A. Couloumbis, "Karamanlis & Papandreou: Style & Substance of Leadership", *Yearbook*, 1988, ELIAMEP, pp. 129-49.

8

THE ETHNOGRAPHER AS THEORIST: JOHN CAMPBELL AND THE POWER OF DETAIL

Michael Herzfeld

Rodney Needham, lecturing to his students in the early 1970s, praised *Honour, Family, and Patronage* as the best ethnography of a cognatic society ever written. Surprisingly, that evaluation understates the case or, more dangerously, misconstrues the real achievement of John Campbell in turning the traditionally Africanist gaze of Oxford social anthropology on a society that belonged, albeit marginally, in the West. For many, this book has indeed served mainly as a source of insight into agonistic relations and the cosmological grounding of social mores in a society characterized by cognatic kinship reckoning; and it is indeed all of that. But it is also something arguably much more important: a demonstration that social anthropology is in important respects a historical discipline; an exploration of the disjuncture between ideology and social performance; and a superb analysis of the micro-politics of the role of patronage in securing a workable relationship between a state and some of its most marginal citizens.

It was at Evans-Pritchard's urging that Campbell made this move into Europe. Evans-Pritchard, Campbell tells us, was not particularly interested in the idea of a Mediterranean focus, nor did he relish the idea that one of his students might actually be able to learn his field language in his study before setting out.[1] But he did apparently respond with some alacrity to the idea that Campbell could study a transhumant population, the Sarakatsani, that exhibited numerous features of ecological adaptation and social interaction that were not unlike the tribal groups of East and North Africa. No doubt the

---

1 John Campbell, "Fieldwork among the Sarakatsani", in John Campbell and João de Pina-Cabral (eds), *Europe Observed*, Basingstoke: Macmillan (1992), p. 150.

doughty Africanist thought that the classically trained Campbell could thereby complete the remarkable move away from the exoticism of then current anthropology that in certain respects Evans-Pritchard himself had initiated in his *The Sanusi of Cyrenaica*, a work that Campbell acknowledges as formative (and that has under-acknowledged consequences for any serious anthropology of postcolonial European centres of power), without abandoning the classic field posture of long-suffering exposure to exotic peoples and tough conditions that was still *de rigueur* for practitioners of the discipline.[2]

Evans-Pritchard could hardly have predicted that Campbell would not only reproduce his teacher's achievement in historicizing a seemingly timeless society—long before it became fashionable to speak of "allochronism"[3]—but would also reproduce his pedagogical role in training several generations of scholars. Moreover, so determined was Campbell to demonstrate that there were some features the Sarakatsani did *not* share with the Nuer that he sometimes found it hard to accept that other Greek populations might still exhibit these features.

Campbell, however, is a far better listener than it seems Evans-Pritchard ever was, and perhaps this is one of the reasons why he was almost as influential as Evans-Pritchard himself in training a long line of students. He also went further than Evans-Pritchard in at least two respects: first, many of his students were not anthropologists and indeed some of the most distinguished, among them some of the contributors to this book, were historians; and second, his unique combination of critical reading and tolerance for intellectual differences of opinion allowed for an arguably much greater range of "refractions"—to use another Evans-Pritchardian metaphor—of the teacher's vision.

Campbell himself, as far as I am aware, has never made grand theoretical or even methodological claims for his work; in fact, he has written relatively little of a retrospective (or introspective) nature, and in his one essay devoted explicitly to his fieldwork experience he is at some pains to deny any such ambition.[4] Indeed, his personal demeanour, much like his writing style, is self-restrained and modest. Yet it is also, like all good ethnography, a performance—a performance of an intellectual identity that does not reflect some misguided colonial condescension,[5] but a deeply felt ambivalence about the promotion of the-

---

2   E.E. Evans-Pritchard, *The Sanusi of Cyrenaica*, Oxford: Clarendon Press (1949); see also Campbell, "Fieldwork", p. 149.

3   On colonialism and anthropology, see Talal Asad (ed.), *Anthropology and the Colonial Encounter*, London: Ithaca Press (1973); on allochronism, see Johannes Fabian, *Time and the Other: How Anthropology Makes its Object*, New York: Columbia University Press (1983).

4   Campbell, "Fieldwork", p. 165.

5   As at least one author would, mistakenly in my view, have us believe this of

ory to the importance it has acquired in our postmodern age.[6] Doubtless this partly reflected an almost stereotypically British reticence about the potential for innovation that Campbell can hardly have failed to sense in his own work. But it also reproduced a "blank banner", *avant la lettre*,[7] of that mediation between structure and agency, and between theory and description, that has become the hallmark of much social and cultural anthropology in the opening years of the 21st century. It also exemplifies the necessary incompleteness of any anthropological theory, which must always deal with a far higher degree of unpredictability—what today we call indeterminacy—than was then generally recognized, or than we see even today in the natural sciences.

Campbell demonstrated his interpretations by paying close attention to matters of detail. Take the description (itself a source of some embarrassment to him) of how Sarakatsan women never run for fear of tripping and thereby, through self-exposure, fatally damaging their reputations. This modest vignette is a treasure trove of remarkable conjunctures. First, as I noted some years ago,[8] it exemplifies the ways in which personal actions and patterns reproduce larger social phenomena, so that in this case the protection of sexual propriety parallels the defensive posture of the Greek state itself in what I have since come to label "cultural intimacy".[9] It shows how the body registers ideology, especially with regard to gender; this particular focus was to become a major *topos* of the ethnography of Greece, and thus also of the dawning realization

---

Evans-Pritchard; see Renato Rosaldo, "From the Door of His Tent: The Fieldworker and the Inquisitor", in James Clifford and George E. Marcus (eds), *Writing Culture: The Poetics and Politics of Ethnography*, Berkeley: University of California Press (1986), pp. 77-97.

6   The relationship between epistemology and stereotypes is both fascinating and complex. In the 1960s, for example, a distinguished British archaeologist castigated the Anglo-Saxon anti-intellectualism of his colleagues, a stance that, he suggested, resulted in their rejecting the very possibility that earlier inhabitants of the British Isles could have been capable of innovation! See Grahame Clark, "The Invasion Hypothesis in British Archaeology", *Antiquity*, 40 (1966), pp. 172-89.

7   See Edwin Ardener, "Introductory Essay: Social Anthropology and Language", in Edwin Ardener (ed.), *Social Anthropology and Language* (ASA Monographs, 10), London: Tavistock (1971), p. xliv.

8   Michael Herzfeld, *Anthropology through the Looking-Glass: Critical Ethnography in the Margins of Europe*, Cambridge University Press (1987), p. 67. The original passage is in John Campbell, *Honour, Family, and Patronage: A Study of Institutions and Moral Values in a Greek Montain Community*, Oxford: Clarendon Press (1964), p. 287.

9   Michael Herzfeld, *Cultural Intimacy: Social Poetics in the Nation-State*, 2nd edition, New York: Routledge (2005).

that ethnography done in that land so curiously and paradoxically Western and non-Western at one and the same time could speak to the burning theoretical issues of the late 20th century. And although much other work on the training of the body owes (as far as I know) nothing directly to Campbell's example,[10] it is construed in a tradition to which his students did contribute and in which their own students may in turn have been more strongly influenced by Campbell's focus on the moral economy of the body than was apparent at the time.

Since the book was published, many things have changed—not least, to be sure, the lifestyle and status of the Sarakatsani about whom Campbell wrote. One of the largest changes, however, is the growing acceptability of Europeanist work in anthropology (and, conversely, of anthropological research among scholars of European culture and society, although that, alas, is a slower process). To this, the publication of *Honour, Family, and Patronage* undoubtedly made an enormous and indeed decisive contribution, taking as its subject-matter one of the most marginal-seeming societies in a nation-state that itself was constrained by its exclusion from the corridors of autonomous *Realpolitik* and that, by virtue of precisely this marginality, demanded answers to inconvenient questions about the nature of political patronage between nation-states as much as between individuals.

One might almost say that this was such a classic anthropological move—ethnography from the outer edges of power and hence a commentary on the way that power defines its centre—that it was virtually invisible to the non-anthropological Europeanists of its time. Unlike Edmund Leach and Mary Douglas, who with genial impudence applied models derived from supposedly primitive societies to what they revealed as the equally irrational and symbolic worlds of technologically advanced groups,[11] Campbell quietly slipped across the line that divides the West from the Rest and as quietly announced—or, rather, persuasively demonstrated—that this line really did not exist except as an ideological construct, albeit one with tremendous consequences.

This quiet revolution came at a crucial moment for anthropology. Indeed, it was far more important than anyone realized at the time; it was in the vanguard

---

10 See especially Susan Brownell, *Training the Body for China: Sports in the Moral Order of the People's Republic*, University of Chicago Press (1995); Dorinne K. Kondo, *Crafting Selves: Power, Gender, and Discourses of Identity in a Japanese Workplace*, University of Chicago Press (1990); Trevor Hugh James Marchand, *Minaret Building and Apprenticeship in Yemen*, Richmond: RoutledgeCurzon (2001); Loïc Wacquant, *Body and Soul: Notebooks of an Apprentice Boxer*, Oxford University Press (2004).

11 See especially Mary Douglas, *How Institutions Think*, Syracuse University Press (1986); Edmund Leach, *A Runaway World?* New York: Oxford University Press (1967).

of something that was happening with a great deal less fanfare than the critique of colonialism and the so-called "reflexive turn". For the only really effective way to undermine the colonialist underpinnings of anthropology and the particular embroilment of Evans-Pritchard's heritage in the peculiarities of warring British political factions and prejudices was in fact to start doing fieldwork in Europe.[12] Campbell was by no means the first to do ethnographic research in the continent; some, such as Arensberg,[13] had done it far closer to the centres of colonial power, although in a society that was also effectively colonial.[14] But what made his work different was that it imported into Europe a model that was in fact already being subjected to a good deal of internal critique of its colonialist underpinnings by the very school that had created it—the so-called "Oxford structuralists". He thus imported with a seemingly imperial model of otherness a sensitivity to the absurdity of such prejudicial positions—a sensitivity that was to lead him to show both more interest in folklore than many of his contemporaries or immediate successors (he cites numerous songs, tales, and rituals) and considerable impatience with the nationalistic discipline that the study of folklore had become in Greece itself. In *Honour, Family, and Patronage*, moreover, he initiates an analysis of that relationship, not only with regard to Greece, but also among its neighbours—although Wace and Thomson had already identified "political philology" as an irredentist game in the Balkans.[15]

Because the British elite was an obvious, easy, and in some respects entirely justifiable target for post-colonial criticism, its doubts and self-critique were too often overlooked in the rush to judgment, and the more interesting consequences of its expansion—again, and here especially, including Campbell's work—do not appear at all in much of the "critical anthropology" literature. Indeed, anthropologists in general acted as though there were no theoretically productive ethnography being done in the European context, suggesting that its practitioners must necessarily be theoretical followers rather than leaders.

---

12   On the influence of British political theory on Evans-Pritchard's thinking, see Henrika Kuklick, "Tribal Exemplars: Images of Political Authority in British Anthropology, 1855-1945", *in* George W. Stocking (ed.), *Functionalism Historicized: Essays on British Social Anthropology*, Madison: University of Wisconsin Press, 1984, pp. 59-82.

13   Conrad Maynadier Arensberg, *The Irish Countryman: An Anthropological Study*, New York: Macmillan (1937).

14   See, much more recently, Begoña Aretxaga, *Shattering Silence: Women, Nationalism, and Political Subjectivity in Northern Ireland*, Princeton University Press (1997).

15   A.J.B. Wace and M.S. Thompson, *Nomads of the Balkans*, London: Methuen (1914), p. 9.

Superficially, perhaps, Campbell's work might appear to justify this criticism. The form of *Honour, Family, and Patronage* follows, in a compact but therefore also more identifiable variant, the essentially Durkheimian format of Evans-Pritchard's work. But in fact Campbell parts company from Evans-Pritchard in subtle but important ways. His Sarakatsani do not organize their perception of nature entirely on the basis of their existing social relations, as Evans-Pritchard's Nuer appear to do; the Nuer, for example, imagine the natural and spiritual world as divided up into entities exactly like the sub-units of their agnatic clan structure.[16] When Evans-Pritchard tells us that he has offered "a short excursion into sociological theory",[17] he is speaking less of theory in the usual sense than of a model, largely Durkheimian in inspiration, through which the more conventionally theoretical construct of the "total social fact" will be revealed through careful examination of the articulation of cosmology with social organization.

For Campbell, by contrast, cosmology is as crucial to understanding the dynamics of social relations—especially with regard to the *breaking* of rules—as it is determinative of its form. To be sure, Evans-Pritchard's splendid metaphor of "refraction" is present in the idea that divine grace is fractured through the various hostilities and rivalries of social life, but the existence of such hostilities is in turn the product of a cosmological principle, the doctrine of Original Sin. Where for Evans-Pritchard the divine essence, or *Kwoth*, is refracted through the social and material world in a multiplicity of such essences (*kuth*), a phenomenon that is certainly reproduced in the Orthodox Christian world of local saints and icons,[18] Campbell refused the reductionism that the more extreme forms of Durkheimian sociocentrism entail. More interested in the way that cosmology informs social understandings of time and place, he generated an approach that has been consistently more willing to concede to local theologies a central role in defining and shaping social experience.[19]

---

16 See, for example, E.E. Evans-Pritchard, *Nuer Religion*, Oxford: Clarendon Press (1956), pp. 116-17, where there is also a helpful illustration of the refraction metaphor.

17 E.E. Evans-Pritchard, *The Nuer: A Description of the Modes of Livelihood and Political Institutions of a Nilotic People*, Oxford: Clarendon Press (1940), p. 266.

18 See Richard and Eva Blum, *The Dangerous Hour: The Lore of Crisis and Mystery in Rural Greece*, London: Chatto & Windus (1970), pp. 79-80; Michael Herzfeld, "Icons and Identity: Religious Orthodoxy and Social Practice in Rural Crete", *Anthropological Quarterly* 63 (1990), pp. 109-21.

19 See Juliet du Boulay, *Portrait of a Greek Mountain Village*, Oxford: Clarendon Press (1974); Laurie Kain Hart, *Time, Religion, and Social Experience in Rural Greece*, Lanham, MD: Rowman & Littlefield (1992); Charles Stewart, *Demons and the Devil: Moral Imagination in Modern Greek Culture*, Princeton

THE ETHNOGRAPHER AS THEORIST

Does this move make Campbell a theorist? Only those who embrace a fundamentally Cartesian position would insist on the conceptual separation of theory from practice, so perhaps the question makes little sense and should be reformulated thus: what are the theoretical implications of Campbell's treatment of cosmology? Because of the modest framing of *Honour, Family, and Patronage*, few have sought to include Campbell in a theoretical lineage. His emphasis on cosmology as a source of order, rather than its product, has been largely confined to the Greek and a few other southern European ethnographies,[20] and this has had a parochializing effect on its impact on the discipline as a whole. It has been confined by the larger failure of Europeanist work, until very recently, to break out of its intellectual ghetto. Scholars who work in societies without organized, literary schools of theology could easily dismiss such work as irrelevant to their concerns.

The work of Charles Stewart,[21] in particular, suggests why such a dismissal is wrongheaded. Stewart has consistently and persuasively argued against the conceptual separation of church doctrine from folk practice in Greece, suggesting that these apparently antithetical idioms of religiosity share common origins and concerns, and that it is only the former's hegemonic proclivities that have permitted and even reinforced the idea that "folk religion" somehow represents an inferior domain. Stewart's argument should in turn lead us to look for doctrinal principles even in societies that completely lack literate priesthoods claiming the authority to define such doctrines, and to ask how far those doctrines might determine the shape of social interaction.

In this regard, the conceptual position represented by Campbell is closer to the "practice theory" of writers such as Bourdieu (1977) and Giddens (1984) than is usually recognized. It is more usual to see him as a derivative "Oxford structuralist" than as someone who recognizes and even celebrates the dialectical relationship between the seeming fixity of social structure and the inventiveness of ordinary people. Campbell did not himself articulate such a position, to be sure, but he was attracted to it; when I was his student, he urged me to pay attention to the work that Loizos and others, to some extent following Bourdieu, were doing on "matrimonial strategies".[22] Yet his own work

---

University Press (1991).

20 See, most notably, João de Pina-Cabral, *Sons of Adam, Daughters of Eve: The Peasant Worldview of the Alto Minho*, Oxford: Clarendon Press (1986).

21 See Stewart, *Demons and the Devil*; also Charles Stewart, "Hegemony or Rationality? The Position of the Supernatural in Modern Greece", *Journal of Modern Greek Studies* 7 (1989), pp. 77 ff.

22 Peter Loizos, "Changes in Property Transfer among Greek Villagers", *Man* (n.s.) 10 (1975), pp. 503-23.

went further than Bourdieu's in recognizing that a doctrine of seemingly great antiquity would exercise a correspondingly powerful influence on the shaping of everyday social experience. Hirschon's work on the persistence of Orthodox concepts in the organization of social space even among supposedly atheist urbanites wonderfully extends this principle in another anti-Cartesian move, that of rejecting the conceptual dualism implied by the genesis of a discrete sub-speciality of "urban anthropology".[23]

At the same time, Campbell was also attentive to the secular cosmology that we call "nationalism". Like Evans-Pritchard situating his work in the context of the British colonial administration, Campbell situated his analysis of Sarakatsan social life within the geographical and ideological parameters of nationalist arguments about origins. The Sarakatsani were, and are, speakers of Greek, and this fact has a rather peculiar effect on their relationship with the core population of the nation-state.[24] At the same time, uncertainties about their origins allowed representatives of the Romanian and Greek state ideologies to make historicist claims based on dubious renditions of "political philology". Campbell realized that such claims had real political consequences, even though, in accordance with the habits of the time, he regarded much of the ethnological nostalgia of the folklorists with a jaundiced eye.

There is no point in trying to argue that *Honour, Family, and Patronage* is primarily a work of theory. It offers no such pretensions; its rich ethnography would be slighted by such a claim; and its theoretical significance is easier to perceive by hindsight than in any explicit claims made by its authors. But there is a powerful sense in which its theoretical impact on the discipline, actually and potentially, reproduces in an ironic instantiation the type of theory that it most fully, I suggest, embodies: an emergent theory of practice. We should not forget, after all, that John Campbell and Pierre Bourdieu both moved within the orbit of Mediterranean scholarship fostered by J.G. Peristiany.

Nonetheless, such a characterization calls for further explanation. *Honour, Family, and Patronage* has clearly exercised a great influence on subsequent ethnographic research in southern Europe and elsewhere, both through John Campbell's direct teaching of his many students and through the book's circulation as an exemplary study of a cognatic society. Thus the way in which the book generates theoretical insight is, as practice theorists like to say,[25] *emergent*

---

23 See Renée Hirschon, *Heirs of the Greek Catastrophe: The Social Life of Asia Minor Refugees in Piraeus*, Oxford: Clarendon Press (1989), p. 233.

24 See Muriel Dimen Schein, "When is an Ethnic Group? Ecology and Class Structure in Northern Greece", *Ethnology* 14, pp. 83-97.

25 See, for example, Ivan Karp, "Agency and Social Theory: A Review of Giddens", *American Ethnologist* 13 (1986), pp. 131-7.

in the actual production of intellectual knowledge. It does not offer a prior template for the working out of specific problems, nor does it provide a formal set of explanations capable of being reproduced across a wide array of the world's societies. Instead, its advance on the Oxford structuralism to which it is usually attributed *emerges* in reading and emulation.

In this respect, its impact is curiously consistent with practice theory itself: rather than offering new theory as a framework, it repays later re-readings with a growing sense of how its author articulated a complex dynamic that cannot be produced through the sociocentric methods of the structural-functionalists. While some of this shift is already present in Evans-Pritchard, whose rejection of his own mentor Radcliffe-Brown's anti-historical emphasis on the "nomothetic" potential of anthropology was itself a profoundly anti-positivistic theoretical move, Campbell's achievement is more subtle and is more directly grounded in the peculiar historical contingency of having worked in a European society, on the very margins of the colonial project that initially generated anthropology itself.

Such ethnographic reworkings of theoretical positions have traditionally been of great significance in the history of social anthropology itself. Another illuminating example is provided by Nur Yalman's *Under the Bo Tree*, an exemplary demonstration that structuralists could (so to speak) structure an ethnography.[26] This was an achievement precisely because it would hitherto have seemed to be a contradiction in terms. In a strikingly similar way, *Honour, Family, and Patronage*, while cast in the classic format of an Oxford structuralist monograph, shows how the writing of ethnography could generate the right kind of theory-practice synergy in ways that go far beyond classic structural-functionalism.

It is true that Campbell, faithful to the conventions of anthropological writing in which he was trained, often seems to generalize about ideal-typical postures, especially with regard to gender roles. But that characterization would be misleading. Not only does he often illustrate his generalizations with vivid ethnographic examples that permit a critical resistance (and that help to historicize the otherwise timeless shepherds), but he also shows, without using the language of social poetics as such, that many of these scenes are indeed performances of moral norms. He also captures the underlying ambiguity that makes such multiple interpretations possible; for example, in describing the affective bond between mother and son as both occasionally tense but always one of complete solidarity, he delicately points up the tension between a mother's pride in her son's masculinity and her disapproval of some of the escapades in

---

26 Nur Yalman, *Under the Bo Tree: Studies in Caste, Kinship, and Marriage in the Interior of Ceylon*, Berkeley: University of California Press (1967).

which it inevitably involves him.²⁷ He thus shows us the domestic source of one of the most important areas of ambiguity and contingency in social relations on the larger stages on which men, in particular, must constantly perform. In a society where no one is sure that others are what they seem to be (Campbell is a master at documenting the lack of fit between appearances and the realities they are performed to obscure), the public display of adherence to a formal role is socially often more important than the precise calibration of one's real actions to it. When a Sarakatsan throws a stone to alert another man that he is being observed as he cruelly beats his daughter, the ethnographer is treated to a performance of discretion and secrecy, and soon comes to appreciate that secrecy is an end in itself; indeed, a reputation for secretiveness is an enviable one in many societies in which resources are similarly the objects of sometimes violent competition.²⁸ In short, performance trumps instrumental efficiency, especially in a society in which the idea that others' motives are unknowable is as axiomatic as is the assumption that most people's motives are of the lowest. Passages such as these illustrate a richness in Campbell's ethnography that, in my view, sets a standard of meticulous attention to detail that is difficult to achieve even with the modern recording methods that he either eschewed or simply did not have the opportunity to enjoy. Yet such detail, as the Greek anthropologist Efthymios Papataxiarchis has recently remarked, is essential to understanding the ways in which, at widely differing levels of social integration, a sense of unchallengeable collective identity is produced and reproduced.

Indeed, Paptaxiarchis has perceptively offered this comment: "First of all, this material, transcending the 'surface level' of studying the content of collective identity, contributes to our understanding of the symbolic mechanisms of culturally determined means by means of which identities are assembled at different scales of integration."²⁹

---

27   Campbell, *Honour, Family, and Patronage*, p. 168. This passage offers a classic example of Campbell's remarkable ability to offer a generalization based on locally expressed norms while also hinting at the forces that offer individual actors in comparable situations a range of possible responses. It is this contingent variability that allows for the play of reputation and gossip; Sarakatsani understand perfectly that no two individuals will interpret the prevailing norms in identical ways, or follow them to a similar degree.

28   Campbell, *Honour, Family, and Patronage*, pp. 190, 192.

29   Evthymios Papataxiarchis, "Ta akhthi tis eterotitas: Dhiastasis tis Politismikis Dhiaforopiisis stin Elladha tou proimou 21ou eona", in Evthymios Papataxiarchis (ed.), *Peripeties tis Eterotitas: I Paraghoyi tis Politismikis Dhiaforas sti Simerini Elladha*, Athens: Alexandreia (2006), pp. 1-85, and especially p. 26.

THE ETHNOGRAPHER AS THEORIST

These identities are emergent in the performance of identities of various kinds, and are beset, as Campbell realized from the start, with ambiguity and contingency—the very features of social life that give substance to agonistic social relations, because they encourage ceaseless conflict over interpretation. Thus, downcast eyes do not necessarily mean chastity, and may not be accepted as evidence of a good character; but an impudent stare would completely undo any good that chastity might otherwise have achieved. Moreover, a mother's inappropriate laughter can ruin even her relatively modest daughter's reputation, as Campbell notes.[30] Juliet du Boulay, another Campbell student, elaborated on this theme, while yet another, Renée Hirschon, showed how the same attitudes pervade even "sophisticated" Greek society, providing a cultural specificity for which a globally dominant morality of more Calvinist inspiration has much less tolerance.[31]

Body posture, then, is the performance of a moral claim. In it, moreover, the principles articulated are sufficiently conventional to make any substantial departure from them worthy of (usually derogatory) comment. Thus Campbell's description of the way a woman will milk ewes, gently persuading them to accept the lambs of ewes that had died in childbirth as their own,[32] provides a kind of benchmark. What he does not specifically say is that some women might be able to exaggerate this performance in ways that elicit approving comment but could also presumably raise the suspicion of an intention to disguise a lewd or aggressive personality—just as men who push the edges of normative public aggression both risk censure for going too far and yet also earn praise for daring to risk precisely that outcome. This is the play of convention and invention that I have called "social poetics", in a language that owes more to Jakobsonian-derived semiotics than to Oxford social anthropology, and that also emerges in the emphasis on contingency in Thomas Malaby's work on gambling in a Cretan town.[33] It emerges forcefully and clearly from the ethnographic subtleties of Campbell's portrayals. While it is true that Evans-Pritchard himself emphasized the play of "idiom" and reality, notably in the politics

---

30 Campbell, *Honour, Family, and Patronage*, p. 169.

31 Juliet du Boulay, *Portrait of a Greek Village*; Renée Hirschon in this volume and "Greek Adults' Play, or, How to Train for Caution", *Journal of Modern Greek Studies* 10 (1992), pp. 35-56. See also the extended discussion of apprentices' training in Michael Herzfeld, *The Body Impolitic: Artisans and Artifice in the Global Hierarchy of Value*, University of Chicago Press (2004).

32 Campbell, *Honour, Family, and Patronage*, p. 32.

33 Thomas M. Malaby, *Gambling Life: Dealing in Contingency in a Greek City*, Urbana: University of Illinois Press (2003).

of agnatic self-identification, Campbell takes this far beyond kinship and into the realms of gender, politics, and ritual.

Yet the Evans-Pritchardian influence was also a burden. It provided a context of comparison that was not entirely favourable to the development of anthropological interest in European societies. If Campbell's influence has been largely overlooked outside the rather introspective world of Europeanist anthropology, it is, I suggest, the result of a historical accident: anthropology's move into Europe anticipated by a couple of decades the emergence of a more fashionable kind of disciplinary self-awareness and was not immediately connected to it. Had the call for greater reflexivity emerged before anthropologists began working on European themes in earnest, rather than as an eccentric minority, Campbell's work would very possibly have been seen instead as pioneering the anthropological examination of Europe as a political and cultural construct, and might well have formed part of the genealogy of the emergent call for critical awareness of the discipline's own place among the phenomena it studies.

One effect of this understated and unrecognized consequentiality is that, while Campbell is rarely cited as a source of theoretical innovation, much of what he—and others following with a similarly cautious sense of criticism in the footsteps of Evans-Pritchard—did with the complex inter-relationships of ecology, social order, and cosmology became the received wisdom of his students and of their own pupils. Because Europeanist work was regarded as a minor luxury by most anthropologists, one will rarely find *Honour, Family, and Patronage* mentioned in work done outside Europe (or, more broadly, the circum-Mediterranean world). One of the few anthropologists to take the specifically theoretical implications of Campbell's work seriously, Robert Paine,[34] was himself partly a Europeanist, concerned with societies—especially the Norwegian Sami—that were, and are, as marginal to the centres of power as were the Sarakatsani.

Paine is predominantly a "transactionalist", in that his approach is representative of the work developed late in the heyday of the Manchester School,[35] and he is thus, like Campbell, an early advocate of focusing on what came to be called "practice". More particularly, he focused on what he called "high-wire politics"—the performative maintenance of a pose of courting danger by distorting or flouting the rules of society. Such actions, which are commonly as-

---

34   Robert Paine, "High-Wire Culture: comparing Two Agonistic Systems of Self-Esteem", *Man* (n.s.) 24 (1989), pp. 328-39.

35   See Bruce Kapferer (ed.), *Transaction and Meaning: Directions in the Anthropology of Exchange and Symbolic Behavior*, Philadelphia, Institute for the Study of Human Issues (1976).

sociated with demonstrative forms of masculinity around the world,[36] not only assign a high value to risk-taking; they instantiate it. A dancer who aggressively courts potential disaster by testing the limits of his athleticism, a raconteur who embroiders his stories with barely believable spice, a villager who challenges the power of the educated and the well-connected: these actions all entail both enhanced rewards for success and a correspondingly high risk of failure.

Paine's essay, which draws its Greek material from *Honour, Family, and Patronage*, introduces a strong comparative element by bringing in the parallel case of the Marri Baluchi of western Pakistan. Paine had already demonstrated a considerable interest in theoretical issues associated with the negotiation of power in everyday social interactions, so that this piece became part of his own contribution to anthropological theory. Yet it is clear that it owes a great deal to Campbell's ethnographic description and analysis, as Paine himself is careful to acknowledge. Those of us who, unlike Paine, worked in Greece may have missed this dimension of theoretical potential, since what we saw was a pattern already described by Campbell and thus domesticated for us by his expert description. My own focus on the agonistics of animal-theft, Malaby's description of how coffee-house waiters embody the tension between high-wire performance and the fear of embarrassing failure, and Cowan's vivid account of how gender ideologies are tested to the extreme in dance events among an emergent northern Greek bourgeoisie all illustrate the same set of principles.[37] All of us, I suggest, found more theoretical explicitness in our local informants' commentaries than we did at first in Campbell's own account.

Yet the hidden arguments in that account are crucially important. Consider, for example, Campbell's descriptions of male braggadocio, especially in the face of agonistic challenges. Campbell pointed out that men would take care to ensure that their particularly aggressive outbursts of threats of violence would take place in the company of unrelated men. These men (and occasionally women) could be counted on to intervene in any rapidly escalating dispute, not only, I suggest, to avert homicide and all the complications that it would entail, but also to provide the protagonists with a culturally plausible excuse for *not* pursuing their goal of revenge to its fatal conclusion.

---

[36] A very useful general overview, although of decidedly functionalist cast, is to be found in David D. Gilmore, *Manhood in the Making: Cultural Concepts of Masculinity*, New Haven: Yale University Press (1990).

[37] Jane K. Cowan, *Dance and the Body Politic in Northern Greece*, Princeton University Press (1990), pp. 171-205; Michael Herzfeld, *The Poetics of Manhood: Contest and Identity in a Cretan Mountain Village*, Princeton University Press, pp. 163-205; Malaby, *Gambling Life*, pp. 76-92, 134-5.

As one of my Cretan informants expressed it, "When you hold someone back, he can afford to be brave!"[38]

All of this is clearly present in Campbell's description, especially the recognition by informants and anthropologist alike that the display of defiant masculinity relies on the presence of a restraining audience. Campbell thus acknowledges the role of local recognition in his own perception of this dynamic. He does not offer it as a social theory in any formal sense. In his precise and measured prose, however, we can see clearly that his Sarakatsan interlocutors were quite articulate about the social principle in question, and were prepared to generalize it. They could interpret each such action as part of a pattern of self-regard in which saving face is at least as important as exacting vengeance. What Campbell significantly did was to extract these implications from the flow of everyday activity and render them accessible as a heuristic and comparative model.

Moreover, while Paine emphasizes the aspect of high-wire risk-taking in agonistic social relations, and while he certainly acknowledged the importance of the audience in generating reputation out of such performances, he did not dwell on another aspect of Campbell's treatment of such encounters: the realization that the risk might not always be as great as appears, and that, in fact, the very witnesses for whom the key actors produce these performances are also the guarantors and managers of the *limits* to that risk. They know perfectly well that it is their presence that both legitimates and defuses the angry display of violent intentions and provides the protagonists with an excuse for their eventual failure to draw blood.

Campbell has himself reflected on the implications of his analyses of Greek masculinity for an understanding of the actions of the guerrillas, or *kleftes* (klephts), who were supposedly the backbone of the Greek struggle for independence.[39] In this respect, he attempted a form of diachronic comparison. I do not intend here to engage the usual arguments about whether the *kleftes*' primary interests were in national independence, but rather want to suggest that their opportunism—derided by many of the Philhellenes who sought to stiffen

---

38 See Campbell, *Honour, Family, and Patronage*, p. 97; Herzfeld, *Poetics of Manhood*, pp. 51, 61.

39 J.K. Campbell, "The Greek Hero", in J.G. Peristiany and Julian Pitt-Rivers (eds), *Honor and Grace in Anthropology*, Cambridge University Press (1992), pp. 129-49. He also addressed the issue of solidarity and nationalism in an important but brief piece, "Regionalism and Local Community", in Muriel Dimen and Ernestine Friedl (eds), *Regional Variation in Modern Greece and Cyprus*, in *Annals of the New York Academy of Sciences* 268 (1976), pp. 18-27.

their backbone by joining the cause[40]—similarly relied on a greater concern for avoiding death than most accounts recognize. Much has been made of the slogan "Freedom or Death" in the official historiography of Greek independence; any attempt to question this slogan is seen as a slur on the national cause. Yet it is abundantly clear that many *kleftes* were not even Greek-speaking, and that their primary loyalties were more local and more redolent of the self-interest (*simferon*) that is also a major topic in *Honour, Family, and Patronage*. They thus were understandably reluctant to expose themselves to what they saw as the foolish heroism and unproductive innocence of the foreign Philhellenes. Campbell understood this reasoning and explained it with great clarity:

> At first sight this mode of warfare may seem less than heroic; yet it is individual irregular warfare in which the warrior moved and decided his own path, balancing his courage, his prudence, and technical prowess with his gun. The safety and survival of the captain, whose name and personality stood for the continuity of the band, were a first concern and therefore his position was generally carefully concealed. Yet he had to exhort and inspire his men by his vocal and personal encouragement. As in the case of a head of family in the civil society of the village his loss threatened the dissolution of the group. And it was the task of the young *pallikari* hero, not the leader, to die if that sacrifice was necessary.[41]

After-the-fact canonization was another matter, since this formed part of the strategy of survival in the new realities created by the foundation of the nation-state and its opportunistic calibration to the values and historical vision of its Western patrons—it was, indeed, an extension of the unctuous self-abasement that is so central a part of the performance of clientage at the local level. At the time of the conflict with the Ottoman forces, however, many of the *kleftes* were more interested in both saving their own lives and enriching themselves and their families than in dying for an abstract and, from their perspective, hopelessly quixotic cause. That their performances of devil-may-care heroism outlived any memory of their pragmatism owes more to their success in capturing the imagination of those in power at the end of the conflict than it does to any widespread willingness to place their lives at real risk, although on occasion, when it seemed appropriate, they were willing to do so.

The historiographic adumbration of the *kleftes* to an ideology of heroism is thus very much like the invocation of fate in their own cultural universe: they do not resign themselves to the inevitability of disaster in advance, but their admirers invoke overwhelming external forces to explain that disaster once it has happened and clearly cannot be reversed. In social life, the attention that Sarakatsani

---

40 See especially William St. Clair, *That Greece Might Still Be Free: The Philhellenes in the War of Independence*, London: Oxford University Press (1972).

41 Campbell, "The Greek Hero", p. 140.

(and Cretans) pay to the audience context is not merely a way of avoiding death, and Campbell emphasizes that the survival of a male household head is also a matter of protecting his immediate family from the ridicule and opprobrium that a heedless death would surely bring in its train. Campbell's willingness to explain a historically puzzling pattern by reference to values shared with a population studied in modern times is not reductive; but it is theoretically valuable precisely because it removes analysis from the simplifications of both nationalist hagiography and supercilious foreign incomprehension.

This is only possible because the enabling ethnographic case is presented with such meticulous care. Once again, the abstract principle is instantiated in the action: just as the performance of risk-taking itself instantiates the risk itself (since the performance can always fail), so, too, reliance on bystanders' intervention not only reduces the risk of sudden death but also performs the awareness of a man's responsibility to his family *not* to die because of his heedless pride.

Campbell's writing captures this dual contingency with remarkable clarity. He shows us both the realities of risk that all agonistic encounters entail and the audience participation that, in fact, limits the real dangers while colluding in perpetuating their apparent significance. The fact that he is then able to transfer that insight to a historical case suggests that, while he has little interest in the kind of Radcliffe-Brownian generalization that he had been taught to abjure, he perceives in these transhistorical parallels something of a heuristic model, capable of generating new insights. This is what also allows him, in the same essay as that in which he discusses the *kleftes*' mode of warfare, to discuss a similar range of values and attendant actions in the *Iliad*. Unlike nationalistic folklorists, who sought evidence of unbroken cultural continuity and used that evidence to support irredentist claims, Campbell was interested in discovering what concepts of responsibility the comparison might yield, especially—but not necessarily—given evidence for social continuity between the two societies in question over a very long period of time. In this concern with responsibility, here specifically confined to the ideal-typical figure of the male hero, he was also working very much within an Evans-Pritchardian paradigm.[42] There is one important difference, which springs from Campbell's specific focus on the heroic: his knowledge of the long European tradition and of the vernacular songs of the modern Greeks gave his analysis a philological richness that few anthropologists have ever matched.

Campbell himself never, to the best of my knowledge, sought to generalize these insights to a larger geographical frame of reference as Robert Paine has

---

42 See, in particular, E.E. Evans-Pritchard, *Oracles, Witchcraft and Magic among the Azande*, Oxford: Clarendon Press (1937).

done. Paine, in focusing more one-sidedly on the risk of death, de-emphasizes the factors that actually lessen that risk, and thus loses some of the subtlety of Campbell's analysis of local social calculation. Paine seems to have been concerned to address an aspect of social relations that could be contrasted with the "Western" fear of contingency on the one hand and discovered in the contexts of very different gender ideologies on the other, and this was a worthwhile exercise in its own right, intelligently executed and elegantly presented. It did, however, rather unfortunately occlude the *limits* of risk to which Campbell was so subtly attentive. What he did achieve, as few others have done, was to show the relevance of Campbell's work for the understanding of very different social and geographical contexts. If, then, we return to Campbell's text, but now with Paine's comparative perspective in mind, we may be able to articulate a heuristic theoretical proposition that will generate new perspectives far beyond the confines of Greece.

Such a move was not a concern at the time of Campbell's fieldwork. He amply documents the almost anti-theoretical stance of Evans-Pritchard—itself, I suspect, a somewhat self-consciously mannered extension of British understatement and distrust of the obviously cerebral (see, for another example of this, Leach's distinctly Anglocentric commentary on the intellectual acrobatics of Lévi-Strauss).[43] But since the publication of *Honour, Family, and Patronage* there have been numerous developments that have made such protestations of intellectual innocence untenable. Prominent among these is the now widespread interest in an anthropology of the body, reviving an old concern in a modern intellectual universe. This focus is particularly strongly articulated in the writings of Jane Cowan and Thomas Malaby, both already mentioned.

In addition to a Maussian heritage transmitted in the works of Evans-Pritchard and Campbell himself,[44] these authors were evidently influenced by some of the new work emerging on the anthropology of the body, notably in American medical anthropology, and by the rise in the 1970s of a more attentive anthropological concern with gender. I have engaged with both these former students of mine over long years and learned a great deal from their insights. It is important to signal the "genealogical" connection here, if only because it underscores the formative role played by Campbell's original work; as I have already noted, he was already attentive to bodily stance, at a time in the history of our discipline when he himself was (as I can ruefully recall) quite sceptical about the utility of electronic equipment of any sort. His deep sensitivity to

---

43   Edmund Leach, *Claude Lévi-Strauss*, London: Fontana/Collins (1970). See also my comments in note 5, above.

44   That heritage is also instantiated in both authors' close attention to the ecological fact of seasonal change and its impact on the forms of social life.

his informants' preoccupations nevertheless led him to a nuanced appreciation of how the carriage of the body—whether as an expression of chastity, a demonstration of virile aggression, or in a staged performance of restrained violence such as I have just been discussing—both expressed and articulated an underlying ideology of personhood. Here again we see how his work displays an awareness of the double articulation of a morally inflected cultural form with the play of risk and avoidance, here displayed in bodily comportment and understood as such by local informants. This dimension of his work is particularly innovative in relation to Evans-Pritchard's ethnographic writings. Whether one wishes to attribute theoretical sophistication to Campbell's Sarakatsan informants or to Campbell himself is perhaps immaterial; his preference for backgrounding his own role in the formulation of this vivid account effectively pushes into the foreground the embodied production of images in the social interactions of his Sarakatsan interlocutors. Even Cowan's nuanced account of the relationship between gender ideology and embodied movement would not be so persuasive had Campbell not burned into our inner consciousness images of the Sarakatsan woman who does not run for fear of exposing herself; of the eccentric male who rips his shirt into shreds at weddings; or of a woman's harshly incontinent laughter that burdens her daughter with an unwanted inheritance of ridicule.

Campbell's contribution to anthropological theory thus continues, for the moment, to be most palpable in work conducted in his old stamping grounds, in Greece. As it diffuses outward, its already somewhat muted articulation will presumably become more diffuse, mingling with concerns of which anthropologists of the 1950s and 1960s had not remotely dreamed, but to which John Campbell's intellectual generosity makes his theoretical contribution especially germane. Given the new respectability of Europeanist work, however, it is to be hoped that his distinctive contributions, as I have tried to outline them here, will be given their due outside the narrow confines of a geographical specialization.

If there is something slightly defensive in his insistence that "the discipline was conscious of itself but not yet self-conscious, not yet given to questioning the validity of what it was doing", and that "the significance of theoretical discourse for most anthropologists was its usefulness to give precision to the structural abstractions they hoped to achieve in the interpretation of their field material",[45] this should not obscure either the theoretical importance of his own contribution or the independence and originality he displayed in pushing the frontiers of anthropological imagination beyond the genealogical limits of an Africanist sensibility. By bringing Africanist models of ethnography into the

---

45   Campbell, "Fieldwork", p. 149.

THE ETHNOGRAPHER AS THEORIST

domestic space of Europe, albeit at its outer edges, and by gently nudging his readers toward a rethinking of the theoretical postures that had undergirded his original ethnographic project, he has already exercised a far greater influence on the theoretical pluralism of anthropology than his own personal modesty would ever allow him to claim. But if, in the end, his greatest contribution was to set extraordinary standards for the writing of ethnography, who would wish to argue that this was a lesser achievement? Paradoxically, however, this was an achievement of theory as much as of ethnography. It rendered as a palpable and accessible practice a transgression of the old colonial boundaries between those who were legitimate objects of anthropological concern and those who claimed immunity from such inspection. In so doing, John Campbell revealed the importance of seeking cosmological models in the most mundane and familiar social practices of Western societies, returning the intense focus on matters of detail to those intimate dimensions of our own professional and political environments that had seemed the least propitious objects of such an exercise.

BIBLIOGRAPHY

Ardener, Edwin (1971) "Introductory Essay: Social Anthropology and Language", in Edwin Ardener (ed.), *Social Anthropology and Language* (ASA Monographs, 10), London: Tavistock, ix-cii.

Arensberg, Conrad Maynadier (1937) *The Irish Countryman: An Anthropological Study*, New York: Macmillan.

Aretxaga, Begoña (1997) *Shattering Silence: Women, Nationalism, and Political Subjectivity in Northern Ireland*, Princeton University Press.

Asad, Talal (ed.) (1973) *Anthropology and the Colonial Encounter*, London: Ithaca Press.

Blum, Richard and Eva (1970) *The Dangerous Hour: The Lore of Crisis and Mystery in Rural Greece*, London: Chatto & Windus.

Brownell, Susan (1995) *Training the Body for China: Sports in the Moral Order of the People's Republic*, University of Chicago Press.

Campbell, J.K. (1964) *Honour, Family, and Patronage: A Study of Institutions and Moral Values in a Greek Montain Community*, Oxford: Clarendon Press.

—— (1992) "The Greek Hero", in J.G. Peristiany and Julian Pitt-Rivers (eds), *Honor and Grace in Anthropology*, Cambridge University Press, 129-49.

—— (1976) "Regionalism and Local Community", in Muriel Dimen and Ernestine Friedl (eds), *Regional Variation in Modern Greece and Cyprus*, in *Annals of the New York Academy of Sciences* 268, 18-27.

—— (1992) "Fieldwork among the Sarakatsani", in John Campbell and João de Pina-Cabral, eds , *Europe Observed*, Basingstoke: Macmillan, 148-66.

Clark, Grahame, "The Invasion Hypothesis in British Archaeology", *Antiquity*, 40 (1966), 172-89.

Cowan, Jane K. (1990) *Dance and the Body Politic in Northern Greece*, Princeton University Press.

de Pina-Cabral, João (1986) *Sons of Adam, Daughters of Eve: The Peasant Worldview of the Alto Minho*, Oxford: Clarendon Press.

Douglas, Mary (1986) *How Institutions Think*, Syracuse University Press.

du Boulay, Juliet (1974) *Portrait of a Greek Village*, Oxford: Clarendon Press.

Evans-Pritchard, E.E. (1937) *Oracles, Witchcraft and Magic among the Azande*, Oxford: Clarendon Press.

—— (1940) *The Nuer: A Description of the Modes of Livelihood and Political Institutions of a Nilotic People*, Oxford: Clarendon Press.

—— (1949) *The Sanusi of Cyrenaica*, Oxford: Clarendon Press.

—— (1956) *Nuer Religion*, Oxford: Clarendon Press.
Fabian, Johannes (1983) *Time and the Other: How Anthropology Makes its Object*, New York: Columbia University Press.
Gilmore, David D. (1990) *Manhood in the Making: Cultural Concepts of Masculinity*, New Haven: Yale University Press.
Hart, Laurie Kain (1992) *Time, Religion, and Social Experience in Rural Greece*, Lanham, MD: Rowman & Littlefield.
Herzfeld, Michael (1988) *The Poetics of Manhood: Contest and Identity in a Cretan Mountain Village*, Princeton University Press.
—— (1987) *Anthropology through the Looking-Glass: Critical Ethnography in the Margins of Europe*, Cambridge University Press.
—— (1990) "Icons and Identity: Religious Orthodoxy and Social Practice in Rural Crete", *Anthropological Quarterly* 63 (1990), 109-21.
—— (2004) *The Body Impolitic: Artisans and Artifice in the Global Hierarchy of Value*, University of Chicago Press.
—— (2005) *Cultural Intimacy: Social Poetics in the Nation-State*, 2nd edition, New York: Routledge.
Hirschon, Renée (1989) *Heirs of the Greek Catastrophe: The Social Life of Asia Minor Refugees in Piraeus*, Oxford: Clarendon Press.
—— (1992) "Greek Adults' Play, or, How to Train for Caution", *Journal of Modern Greek Studies* 10 (1992), 35-56.
Kapferer, Bruce (ed.) (1976) *Transaction and Meaning: Directions in the Anthropology of Exchange and Symbolic Behavior*, Philadelphia, Institute for the Study of Human Issues.
Karp, Ivan (1986) "Agency and Social Theory: A Review of Giddens", *American Ethnologist* 13, 131-7.
Kondo, Dorinne K. (1990) *Crafting Selves: Power, Gender, and Discourses of Identity in a Japanese Workplace*, University of Chicago Press.
Kuklick, Henrika (1984) "Tribal Exemplars: Images of Political Authority in British Anthropology, 1855-1945", in George W. Stocking (ed.), *Functionalism Historicized: Essays on British Social Anthropology*, Madison: University of Wisconsin Press, pp. 59-82.
Leach, Edmund (1967) *A Runaway World?* New York: Oxford University Press.
—— (1970) *Claude Lévi-Strauss*, London: Fontana/Collins.
Loizos, Peter (1975) "Changes in Property Transfer among Greek Villagers", *Man* (n.s.) 10, 503-2.
Malaby, Thomas M. (2003) *Gambling Life: Dealing in Contingency in a Greek City*, Urbana: University of Illinois Press.
Marchand, Trevor Hugh James (2001) *Minaret Building and Apprenticeship in*

Yemen, Richmond: RoutledgeCurzon.

Paine, Robert (1989) "High-Wire Culture: Comparing Two Agonistic Systems of Self-Esteem", *Man* (n.s.) 24, 328-39.

Papataxiarchis, Evthymios (2006) "Ta akhthi tis eterotitas: Dhiastasius tis Politismikis Dhiaforopiisis stin Elladha tou proimou 21ou eona", in Evthymios Papataxiarchis (ed.), *Peripeties tis Eterotitas: I Paraghoyi tis Politismikis Dhiaforas sti Simerini Elladha*, Athens: Alexandreia, 1-85.

Rosaldo, Renato (1986) "From the Door of His Tent: The Fieldworker and the Inquisitor", in James Clifford and George E. Marcus (eds), *Writing Culture: The Poetics and Politics of Ethnography*, Berkeley: University of California Press, 77-97.

Schein, Muriel Dimen (1975) "When is an Ethnic Group? Ecology and Class Structure in Northern Greece", *Ethnology* 14, pp. 83-97.

St. Clair, William (1972) *That Greece Might Still Be Free: The Philhellenes in the War of Independence*, London: Oxford University Press.

Stewart, Charles (1989) "Hegemony or Rationality? The Position of the Supernatural in Modern Greece", *Journal of Modern Greek Studies* 7, 77-104.

—— (1991) *Demons and the Devil: Moral Imagination in Modern Greek Culture*, Princeton University Press.

Wace, A.J.B. and M. S. Thompson (1914) *Nomads of the Balkans*, London: Methuen.

Wacquant, Loïc (2004) *Body and Soul: Notebooks of an Apprentice Boxer*, Oxford University Press.

Yalman, Nur (1967) *Under the Bo Tree: Studies in Caste, Kinship, and Marriage in the Interior of Ceylon*, Berkeley: University of California Press.

9

MARITAL FAILURES: GLIMPSING THE MARGINS OF MARRIAGE IN GREECE

Roger Just

Thirty years ago, between April 1977 and April 1980, I conducted under the supervision of John Campbell a total of twenty months' anthropological fieldwork on the tiny Ionian Island of Meganisi, part of the *nomos* of Leukada, Greece. There were three villages on Meganisi—Spartochori, Katomeri and Katomeri's small port offshoot, Vathy—each of them at the time a separate commune or *koinotita*.[1] Throughout most of my fieldwork, however, I was resident in Spartochori, moving to Katomeri only for the last two months of my stay. One of the routine tasks I undertook in Spartochori was gradually to compile a village and household census with the names, ages, sex, kinship connections and household membership of every villager. This, for a variety of reasons, was a slow and complicated task. Official statistics were of little use, for people were coming and going all the time. Sailors were regularly away at sea for up to a year; students, often with their entire family, shifted to Athens for the duration of their studies, returning only for the summer months; the members of Spartochori's small but growing educated and professional elite were resident in Athens but regularly visited the village; and villagers were continually setting off to or returning from outposts they had established in the United States, Canada, South Africa or Australia. Keeping track of everyone was not easy. Further, as in many areas of rural Greece, information was a guarded commodity. People were disinclined to discuss their personal details with me, and they were equally cautious about discussing those of their co-villagers lest they be accused of "gossiping". Finally, I was certainly in no

---

1   The three *koinotites* were subsequently amalgamated into a single Deme of Meganisi.

position to demand from people their dates of birth, lists of their kin or the nature of their domestic arrangements, for, apart from the obvious constraints of politeness, I had no authority within the village. For those with whom I had not struck up a particular friendship, I was simply *to pedi*, "the boy"—or, more specifically, Nikos's boy, since I rented a room from Nikos and worked for him (gratis) in his coffee-shop.

My village and household census had therefore to be slowly pieced together from fragments of information, casual conversations, chance remarks, anecdotes and, of course, straightforward observation. Nevertheless, by two-thirds of my way through fieldwork I had a near complete record of Spartochori's demography and of its inhabitants' kinship connections. I could not hope, however, to repeat the same for the other two villages, Katomeri and Vathy, for although they were only half an hour's walk from Spartochori, there was little social exchange with them. On the whole, Spartochoriots and Katomeriots held each other in mutual contempt and kept their distance, and there were few kinship connections between them that might have allowed me some privileged, or at least rapid, entry into the Katomeriot community. I was therefore delighted when, during my second summer on the island, a number of Katomeriot university students who were back from Athens and who had some idea of what I was trying to do as an anthropologist asked me whether they could be of assistance—although, to be honest, I did not think at the time that much would come of it. I took their offer of assistance as a polite, albeit welcome, gesture. Nevertheless, I suggested that they might try to find out for me what the real population sizes of Katomeri and Vathy were, giving a breakdown by sex and approximate age. This, they said, could easily be done since they "knew" everyone there.

Somewhat to my surprise, a week later they returned with a neatly written-out sheet of paper giving me the number of men (*andres*), women (*gynaikes*) and male and female children (*pedia*) for both Katomeri and Vathy. I immediately realized, however, that I had failed to give the students sufficient instruction. Up until what age, for example, had they classified someone as a *pedi*, a child, rather than as a man (*andras*) or a woman (*gynaika*)? Eighteen, twenty-one, or what? Whereupon followed a conversation in which both I and the students became increasingly confused, for we were talking at cross-purposes. Eventually one of the students, frustrated by what seemed to be stupid questions on my part, said, "Look, some of the *pedia* might be babies—they've just been born. Others might be ten or fifteen; others thirty or forty!" Somewhat taken aback, I asked what, then, was the difference between a *pedi* and an *andras* or a *gynaika*? The students' answer was simple: an *andras* or *gynaika* was married; a *pedi* was not.

MARITAL FAILURES

Terms

Social classifications are not dependent on linguistic classifications; nor are they necessarily even represented in language (Ellen, 2006). Nevertheless, the students' use of *"pedia"* (pl.) to refer to unmarried "adults" was telling, and it is worthwhile briefly considering that term (and related terms) since in fact the meaning of *"pedi"* (s.), like the meaning of so many common words, is highly context-sensitive. Standard dictionary entries for *"pedi"*—which is grammatically neuter—translate it as "child", i.e. its referent may be male or female. In day-to-day speech, however, this was not necessarily the case. Again for the purposes of my census, from time to time I would ask people how many children they had (*"Posa pedia echeis?"*) and I would be told one or two or three. It was only when someone added *"kai duo kopelles"* ("and two girls") that I realized that much of the information I had collected was wrong. In common parlance *"pedi"* often meant "boy" (despite the fact that a sex-specific term for "boy", viz *"agori"*, exists), and if one wanted to dispel any ambiguity then the more specific terms *"kopella"* (girl) or *"koritsi"* (little girl) had to be used to designate a female child or unmarried young woman (cf. Cowan 1990: 51 n.7). In short, there tended to be an asymmetry, with the paired terms being *"pedi"/"kopella"* rather than *"agori"/"kopella"*. On the other hand, as a term of address *"pedi"* was regularly used in a non-sex specific way. Women and girls could be affectionately or familiarly addressed as *"pedi mou"*, "my child", just as easily as could men or boys.

This, however, raises a more important point. As a term of address, *"pedia"* (let me translate it in this context as "boys") can be used with absolutely no reference to age, or, indeed, marital status. A group of seventy- and eighty-year-old grandfathers might be hailed with the words, *"Pos pame, pedia?"* ("How are we going, boys?"). The same might apply to a group of grandmothers. *"Pedi"* and *"pedia"* are to that extent generic terms of address. They can also serve as generic terms of reference, as in the phrase *"Ola ta pedia sto chorio mas"*, which could perhaps be rendered as "All the "people" in our village" or "Everyone in our village". Nevertheless such greetings and phrases, while usually affectionate, are certainly familiar, and in any social situation that entails a degree of hierarchy then their familiarity and the linguistic shadow of infantilization they cast will mean that they are used asymmetrically. A boss might address his workers as *"pedia"* (boys), but a worker would not address his boss as *"pedi mou"* ("my boy/child")—in just the same way, we might note, as a father or mother might address their son (or daughter) as *"pedi mou"*, while children would be very unlikely to address their fathers or mothers in that way. In this respect it is perhaps also worth noting in passing that the standard term of reference and address for a slave in ancient Greek was "*pais*", i.e. "child", the term from which modern Greek "*pedi*" derives. In that case linguistic infantilization was a clear marker of the absence of autonomy and self-determination. In classic structuralist mode we might say that *andras* : *pedi* :: married : unmarried :: adult : child :: superior : inferior.

Within the relatively egalitarian world of the village, however, "*pedi*" remains a largely affectionate term, albeit a somewhat proprietorial one—hence my own designation as "Nikos's boy", which was not intended as an insult, but which did underscore my apparent dependency on Nikos as some sort of a member of his household as well as the fact that, as an unmarried man, I was not the autonomous head of my own household. But as I have suggested, language is not the crux of the matter. We need to turn to sociological considerations.

The necessity of marriage

For my Katomeriot students, the distinction between "adults" and "non-adults" was self-evident. To them, "*andras*" actually meant a married man, "*gynaika*" a married woman,[2] and anyone, regardless of their age, who was not married was still a *pedi*. I should have guessed this, for all the ethnographic literature on Greece (not so very extensive back in 1980) either stated or strongly implied the inevitability of marriage for both men and women as part of a "natural" process of maturation—though the significance of marriage and of adulthood was rather different for men and for women. In fact the possibility of non-marriage was scarcely mentioned in Campbell's account of the Sarakatsani (it went without saying), but the significance of marriage for the transition of men to full adult status was made quite clear:

> The diminished authority of the father is the inevitable outcome of his sons' assumption of adult status which, in this community, is incompatible with subordination. Marriage completes the process by which a son asserts his individuality . . . (1964: 180)

Both Loizos (1975: 70) and du Boulay (1974: 91) also pointed out the universal expectation and the social necessity of marriage for both men and women in their respective communities (Argaki, alias "Kalos", in Cyprus, and Ambeli in Evia), and for du Boulay, women's marriage and motherhood (which could be assumed quickly to follow) were essential to her interpretation of women's redemption from their original state of pollution or sin (1974:112ff. &135; cf. du Boulay 1986:162-3).

---

2   By way of further linguistic comment, it might be noted that in Greek the terms *andras* (man) and *yineka* (woman) double as the standard terms for "husband" and "wife" (although there is a non sex-specific term for "spouse", *sizugos*). Cf. Faubion 1993:177.

MARITAL FAILURES

Aschenbrenner, too, mentioned "the central preoccupation" of households in Karpofora (Messenia) to marry their children, particularly daughters (1976: 215), and Bialor notes that in Vovoda (northwestern Peloponnese) the "expectation is that all biologically normal people will marry, even those who, usually for reasons relating to the dowry, must defer marriage until well into middle age" (1976: 232).

Subsequent ethnographic accounts (published after I had completed fieldwork) reiterate with greater or lesser elaboration both the universal expectation of marriage and its critical role in the achievement of adulthood for both men and women. Loizos makes the first point succinctly for Argaki: "Everyone was expected to marry" (1981:70). Salamone and Stanton point out that in Amouliani (Halkidiki) "no man . . . is even considered a mature adult until after his marriage and the establishment of his own nikokyrio [household economy]" (1986:103). In Hirschon's account of Yerania (a working-class suburb in Piraeus inhabited by Asia Minor refugees and their descendants), marriage for both men and women "was not considered to be an optional matter, nor one of choice, but rather a matter of destiny". Moreover, it "was seen by all as a turning-point in the life cycle, conferring on the young the status of recognized adulthood . . ." and "was the only accepted means of establishing full adulthood and maturity" (1989: 107). A woman's destiny "was to bear children and raise her family as mistress in her own household and no acceptable alternative existed" (ibid.), while for men "[a]n unduly prolonged bachelorhood indicated avoidance of the full status of adulthood, suggesting certain deficiencies in character: weakness, frivolity, and, ultimately, lack of masculinity" (ibid.: 109). Dubisch states that while little ethnographic attention has been given to the role that marriage plays for men, it is nevertheless obvious "that a Greek man cannot achieve full adult status until he is married. . . It is his "destiny" also to be married" (1991:45). And while Cowan, like Dubisch (ibid.)—and, indeed, like du Boulay (1974:121 and 262)—emphasizes the somewhat different consequences of marriage for women and for men, she also reports that in Sohos (Macedonia) "the importance of marriage in the achievement of full social adulthood is stressed for both males and females" (Cowan 1990:50).

And thus it was on Meganisi. To be a bachelor or spinster was no-one's ambition. Indeed "bachelor" and "spinster"—"unmarried adults" as we might now ponderously say—were not recognized social categories in rural Greece; or rather, inasmuch as they were recognized, they were recognized only in terms of a failure to have achieved or completed the normal and expected "destinies" of adult human beings. As Cowan observes, "A girl who reaches her mid-twenties without marrying risks being labelled an "old maid" (*yerondokori*, literally "old girl/daughter") (1990:50)—or alternatively "*megalokopela*" ("big/grown-up girl") (Kirtsoglou 2004:141), the only terms readily available in Greek for mature unmarried women. Their negative connotations are obvious. As for unmarried men, even in their fifties they might be termed *"eleutheroi"*, literally "free", as if they were yet to be spoken for—but not as if they had opted for an alternative social role. Given its near-comprehensiveness and the lack of any socially approved alternatives,[3] the Greek marital system was (in the pristine sense of the word) totalitarian. As Kennedy, writing on the aspirations of women in Hatzi (Crete), somewhat ruefully remarks:

A significant aspect of their awareness . . . is that they see no role models within their own social setting which suggest ways to obtain rewards that compensate for the negative consequences of moving outside their social role. Moreover, they view their options for personal freedom as tied directly to their marriages and the economic reality outside it (1986:127).

Nevertheless, failures occurred, and in this paper I want briefly to consider some of the causes and consequences, both practical and symbolic, between such failure and what amounts to the infantilization of those who, for whatever reasons, failed. Given the normative status of marriage, however (which at the time, I suspect, was internalized by ethnographers almost as much as it was by those about whom they wrote), one has genuinely to scour the literature in order to discover their traces.

Failure

As mentioned above, the inevitability of marriage goes almost without saying in Campbell's account of the Sarakatsani—except for a half sentence in which Campbell notes that "should a daughter remain unmarried she too will receive something, a half share [of a dowry portion], with which, like her parents, she passes into the family of her youngest brother" (1964:189). On the assumption that this is not a hypothetical case, and given that, ideally, among the Sarakatsani all the sisters in a family should marry before even the oldest brother might take a wife (although in practice one sister generally remained unmarried after the eldest brother had married) (ibid.), it might be supposed that if there were still a sister unwed by the time her youngest brother had married and had a family into which she might be placed, then she was indeed a casualty of the system and was someone who would never marry.

To revert to my own data, out of a total permanent (or "core")[4] population of 551 (288 females and 263 males) for Spartochori in 1977-80, there were 12

---

3   The obvious exception is the case of women (and men) who entered celibate holy orders—nuns and monks (but not priests). See Iossifides, 1991.

4   I used the term "core" population as a rough and ready way of distinguishing

unmarried women and seven unmarried men who, either by reason of age or because of other factors (discussed below), could with some degree of confidence be considered as permanent bachelors or spinsters (see Just 2000: 80-9). This is not an entirely insignificant proportion of the village population—3.4%. Du Boulay also mentions that in Ambeli, out of a population of 144 there were six permanently unmarried villagers, or 4.2% (1974:91). Unfortunately most other ethnographic accounts do not provide numerical data, although Dubisch, in a foot-note, mentions two unmarried men in her village on Tinos (1991:45 n. 24) and Loizos mentions the existence of non-married and non-marriageable persons in "Kalo" (1975:70)—as does Hirschon for Yerania (1989:107).[5] In this situation, a resort to national statistics is warranted.

I take the data from the 1971 census (included in the 1981 *Statistical Yearbook of Greece*) as those being roughly compatible with the dates of the ethnographic research I have been discussing. The data are interesting. In what was classified as the population of "rural Greece",[6] for the age group 35-44 (within which, according to stated norms, one might expect most men and women who were going to marry to have been married), 7.8% of men and 7.2% of woman had never married.[7] Interestingly, in the 45-55 category the "never-married" percentage falls to 4.5% for men and 5.2% for women. Finally, among those over 65—by which age it could surely be assumed that anyone who was ever going to marry had married—3.6% of men and 4.0% of women were ending their lives without ever having married. Given that my own data from Spartochori and du Boulay's data from Ambeli relate to small populations, it is at least interesting to note that the percentage of both villages' populations considered to be non-married and non-marriageable roughly coincides with the overall statistics for rural Greece. The data for Greece as a whole in 1971 showed an

---

    those whose year-round place of residence was Spartokhori from those living for some part of each year in Athens or some other urban centre.

5   Bialor (1976).

6   The census report defines this category as populations living in centres of less than 2,000 people.

7   The 1971 census (and the 1981 census) record the population of Greece by age, sex, and marital status. The age groups, however, are given in unequal divisions: 0-14, and then by five-year groupings (15-19 etc.) up to the age of 34. After 35 years, there are ten-year groupings (35-44 etc.) up to the age of 64. The next grouping is 65-79, and the final grouping is 80+. In the discussion below I have regularized the groupings between 15 and 65 into ten-year age-groups (e.g. 25-34). The headings in the census for marital status are "single", "married", "widowed", "divorced" and "not declared". In the discussion below, I have amalgamated "married", "widowed", and "divorced", so that comparisons are between those who are or at some stage have been married, and those who have never married.

175

even greater percentage of "never-married" than the data for rural Greece. In the 35-44 age group, 10.2% of males and 9.2% of females had never married, while in the 45-54 age group this fell to only 6.0% for males and 7.2% for females. In the 65-and-over category, 4.9% of males and 5.1% of females were ending their lives never-married. Normative expectations of marriage and the lack of socially approved alternatives are therefore one thing; the reality of the situation is perhaps another—and at the very least, the gap between the universal expectation of marriage and the statistically evident failure of a significant proportion of the population to marry invites some comment.

Eugenics

Again, one has to rely on snippets of ethnographic data to provide some clues about those who did not marry. As mentioned above, Bialor states that the expectation in Mavrikion (Peloponnesos) was that "all *biologically normal* individuals will marry" (1976:215, my emphasis) —but not, one thereby assumes, biologically "abnormal" individuals. No data, however, are provided to back up what might, after all, be only Bialor's supposition. Loizos, however, makes a similar observation: "In the village [of Kalo/Argaki, Cyprus] all children of both sexes, *if not seriously deformed or handicapped*, must marry, and do marry" (1975:70, my emphasis), and Hirschon qualifies her observation that in Yerania marriage was considered imperative for all men and women by the parenthesis "excepting only the physically and mentally handicapped and those who entered celibate monastic communities" (1981:107). Du Boulay gives a little more detail: of the six adult individuals in Ambeli who remained unmarried, two men and four women, "Three of these are crippled through, variously, polio, meningitis, and laming through an unknown disease; two through severe mental illness; one through the necessity for her to look after her old parents and mentally ill siblings" (1974: 262, and 91). Finally, of the two adult individuals whom Dubisch mentions as unmarried, one was "retarded" (1991:45 n.24).

In Spartochori, disabilities of one form or another appear similarly to have accounted for many (but by no means all) of the cases of non-marriage—and I suppose there are very few, if any, communities or societies in the world where serious physical or mental disability does not constitute a substantial impediment to marriage (despite the strenuous efforts currently being made in much of Europe to ensure a "normal" life for those with disabilities). A question remains, however, about how serious a "serious handicap" had to be in rural Greece to preclude marriage; or, to put the matter another way, whether in rural Greece of the 1970s and 1980s we are not dealing as much with cultural prohibitions as with insuperable physical or mental disabilities. At the time of my fieldwork, the Spartochoriots seemed to me to practise a quite ruthless form of folk eugenics, and I doubt they were exceptional in this respect. Hart recounts that the local doctor in the village of Richia (Peloponnese) commented to her on the degree to which local villagers viewed physical illness as a matter of "shame", proffering the example of a 15-year-old girl who had contracted tuberculosis but whose father feared that there would be a "rumour that she was seriously ill, that the family was tainted, and [that this] would ruin her chances for marriage" (1992:86 n.14). At all events, in Spartochori, anyone who was in any way physically "challenged" (as we might now say—the Meganisiots simply said "*arrostos*", "sick") could expect to remain unmarried (and celibate), and given that marriages were still substantially arranged, or at least involved the collective considerations of both the potential groom's and bride's families, individuals thus condemned had little chance of taking any personal initiative that might circumvent their fate.

Moreover, in what might be considered a fairly competitive marriage market in which, again, collective family reputations were at stake, the disqualifying disabilities for marriage did not have to be so very great. One old woman, for example, was simply lame, one leg a little shorter than the other. Whether, as in the cases du Boulay mentions, this was because she had suffered some affliction, or whether her disability was congenital, I do not know—but as my host, Nikos, explained to me, it was a pity, but in her youth no man in the village had been willing to "take" her. As it happens, I registered such village prejudices quite directly. For two summers I worked in Spartochori as a crew member for a fisherman called Alkis. I am quite badly myopic, but since my teens I have worn contact lenses. Alkis did not know this, but one day on the boat I got a speck of dirt caught on one of my lenses, and so removed the lens, licked it clean, and reinserted it. Alkis showed no surprise. He had heard about contact lenses, which even then had begun to be advertised in Greece. He was, however, interested in my disability, and asked me how short-sighted I was. I gave him as good an account as I could, whereupon he took it upon himself to advise me in no uncertain terms that, given the degree of my affliction, I should make sure that I never married.

Mental disabilities of any sort were equally an impediment—and, in fact, were scarcely distinguished from physical disabilities, both being classified as *arrostia*, "sickness". Their actual seriousness was, of course, difficult to judge. Like most villages, Spartochori had its "village idiot"—virtually an institutionalized position. In fact it had three—men categorized (and dismissed) by the village as "*trelloi*", "crazy". While I am in no way qualified to assess the degree of their disabilities, to a layman the first certainly appeared to have many of the stereotypical attributes of someone we might call "crazy". He was not "dumb" or moronic. Indeed, he could be quite cunning. But he wandered around the village in a dishevelled state, cackling and talking to himself, and accosting anyone who might pause near him—and he was quickly shooed away by other men whenever he approached or tried to enter a coffee shop (which he often did whenever he had managed to beg a few coins from a stranger).

This last point is not trivial. The coffee shops (there were four in Spartochori) were where men publicly socialized—a very necessary part of their male role as village equals. And they socialized by smoking and drinking together. Indeed, in the late 1970s and early 1980s almost every adult male in the village smoked, and Spartochoriot adult males were also fairly heavy drinkers (although they showed no toleration for anyone who was drunk).[8] But smoking and drinking were not simply male pleasures. They had iconic status. Men smoked and drank; women and children did not. And men would regularly place a cigarette in their mouth or raise a glass whenever I tried to take a photograph of them. Of course younger unmarried men also smoked and drank, but they avoided doing so in the close presence of their fathers, for both actions, particularly smoking, were tantamount to a symbolic assertion of the full autonomy of male adulthood. Consistently with their status as non-adults, however, those considered "*trelloi*" were permanently denied the right to smoke and drink. Moreover, no adult male, however addicted to tobacco, would ever ask for a cigarette or "borrow" a cigarette from a fellow villager, let alone a stranger. The exceptions, again, were those judged to be *trelloi*, and while this might be explained in economic terms (since those who were "crazy" would normally also be unemployed and have no money to buy cigarettes) they were also amply demonstrating their total disregard for the fundamental moral rule of adult male conduct: never be beholden, never beg. After they had been denied the right to smoke and drink in the first place, their attempts to cadge a cigarette or a glass were then considered infantile.

Spartochori's other two *trelloi*, a pair of brothers, were, to my layman's gaze, more marginal cases than the first—in fact quite literally so, since they were effectively exiled from the village and spent most of their time camped out in a hut shepherding a small flock of sheep and goats. I encountered them many times on my walks, and they seemed perhaps a little odd. They were, of course, unmarried. They were again, understandably, rather dishevelled and rather dirty. They were also perhaps excessively excitable and talkative, and they usually asked me for a cigarette. But although I must again emphasize that I have no qualification to dispute the villagers' judgement that they were "crazy", I

---

8   My rough estimate is that most adult males were drinking well over half a litre of wine a day (although many preferred beer), and perhaps a third of a bottle of ouzo.

could not help feeling that whatever the villagers' initial basis for their judgement, were I, for example, to be similarly deprived of any normal human intercourse and exiled into near-solitary and life-long rural confinement—or, like the first "village idiot", rebuffed in my every attempt to participate in regular social life—then I too might go a little mad. Even as a layman I am willing to suggest that whatever the "natural causes" of these men's conditions, the social consequences of their classification as "crazy" played some part in their behavioural abnormality.

In this respect, the saddest case I encountered was a young man whom I came to know quite well. He was about 18 years old at the time and suffered from a very minor form of epilepsy (well under control through the administration of drugs). He also exhibited what I can only describe as a slight social gaucheness—a tendency to laugh a little too much when something was funny, to be a little too emphatic when something required emphasis. In Bourdieu's terms, he did not have a particularly good "feel for the game" (1990:80-82). But in other respects he was a tall, strong, healthy and quite good-looking young man, and despite his social ineptitude, he was certainly not unintelligent (at least I choose to think not, since I lost at least a hundred consecutive games of backgammon to him). And yet his minor medical affliction (known to the village) was sufficient to ensure that he would never marry—a cause of particular sorrow to his parents, since he was their only son, and surely a cause of anxiety for him, since he lived his life knowing that he was condemned never to take his place in society as a married man and a full adult. He too was not allowed to smoke (which he made a virtue of by pointing out the health risks of the habit). Nor was he allowed to drink, although since he was well liked, he was allowed in the coffee-shops and men would buy him a soft drink. But it does not take a great deal of imaginative licence to suspect that the social infelicities that compounded his reputation as being a little "sick" were at least in some part the consequences of a desperate compensatory attempt to appear "normal", to play the standard extrovert male role—which, unfortunately, then ended up verging on parody.

Social causes

But beyond the casualties of such "eugenics", there were, of course, "social" casualties—or perhaps the casualties of history. For the most part these were elderly women—women who, I suspect, in an earlier and harsher period[9] had

---

9 At least in Spartokhori, by 1980 dowry was no longer either a determinant of, or a necessity for, marriage. Age and physical and attraction were substitutes. See Just 1985.

not had dowries provided for them and were therefore unable to make an honourable match. There were, for example, two sisters in Katomeri (whom, perhaps not surprisingly, I never met), resident in the household of their brother, himself a married man with children. I do not know the full story, although I do know that the problem had been economic. My guess is that since their brother had been (and was) a Communist who had spent a considerable number of years after the Civil War detained in exile on the island of Makronisi, he had been absent from the village during their marriageable youth and had therefore been unable to fulfil his traditional duty of providing his sisters with dowries and/or arranging suitable marriages for them. They became, as a result, his permanent wards, for although it was possible, even commonplace, for widows to live alone and maintain an independent household, the same did not apply to unmarried women, even supposing they had the financial resources to do so. In Spartochori, one household also consisted of a widow and her four unmarried children, two sons and two daughters, all of them in early middle age. Given the late age of marriage for men, it was possible that the sons might still marry, but it seemed doubtful that the daughters would (and they too were scarcely to be seen). Again, I do not know the full story, for this is precisely the sort of situation that villagers were extremely cautious about discussing, but I know the family had been poor, and I assume the father had died prematurely. By the time of my stay, both brothers were employed as sailors on good wages, but they might well have been unable (or unwilling) to provide their sisters with dowries at the appropriate time. There were also a few unmarried men in their fifties in both Katomeri and Spartochori who sadly confided to me that "they had waited too long"; they had delayed their marriages and then suddenly found that "their youth had gone". These were all, notably, youngest sons—a point to which I shall return. Such men and women were not treated as children, but in a context in which marriage was a universal expectation and constitutive of adulthood, they were marginalized. They were granted the quasi-honorific title of "*Thios*" or "*Barba*" ("Uncle"), or "*Thia*" ("Aunt"), by which any adult man or woman over, say, fifty years of age might expect to be addressed; but they were also universally pitied, and as the recipients of pity rather than respect, the men kept a low profile in village affairs while the women became virtually non-persons scarcely to be seen. In short, they occupied a grey area in the world of adults, without prestige or influence, since, by definition, they represented no one except themselves.

Here, a nexus of social and cultural factors related to marriage and also widely commented on in the literature on rural Greece of the period needs to be borne in mind: the necessity of dowry; the obligation on brothers to assist in the provision of their sisters' dowries; and the consequent late age of marriage for men. In fact what historically constituted women's dowries in Greece (and Cyprus) in terms of the type of property conveyed on marriage, the proportion of a family's wealth it accounted for, and even the degree of its social necessity shows enormous regional variation. On all three counts it shows an equally high degree of variation over time.[10] Nevertheless, inasmuch as generalizations can be made, the provision of dowry of some sort was a critical factor for the successful conclusion of women's marriages in most parts of Greece at most periods. The majority of unmarried adult women who appear in the national statistics for 1971 are, I suspect, like the two sisters in Katomeri, the negative correlate of this requirement—women who were not provided for.

That in most parts of Greece the obligation to dower a woman fell not only on her parents but also on her brothers meant, however, that men's marriages too were affected by the dowry system. In some communities the rule was that all sisters should marry before any of their bothers could wed, and in some communities there was also, ideally, a sequence of marriage, with older sisters marrying before younger sisters and older brothers before younger brothers. The rule or convention was justified by a general notion that brothers should act as their sisters' guardians and protectors, as well as by the economic contributions they might be required to make to their sister's dowries while remaining members of their natal household; but given the time it might take to accumulate an acceptable dowry for a woman, a youngest son who had a youngest sister, say, fifteen years his junior might see the possibility of his own marriage very significantly delayed. Something of the possible complexity (and strains) of such situations is nicely recounted by Bernard for Kalymnos:

[A] Kalymnian boy from a large and highly respected family wanted to marry a girl from a family whose social status was equivalent to his own. There were no social problems, so the engagement was announced. Then the boy's father became seriously ill and the medical expenses consumed the family's dowry for the boy's younger sister. The engagement was threatened because the boy wanted to work for several years before marrying in order to fulfil his obligation to his younger sister.

In order to avoid a long engagement . . . the girl's family gave the boy full power over his future wife's dowry. The couple was married, and the dowry was transferred to the bride's new sister-in-law who married, gave her husband the dowry, who gave it to his sister. The one dowry, in fact was *said* to have been used to marry five couples . . . (1976:296).

---

10   The topic is too large to be dealt with here. For overviews, see Couroucli 1987; Papataxiarchis 1998. For collected essays, see Piault 1985. For an historical account, see Sant Cassia and Bada 1992. See also Loizos 1975.

In this case the story has a happy end due to the exercise of a deal of ingenuity; in other communities not so open to the manipulation of requirements, tragedy might well have replaced comedy.

In Spartochori there was no strict rule that brothers had to delay their own marriages until all their sisters were wed; nor was there any strict age-sequence for marriage. Nevertheless, responsibilities were still felt towards sisters, and since brothers set up their own neolocal households on marriage (no married brothers ever cohabited), thus acquiring new responsibilities towards their own wives and children, it seems that a disproportionate burden could fall on youngest sons, especially if their father were dead (which was likely to be the case by the time their older brothers had married). It is thus likely that they ran some risk of finding themselves too old to attract a bride by the time they felt at liberty to marry. At the very least, it is significant that the three late middle-aged unmarried men in Spartochori who sadly told me that they "had waited too long" were all, as I have mentioned, youngest sons who each shared a household with an elderly widowed mother.

But, given the specific historical period with which I am concerned, a further factor may have come into play—emigration. The concern aroused in villages by accelerating rural to urban migration of young men during the 1960s has been discussed by du Boulay (1983) in relation to dowry inflation. In Spartochori, it was registered not so much by the inflation of dowries as by a significant drop in the age of women's marriages as parents became anxious that their daughters might find themselves "*sto raphi*", "on the shelf".[11] Rural to urban migration, however, is the smaller part of the story, for between 1949 and 1969, Greece experienced massive external migration to other parts of Europe and to Australia, Canada, the Unites States and South Africa (Vgenopoulos 1985: 42-8).[12] Insofar as it is possible to piece together the life histories of those who had emigrated outside Greece from Spartochori, it seems that many young men went before they were married with the intention of establishing themselves economically in their new locations before sending back for a bride or returning to Spartochori to find one. Needless to say, however, some proportion of them married overseas—though it was virtually impossible to arrive at any meaningful figures. Here it may again be useful to look at national statistics to see whether such male emigration may have affected women's marriage rates.

According to the census, in 1971 there were more males than females in Greece under the age of 25: approximately 1,054 males for every 1,000 females. This imbalance then reverses in the 25-34 age-group, with 1,096 females for

---

11 See Just, 1985.
12 The estimate is 1,179,076.

every 1,000 males. From then on the numerical imbalance in favour of females continues with 1,056 females to 1,000 males in the 35-44 age-group; 1,097 females for every 1,000 males in the 45-54 age-group; 1,071 females for every 1,000 males in the 55-64 age group; and 1,286 females for every 1,000 males in the over-65 age group.

Differential mortality rates between male and female infants may in part account for the reverse in the imbalance between males and females after the age of 25, although there is not much difference in the ratio of males to females in the 0-14 age group (1,056 males to 1,000 females) and the 15-24 age group (1,051 males to 1,000 females). Similarly, the excess of females over males in the 65+ age group (1,286 females to 1,000 males) can be explained by women's relative longevity. Nevertheless it is clear that in 1971 an imbalance whereby the number of females exceeded the number males becomes apparent after the age of twenty—that is to say, exactly the age at which one might expect single males to have emigrated overseas or to Europe. And it is an imbalance of nearly 10% in the 25-34 age category (1,096 females for every 1,000 males). In fact, up to the age of 44 the percentage of unmarried women resident in Greece was actually less than the percentage of unmarried men—which is readily explainable in terms of the considerably later age of marriage of men than of women.[13] After the age of 45, however, not only does the absolute number of women exceed that of men (1,097 women for every 1,000 men in the 45-54 age group), but so too does the proportion of unmarried women to unmarried men (6.0% of men in the age group, and 7.2% of women)—and it continues thereafter to be higher for women. Admittedly these sorts of calculation are extremely crude, and the difference between marriage rates for women and men are not great (1.2% in the 45-54 age group); but the national figures give some support to the anecdotal evidence that marriageable men had left Greece and that this had affected women's chances of marriage.

Coda

I have briefly examined, in so far as it is possible to do so, an area of post-war Greek social life that is marginal in two respects: it lay outside the emphatically stated norms of the period, and, consequently, it appears as shadow only occasionally to be glimpsed in ethnographic accounts. But precisely because Greek society from the 1950s through to the 1980s appears to have placed such heavy

---

13 Between the ages of 25 and 34, 80.7% of women were married (or had been married), whereas only 62.6% of men were married (or had been married). Between the ages of 35 and 44, the unmarried rate begins to even out, with 90.8% of women in that age group at some stage married, and 88.8% of men at some stage married.

emphasis on the role of marriage not only as its central institution but also as definitional to the formation of full adult human beings, it seems important to note that a significant proportion of Greece's population failed to marry and, rather than constituting some alternative to normative roles, were thereby effectively condemned to the status of non-persons.

The factors I have suggested that most probably account for these "casualties"—a fear of any physical or mental disability, the necessity of dowry for women, the obligation that fell on brothers to assist in the provision of dowry and, possibly, a demographic imbalance between eligible males and females as a result of post-war migration—could all be seen to contribute to a casualty rate that was merely the aggregate effect of the accidents of individual life-histories. After all, no system of values and practices ever fully achieves its aim—but the aim of the system was to achieve marriage, not impede it. There was at least one area of Greece, however, where the effects of both dowry and emigration in creating a class of unmarried persons, particularly women, appear to have been explicitly recognized as part of the marital system itself. Vernier (1991) describes what he considers to be a unique system of dowry, marriage and inheritance in operation on the island of Karpathos in the 19th century and with diminishing vigour throughout the first half of the 20th century. In brief, property was passed down two lines, patrilineally for men, matrilineally for women. First-born sons inherited from their fathers; first-born daughters inherited from their mothers; and ideally first-born sons married first-born daughters. The other children of both sexes were disinherited. For younger sons, the solution lay in emigration, both overseas and to other parts of Greece (thus relieving pressure on scarce agricultural resources). Some younger daughters also emigrated, but the majority remained on the island where they worked as unpaid domestic and agricultural labour for their eldest and married brothers or sisters. Importantly, as most part they lacked dowries, and given the shortage of men, they also remained unmarried—although the proportion of unmarried younger daughters begins to decrease as forms of wealth other than land become available. Nevertheless, the proportion was extremely high. According to Vernier's figures, the percentage of younger daughters born between 1885 and 1904 who remained unmarried was 61.9%; for those born between 1905 and 1924 it was 50%; and for those born between 1925 and 1934 it was 34.6% (1991:153). Even at the time of his fieldwork in 1975, 76% of younger daughters from shepherding families were unmarried (1991: 152 n.3). Although we are concerned here with women rather than men, the "structuralist" formula I presented earlier whereby it could be claimed that "married : unmarried :: adult : child :: superior : inferior" is fully and systematically played out. The dominant class of married eldest siblings literally reproduced at each stage for the next generation a celibate class of servants for its own eldest children (1991:63).

The Karpathiot system could thus be seen as a peculiarly institutionalized version of tendencies inherent in Greek society as a whole that worked against the achievement of the ideal of marriage: the disadvantage that younger siblings might suffer in relation to both receiving and providing dowries; the resort to overseas migration by young men. But Greece nowadays is a different country. There are intimations that marriage is no longer "destiny", and that there are perhaps other routes to adulthood. Even by the mid-1980s the Athenian gay community—admittedly in the trendy bars of sophisticated Kolonaki—was conspicuous, and although Faubion comments, "As a figure, as a trope, the "homosexual" was in 1986 and 1987 among the general Greek public still predominantly nothing more than a trope of limitation, an ironic negation of sexual meaning" (1993:229), it is clear that a male role that openly precluded marriage was in the process of formation. His composite portrait of "Maro", an Athenian woman of around thirty from a prominent Athenian family, is also suggestive of changes beginning to occur in the mid- to late 1980s. Maro has never been married, and while she acknowledges that this is not the "normal condition" for a woman of her age and, furthermore, that she would like to have a child and be happily married, her opinion of Greek men and her own desire to learn how to live "for herself" seem to preclude marriage (1993:173). This is not the formation of any new ideal or destiny, but it is the measured and deliberate rejection of old ones.

Kirtsoglou's later ethnographic study of female same-sex relations in a Greek provincial town points in a similar direction. Nena and Stasa, two women in their fifties, have had a long-term relationship for twenty-five years. They conceal rather than flaunt that relationship, and "do not particularly like to be thought of as lesbians" (2004:141), but while they are in no sense activists for change, their rejection not only of the inevitability but of the desirability of marriage is clear: "Do you think those who actually married are happier? They were loaded with a husband to carry on their backs, to wash, to feed and listen to his whining." (2004: 143)

It is, however, again at the national level that acknowledged changes in the nature of marriage in Greek society can most easily, albeit crudely, be registered. The 2001 census includes new categories. To the established "single", "married", "divorced" and "widowed" breakdowns of the population are added "persons living in consensual union"; then, under that heading, "single", "married", "divorced" and "widowed" are reiterated for those within the consensual union category. Moreover, under "Selected social indicators" is included "lone parent". The precise nature of those consensual unions (i.e. heterosexual or same-sex) cannot, of course, be determined from the census (and neither can it accurately be determined whether "lone parents" are the result of divorce, widowhood, or a deliberate choice of single parenthood). Suffice to say, however, that numbers are now sufficient for the inclusion of categories that break with the long held assumption that marriage is the critical marker of independent adulthood. In the 30-34 years old age group of 274,945 unmarried persons, both male and female, in 2001, 17,593, or 6.4%, are now living in consensual unions. No doubt the bulk of these will transform into marriages in due course, but the shift in social values is still evident. Finally, if we compare the 2001 census with the 1971 census, then although overall non-marriage rates have not dramatically changed, other things have.

If we again take the 45-54 age group, the ratio of women to men is now almost equal: 1,008 females to every 1,000 men (as opposed to 1,097 females for every 1,000 males in 1971). The effects of male emigration would seem to have petered out. If we compare the proportion of unmarried men with the proportion of unmarried women in this same age group, then the sexual imbalance has gone into reverse: 8.3% of men unmarried (as opposed to 6.0% in 1971), but only 5.6% of women unmarried (as opposed to 7.2% in 1971). Perhaps somewhat ironically, a greater proportion of women, at least, appear to have achieved their "destiny" today now that it is no longer carries with it quite the same imperative than thirty years ago when that destiny brooked no ideological challenge.

BIBLIOGAPHY

Aschenbrenner, S. (1976) "Karpofora: Reluctant Farmers on a Fertile Land", in M. Dimen and E. Friedl (eds), *Annals of the New York Academy of Sciences*, Vol. 268, 207-21.
Bernard, R. (1976) "Kalymnos: The Island of the Sponge Fishermen", in M. Dimen and E. Friedl (eds), *Annals of the New York Academy of Sciences*, Vol. 268, 291-307.
Bialor, P.A. (1976) "The Northwestern Corner of the Peloponnesos: Mavrikion and its Region" in M. Dimen and E. Friedl (eds), *Annals of the New York Academy of Sciences*, Vol. 268, 222-35.
Bourdieu, P. (1990) *The Logic of Practice*, Cambridge.
Campbell, J.K. (1964) *Honour, Family, and Patronage. A Study of Institutions and Moral Values in a Greek Mountain Community*, Oxford.
Couroucli, M. (1987) "Dot et société en Grèce moderne", in G. Ravis-Giordani (ed.) *Femmes et patrimoine dans les sociétés rurales de l'Europe méditerranéenne*, Paris, 327-48.
Cowan, J. (1990) *Dance and the Body Politic in Northern Greece*, Princeton.
Dimen, M. and E. Friedl (eds) (1976) *Regional Variation in Modern Greece and Cyprus: Toward a Perspective on the Ethnography of Greece. Annals of the New York Academy of Sciences*, Vol. 268.
Du Boulay, J. (1974) *Portrait of a Greek Mountain Village*, Oxford.
—— (1983) "The Meaning of Dowry: Changing Values in Rural Greece", *Journal of Modern Greek Studies*, 1, 43-270.
—— (1986) "Women—Images of their Nature and Destiny in Rural Greece", in J. Dubisch (ed.) *Gender and Power in Rural Greece*, Princeton, 139-68.
Dubisch, J. (ed.) (1986) *Gender and Power in Rural Greece*, Princeton.
—— (1991) "Gender, Kinship, and Religion: "Reconstructing" the Anthropology of Greece" in P. Loizos and E. Papataxiarchis (eds), Princeton, 29-46.
Ellen, R. (2006) "Anthropological Studies in Classification" in R. Ellen, *The Categorical Impulse: Essays in the Anthropology of Classifying Behaviour*, Oxford, 31-7.
Faubion, J.D. (1994) *Modern Greek Lessons. A Primer in Historical Constructivism*, Princeton.
Hart, L.K. (1992) *Time, Religion, and Social Experience in Rural Greece*, Lanham, MD.
Hirschon, R. (1989) *Heirs of the Greek Catastrophe. The Social Life of Asia Minor Refugees in Piraeus*, Oxford.

Iossifides, M. (1991) "Sisters in Christ: Metaphors of Kinship among Greek Nuns", in P, Loizos and E. Papataxiarchis (eds) *Gender and Kinship in Modern Greece*, Princeton, 156-79.

Just, R. (1985) "A hommes plus riches, épouses plus jeunes. Le cas de Meganisi, île ionienne", in C. Piault (ed.) *Familles et biens en Grece et à Chypre*, Paris.

—— (2000) *A Greek Island Cosmos. Kinship and Community on Meganisi*, Oxford and Santa Fe.

Kennedy, R. (1986) "Women's Friendships on Crete: A Psychological Perspective", in J. Dubisch (ed.) *Gender and Power in Rural Greece*, Princeton, 121-38.

Kirtsoglou, E. (2004) *For Love of Women. Gender, Identity and Same-Sex Relations in a Greek Provincial Town*, London and New York.

Loizos, P. (1975) "Changes in Property Transfer Among Greek Cypriot Villagers", *Man N.S.* 10 (4) 503-23.

—— (1975) *The Greek Gift. Politics in a Cypriot Village*, Oxford.

—— (1981) *The Heart Grown Bitter. A Chronicle of Cypriot War Refugees*, Cambridge.

Loizos, P. and E. Papataxiarchis (eds) (1991) *Gender and Kinship in Modern Greece*, Princeton.

National Statistical Service of Greece, *Statistical Yearbook of Greece 1981*, Athens, no date.

—— (1994) *Statistical Yearbook of Greece 1991*, Athens.

—— *Statistical Yearbook of Greece 2004* http://www.statistics.gr/.

Papataxiarchis, E. "The Devolution of Property and Kinship Practices in Late and Post Ottoman Ethnic Greek Societies", *Mélanges de l'Ecole Française de Rome* 110 (1): 217-41.

Piault, C. (ed.) (1985) *Familles et Biens en Gréce et a Chypre*, Paris.

Salamone, S.D. and J.B. Stanton (1986) "Introducing the *Nikokyra*: Ideality and Reality in Social Process", in J. Dubisch (ed.) *Gender and Power in Rural Greece*, Princeton, 97-120.

Sant Cassia, P. and C. Bada (1992) *The Making of the Modern Greek Family. Marriage and Exchange in 19th Century Athens*, Cambridge.

Vernier, B. (1911) *La genèse sociale des sentiments. Ainés at cadets dans l'île grecque de Karpathos*, Paris.

10

PRESENTS, PROMISES AND PUNCTUALITY: ACCOUNTABILITY AND OBLIGATION IN GREEK SOCIAL LIFE

Renée Hirschon

In this contribution, I wish to show how perspicacious John Campbell was in identifying values associated with prestige and honour, and the notion of self regard *(egoismos)*, among Sarakatsani shepherds when he lived with them in the late 1950s. His seminal work *Honour, Family and Patronage* (1964) is a powerful comprehensive account and provided insights into Greek society for a generation of social anthropologists. In that classic monograph, he flagged up the most important social institutions which even today are salient for our understanding of contemporary Greek society, namely, the family and networks of patronage, and together with these, the central importance of a constellation of values and attitudes surrounding the notion of "honour".

My own fieldwork (around 1969-72) was located in an urban slum with few apparent similarities to the transhumant shepherds of Epirus, but much of the material that I gathered corresponded with Campbell's findings. This chapter examines the elements identified by Campbell as values stressing independence and autonomy, the denial of hierarchical relations, and a clear sense of self-confidence and equality. I wish to argue that these assertive values based on self-regard in a highland shepherd community have different expressions, depending on social action and on context. In my understanding of "honour" in Campbell's account, the essential common elements are a sense of dignity and independence, expressed as a concern with not being beholden to others.[1]

---

1   For a fuller discussion, reference should be made to a number of related issues. These are the notion of freedom, the concept of the individual, of personal

I suggest that these are widespread cultural concerns in Greek society that appear as transformations in different social and cultural contexts. This chapter aims to show how gift-giving, certain aspects of verbal behaviour, and lack of punctuality, can be better understood in terms of a particular emphasis—the premium placed on cultural notions of personal autonomy and its relationship to obligation. It is important to stress, however, that the unit of reference is not an individual in the Western sense (Hirschon, in press 2008), for in the Greek context social action and values and the construct of the human subject should always be seen as embedded in family loyalty and identification.

The ethnographic material is culled over time and from various contexts, part of my varied personal and professional experiences in Greece dating from the late 1960s, in different social classes, in widespread parts of the Athens-Piraeus metropolis (from Kolonaki to Kokkinia), in provincial centres (Mytilini) and in island settings (Karpathos, Rhodes, Aigina), as well as from my reading of colleagues' work on various parts of Greece. Inevitably this is an over-generalized account to make a specific point, and cannot do justice to the variations within the overall cultural pattern I wish to describe. I am aware of the significance of class and regional differences, but these can only be explored in a much larger study. My epistemological position lies within what Herzfeld has called the "militant middle ground" (1997: 165ff), especially in the insistence on recognizing the diversity within the populations we study (ibid.: 167, 170-1). It would be a mistake to charge the approach taken here with essentialism, since it does not posit any inherent or immutable quality to a people's worldview. On the contrary, I hold that cultural features are transmitted and acquired through processes of socialization and ongoing sociability; they are essentially malleable and dynamic but are also resilient and persistent.

The exercise I embark on here is inspired by the assumption that every culture has a logic, a rationale, and a set of practices and meanings which may for the outsider be incomprehensible or obscure but for the insider be self-evident and common sense. This is the challenge par excellence for the exercise of the social anthropologist's skills in interpretation, to "make sense of" the apparently puzzling aspects of the social conduct of others. Thus it is an attempt to advance an understanding of the ways in which central values that inform Greek social life have particular expressions.[2]

---

identity, the character of family and kinship ties. All are topics which in themselves merit full scale attention, and cannot be dealt with here. I address some of these issues in Hirschon in press, 2008. See also Herzfeld 2002.

2   My approach here is clearly hermeneutic/interpretive and also has as its theoretical reference aspects of Max Weber's work, an empathetic "*verstehen*" grasp of the subject matter. I find a "holistic" approach productive for Greek society

PRESENTS, PROMISES AND PUNCTUALITY

My aim is to demonstrate how the culturally defined premium placed on personal autonomy helps to explain the particular characteristics of apparently unrelated dimensions of social conduct: the style and cultural expression of presents, of promises and threats, and of the disregard of punctuality in Greece. My analysis is also a personal quest, for the topics dealt with here have long puzzled me, and have directly affected my professional and personal life in various social settings in Greece.

Presents, or how to ignore a gift

It is part of the experience of all who live in Greece that giving is far more difficult to achieve than receiving, and this generates a sense that one cannot repay the kindnesses offered. The well known hospitality of Greeks and their insistence that a stranger or guest should receive and not give creates tension around ways in which to reciprocate. The difficulties of how to deal with the overabundant hospitality of communities as far apart as Macedonia (Cowan 1990:64-7) and the Aegean islands (Herzfeld 1987; Kenna 1992) illustrate well the dilemmas of the stranger, the guest and the fieldworker. Hospitality is lavishly offered, but how can one reciprocate?[3] A return gift or small present of any kind is likely to be met with an embarrassed gesture of acceptance, or more tellingly, with the phrase, "But there was no need" (*ma dhen itan anagki*).

A paradigmatic example of the style of gift giving suitable for our analysis is that which takes place on the occasion of name day celebrations. Though these have undoubtedly changed in significance in the past few decades, nonetheless such occasions are still major family events for many Greeks, celebrations which involve the wider community in ways that are profound and symbolic of deep elements in the cosmology (see Hirschon, in press, 2008). Here, I concentrate on customary conventions which provide a clear picture of the accepted cultural practice before the insidious inroads of Europeanization which have accompanied Greece's EU membership in 1981, and my focus is on only one aspect of the celebration, the style in which the gift is presented and re-

---

	in seeking to interpret the relationship between worldview, ideas and values (part of the cosmology, the cultural endowment of a social group) and the observed actions which may present puzzles and paradoxes to the outsider. Also incorporated in my approach is the notion of "ethos" pioneered by Bateson in his innovative ethnography of Highland New Guinea, *Naven* [1936] (1958).
3	Building on Mauss' model, Sahlins (1974) developed a wider scheme which includes forms of "balanced" and "delayed reciprocity". This accommodates cross-cultural differences in forms of reciprocal exchange, and provides a possible application for solving the asymmetry of the exchange between guests and hosts in the Greek context (see Herzfeld 1987:78,84; Kenna 1992:140-1).

ceived. "Style", as a focus, is far from being a trivial matter but can be seen as a revelatory index of prevailing themes (see Herzfeld on "social poetics", 1997).

The expected and accepted practice was to visit the celebrant's house, uninvited, taking a wrapped present. The expected and acceptable gift was equally standardized and easily identifiable, usually a box of confectionery or a wrapped bottle of liqueur. Since the latter quite commonly remained untouched it could be—and often was—offered to someone else on another name day occasion. Usually the visitor entered the room and placed the gift unobtrusively on a table near the door, and did not present it to the host/ess. It would stay there, generally ignored, not unwrapped or commented on, and its presence apparently went unnoticed. The visitor would be offered a standard treat, a *kerasma* (see Cowan 1990: 65-7) consisting of a chocolate, a small glass of liqueur, and a glass of water, and would offer wishes for "Many Years" *(Chronia Polla)* to the celebrant. At the end of the name day visit, people again exchanged wishes for health and for long life, the visitor would leave and the gift would usually not be referred to. On other occasions, too, little attention was paid to gifts, certainly not in the presence of outsiders or of the giver. In private, however, the recipient might discuss a particular gift with family members or a close friend, especially at weddings, where gifts were not standardized as for name days. In such discussions, the conversation centred on the cost of the gift and, significantly, the degree of obligation implied by it.

The public indifference to the offering of a gift is highly significant. Unlike the conventions in some other cultures, especially among the Japanese (see below), the Greek response is far from a spirit of gracious acceptance. On the contrary, it seems that in most Greek circles the prevalent reaction to a gift was actually to make no response. If at all possible, a gift would be ignored. At the most, a gift would be acknowledged perfunctorily, as already noted, in the characteristic and telling phrase "But there was no need". In this way the rhetoric, style and character of this exchange of receiving the gift makes it appear as redundant, even unwelcome. I am provoked to pursue this cultural conundrum, and hope to present an explanation in which the reluctance to acknowledge gift giving in Greek context can be seen "to make sense"—flagging up what I infer is a structural tension between the two actors in giving and receiving.

The central notions around which my interpretive analysis is organized are those of reciprocity and obligation as suggested in Marcel Mauss' classic study *The Gift* ([1950] 1990). Exchange depends on the recognition of "the obligation to reciprocate" (1990: 8). Even though Mauss focus is on "archaic societies", the monumental impact of his work on exchange has highlighted the importance of the pervading notion of obligation which has achieved the status of an analytical tool (see Douglas in Mauss 1990: vii-xviii). According to the Maussian model, the act of gift-giving implies three linked exchanges: that of offering, that of receiving, and that of returning the gift, and these are linked together by an imperative, the recognition of the notion of obligation (ibid.:13-14).

Recognition of obligation, therefore, is the key, providing the structural principle which orders the essence of gift exchange. Although Mauss does not elaborate on the difference in status between the subordinate and super-ordinate positions associated with exchange, his analysis does include the recognition of honour, rivalry, and the resolution of hostility which are involved in all exchange relationships. In my understanding of the Greek context, the key lies here: once a gift is accepted, the receiver is under obligation to return it and until doing so, s/he occupies a structurally inferior position. As Campbell noted, ".. to be grateful is to be obliged (*ypochreomenos*), and this is an admission of inequality and even of weakness" (1964: 95). At the structural level, then, the notion of obligation is a nexus which generates ongoing exchanges in which the actors seesaw between superior and inferior positions depending at which point in the chain of exchanges they are. Metaphorically, social actors are trapped on a seesaw of perpetual motion: what is down has to come up as one gift is countered by another.

The analysis in this paper, therefore, takes into account the structural dimension, i.e. status differences between two actors in an exchange, as well as the cultural dimension, i.e. the values and ideas which imbue that exchange with meaning. Since I suggest that the notion of obligation is a highly developed indigenous one in Greece, an explicit and charged concept which—I contend—constitutes an ordering principle, the analysis must consider both dimensions. My approach predicates linguistic expressions and phrases as central elements in the particular cultural mindset (see Herzfeld 1997:143-8) or "ethos" of the society. Here, the Greek word for obligation, *ypochreosi*, reveals the tension generated by this notion, for the word itself incorporates the idea of "debt", *chreos*. Thus, in Greek, the notion of obligation is one of "indebtedness", having its root in the notion of debt: *ypo=* in or under, *chreos=* debt. To be obliged, therefore, entails being *in debt* or rather, literally, "under debt" (Hirschon 1992: 45-7, and Hirschon 2001 for effects on linguistic politeness).

Furthermore, the structural principle is immediately evident in the word itself, since the relationship of creditor and debtor is never one of equality, and so neither is the relationship between those involved in any exchange in which a sense of obligation resides. Greeks are verbally explicit about the abhorrence of "being under obligation" *(to na'sai ypochreomenos)*. Herein, I argue, lies the clue to understanding the stylistic indifference that Greeks affect when a gift

193

is presented. The cultural awkwardness begins to make sense for it is an inevitable consequence of the abhorrence of obligation, of being "in debt", and the erection of structural asymmetries of superior and inferior statuses in a society where an ethos of egalitarianism prevails, and there is a reluctance to concede to hierarchy. Using the term "no need" when faced with the gift surely refers to cultural ideals of independence, autonomy and self-sufficiency, and the ability to provide not only for oneself but also for the guest without thought of return (see du Boulay 1974: 38-40 for the notion of the house as a cornucopia and of household self-sufficiency).

I am arguing that the culturally acceptable style of gift presentation in Greece, in which the gift is practically ignored, is a direct reflection of an indigenous "problem", that is, the culturally defined abhorrence of status differences and hierarchical relations in everyday life. The "problem" from the Greek point of view, therefore, is the open recognition of inequality of status or rank implied in gift exchange. Along with many others who have studied Greek society, I argue that the reluctance to accept hierarchy and the abhorrence of rank difference is a major issue.[4] In what several anthropologists have generally characterized as the "agonistic" and competitive spirit of the society (e.g. Friedl 1962: 75-6, Peristiany 1965:188,190; Herzfeld 1985), Greeks do not easily concede hierarchy in informal settings. They do so only in specific institutionalized contexts or those which may be instrumentally useful and which are defined by the individual (e.g. with powerful persons). The turbulent and unpredictable nature of most areas of social life arises from the fact that authority, especially that of the state, is more readily questioned than accepted; similarly, challenges to the status quo are a cultural norm.

Two examples provide useful demonstrations. On a recent journey, I complained to the duty policemen at a provincial airport departure lounge that non-smoking signs were being contravened in all the waiting areas, so there was no smoke-free area for non-smokers. His response was enlightening. In a supercilious tone, this officer of the law stated firmly, "Madam, here in Greece, the laws are not strictly applied" (*Edo stin Ellada, kyria mou, oi nomoi then tirountai afstira*). His response put me in my place as a foreigner who was obviously not conversant with "Greek ways", and it exposes the themes I pursue in this analysis, those of "unaccountability", autonomy, and reluctance to accept authority.

---

4 This theme can be traced in many of the established anthropological monographs and articles. Peristiany (1965:186-7) was one of the first to note the significance of rank in organizational settings as it affected the sense of self-regard. See Herzfeld's 2004 study of apprenticeship in Crete, and for its linguistic correlates see e.g. Hirschon 1992: 22-8; 2001.

The latter theme, a cultural predisposition to challenge the authority of others and the necessity of asserting one's own worth, is revealed in a common response, characteristically voiced in Greek interpersonal conflicts: "And who are you?" (*Kai pios eisai esy?*) (Hirschon 1992: 40). This phrase, I argue, is the quintessential expression of that value identified by Campbell and other anthropologists as self-regard, *egoismos*. Peristiany noted the concern with equality (*isotimia*) in the Cyprus villages he studied, concluding that "hierarchical relations are resented and resisted", and illustrated this attitude with the phrase used in Cyprus, "You have a moustache, and I have a moustache" (*K'esy moustaki, k"ego moustaki*) (1965:177-8). Cowan shows how forms of dance may express the rhetoric of "defiant masculinity" in a Macedonian town (1990:173-80). In many ethnographic studies, the cultural emphasis on self-regarding values, on independence, on the denial of hierarchical relations, and a clear sense of assertive self-confidence are clear. However, all these elements should only be understood in the context of the primary unit of personal loyalty and identification, that of the family.[5]

In Kokkinia, for example, a similar sentiment was revealed in the local men's aspiration for self-employment, when they said that they preferred not to have "anyone over their head" (*na min echis kanenan pano sto kefali sou*) (Hirschon [1989]1998: 84-98). As a pronounced cultural value in this urban proletarian environment, self-employment can be shown to have its roots in the same set of preoccupations—independence, autonomy, self-determination—as those of Sarakatsani shepherds and Cretan artisans. It is the urban transformation in a wage labour economy of what Campbell and others have identified as assertive masculine values in Greece's rural areas.

The transformation of values in the urban context should also be assessed from a gendered perspective. The austere regime guided by the notion of shame (*ntropi*) which constrained the lives of Sarakatsan women (Campbell 1964:276-8) might have appeared at first sight to be irrelevant in Kokkinia where urban living was informed by values of fashion and competitive rivalry for prestige and economic success. Nonetheless, in the early 1970s female chastity and sexual propriety were foremost concerns among most families (Hirschon [1978]1993), and the gendered division of labour was held up as an ideal. It was therefore highly

---

5   This point is also evident in most Greek ethnographies. In addition, we should note that these are culturally articulated values which do not correspond with the same terms and notions espoused in the late capitalist societies of the developed West, or have the same social consequences. I have argued elsewhere that constructs of the human subject and of personhood require a more nuanced analysis in which the quality of individualism and what constitutes it in the Greek context must be carefully examined (Hirschon, in press 2008; see also Herzfeld 2002).

significant that those women who were forced to supplement the family income by becoming reluctant members of the labour force expressed their preference for lower paid work in factories to the better paid jobs in domestic service. The implications of relative status vis-à-vis another woman, and the risk of criticism for their housekeeping abilities, among the main criteria of female prestige and identity, made these jobs less desirable, despite their better remuneration (Hirschon [1989] 1998: 98-104). Just as men were concerned with their status in a highly competitive society and responded according to the prevalent values protecting their sense of dignity and self-regard, women responded in accord with values associated with the prestige attached to their womanhood.

Analytically and in abstract terms the central question relates to that of hierarchy as an ordering principle in Greek society. It is enlightening, therefore, to take as an instructive contrast the Japanese case where both the notion of hierarchy and that of status inequality are quite differently perceived and articulated. Students of Japanese society emphasize the overt recognition of rank differences and their explicit codification in terms of address, interpersonal conduct, and social organization. An interesting reflection and clear cultural expression of this fundamental concern among Japanese is the style of gift giving, quite different from that prevalent in Greece. Dore's classic study *City Life in Japan* (1985) devotes considerable attention to reciprocal gift exchanges, while a recent study (Rupp 2003) devotes a whole monograph to the topic of gift-giving in its many contexts. The overall picture is one in which the Japanese devote attention to the gift at the time of its offering during which they openly express their appreciation. The obligation attendant on the exchange is explicitly recognized, even though they may not feel entirely comfortable about this. A further interesting contrast is the degree of formalization of the exchange, the detailed attention to wrapping of a gift, later speculation about its cost and the matching of the return gift, as well as the timing of the return (see Hendry 1989; Rupp op.cit.). All of these elements of style are culturally prescribed concerns in the Japanese case. By and large, these features are given little overt attention in the Greek practice of gift giving. Significantly for our argument, too, is that there is generally only a limited acceptance of rank differences in specific contexts in Greek society. Whereas the principle of hierarchy and its cultural acceptance are seen to pervade all aspects of Japanese social life (also modified by context), they are a far more problematic and ambiguous dimension in Greek social relations.

Verbal play

I can further illustrate the ramifications of the cultural emphasis on personal autonomy with reference to freedom of expression, by examining aspects of linguistic conduct where the notion of obligation—or rather the absence of it through a lack of accountability—operates. In my early fieldwork in Kokkinia, I was fascinated by the discourse of adults and children and, in particular, the way in which adults used unfulfilled promises and threats, and the frequency and extent of their gratuitously false stories. My experience was reinforced by bringing up a young child in a circle of academic colleagues in a provincial town (Mytilini) in the late 1980s, which alerted me further to this cultural practice, what can ethnocentrically be called "verbal irresponsibility".

In trying to make sense of what constitutes a lack of accountability for verbal utterances (Hirschon 1992), I concluded that a Greek speaker has a greater degree of freedom to dissociate words from actions than in my own speech community (middle-class English-speaking "colonial"). There was (and is) a different relationship between word and action, what academic colleagues and I referred to in shorthand as "*logos*" and "*praxis*". For my contrastive English speech community, ideally a close correspondence should exist between what you say and what you do, between stated intention and performed action. Similarly, value is placed on honesty, and emphasis is given to face value representations, another dimension in which these two speech communities differ. Anthropological attention has focused on teasing and deception in Greek villages, on lying and its social uses, particularly by Friedl (1962:79-81, 1972) and du Boulay (1974, 1976), and on tactics of concealment and dissembling in urban contexts (Hirschon [1989] 1998: 176-81; Herzfeld 2004: 47-9, 95-6,100,105, 107ff.). The implicit comparative framework of all these anthropological studies shows nonetheless how culture-bound are assessments of the (linguistic) conduct of "others". Sifianou's revealing study shows how attributions of hypocrisy and falsity abound in Greek views of the English speaker, particularly with regard to politeness (1992:13, 42-3).

In attempting to unravel the conundrums of Greek verbal play (Hirschon 1992), I followed Searle, a philosopher of language whose approach is compatible with an anthropological perspective. He reminds us that "meaning is more than a matter of intention, it is also a matter of convention" (1971: 46) and shows how any attempt to understand speech acts requires knowledge and familiarity with the "rule governed skills" of that language. Consequently, we must not only confront the question of context, but also the relationship between the form of utterances and their function, i.e. the conventions under which they operate.

The contexts in which promises made by Greek adults to children are much like ones which English speakers make, but there appears to be greater scope for default. "If you stop crying, I'll take you for a walk—buy you an ice cream—tell you a story" are all conditional formulations used by adults everywhere to control children. Since they are essentially bribes and bargaining ploys, there is some leeway for non-fulfilment of the promise. The difference in the Greek case is the prevalence and frequency of gratuitous promises made without any apparent conditions, but left unfulfilled. Similarly, I noticed the negative statements of intention, i.e. threats, which expressed some kind of violent sanction upon a tiny offender, but which were never carried out. In my neighbourhood in Kokkinia, spine-chilling threats reverberated from courtyards and doorways but were never followed through in action (for examples, see Hirschon 1992:38-40; see also Friedl 1962:82). Parents were affectionate and indulgent and found physical discipline abhorrent. Adults could, however, express their anger and frustration to children in the same way as they could make promises—without there being a necessary commitment to action.

This led me to consider that such utterances constitute formally what appear to be statements of intention but do not work as such, and again, following Searle, I noted the distinction between promises and statements of intention. I suggested that the different approach to intentional statements in Greek usage could be attributed to a cultural premium placed on personal autonomy/independence, the reluctance to accept the obligation to follow through a stated intention, and a consequent lack of accountability.

The first question which we have to face is whether a correspondence exists between apparently similar speech acts in two different language communities. In the use of language in my constrastive English speech community, statements of intention also entail commitments to action, at least normatively. Ethnographic evidence suggests that the Greek equivalents of these statements of intention, specifically promises, threats and lies, do not entail the same degree of accountability. I therefore concluded that in Greek usage, utterances which seem to constitute statements of intention do not operate or function as such. Although they may syntactically correspond to the English forms, the function of these statements of intention is rather different. Expressing intentionality, they have the same grammatical form and implication, but the convention of usage is so different as to suggest that these statements should constitute another category in terms of function. I therefore suggested a taxonomic refinement for Greek usage, in that statements of intention contain, as a subcategory, statements of affect which resemble them syntactically but not in function, since they are not binding in terms of action (ibid.:43-5). I concluded, therefore, that what appeared to be statements of *intention* were actually statements of *affect* which expressed particular emotional states and dispositions, but did not entail commitment to action.

Lack of accountability is another striking aspect of adults' verbalizing with children, viz. verbal fantasy contained in false stories which are frequently told by adults to children, but never resolved (specific examples are presented in Hirschon 1992:40-2). It seemed often that they would answer children's questions with whatever sprang first to mind and create fantastic scenarios without any provocation.

One significant issue in these cases of verbal fantasy, teasing and lies is that indications are not given to resolve the puzzles set up in the child's mind. In an English speech community, similar games are played, but it is customary here for the "frame" to be set by the phrase "Only joking". In the Greek case, the verbal fantasy is often presented as serious, can be long-drawn out, and is seldom marked explicitly as a "joke" (ibid.: 42-3). Since only the "joker" knows whether the statement is true or not and the listener must try to figure it out, this can also be seen to constitute a contest over relative status position. Obviously, though, other non-verbal cues are also simultaneously given. Greek speakers have pointed out to me that non-verbal indicators such as intonation, body language and gestures play a very important part in communication and in interpretation, particularly in issues related to politeness (Hirschon 2001). While it is impossible to assess comparatively, non-verbal signs are an essential element in effective communication in all language groups and must also be passed on to children at an early stage.

One may infer that the rules governing Greek speech acts allow a great variety of verbal expression, since it is not necessary to follow through with action.[6] Consequently, too, playing games with words in the form of verbal fantasy is also more of a cultural activity than in a language group where a literally bound convention of verbal conduct prevails. Since the utterance does not entail a definite commitment to perform the action, the speaker may simply express transient states of affect or any fantasy of the moment. Indeed this provides for the speaker a degree of freedom with words, and an "elastic" use of language where direct accountability and face value statements are not always normative expectations. Given that Greeks enjoy considerable freedom in their verbal utterances since they are not absolutely bound by them, problems of interpretation are posed, both for insiders and outsiders. "I'll see you tomorrow" is a statement of intention in form, and also conveys the sentiment that the speaker *wishes* to meet the next day. However, actualization of the intention in the Greek context is best left as an open question.

Scott's (1985) compelling analysis of "everyday forms of resistance" in a Malaysian peasant community may shed light on the historical dimension of "verbal non-accountability" as an aspect of Greek culture. In Scott's exami-

---

6   Mackridge has commented on the particular richness of the language in its literary and verbal forms, poetry being notably a flourishing genre (1992: 111-20).

nation of power differentials, exploitation and class conflict, he characterizes some of the everyday forms of resistance as "foot dragging, dissimulation, false compliance, pilfering, feigned ignorance, slander...." (ibid.: 29), and noted a performative dimension which included "false" or "calculated" deference (ibid.: 278, 285). In the Greek case, an interesting possibility for interpretation lies in the power inequalities of the past. The Ottoman empire's domination of its subjects may have had similar concomitants; notably, the kind of non-accountability highlighted in this paper is also stereotypically associated with the Balkans and Middle East, regions which were long under the imperial regime with its constant extraction of taxes and varying periods of oppression. "Verbal non-accountability" in its various forms (deceit, lying, dissimulation) can therefore be understood as part of a survival strategy as well as a mode of resistance to outside domination. Such forms of everyday resistance may be seen as historically rooted and incorporated among cultural predispositions that become part of the socialization process. Children may also participate in this kind of verbal play, in a way that matches those of adults, where they perform and dramatize and soon acquire a sense of caution about the face value weight of verbal statements. Clearly, this kind of linguistic conduct has social consequences which are historically and culturally explicable.

This returns us to questions about the relationship between intention, action and obligation, and issues of interpretation. The social consequences of this nexus—intention-action-obligation—leads inevitably to a degree of caution, suspicion and cynicism, in what might be called a "doubting Thomas" syndrome. This attitudinal disposition is a feature which extends into all aspects of Greek life from the most formalized and bureaucratic to the intimate dynamics of home life. "Don't believe it until you see it" (*mechri na to deis, mi' to pisteveis*) is a principle which Greeks say that they need to employ in all social contexts; it is expressed explicitly, and is especially evident in responses to electoral promises by party politicians. This saying expresses the kind of cynicism and suspicion that was recognized early in anthropological descriptions of Greece, and has been invoked to explain the tendency to adopt "conspiracy theories".[7]

In an analysis of bureaucracy, Herzfeld has explored its symbolic roots in the context of the ideology and practice of accountability (1992). I have argued that lack of accountability can be traced to patterns of verbal socialization of children where an early attitude of caution is instilled into children's minds regarding any kind of verbal utterance (Hirschon 1992: 47-52). The existential knowledge that words are not to be taken at face value is propagated and the

---

7   See the subtle analysis by Sutton 2003. Stewart notes the values of autarky, cleverness and cunning among Naxiot villagers (199:62-3), and illustrates them with a paradigm case in the context of local politics (ibid.:64-6).

message also has ontological implications (ibid.). Despite this conditioning, however, it is nonetheless a common complaint that "people do not do what they say they'll do".

In the Greek case it is clear that the link or continuum between word and action, between statement of intention and commitment to act, is variable. There is a hiatus since the verbal utterance of a promise, or a threat, or an undertaking to do something, to be somewhere, may remain hanging, suspended in the realm of "*logos*" without any necessary impulse for the equivalent action to become manifest in "*praxis*". I maintain that this is a pervasive feature in Greek culture, and while it does show variation, it is not confined to a particular class or region. There are undoubtedly different styles and genres through which verbal laxity or non-accountability is expressed, just as it is necessary to specify the class and regional parameters of linguistic conduct in any English-speaking speech community.

To sum up my argument then, phrased in general terms, many Greeks act as though they are not under absolute obligation to follow through from their verbal utterances. Although the performance view of social life stresses that words are an assertion of the person, it would also appear that the issue is far more complex: verbal rhetoric needs to be seen in the context of the rhetoric of social action. Ethnographic evidence of the disjunction between words and actions exists, and suggests that the notion of "detachability" is useful. As I understand it, a Greek speaker is not necessarily bound by words; somehow, a sense of self can stand apart from one's words, depending on context and occasion. Verbal utterances are detachable from the person's set of inviolable commitments, those aspects of self that comprise the person and his/her own image of self.

Punctuality, or the freedom to turn up when you feel like it

Attitudes to punctuality, described here briefly, reinforce my perception that the key to understanding patterns of conduct such as "verbal irresponsibility" and the awkwardness with gifts is to be found in the attitude to obligation, and linked to the recognition of social hierarchy, to issues of personal autonomy and commitment in Greek society. In my view, punctuality—or rather the lack of it—can also be understood in these terms, and I present here a tentative attempt to grapple with a problem encountered by all who have dealings with Greece.[8]

---

8   This very limited attempt touches on an enormous subject, viz. the structuring and significance of time in Greek society. Deserving extensive analysis, it is understudied in the main; see, however, two noteworthy studies, Hart 1992, du Boulay 1995.

Everyone soon learns that appointments are not strictly adhered to in Greece, indeed in many cultures of the Mediterranean and beyond. It is one of the things that strike visitors to Greece who can say appreciatively, though quite inaccurately, "How relaxed is the way of life here". I argue that one aspect of Greek attitudes to time, the widespread lack of punctuality, makes sense when seen in the context of the pervasive cultural values already noted. An interesting feature, which poses difficulties for anyone who has to operate in a formal and institutionalized context, is the conflict set up between absolute time schedules essential for the smooth operation of any organization and the reluctance or inability of individuals to keep to these timetables.

Experience in a particular Greek university department some years ago included ongoing misunderstandings and confrontations over time schedules and their violation. An early experience provides an illustrative example. In September 1987 the seven staff of the newly inaugurated Department of Social Anthropology had two days in which to select 20 students for places on the postgraduate course. Thirty candidates had to be interviewed, selections had to be discussed, and other matters such as course organization had to be covered. With a tight schedule, the interviews were scheduled from 9 am on the first morning, but at the specified time only two members of staff were present. By 9.30 four of the seven staff had appeared, and several candidates were waiting. The interview sessions did not start before 10 am, and each lasted more than the allocated time, further putting out the schedule for the rest of the day. The following day, after two hours of discussion on selection of candidates, with only half the agenda covered by late morning, a 15-minute break was agreed on, and staff were urged to be punctual. All were late returning, and after half an hour, only five of the seven had returned. The working session could not proceed, however, because everyone's opinion had to be considered. The group had to wait until finally the two errant staff members returned after an hour and a half!

In an educated speech community, that of a university department for example, the issues surrounding personal autonomy and hierarchy are further complicated by the elaborated code of communication, which also has its gendered dimensions. The flourishing nature of rhetoric was revealed in academic encounters where "*logos*" (a loaded concept, conveying both the "word" and "rationality") takes an extreme form. It is through verbal performance in this primarily male arena (it was noticeable that female academics of my acquaintance expressed themselves differently from males) that the "rational being", *o logikos anthropos*—he who possesses *logos*—asserts his worth, independence, and sense of self-regard. Lengthy speeches could not be interrupted, for affront is taken when freedom of expression is interrupted.[9] For the everyday functioning of the Department, therefore, maintaining a timetable was a secondary consideration, the cultural pattern of elasticity prevailed and, as elsewhere, the connection between "*logos*" and "*praxis*" was problematic and unpredictable. The crucial link between word and action varied for individuals, a variability that could be explained in terms of the individual's attitudes to personal autonomy, to obligation and to acknowledgment of hierarchy.

Overall, these features continued to be characteristic in the pattern of Departmental organization. Short meetings were impossible since everyone had the right to speak in the expected rhetorical style (they often lasted for four to five hours). Meetings could never start at the scheduled time because a majority of colleagues would not be present. Meetings would often be held up because, even when a majority was present, the one person essential for discussing a particular issue would be the last to arrive. My attempts as Head of department to sensitize colleagues to the need to keep schedules were unsuccessful, even though all of them had had several years of education in France, USA or UK. My colleagues' own explanations of why they were consistently late ranged from attributing it to self-confessed bad management or lack of organization, to the trite slogan of the "academic quarter-hour" (*to akademaiko tetarto*), itself a continental European (German academic) reference point. But this did not constitute an explanation, only an excuse. One colleague's comment was revealing, however: "Time itself is not important," he said. "What is important is getting the work done". Like many others, he would say that the time given for an appointment is only an approximation: "5 o'clock" means "some time after 5" and, anyway, "no-one expects accurate timing" and so "there's no problem".

In order to draw my argument together, I define punctuality as the recognition of obligation and of accountability; it entails the expression of commitment to an agreed time schedule, in essence the obligation to be on time and the recognition of an obligation not to keep others waiting. It is a commitment to action following a statement of intention so that, in this sense, the link with "verbal irresponsibility" becomes clear. I argue, then, that lack of punctuality is another expression of the disjunction in the relationship between intention-action-obligation. Promises unfulfilled, threats unexecuted, and turning up late (or not at all) are all expressions of the same phenomenon—the loose attitude to, or even the denial of, the obligation to follow through from words to action. It is a way of maintaining a sense of autonomy and freedom of action, of

---

9   Television discussion panels are a striking current example, where all four or five speakers insist on making their points simultaneously, the effect being to produce a babble of competing voices and incomprehensible sound.

not being beholden to outside expectations. The interpretation of attitudes to time in Greek society requires much deeper and more extensive analysis than is possible in this limited reference to a single aspect. In the present analysis, the relevant point is that consistent unpunctuality can be understood in the context of other characteristic forms of social conduct, whose common denominator is their relation to a sense of personal autonomy.

Conclusion

I have already referred to the etymological significance of the Greek word for "obligation", having its root in the notion of debt: *ypo=* in or under, *chreos=* debt. To be in debt is to owe something, to be beholden to someone else. It is a bond and in essence a limitation on freedom. Furthermore, for one to be under obligation or in debt implies a relationship of inequality. In structural terms, the debtor is inferior to the creditor, the recipient of a gift to the donor. In all situations involving the notion of obligation the inequality of rank or status is inherent, and I further suggest that the binding notion underlying obligation, in both social and emotional terms, places a limitation on the sense of personal autonomy that an individual has.

These general characteristics surrounding the concept of obligation have particular impact in the context of Greek social organization and values. Ethnographies of Greece have shown the central place that values of self-regard and independence occupy, illustrating their expression in different communities: Sarakatsan and Cretan shepherds, mountain and plains villages, island communities. For men in the poor district of Kokkinia settled by Asia Minor refugees in the 1920s, the most important concern in the economic sphere in the 1970s was to achieve self-employment. The telling phrase used to describe their aspirations was "not to have anyone above their heads", and I argue that this is an expression of the urban transformation of a constellation of values identified by Campbell.

I have tried to document the transformations of what I suggest is a wide cultural emphasis on the sense of personal autonomy, independence, and consequent self-regard. This can be seen in various contexts and aspects of social action, but stands in tension with the reluctance to recognize hierarchy and a sense of obligation. I have focused on ways in which exchange through gift-giving is disregarded, on various forms of "verbal unaccountability", on the lack of concern for punctuality. I hope that I have managed to "make sense" of these disparate features of Greek life, by showing how they derive from the sentiment of self-regard associated with the quintessential value of honour, first identified by John Campbell some fifty years ago in his ground-breaking study of Sarakatsan shepherds, and whose findings are by no means limited to that time or social context.

Acknowledgements

Contrary to the spirit of the foregoing analysis, I am happy to express my deep gratitude to Michael Herzfeld and David Sutton for feedback at a late stage in the drafting of this chapter, and I fully recognize my obligation to them! I have tried to improve the text in the light of their comments, but the remaining shortcomings are my responsibility. I am also grateful to Joy Hendry for a helpful discussion on the Japanese case.

BIBLIOGRAPHY

Bateson, G. [1936] (1958) 2nd ed. *Naven*, Stanford University Press.
Campbell, J.K. (1964) *Honour, Family and Patronage*. Oxford, Clarendon Press.
Cowan, J. (1990) *Dance and the Body Politic in Northern Greece*, Princeton University Press.
Dore, R.P. (1958) *City Life in Japan: A Study of a Tokyo Ward*, Berkeley, University of California Press.
Du Boulay, J. (1974) *Portrait of a Greek Mountain Village*, Oxford, Clarendon Press.
—— (1976) "Lies, Mockery and Family Integrity" in J. Peristiany (ed.), *Mediterranean Family Structures*, Cambridge University Press, 389-406.
—— (1995) "Time and Society in Rural Greece" in *Brothers and Others: Essays in Honour of John Peristiany*, Athens, EKKE, 147-62.
Friedl, E. (1962) *Vasilika: A Village in Modern Greece*, New York, Holt, Rinehart and Winston.
—— (1972) "Paidi kai Oikoyenia", *Iatriki* (Athens) vol. 21 (1), 113-14.
Hendry, J. (1993) *Wrapping Culture*, Oxford, Clarendon Press.
Herzfeld, M. (1985) *The Poetics of Manhood: Contest and Identity in a Cretan Mountain Village*, Princeton University Press.
—— (1987) "'As in Your Own House': Hospitality, Ethnography, and the Stereotype of Mediterranean Society" in D. Gilmore (ed.), *Honour and Shame and the Unity of the Mediterranean*. Washington, DC, American Anthropological Association, 75-89.
—— (1992) *The Social Production of Indifference: Exploring the Symbolic Roots of Western Bureaucracy*, New York, Oxford, Berg.
—— (2002) "The European Self: Rethinking an Attitude" in A. Pagden (ed.) *The Idea of Europe: From Antiquity to the European Union*, Woodrow Wilson Centre and Cambridge University Press, 139-70.
—— (2004) *The Body Impolitic: Artisans and Artifice in the Global Hierarchy of Value*, University of Chicago Press.
Hirschon, R. [1978] (1993) "Open Body/Closed Space: the Transformation of Female Sexuality" in S. Ardener (ed.), *Defining Females: the Nature of Women in Societ*, Oxford, Berg, 66-88.
—— [1989] (1998) 2nd ed., *Heirs of the Greek Catastrophe: the Social Life of Asia Minor Refugees in Piraeus*, Oxford, New York, Berghahn.
—— (1992) "Greek Adults' Verbal Play or, How to Train for Caution", *Journal of Modern Greek Studies*, vol. 10, 35-56.
—— (2001) "Freedom, Solidarity and Obligation: the Socio-Cultural Con-

text of Greek Politeness" in A. Bayraktaroglu and M. Sifianou (eds), *Linguistic Politeness Across Boundaries: the Case of Greek and Turkish,* Amsterdam, Philadelphia, John Benjamins Publishing, 17-42.

——— (in press, 2008) "Indigenous Persons and Imported Individuals: Changing Concepts of Personal Identity in Contemporary Greece" in C. Hann (ed.) *Eastern Christianities: Anthropological Perspectives,* Berkeley, University of California Press.

Kenna, M. (1995) "Saying "No" in Greece: Some Preliminary Thoughts on Hospitality, Gender and the Evil Eye" in *Brothers and Others: Essays in Honour of John Peristiany,* Athens, EKKE, 133-46.

Hart, L. Kain (1992) *Time, Religion and Social Experience in Rural Greece,* Lanham, MD, Rowman & Littlefield Publishers.

Mackridge, P. (1992) "Game of Power and Solidarity—Commentary", *Journal of Modern Greek Studies,* vol. 10: 111-20.

Mauss, M. [1950] (1990) *The Gift: the Form and Reason for Exchange in Archaic Societies,* transl. W.D. Halls, London, New York, Routledge.

Peristiany, J. (1965) "Honour and Shame in a Cypriot Highland Village" in J. Peristiany (ed.), *Honour and Shame: the Values of Mediterranean Society,* London, Weidenfeld and Nicolson, 173-90.

Rupp, K. (2003) *Gift Giving in Japan: Cash, Connections, Cosmologies,* Stanford University Press.

Sahlins, M. (1974) "On the Sociology of Primitive Exchange" in M. Sahlins, *Stone Age Economics,* London, Tavistock, 185-276.

Scott, J. (1985) *Weapons of the Weak: Everyday Forms of Peasant Resistance,* New Haven, London, Yale University Press.

Searle, J.R. (1971) "What is a Speech Act?" in J.R. Searle (ed.), *The Philosophy of Language,* London, Oxford University Press, 39-53.

Sifianou, M. (1992) *Politeness Phenomena in England and Greece: A Cross Cultural Perspective,* Oxford, Clarendon Press.

Stewart, C. (1991) *Demons and the Devil,* Princeton University Press.

Sutton, D. (2003) "Poked by the 'Foreign Finger' in Greece: Conspiracy Theory or the Hermeneutics of Suspicion?" in K. S. Brown and Yannis Hamilakis (eds), *The Usable Past: Greek Metahistories,* Lanham, MD, Oxford, Lexington Books, 191-210.

11

BREAD AND SHEEP: A COMPARATIVE STUDY OF SACRED MEANINGS AMONG THE AMBELIOTS AND THE SARAKATSANI

Juliet du Boulay

Both the history and the literature of Greece bear witness to the enduring influence of its Byzantine heritage, and the more recent development of ethnographic studies in Greece continues to find evidence of the way in which Orthodox Christianity still shapes many aspects of popular symbolism.[1] But no single influence is likely to have been more formative in this respect than the Orthodox liturgy, whose texts have remained substantially as they are now since the 15th century,[2] and whose enactment has continued in much the same way in cities and villages not just in Greece, but throughout the Orthodox world.

In a book soon to be published[3] I have sought to explore the connections between the Orthodox liturgy and the symbolism of everyday life in Greek culture. For this purpose I have focused on the village of Ambeli, whose ethnographic portrait I painted in 1974;[4] but despite this local limitation, a striking

---

[1] For recent examples see L. Kain Hart, *Time, Religion and Social Experience in Rural Greece*, Lanham: Rowman and Littlefield, 1992; C. Stewart, *Demons and the Devil: Moral Imagination in Modern Greek Culture,* Princeton University Press, 1991.

[2] R.F. Taft, *The Byzantine Rite: a Short History*, Collegeville, Mn.: The Liturgical Press, 1992.

[3] J. du Boulay, *Cosmos, Life, and Liturgy in a Greek Orthodox Village,* Evvia, Greece: Denise Harvey Publishers (forthcoming).

[4] Juliet du Boulay, *Portrait of a Greek Mountain Village*, Oxford: Clarendon Press, 1974. Reprinted as paperback, 1979. Reprinted 1994, Limni (Evvia, Greece), Denise Harvey Publishers, 1994.

feature of the material is the richness and variability of the everyday symbolism in contrast with the relatively constant and unchanging character of its liturgical sources. Thus while the book has focused on the necessary initial task of showing the integral symbolic connections between popular and liturgical imagery within a single community, there remains a longer-term comparative task of tracing the way in which the same liturgical sources give rise to varied symbolic imagery in different kinds of community.

The occasion of a *Festschrift* for John Campbell is therefore an opportunity to explore how this longer-term task might be approached, using his extraordinarily sensitive observations on the everyday symbolism of Sarakatsan shepherds[5] as the basis for comparison with the mountain village of Ambeli, where subsistence farming was the primary way of living. His work in the 1950s and mine in the 1960s and early 1970s are distinguished less by historical change during the intervening decade, which was slight compared with what came after, than by the very different ways of making a living in the two communities. Both stand as exemplars of ways of life now rare in Greece since the flight to the cities and the growth of trade with Europe, but of continuing importance as ethnographic types, and I refer to both in the ethnographic present.

The people of Ambeli live in a world which is both sacred and material, by no means defined by hard and fast boundaries, but rather by categories which are permeable and capable of infusing each other at any moment. Thus the sacred presences of the village, Christ, the saints and the Mother of God, not being confined to church, may be met in the way; and the nereids, the evil hour, the demons in their various manifestations, are also not just presences inhabiting the human heart but may be encountered, seen and heard. Nowhere, however, is this infusion of categories so clear as in the charter for village life, the origin myth of the Fall.

According to this understanding man was created to live in a harmonious relationship with his creator in a world which was paradise. Nature gave her fruits freely—"Whatever you wanted you had, roast chicken, whatever you wanted"—stones were bread, there was abundant water, and no struggle to live. But there was a condition for this blessedness—obedience to God; and harmony with God once having been ruptured, the curse which then fell upon man is related in terms of a consequent rupture of harmony with the created world: "You, Adam, with blood and with sweat shall you till the fields, and you Eve, with pain and agony shall you bear children". Thus the essential element of the Fall is an initial disobedience which breaks the primal harmony; it can

---

5   J.K. Campbell, *Honour, Family and Patronage*, Oxford: Clarendon Press, 1964, 6.

only be expiated, and harmony between man and God restored, through obedience to a pattern of work and the making of a family, and to death.

The relationship with the earth, then, is the locus of the spiritual drama lived by the villagers every day. "Do we have things otherwise now?" a villager will say, as he shouts at recalcitrant mules and exerts all his strength on the plough as it turns over the thin covering of earth on stony ground, and indeed the question answers itself. It is because of this that the main produce of this labour, the winning of bread, is for these subsistence farmers a symbolic as well a material act, for the bread in the houses is not only a promise of life for the coming year, but an image of the reversal of the curse and the overcoming of the hostility between man and the wild by the obedient living through of that original punishment.

Bread, then, is prototypical of food and hospitality, and its growing and harvesting, its giving and receiving, are central to the maintenance of the village household; and since it is part of the general interpenetration of sacred and material that the rhythms of the natural world run indivisibly with the sacred rhythms of the liturgical year, bread is central also to the sacred life lived within the households. This sacred life, incarnated in basic patterns of fast and feast involving both regular days and seasons and applying not just to food but also to work, is composed of a series of interlocking cycles—from Great Lent to Easter, from Easter to Pentecost, from the first feast of the Lord at the Exaltation of the Cross on 14 September to the last at the Transfiguration on 6 August, and so on; but all these cycles are held within the single sweep of the agricultural year which begins in early September, and it is no accident that this cycle is identical with that of the Mother of God. In the autumn when the first rains have refreshed the earth, when the harvest is over and the fields are being prepared for the first ploughing, the birth of the Mother of God is celebrated in the first major festival of the Church's year on 8 September. And at the end of the agricultural year a similar correspondence is seen, for when the earth is falling to rest at the end of the high summer on 15 August, the final festival of the liturgical year is celebrated, in the Falling Asleep of the Mother of God. Thus the earth that bears the wheat which in the eucharist becomes the body of Christ is seen as an analogy to the Mother of God who bears Christ himself, so that from the birth of the Mother of God to her Dormition, and from the sowing of the wheat to its harvest, there is a continuum between the sacred and the material understanding of bread. Bread is honoured by the villagers as "the body of Christ" whether in the liturgical setting or out of it, and it is for this reason that the greatest agricultural festival of the year is the harvest of the wheat, for here the grain that is brought in is the staff of life not only for the household but for the eternal life of the soul.

The understanding of bread as the body of Christ gains particular power from the fact that in the villages it is the work of man that, in addition to its origin in God and in the natural world, is the third indispensible element in its production—it is the flour from wheat grown on the peoples' own land, and baked with the housewife's own hands, that is used in the liturgy. The great round loaves of the peoples' daily bread, wrapped in cloths and perched on the beams for the week's eating, although they differ in the manner of their preparation, are not in their material substance different from those loaves which, closely kneaded and stamped with a special seal, are consecrated in the liturgy as the Holy Mysteries. In this way the ear of corn gathered in at the harvest, which will become the bread both of the household and of the eucharist, is, of all the foods eaten, the one which most completely links the natural world with the divine.

The harvesting of the many crops is spread over a period of several weeks and the whole period is noticeable for a growing sense of completion and fulfilment, even while it involves long hours of exhausting work at the hottest time of the year. But the climax is reached when the villagers, as one, "enter in" as they say, "to the [wheat] harvest". The previous evening the threshing floors will have been dampened with water and sprinkled with chaff to make a hard surface, and the next day a number of families gather with their mules or horses so that several animals together may trample the brittle stalks while a man or boy runs behind them with a whip keeping them going, and other family members rest in the shade. Five times during the threshing, which takes all day, several people go through the mixed up stalks and grain with long-handled wooden forks and shovels turning over and bringing to the top anything untrampled. At first the workers move forward in rows, but the last time they move forward in a single line from the inside out, "fork first, shovel after", coiling "right-handed" from the centre until they have covered every last piece of ground. At the end of the day everyone sweeps together the chaff and loose grain into a long mound, ready for the winnowing next day, which they then mark diagonally with a rope in the imprint of an X (the initial letter in Greek for Christ).

The day is marked as one of celebration from the moment at dawn when the housewife rises to make bowlfuls of *loukoumádes* or batterpuffs, and throughout the day this refreshment—a festive food traditionally served only on name days and feast days—together with a sprinkling of honey and little glasses of raki, is served to all present as well as to any passer-by who can be haled in, and at noon a meal is served on the threshing-floor by the housewife whose harvest it is. While the evening meal is traditionally a cockerel—those birds being fat at this season—the midday food is always green beans stewed with tomatoes and oil, but it is brought out in ceremony from the house in due order, the harvest bread coming first. This bread is made in the same way as bread for a wedding or for the New Year in a large round copper dish which has been smeared with olive oil, and after baking is anointed with honey and sprinkled with sesame seeds. The decoration of these breads however varies with the occasion, and the harvest bread is imprinted all over before baking with crosses made with a fork. Thus the cooked food from the house, led by the festival bread with its decoration of crosses, emerges from the house, to meet the gift of the sheaves of wheat brought in from the wild, and this meeting between wild and socialized takes place on the threshing floor which, placed at the edge of the village, marks the boundary between the two worlds. This is one of the great moments of reconciliation when through the medium of toil the natural world has produced her bounties for man, and the reconciliation of the wilderness with the socialized world, for however brief a moment, returns the world to its unfallen state and reintegrates the garden of nature with its archetype in the garden of paradise. This movement from the fallen world to the paradisal one is in fact parallel with the movement in the Divine Liturgy when the bread of the houses is blessed as the body of Christ, and it is because of this complex of meanings that the day is one of such high celebration, and because of this that the words "We are threshing tomorrow!" in fact mean, "Come and celebrate with us!"

In spite of a broad division between the work of men on the land and the work of women in the houses, women play a considerable part in the fields, and it is a shared effort that produces the spontaneous outburst of rejoicing at the harvest; and because of the part played by wheat as a food which preeminently unites the physical and spiritual worlds, bread is, above all other forms of food and in all sorts of different forms, used to define and express the meaning of the great variety of ceremonial occasions.

First and most basic of these ceremonies is the family meal, especially the cooked meal eaten in the house, for this involves not only material sustenance but also a communion between all the individual members of the house, and between the house and all those elements which have brought it into being—the land which produces the food, the forefathers from whom the land was inherited, and the sacred world on which all depends. No meal begins before everyone is gathered, sitting round on stools at the low tables set in front of the fireplace, where the single copper pot sits on its tripod over the flames, and always a good wish or blessing is given by the householder—"Good appetite", "Welcome", or very often "All holy Mother of God, come and let us eat together". Both at the beginning and at the end of the meal the sign of the cross, made by all present, acknowledges the original source of the life that is given them, while on the table is evidence of family toil on family land—usually a stew of vegetables, or beans, chickpeas or lentils, little glasses of wine, perhaps cheese, and, in season, salads of tomatoes, cucumber and lettuce. But whatever else might vary, always without fail one of the great round loaves is produced, signed briefly with the sign of the cross, and cut generously into wedges or slices which are piled up on the table and eaten by everybody as an accompaniment to the main dish.

At the end of the meal, when the plates are taken away, the larger pieces of bread are gathered up, to be kept for a future meal or given, usually as their only food, to cats and dogs. After this, the tablecloth is gathered up from the corners to preserve all the remaining breadcrumbs, and these are given to the hens. Bread is never thrown away— "It comes from the ground, it is given by God, it is our chief food, it becomes the *antídoro*" (see below). According to the universal saying, "One must honour bread": it must be eaten, not wasted, and in particular it must not be left on the ground to be trodden underfoot.

Bread, then, is in the most basic sense the food of man—very often during the course of work outside it is virtually the only food, eaten in large quantities accompanied only by a little cheese or some olives, and draughts of water from, if possible, a nearby spring. The definition of superlative water is that it creates a hunger for "three great loaves". Thus to eat bread is to live, to live is to eat bread, and this is enshrined in the phrase "to eat bread" which is used not only to indicate "We are eating a meal", but also, in a different sense, to denote old people. In this context it is a phrase which involves a series of nuances, from "I have eaten my bread" in the sense of "I have lived [and am now ready to die if I have to]" to the more frequent meaning of someone who is in a sense living too long, "He (or she) eats [but cannot work]". Thus to live does not just mean to eat bread, it means to work to produce that bread: to eat without working means that a radical balance has gone astray.

If the growing and harvesting of the wheat is a part of this process, so also is the baking—an arduous and recurrent task involving considerable skill if a series of perfect loaves is to be regularly produced in all conditions of temperature and humidity. For its rising, *prozými*—a piece of naturally leavened dough kept aside from the previous baking—is mixed with the new batch, and large loaves are pummelled and kneaded and set to rise in the separate compartments of a long wooden trough. When the bread has risen for the second time, the beehive-shaped mud oven in the yard is fired—using dead brushwood left over from the evergreen branches cut as winter feed for the animals—and on its becoming hot enough, the glowing embers are raked forward with the use of a long pole finished with a mop-head of strips of material. Each loaf is quickly scored with the letters I X (*Iisoús Hristós*, Jesus Christ), pierced with the knife top and bottom, signed—with a quick motion of the hand—with the cross, and placed on the oven floor, the mouth of which is then banked up with the glowing embers, and closed on the outside with a sheet of tin.

The sign of the cross is used in all sorts of activities, but bread is distinguished by being actually marked with the initials of Christ; in this, and in the "piercing"—an action specifically avoided on certain sacred times because of its resemblance to the piercing of Christ—there is more than an echo of the Orthodox liturgy.

One feature of the bread for the eucharist is that it is stamped with a seal patterned in the form of a cross whose central square, the Lamb, holds the initials representing the words "Jesus Christ Conquers". The right and left sides of this piece of bread are designated as if the bread were Christ, facing the priest—the right hand of Christ thus being on the priest's left:

	IC XC	
right		left
	NI KA	

Further squares on either side of the Lamb are cut with symbols representing, on the left, the nine orders of saints, and on the right the Mother of God. This loaf, called a *leitourgeiá* (liturgical bread) or *prósphoro* (bread that is "offered" to Christ) is, during the *proskomédia* (the service of preparation before the full liturgy begins), taken by the priest who with a little implement in the shape of a spear cuts out the "Lamb", the central square of bread which represents Christ. This he does by making four incisions—on the right, the left, the upper part and then the lower part—accompanying his actions with quotations from scripture: with the first incision, "He was led as a sheep to the slaughter"; with the second, "And as a blameless lamb before his shearers is dumb, so He opened not his mouth"; with the third, "In his humiliation justice was denied him"; with the last: "And who shall declare his generation?" Then with the words, "For his life was taken up from the earth," he severs it from its crusted base. After removing the Lamb from the *prósphoro*, the priest places it upside down and makes two deep cross-wise cuts saying, "The Lamb of God, which takes away the sins of the world, is sacrificed for the life and salvation of the world". Inverting the Lamb again so that the seal is uppermost, the priest pierces the Lamb in its right hand side, saying, "One of the soldiers with a spear pierced His side, and forthwith there came out blood and water. And he who saw it bare record and his record is true." After this, pieces are taken out of the other sections of the loaf for the Mother of God, for the nine orders of saints, and for the living and the dead.

The explanation given by the villagers for the piercing of the household bread top and bottom carries no reference to the liturgy, for it is said to be "so that it shouldn't rise too much". However, in other ways this household bread, marked with the initials of Christ and pierced top and bottom with a knife, bears a striking resemblance to the bread of the liturgy, marked, similarly, with the initials of Christ, and pierced top and bottom with a spear. In this commonplace action by the housewife, therefore, it seems likely that there is being commemorated, however briskly and with however practical an explanation for the piercing of the bread, the sacred actions of the priest in the Preparation which precedes the liturgy. This connection is strengthened by the universal statement that the meal of the earthly family images the divine feast of the holy family in heaven ("As we are eating down here so they are eating up there"), and so is on its own level an image of the eucharist itself. In this way the eucharist is revealed as perfected in the liturgy but already present at a lower level and enacted throughout the whole of life. And while this implied correspondence between the bread for the meal and the bread for the eucharist is not explicitly referred to, this correspondence appears to be part of the people's implicit symbolic universe, as witnessed by their commonplace reference to wine as the blood of Christ and bread as his body.

If this symbolic parallel is true of the household bread, still more is it true of the liturgical loaves baked by the women for the liturgy. The maker must not be menstruating when she makes the liturgical bread, though this does not apply in the baking of the household bread, and in addition she must be "pure" in the sense of not having had sexual intercourse for eight days. The piece of dough kept back from a previous baking, which acts as "starter" for the subsequent batch, must also be taken from bread made when the maker was pure. But otherwise, as already described, the bread for the liturgy—like the household bread—arises as part of a communion, a direct relationship, with the land itself. It is the product of the householder's own toil, won from the earth and harvested by his own hand.

The procedure for baking the liturgical bread differs also in certain respects from that followed for normal bread; it is sifted twice (ordinary bread being sifted only once), passed through a finer sieve than that normally used, baked for a shorter time, and the top is imprinted with the large wooden seal as described above. The result is a dense, neat round loaf, smaller, paler and flatter than the robust household loaves, and it is this liturgical loaf that is given into the sanctuary before the beginning of the liturgy. The women do not necessarily bring such a loaf to every liturgy, but they will give one on their men's name days or on other days of their own choice, and three or five on the great memorial days commemorating family members. So at every liturgy several women will be seen going to the sanctuary, each one carrying some pieces of incense in a twist of paper, a little bottle of communion wine, a small amount of money, a loaf of liturgical bread wrapped in a blue and white cotton napkin, and a candle. Pieces of one or more of these loaves are used for the eucharist, the other loaves being blessed in the *proskomédia*, and then cut up for the *antídoro* or blessed bread which is lifted over the cup of the sacrament after the consecration and given out to all the congregation at the end of the liturgy. Thus even if the housewife's offering is not actually used for the eucharist itself this does not diminish the significance of her action, for this lies in the giving of a gift which is then blessed. In their periodic offering of this bread the individual households are related directly to the "Holy Gifts" in the action of the liturgy, and also, in the giving of the *antídoro*, they stand alongside Christ himself as the hosts of a symbolic meal eaten by the community as a whole.

The symbolism of the wheat is further elaborated in two additional contexts: the memorial services for the dead, and the feasts commemorating the saints. The wheat for the saints' days needs to be boiled and left plain, while that for the dead has walnuts, raisins, sugar, parsley and pomegranate seeds mixed in, but the significant difference in this context is that while the wheat for the saint has first to be bruised so that it bursts during the cooking, it is important that the wheat for the dead should remain whole. The difference is critical, for while the unburst corn, closed in on itself and as yet unfruitful, is appropriate for grief, the bursting of the bruised corn calls to mind the germination of seed and the bursting of the buds in spring and signifies "joy".

It is plain from these three ways in which wheat is understood that it is being seen in three different aspects, as an image of life, death and resurrection: the ripened corn of the new harvest representing the eternally renewed gift of life to man, with Christ himself the principle of the resurrection which takes place within it every year; the seed corn of the dead, unburst and in its "mourning" state, representing the body which must be buried before it can rise again into life; and the burst corn, signifying the joy of the saints, representing the lives which, having born fruit, are now with Christ in paradise. Thus, as indicated earlier, the gift which the earth gives to man—the wheat or bread of his material and spiritual existence—reflects on its own level the gift given to man by the Mother of God in the birth of Christ.

Bread, then, in this scheme of things, possesses a multidimensional symbolic nature, and it is for this reason that bread is the food used, in numerous different forms and under numerous different designations, to mark a great variety of ritual occasions. There is no space to detail these here, but in brief they consist of *ártos*, a sweet bread given to the church on various occasions; numerous ceremonial *píttes* (s. *pítta*) made for various occasions—weddings, engagements, St Basil's day, the harvest—and with appropriate decorations either imprinted or in moulded dough; and *kossónes* or *kouloúria* which are special breads made for children.

In this way bread celebrates at every meal the completed work of man and God, and in the great festivals it is used to mark the event and distinguish its nature at turning points in the life cycle. And while it features in the great events of joy and celebration, it is no less important at funerals and memorial services at which food for both the living and the dead is a central theme, and huge quantities of flour are used. At these memorials—of which there are five in any one cycle—a number of liturgical loaves are baked, one for the eucharist which together with four others is sent into the sanctuary. But in addition to this, at memorials there are a great quantity of breads called *kommátia* (pieces) or *psyhónia* (soul-loaves), made with a little oil and either formed in one piece in large open copper trays and divided into diamond shapes before baking, or else shaped separately into tiny loaves, each one crossed with a fork and sealed with a small seal bearing the central letters of the liturgical seal: IXNK, Jesus Christ Conquers. Those for the married dead are distributed at the end of the memorial service, and at the memorial meal, while for the unmarried dead, trays of *píttes* replace the *kommátia* at the end of the service. These breads are also sent, along with corn and wine, to the houses in announcement of a forthcoming memorial, and they are always received with the words "May God forgive him", and *píttes* are also given, along with any remaining *kommátia*, to all the guests from other villages as they depart. Remembering that in such a society these journeys are on foot or on mule or horseback, often over mountainous paths and perhaps in the gathering dark, such a gift of bread has considerable meaning. And given that many of these visitors from other villages are in certain respects "strangers", with all the significance that such a person carries, this gift of bread for sustenance on the journey home is itself a sacramental act.

Bread, then, never losing its relationship with the liturgy and its inner nature as the body of Christ, and predominant also as the staple of physical existence is the supreme symbol of life. It is the food which not only nourishes the individual and celebrates the life of the household, but also celebrates and defines the great rites of passage and links the whole community together in acts of sharing and of hospitality which find both their origin and their completion in the eucharist. In this way it carries a universal symbolism at the same time as being capable of taking on and expressing the character of a great range of events—mourning or celebratory, fast or feast. Bread is food in the most profound sense, crossing the boundaries between grief or joy, matter and spirit, and being a chief medium of commensality, such that a natural invitation to an unexpected guest who finds his hosts eating is: "Come! We are eating bread!"

Within this frame of reference, then, bread carries a great weight of symbolic association, not as a metaphor but, in the Orthodox sense of the term, as an icon of the divine. It does not "stand for" the redemption of the fragmented social world, it already takes part in it; it does not, in the eucharist, represent or take the place of Christ, it becomes Christ's gift of himself to his people. Bread thus becomes a composite symbol of enormous power: in the work needed to produce it man is fulfilling the conditions of the curse laid upon him at his Fall (in the villagers' words, "with toil and with sweat shall you till the ground"), and in this sense the completed loaf is an image of obedience; in the completion of the wheat harvest on the threshing floor it is a symbol of the true harmony between the house and the natural world; in the growing of the wheat and the baking of the bread it is a symbol of the symbiosis of the work of the man in the fields and the woman in the house; in the contrast between the everyday loaf, the decorated *pitta*, and the various breads associated with death lie the difference between fast and feast, celebration and mourning; in the bread of hospitality and of festival lies the reconciliation between the house and the outside world; and in the bread of the eucharist is the gift of union between God and man.

The critical element, however, in all these relationships is work—work of both man and God—and it is because of this that bread and work cannot be separated. It is this that accounts fundamentally for the persistent value placed on growing wheat for the house rather than earning cash and buying bread, for in the many-stranded relationship between God, man, and the world, an essential link is short-circuited and then broken if man abandons the land, goes elsewhere to work for money, and with that money buys his bread. In this way the work on the land which produces the bread, and the eating of the bread itself, are activities which are ordered in such a way as to recognize the needs of both body and spirit, integrating temporal actions with symbolic meanings, and releasing these actions into a dimension of experience which involves far more than the simple struggle to survive.

So through the medium of bread, gained by the sweat of man's brow, the eucharist, the family meal, and the acts of sharing and giving described above, bring together themes of work and festival, and reveal festival not as the antithesis of work, but as its apotheosis. Work, carried out in obedience to the divine command, has as its fruit the bread of reconciliation and hospitality, and it is in this context that the unavoidable and tyrannous work of subsistence living is redeemed from the customary connotations of the Greek word for work, *douleiá*, or slavery, and brought into the realm of *leitourgeía*—an alternative word for work which means public or communal work or service, hence the communal service of God, or "liturgy". That is why, in discussion about the relative merits of buying or making bread for the church, the conversation was ended with the statement, "I may be a stupid old woman, but *I* say that the farmer himself should produce the wheat from his own land to make the liturgical bread. That is what is good."

Comparison of themes between two different ethnographies will always be difficult, for each ethnographer has his own particular focus, but although John Campbell's topic is firstly social and economic, he has a wonderful eye for the sacred dimension of Sarakatsan life and this comes out in extended passages on the sacred nature of the sheep, the family, and the work of the men, as well as in continual incidental observations. Such a comparison, at least in outline, between the Sarakatsan and the Ambeliot sense of the sacred in their primary occupations is thus, I believe, possible.

In their imagery of the sacred, like the people of Ambeli, the Sarakatsani also begin from the myth of the Fall, and the idea of the sin of Adam is a fundamental presupposition. This is presented in terms of the Sarakatsan understanding of sin. Although the Sarakatsani believe themselves to be essentially noble, they see themselves as involved in a world in which sin is inescapable. And while they understand a category of personal sin, the world for them holds a fundamental orientation towards deceit and envy, and this necessitates, on the part of the shrewd and successful man, the use of cunning, deceit, and lies, manifested in petty quarrels and hypocritical posturing. These weigh on the spirit and estrange man from God—"Our sins!" is an exclamation of recognition and sorrow—but they are not characteristics for which the Sarakatsani feel themselves to be personally responsible, for they are "ancestral sins", "the sins of Adam", they are the way the social world constrains a man to be. Responsible or not, however, the Sarakatsani experience these sins as a real grief, saying, "If only we had trust in one another", and they take the remedy seriously: to be reunited with the grace of God which, initiated in baptism, is periodically renewed in the sacraments. "A weight has left me" (p. 351) is quoted as the comment of a man on leaving church after the Easter communion. The "weight" is the weight of ancestral sin.

However, there is a continuum of sacred experience linking the sacramental life in the eucharist with the shepherd and the sheep, rather than with bread, and it is the interpenetration of this sacramental life of the eucharist with the nobility of the shepherd and the life and death of the sheep which is chiefly explored in the following pages.

BREAD AND SHEEP

Nothing has been said about the sheep in Ambeli, not because in the early 1970's there were none there, but because there were so few that they formed the main occupation of only one family, and all other sheep were of the order of household animals kept in ones, twos and threes in the stable on the ground floor of the houses. With the Sarakatsani, however, it is a different matter, for as seen by John Campbell in the mid-1950s (1954-55), these transhumant shepherds of the Zagori graze huge numbers of animals on the mountains, and their ideas of manhood and honour are based largely on the way they understand their relationship with the sheep that are their life and their livelihood. For these people, nevertheless, bread also carries an important symbolism, not as the product of their toil, for the maize or wheat for their bread is bought or bartered, but as the staff of life and in the familiar sense in which "all food is in a generic sense bread" (p. 117). "Come, let us eat bread" cries the master of the wedding ceremonies" (p. 117). Some of the documented rituals of bread recapitulate the themes outlined in the earlier part of this paper. There is ceremonial bread at a wedding, when each guest will bring a circular loaf with symbolic ornamentation on the crust, and when the "bread of the bride" baked by the women of the groom's family is presented together with wine, in return for the same elements prepared and presented by the bride's family. On return from church on Holy Thursday younger women make *psyhoúdia*, reminiscent of the *psyhónia* of Ambeli—small breads, which together with cooked beans and wine are taken to neighbours' houses and received by them, one for each person, for the forgiveness of the dead. A woman is said to fear to let another woman see her kneading bread for fear of the evil eye preventing its rising; *antídoro* brought from church on Holy Thursday is kept for the year, along with a bag of phylacteries—salt, incense and boxwood—blessed on that day; the efficacy of these materials depends on the owner having a "good heart", and in that sense they are not charms. Only older women past the age of sexual desire are thought of as having a "pure soul" and as being permitted to make the bread taken to the church at Easter.

These recapitulations, sparse as they are, are illustrative, for in both communities they indicate the centrality of bread, and the role that decorated bread plays in a key ritual occasion such as a wedding, while the making and giving to houses of bread for the dead on Holy Thursday, together with emphasis on forgiveness, exactly mirror a similar custom in Ambeli before a great memorial day. So although the cultivation of wheat among the Sarakatsani is not emphasized or even possible, bread for them appears to have a similar though not so critical role as for the people of Ambeli, marking great events and symbolizing community and commensality both among the living and between the living and the dead.

With the sheep, however, the roles are reversed: sheep are prototypical in a way which cannot be said of the agricultural people of Ambeli. Near the beginning of the book John Campbell says: "Sarakatsani are deeply concerned about three things; sheep, children (particularly sons), and honour...The three concerns of the Sarakatsani are mutually implicated. The sheep support the life and prestige of the family, the sons serve the flocks and protect the honour of parents and sisters, and the notion of honour presupposes the physical and moral capacities that fit the shepherds for the hard and sometimes dangerous work of following and protecting their animals" (p. 18). Thus it is sheep, intimately interwoven with ideas of prestige, honour, and manliness, that are the life of the family, not bread.

Of these sheep the first thing to be said is that they "are peculiarly God's animals", and their shepherds, made in his image, are essentially noble beings (p. 26). Sheep are docile, enduring, pure, intelligent, and courageous, and to match this their guardians ought to be noble, fearless, devoted, and ritually pure. The position of honour, on which the future of the group of cooperating families (*stáni*) principally depends, is the care of the milking ewes, and those chosen for this position should ideally be young men, unmarried and therefore virgin—men in the heroic mould (*pallikári*), in the prime of their life before marriage claims them, with its cares, sensualities and involvement in the sins of the world, and its intimations of ageing and death. Thus it is the purity and virtue of the sheep that call up the purity and virtue of the shepherd, and a tale based on the presence of flocks at the birth of Christ encapsulates this. In this tale God, who was in the cave with the Mother of God, came out of the cave to find fire, and passing through a flock of sleeping sheep with its shepherd, he took a burning ember, and, returning, he blessed the sheep that they should be his own for all time.

Care of the sheep is indeed a task which calls up all the skill of the shepherds. At lambing time, for two to three weeks the shepherd works without sleep. By day or by night, ewes about to give birth tend to wander away from the flock and the shepherds need to be present to make sure that the new born lambs do not get separated from their mothers, that the ewe cleans the lamb, the lamb finds the udder, and both learn to recognize each other by their smell. For the rest of the year the work is no less demanding, less exhausting but more perilous. The shepherd must be out in the mountains on dark nights, in bad weather, risking precipices and swollen rivers, subject to demonic attack and guarding against predation by wolves or wild dogs. And care of the sheep is perhaps even more exacting in summer than in winter, for as they eat better during the cool hours, they must be taken to graze after midnight for two to three hours, and the areas of good grass are separated from one another by broken limestone ridges which in the darkness require a sure foot and steady nerves. Animals sometimes need to be rescued from precipices or crevasses, and in case of injury the limb must be splinted and the animal carried down the mountain. In these cases, both metaphorically and literally, the good shepherd must be willing to risk giving his life for his sheep.

As part of this reality there is, in addition to the complex of values noted above, an extraordinary emotional bond. Notwithstanding the large size of the flocks, a shepherd scans his animals rather than counting them, knowing instantly if any is missing. *Sevntás* is a word used for the shepherd's feelings on lambing and milking, a word described by John Campbell as a mixture of "love, longing, anxiety and envy". From 1 February when first lambs are weaned, there is intense competition to see which shepherd is the best milker and can extract the most milk before his hands go into cramp. There is huge concern lest the animals contract a disease that turns their milk to water, and the evil eye and attacks of the devil are greatly feared. For this a viper's head or an egg died red on Holy Thursday is a good apotropaic. The purity of the shepherd is guarded if he washes his hands after sex and before milking, and before he begins to milk he will always make the sign of the cross.

The man of honour needs, then, to be a skilled shepherd—fearless on the high ridges, caring devotedly for a sick or injured sheep, skilled in grazing, staunch in defence of his flock. Courage and intelligence in all these situations are the vital attributes, but it remains true that the ideal of manhood, the *pallikári*, is the young man who, holding these qualities in good measure, is yet free from the corruptions of the social world, and such a man is the shepherd who spends his days and nights with the sheep in the mountains, free to live by the ideal standards of honour, aloof from the necessity of deceit and lies, innocent of harming others, protected from evil by the purity of his life and the power of his virginity. And in this context a story told in Ambeli of a shepherd boy is remarkably revealing. This boy living a pure and solitary life in the mountains was granted the gift of communion with his animals, as a result of which they were docile and easy to manage, and came to his call. However, coming one day into the village and—a further irony—into church, the boy saw with his uncorrupted vision that everyone present had a saddle (of sins) on their back, while the priest had two. In the course of the liturgy darkness descended and an orgy took place in which he found himself involved, and coming to himself later he found that he had unwittingly had sexual intercourse with his mother. Devastated, he fled back to his mountain fastness, only to find his gift for communion with the natural world lost, his animals wild and uncontrollable, and his peace destroyed. In this way, although in earlier times the people of Ambeli were never dependent on sheep in the way of the Sarakatsani, these values of the purity of the mountain life and the protection from evil that it afforded were once common to both.

Although women play some part in caring for the sheep, particularly the lambs, the natural affinity between the sheep and the men is a fundamental presupposition with the Sarakatsani, and on these shared values the religious life of the Sarakatsani is centred. The Sarakatsani believe in God, and when they talk of this belief they mean "not only that they believe intellectually in his existence, but that they have confidence in Him" (p.323), that he protects his people and has compassion on them. They have a regular if perfunctory prayer life and in the morning and evening will stand before the icon corner and cross themselves and, in the case of the young men and the women, say also a short prayer. Throughout the day the sign of the cross is used when occasion presents—always before beginning milking, before setting out on a journey, before a meal, and for instance after the successful conclusion of a difficult task. And, as is common with all Orthodox, the Mother of God, the *Panagía*, is the one to whom both men and women turn in the horror of some shock or loss, for she is the figure of compassion and comfort. Saints are venerated also, especially the Prophet Elias, St Theodore and St Paraskevi, and above all St George and St Demetrius. In honour of St George a lamb is always killed by all but the poorest families, and his day on 23 April is the signal for the annual migration to the mountains to begin, while 26 October, the day of St Demetrius, heralds the beginning of the return journey. Both these saints are mounted on horses, both carry a lance, and both are concerned with the pastoral life, so it is said of them, "We honour them because we are like them" (p. 343), and the keeping of vows made to saints in time of trouble is given great ritual importance. The Sarakatsani never kill their own lambs or sheep solely to feed themselves, but only on important ritual occasions such as the fulfilment of a vow, a marriage, and on certain religious feasts—a lamb is always killed in honour of St George, otherwise principally at Easter, Christmas, and the Dormition of the Mother of God.

The Sarakatsani are not regular churchgoers; the mutual distrust between them and the villagers of Zagori is too great, the Sarakatsani seeing the villagers as lacking in honour, the villagers seeing the Sarakatsani as uncivilized. But they will go to church for communion once or twice a year, believing with longing, as has been said, that the power of Christ's sacrifice in the eucharist is the only way whereby sin may be overcome and man reunited with God. Easter is particularly when the Sarakatsani receive communion, and Holy Week is a time of immense feeling and huge anxiety as they live through the events of the Passion, in the present tense: "They have seized him", "he is being judged", "Now they are crucifying him" (pp. 347-8). It is the sacrifice of Christ that is for the Sarakatsani the foremost evidence for his concern and compassion for men, and they love him for this, seeing their own responsibility reflected in his suffering for their sins, saying, "He died for us" (p. 349). However there are also strands of identification which link them with Christ, in that in Christ's persecution and humiliation, suffering though never losing his nobility, they see their own experience reflected, and it is with this in mind that they say of him "He is our brother", and say also that, having a woman as his mother, Christ was "a man, then, like us" (p. 349). And a further identification lies in the fact that Christ, in being born of a virgin and a virgin himself in his life, embodies in their entirety the values that the Sarakatsani aspire to in the years of youthful manhood before marriage.

Their brotherhood with Christ is, then, key to the Sarakatsan religious understanding, and Christ's special identification with shepherd people is reflected also in various folk stories. God's blessing of the sheep at the birth of Christ has been already been recounted, but there is a further story that it was Christ who made the first shepherd's flute, and a shepherd is recounted to have played a critical part at the crucifixion. It was a gypsy who forged five nails for this act, but it was a Sarakatsanos who took the fifth nail and drove it up the blacksmith's backside. And once again a similar story is told by the people of Ambeli, but with the difference that the fifth nail was taken by a shepherd who hid it in his bass clarinet.

So sacrifice and nobility are key themes in the Sarakatsan understanding of Christ, whose sacrifice is a condition for the eucharist and for all reunion with God (pp. 346-53). The sign of the cross, which they make several times a day, recalls this sacrifice to them, and although they are not often in church their faith is in this way a fundamental aspect of their existence. And it is in their dealings with the sheep, blessed above all other animals and essential to their livelihood and their honour, that this theme of sacrifice which makes them brothers to Christ most enters the fabric of their lives.

In a vivid passage John Campbell describes how the receiving of Easter communion is "an integral part, the climactic happening of the week's events. During this time they have watched Christ suffering, they have identified themselves with Him as He in His sacrifice has identified himself with them. At the end of it all...Christ rises from the dead and they in His blood partake of the life which He has poured out to unite them again to the Godhead" (p. 351). And he goes on to describe the relation of the receipt of the sacrament to the offering of the lamb or sheep which they offer at Easter and at the other festivals mentioned earlier, when they sometimes receive communion. These are the chief times when a Sarakatsanos will kill one of his animals, and, interestingly, the word used is not "to slaughter" as in Ambeli but "to sacrifice" (*thysiázoun* or *kánoun kourbáni*).[6] In a long passage he goes on to describe the complex relationships which make the killing of a sheep take on this nature:

> Other occasions when sheep are slaughtered are similarly religious as well as social events, weddings, baptisms, or the dedication (*táximo*) of an animal to a Saint if men or sheep fall sick. Sheep are never killed for meat but only in the form of a sacrifice. Preferably the animal should be male and "clean", that is a lamb, or ram that has not mounted a ewe. The sheep is believed to know its fate to which it goes quietly and willingly...Of the white Easter lamb they say "we bleed it to honour Christ" (*tó matónoume ná timísome tó Hristó*). A shepherd skins a sheep with swift and confident strokes of a knife but his face is strained and concentrated as he cuts into the artery in the animal's neck. With this sacrificial stroke he gives something of himself. The Sarakatsani are conscious of this element of reciprocity. As Christ pours out his blood to open the way between men and God, so the Sarakatsanos pours out the surrogate blood of his sheep to the same end. And since the sheep is the means of establishing a partial relationship between man and God, those who share its flesh are participating in a form of sanctified communion. And for the same reason God chooses to communicate intelligently with men through the shadow markings on the shoulder blade and the condition of the liver. (p. 352)

In this passage the centrality of the sheep to the religious life of the Sarakatsani is made clear, and the nobility of the sheep, which has called forth the nobility of the shepherd, finds its apotheosis in its sacrifice. The sheep is white, it is ritually pure and in being pure it is innocent, it is noble, it goes "quietly and willingly" to its death. The life for which the shepherd has been prepared to risk his own life is poured out in a conscious act of sacrifice which recalls the sacrificial giving of Christ himself, and it is not only the sheep who suffers but the Sarakatsanos himself, "For with this sacrificial stroke he gives something of himself."

The Sarakatsani, in their belief that God gives all things, ascribe the weather, the rain, the gift of children, and in fact all of life, to the gift of God. But in the meanings attributed to the sheep and the shepherd, and in the complex of honour that is associated with the flock and its well-being, the shepherd is aware of the sacredness of his charges and of his occupation, and of its centredness in the liturgy and in the sacrament of communion. And it is for this reason that he is able to say, as he does, "All our work is with God" (p.322).

It was not part of John Campbell's purpose to explore liturgical parallels to Sarakatsan symbolism, but it is striking that when Sarakatsan and Ambeliot symbolism are compared, obvious parallels emerge between the sacrifice of the sheep, and the actions and words in the preparation of the liturgical bread before the liturgy, which in turn has already been quoted as the symbolic basis

---

6   *Kánoun kourbáni*: make an offering (Corban: Hebrew term used in Leviticus 1.2, Mark 7.11).

of Ambeliot actions in baking the bread of the household. To recapitulate, the priest takes the bread that is to become the Lamb, and, as he makes a series of incisions, says in sequence:

He was led as a sheep to the slaughter.
And as a blameless lamb before his shearers is dumb, so he opened not his mouth.
In his humiliation justice was denied him.
And who shall declare his generation?
For his life was taken up from the earth.
The Lamb of God, which takes away the sins of the world, is sacrificed for the life and salvation of the world.
One of the soldiers with a spear pierced his side, and forthwith there came out blood and water. And he who saw it bare record and his record is true.[7]

Thus the purity, innocence, endurance, and capacity for courageous self-giving that are attributed by the Sarakatsani to the sheep as innate characteristics are attributed by the Church to Christ himself as he goes to his death and as He is commemorated in the preparation for the Liturgy. And in the same way the people of Ambeli, in covering the harvest bread with crosses, signing the mound of threshed wheat with the initial of Christ, and piercing and crossing every loaf of household bread before it is baked, are acknowledging that the bread which they grow, harvest, and bake, is the body of Christ. Thus the different symbolisms clustered round the way of life of the Sarakatsani and the Ambeliots can be referred to the same liturgical image; and further confirmation is to be found in John Campbell's comment following soon after the long passage just quoted: "The wine he [the Sarakatsanos] drinks is indeed the blood of Christ," and, significantly, "the body is seldom mentioned" (p. 353). By contrast, the nature of bread as the body of Christ is frequently on the lips of the villagers of Ambeli, and it is wine as the blood of Christ that is less frequently referred to.

It appears, then, that these two different occupations—subsistence agriculture whose product is the bread which is the body of Christ, and the pastoral life whose product is the sheep which on certain critical occasions give their sacrificial blood as Christ gave his blood to unite man with himself—have sprung from the same Orthodox liturgical symbolism. At first sight the particular liturgical example quoted here may seem surprising, for the preparation of the liturgical bread in the *proskomédia* is not part of the public liturgy, and it may seem too recondite a liturgical source to be known to shepherds or villagers. It is true that village priests are villagers themselves, and oral knowledge of their actions may be passed on through sermons or through villagers who act

---

7   First five phrases from Isaiah 53.7-8, sixth in part from John 1.29, last from John 19.34-5.

as servers. But the example quoted is useful chiefly for its compression, and behind it stands a much more obvious source, central to the religious experience of both villagers and shepherds, from which the language and action of the service of preparation are themselves taken; this is the liturgy of Holy Thursday, when a great cross is brought out of the sanctuary and placed in the centre of the church as the reading of the Twelve Gospels of the Passion reaches the moment of the Crucifixion, and the liturgy of Holy Friday, when the *Epitáphios* bearing the image of the dead Christ is brought out in procession and placed for veneration at the centre of the church. The awestruck comments of the shepherding people at these moments of Holy Week, quoted by John Campbell, illustrate the depth of their understanding as they participate in this event, and it is in these services that the Passion accounts, and Isaiah's prophecy of the suffering servant, from which the *proskomédia* texts are taken, are read and repeated in liturgical commentary and elaboration. Thus the symbolism of the *proskomédia* is also the central symbolism of the Orthodox liturgy as a whole, and it is this symbolism that is embodied differently in the communal life of shepherds and subsistence villagers. It is the same with the symbolism of the Fall. Man in the fields as Adam working off the consequences of the Fall, and the shepherd in the hills whose ideal moment is when he is pure, courageous, self giving and as far as is possible untouched even by involvement in ancestral sin, both exemplify the identification of the people's understanding of the Fall with the pressures and hazards of their different communal ways of life.

While, then, the liturgy is unvarying throughout the Orthodox world, the way its symbolism is picked up in communal living appears to vary according to the way of life of different communities, and it would be interesting to have more examples of the different ways in which this has developed both in Greece and elsewhere. The people of Kokkinia studied by Renee Hirschon[8] have already yielded intimations of this in Greek urban life, even though here the relationship with the natural world is weakened and there is no single occupation which is dominant; and there would probably be similarities and differences also in the Greek islands where the people's concentration is on the sea, with consequent dependent variations in kinship patterning.[9] At any rate it has been my hope in this paper not only to do justice to John Campbell's seminal work, but also to show how the same liturgical imagery finds expres-

[8] R. Hirschon, *Heirs of the Greek Catastrophe: the Social Life of Asia Minor Refugees in Piraeus,* Oxford: Clarendon Press, 1989. Reprinted: New York, Berghahn Books, 1998.

[9] M. Dimen and E. Friedl (eds), "Regional Variation in Modern Greece and Cyprus: toward a Perspective on the Ethnography of Greece", *Annals of the New York Academy of Sciences,* 268: 1-465, 1976.

sion in contrasting meanings and practices surrounding the prototypical activities of two different Orthodox communities. A lay creativity is evident here, which has marked the process by which Christianity has been embodied over the centuries into the culture of the Orthodox world, and it belies any easy assumption that Christianity can be treated for comparative purposes simply as a dogmatic uniformity. On the contrary, these communal developments of Orthodox symbolism raise one of the most interesting questions of social life, affecting all notions of identity, coherence, unity, diversity and change: how meanings can be the same and yet different, different and yet the same.

GLOSSARY

andídoro – blessed bread which is lifted over the cup of the sacrament after the consecration and given out to all the congregation at the end of the liturgy.

douleiá – work.

kommátia – breads made with a little oil and formed in one piece in large open copper trays and divided into diamond shapes before baking. Also before baking, each one is crossed with a fork and sealed with a small seal bearing the central letters of the liturgical seal: IXNK, Jesus Christ Conquers.

kouloúria – circular bread rings.

kánoun kourbáni – to make an offering.

leitourgeía – the work of the people, the Divine Liturgy.

leitourgeiá – liturgical bread or bread that is brought to church on the morning of the liturgy and used for the *proskomédia* or service of preparation.

loukoumádes – batterpuffs, prepared for any festive occasion.

pallikári – a man in the heroic mould.

pítta – festive bread.

prósphoro – bread that is "offered" to Christ, the same as *leitourgeiá*.

proskomédia – the service of preparation before the liturgy.

prozými – a piece of naturally leavened dough kept aside from the previous baking and used to leaven the new batch.

psyhónia – breads shaped separately into tiny loaves, each one crossed with a fork and sealed with a small seal bearing the central letters of the liturgical seal: IXNK, Jesus Christ Conquers.

psyhoúdia – small breads presented by the Sarakatsani to neighbouring houses on Holy Thursday for the forgiveness of the dead.

sevntás – a word used for the shepherd's feelings on lambing and milking, a word described by John Campbell as a mixture of "love, longing, anxiety and envy".

stáni – group of cooperating families among the Sarakatsani.

táximo – dedication of an animal to a saint.

thusiázoun – to sacrifice, used by the Sarakatsani of slaughtering a sheep.

12

SARAKATSANI REFLECTIONS ON THE BRAZILIAN DEVIL

João de Pina-Cabral

The Devil does it in a brutish manner; God, however, is treacherous.
—Guimarães Rosa

This paper deals with the Devil in Brazil, both the way in which the demonic trope operates as a central unifying aspect of Brazilian daily experience and the major role that it plays in Brazilian discourses of national identity. The paper is inspired, in a contrastive fashion, by John Campbell's famous essay on the Devil among the Sarakatsani shepherds of Greece. There is, however, no systematic attempt to compare the two: it would seem foolish to place side by side the worldview of small transhumant shepherd communities with Brazilian national culture seen in the long-term historical perspective. The scales of analysis are completely different and the two contexts are immersed in widely divergent historical settings.

Rather, I chose to be inspired by the way in which John Campbell approached the issue—both in his *Honour, Family, and Patronage* (1964) and in the more widely read article on "Honour and the Devil" that is part of the time-setting volume edited by J.G. Peristiany on *Honour and Shame* (1966). These passages are worth remembering in the context of anthropological history for the way in which they inaugurated a wholly new way of dealing with issues that were previously addressed only by historians and theologians. Without rejecting the influence of classical scholars (e.g. Onians 1951), John Campbell studies matters of belief in the context of lived experience as observed through ethnographic fieldwork.

In these pages, as indeed in much of what the British Mediterraneanists were writing in the late 1950s and early 1960s, one can detect a strong influence of the German sociological school and its preoccupation with person, value and religion.[1] To my mind, rather than any sort of contemplation of "honour and shame" as a culture trait, it is this aspect of those texts that is apt to inspire us today (cf. Pina-Cabral and Campbell 1992). The recent discussions of the Greek Devil that have been carried out by colleagues such as Charles Stewart (1991) show what a rich trend John Campbell's work inaugurated.

In his essay, Campbell is concerned to demonstrate how religious experience moulds daily practice, interacting intensely with it in the way people produce themselves as social actors. He identifies a contradiction between the values of social life (the code of personal worth which guides relations both between males and females and between shepherd families) and the values of religion (the simple, but deeply held forms of Orthodox Christianity to which these people adhered). The two sets of values are mediated tensely by the rhythms of daily life and of the life cycle. He does not argue that the two aspects fit nicely together to form some sort of sociocentric notion of "culture". Rather, he shows how social life is pervaded by a moral tension that ultimately cannot be resolved, leading to a dynamic sense of ethical incompleteness. Few ethnographers since then have managed to examine so thoroughly the way in which personal construction, gender differentiation and religious experience operate conjointly and tensely in social experience. In my analysis of Brazilian demonology, I was inspired by Campbell's unwillingness to resolve ethical dilemma into neatly formulated cultural constructions.

The Sarakatsani lived on the margins of the State and the institutionalized Church. Theirs was a world of considerable personal independence which was not marked by the experience of violently enforced hierarchy and captivity that is such a central part of the Brazilian historical legacy. The discussion that follows will show how, contrary to the Sarakatsani's essentially rural view of their world, largely unmarked by the modern utopia, Brazilian experiences were branded from the onset by the utopian outlook of the Modern Era. The Brazilian Devil is, oddly as it may sound today when speaking of the 16th century, a modern devil.

---

1   In their biographical note to the posthumous edition of Franz B. Steiner's work, Adler and Fardon show how his lectures on Simmel in Oxford in the post-war period were far more influential than had been known up till then, and explain how Steiner actually visited Pitt-Rivers while this one was in the field (1999: 86-100, esp. 97).

SARAKATSANI REFLECTIONS ON THE BRAZILIAN DEVIL

Eden and Hades[2]

A few months ago, I was giving a lift in my car to a lady friend. As we started off from the small town of Valença on our way back to Salvador (the capital of the state of Bahia) the following conversation took place:

João – So, here we go.
C. – With God before us.
J. – And the Devil behind?
C. – No, no; 'cause God is good and the Devil is not evil.
J. – If he's not evil, what is he?
C. – If you treat him well, he works; if not, he breaks it all up, he destroys.
J. – And how do you treat him well?
C. – As a matter of fact, you give him his *ebó*, his rum. ("*Ebó*" is the word for the food, drink and tobacco sacrifice one offers to Afro-Brazilian gods)

I immediately stopped the car and wrote down this dialogue in my notepad, as it seemed to echo perfectly what I was reading just then: Laura de Mello e Souza's famous study *The Devil and the Land of the Holy Cross* (1993). In that historical treatise concerning the work of the Inquisition in Brazil, it is clearly demonstrated that all this demonology finds its origins in the exact moment of "discovery", being reflected in the drama that is constituted by the very process of having to find a name for this "new" land. This is the way the issue was perceived by the Portuguese Crown (as voiced by the influential 16th century chronicler and royal chancellor João de Barros):

And thus, as in this earth I have no further way of avenging myself of the devil, I admonish all of you who read these words in the name of the cross of Jesus Christ to give this land the name which it so solemnly received [Land of the Holy Cross], for fear that same cross, which will be present before us in the final day, accuse you of being more devoted to Brazil wood than to it. (in Mello e Souza 1993: 29-34)

As it happens, his wager was lost and the name Terra da Santa Cruz was indeed supplanted by the name for Brazil wood, from which a red dye was extracted that played such an important role in European clothing habits in the 16th century. Thus, like the cross, the new name was also stained in red, but not with the blessed blood of Jesus: rather, with the vile smell of profiteering. In the very name of the "new" land, therefore, a tension was inscribed that

---

[2] This paper is a sequel to Pina-Cabral 2007, where I explore Roberto DaMatta's famous analysis of the notion of "Brazilian dilemma", in light of a critique of the relation between the binomials person/individual and tradition/modernity (DaMatta 1979). These pages were written in Bahia, where I have been carrying out fieldwork intermittently since 2004. Life around me in Bahia constantly confirmed the intrinsic link between daily ethical confrontations and the demonic trope as inscribed in Brazilian literary and academic traditions.

carried with itself from the start a utopian dimension; a wager with the Devil that, as it happens, was promptly lost.

The New World appeared to the Europeans of the Modern Era as potentially Edenic, so that the evil elements that they subsequently discovered there assumed a surprising nastiness. In the words of Sérgio Buarque de Holanda, the initial "vision of Paradise" brings with itself as a corollary a propensity for a subsequent demonization (1996 [1959]). The polarization of value between Eden and Hades—place of desire versus place of horror, place of fulfilment versus place of falsehood—never abandoned the Land of the Holy Cross. There the possibilities were immense, the dangers tremendous. That is the "dream of Brazil", the fascinating tropical wager that has been leading Portuguese people of all social classes, for centuries, to risk their lives in that far off land.

Oswald de Andrade notes that there is something extraordinarily apposite in the notion that Thomas More's original *Utopia* was based on the description by one of Americo Vespucci's sailors of the island of Fernando Noronha, off the coast of Brazil. This "nowhere land" that is at the same time a "perfect land" is a dream, yes, but a practically oriented dream; that is, one that transports an ethical appeal for a change of the world. "The geography of the Utopias is placed in America. [...] Except for the *Republic of Plato*, which is an invented state, all of the *Utopias* which appear in the horizon of the modern world twenty centuries later and which leave a deep impression on it, are bred of the discovery of America. Brazil left quite an imprint in the social conquests of the Renaissance." (Andrade 1990 [1966]: 164) Historians such as Sérgio Buarque de Holanda and Laura de Mello e Souza have shown how the historical origin of the demonic identification at the beginning of the Modern Era, in the 16th century, was born of a reaction to the tropical utopia.

This relation between the demonic trope and the ethical dilemma that is born of the utopian drive has not simply faded away five centuries later. As Lúcia Nagib has cogently argued in her study of Glauber Rocha's film *God and the Devil in the Land of the Sun*, the image of the interior drylands (*sertão*) turning into a sea that pervades Brazilian 20th century cinema is "the wrenching emotion of an utopian country that might have come into existence, yet was fated to remain unrealized since the discovery." (2006:33)

As a matter of fact, Brazil has been characterized, throughout its history, on the one hand by the persistence of its demonic appearance and on the other by the intense domestication of the demonic trope in everyday life. This is present to this day, both in the religious practices and beliefs whose finality is to seduce the Devil—in the Afro-Brazilian tradition—and in those that aim to dominate or destroy him and her: that is, the Pentecostal version that each day becomes more prevalent throughout the country. Today's outside observer, five centuries later, is confronted with an uncanny sense of continuity.

I was surprised by the insidiousness of the trope in a number of events that surrounded the very production of this paper. A few months ago, as I was giving a postgraduate course in Bahia, I suggested to a student that she should write a critical analysis of an earlier version of this very paper. When the time came for handing in the essays, I received an email declaring that she felt herself obliged to change to another one of the topics I had suggested, even although she had already started researching this one and was fascinated by it. According to her, ever since she had started doing so, all sort of nasty events had started occurring and she felt she could not afford to continue. Although she confirmed that she does not "believe in" the Devil, the latter is such an intrinsic part of the world she lives in that she found it impossible to escape his and her agency.

Demonology is a heterology, tells us Laura de Mello e Souza; "the fascination with the Devil responds to a desire to speak of the other, both external and internal." (1993: 25, 195) And there is nothing surprising about the need for a heterology in colonial Brazil, a place where one was faced with vast numbers of Gentiles and imperfectly converted Christians (Amerindian, African and Jewish), particularly in the light of the old Eusebian theological tradition, which interprets Gentile belief as corresponding to actually existing—demonic—powers (Pina-Cabral 1992). As Cristina Pompa shows, in Brazil, "all the interpretations of the savages' 'religion' by the [17th century] missionaries were formulated in terms of a 'devilish counterfact' in which the Devil, God's mome, constructs the infernal counterpoint to divinity." (2003: 27)

Confronted with this pervasive otherness as well as with the unexpected physical hardship of living in a terrain that had initially seemed so bounteous, the utopian disposition to create a new and better world was temporarily dashed at the same time as the perceived urgency for it was further confirmed. The frustration of the expectations produced by tropical Edenism caused incongruence in the world. Lived experience acquired, thus, a kind of infernal perversity.

The incongruence between the Edenic and the Hadean aspects of the New World might have remained a simple curiosity for Europe, were it not for the constructivism of the human condition. This, however, means that at the very moment human beings come to *live* this incongruence, they end up being formed by it. Thus, incongruence becomes constituent of these men and women. There, then, what was only a game of lights suddenly becomes a game of shadows with sinister implications concerning the life and death of the people involved. As is clearly patent in the missionary correspondence studied by Cristina Pompa or in the Inquisitional reports that Laura de Mello e Souza examines, very early on the "Brazilians" were no longer the "savages"—good or bad—but were all of those who, in the meantime, were being constituted by this new and incongruous land. The reification of identities started even before the collective names that they later assumed were fully consolidated, as we have seen. These reifications accumulate and consolidate.

In short, the game of Eden and Hades is not inconsequent, as human desire is invested in it—the desire for good, for happiness, for strength, for power, for prosperity ... Now, in a context of internal polarization, the dynamic of desire potentiates the impact of its satisfaction and its frustration—in what we might call a "fridge effect". Each new satisfaction places the integrity of the subject in further jeopardy and, therefore, appeals to a frustration. Great goods bring great evils. The Brazil of easy gold, easy sex, abundance is also the Brazil of misery, hunger, slavery and plague.

Once the dualizing game of Brazilian Edenism is set in motion, the incongruence of the land inevitably becomes the incongruence of its people. Thus, the latter are confronted with a social dilemma of being. The demonic aspect of this land, then, is not due to the fact that it also includes destitution—the Devil was also afoot among the Sarakatsani; it is the Edenic and not the Hadean side of Brazil that appeals to a special presence of the Devil. The Edenic appearance creates a dynamic of intensification of desire that can never really be fully satisfied and that gives rise, as a consequence, to a demonic alert, an awareness of perversity.

The demonic game of Brazilian tropicalism is directly connected to the perversions of desire, as Gilberto Freyre turns out to have demonstrated (2003 [1933]). Tropicalism is demonic because it sits on an initially utopian proposition: that we will be able to fabricate a New World where our desires will be satisfied. What produces the demonic alert is the utopianism of those who see a "new" world and want to fashion it into a "better" world—this applies equally to the initial efforts of the Jesuits, the lords of souls; to the boundless greed of the slave owners, the lords of bodies; but also to the erotic and financial mismanagement of the ordinary settler. In short, the dilemmatic condition of this land is not something that is in Brazil, but it is something that is produced there.

In the end, as all worlds are human worlds—and all of them are constitutive of the humans that inhabit them—there are no new and better worlds, there are no final solutions: there are only human worlds. I suppose it is easy for us now, five centuries later, to mistrust modern utopianism in the face of its repeated collapse, and even then there are still many of us that continue to hope.

SARAKATSANI REFLECTIONS ON THE BRAZILIAN DEVIL

Faith or idolatry

As to the religious aspect, Laura de Mello e Souza demonstrates how, from the very first known description of a colonial Afro-Brazilian cult (*candomblé*), the demonic condition integrated a number of strains with diverse origins (1993: 145)—Brazilian religious experience has always involved forms of multilateralism. However, in her impressive study, the author makes abundantly clear that, already then, this was a different Devil from that of erudite Europe, which is the Devil of an increasingly monotheistic God.

'Without devils, there is no God', [...] The existence of the devil was the primary proof of the existence of God, as was appropriately observed by a number of English thinkers of the seventeenth century. The devil has been historically associated to monotheism; the first Hebrews felt no need to personify the malign principle; they attributed its influence to rival divinities. With the triumph of monotheism, in the meantime, it became necessary to explain the presence of evil in the world, as God was so good: [And here she quotes Keith Thomas,] 'Thus, the devil helps to sustain the idea of a divinity which is absolutely perfect'. (1993:249)

Now, the influence that Keith Thomas identifies also works in the contrary direction. As Derrida puts it, the devil too can serve as an "excuse" for God: "radical evil can be of service, infinite destruction can be reinvested in a theodicy, the devil can also serve to justify." (1998: 13) The image of the devil as an absolutely evil being evolves concomitantly with the monotheistic ideal. The evolving conceptions of the devil reflect the change in posture towards God. The Counter-Reformation drive that the Inquisition and the Jesuits espoused involved a wish to stress further the monotheistic conception of God by relation to earlier medieval Ctholic popular notions. However, once God is seen as absolute ("He is all things", as Father António Vieira used to say in his sermons, e.g. 1959: X, 210), He has to be absolutely good and He cannot be visually represented. This affects attitudes towards the Devil as, if God is all and is good, evil is of necessity a problem—since evil has to be good in the last instance, as it is a divine creation.

For the Catholics of the Modern Era, dualism was as much a necessity as an impossibility. This was the problem that had confronted the Church throughout the Late Middle Ages under the guise of the various dualist heresies. We must not forget that the Church that was trying to convert Brazil in the 16th century had been struggling for three centuries to eradicate Catharism from Europe (Lambert 1998) and, earlier still, to eradicate Arianism from the margins of what had once been the Roman Empire. The problem lies at the root of Christianity and the various rational attempts to go round it have proved, in the last instance, to be unsatisfactory, as is present again from the Pope's recent ditherings concerning Hell's actual existence.

The problem that confronts us today, however, is that most authors who study these matters (both historians and anthropologists) place themselves in the position of one who knows what it is to have "faith" in a "God", one immanent God, even when they do not necessarily "believe in" Him. In other words, conceptual precedence is silently granted to a prototype of divinity of the "God" type with whom a "believer" is related through "faith" (an intellectual disposition), the manipulation of icons becoming secondary. As Malcolm Ruel has famously argued, however, such a posture can hardly be taken as a universal of the human condition, which means that these dispositions end up working as what he called "shadow fallacies" (2002 [1982]: 110).

Cristina Pompa develops a similar argument concerning the relationship between Catholic missionaries and Indians in 17th century Brazil: "The concepts of Faith and Belief are born of the Christian choice, for which the 'profession of faith' is an inseparable mark; [...] it is religion (Christian, as it happens) that constructs historically the faith; it is not the faith that identifies the religion." (2003: 349) Thus monotheistic, fideistic (as our Italian colleagues call it) and anti-idolatric predispositions are intimately connected. In the face of such a complex, postulating a figure such as the Devil is a logical necessity. The demonic concept is, thus, silently universalized.

The very history of this monotheistic and fideistic prejudice comes to be inscribed in the modernist theologies produced for themselves by the world religions that do not originate in the Judaic tradition. These are religions that have to face the hegemony of the monotheistic prejudice and who become dependent on the interpretations that missionaries, historians, sociologists and anthropologists have made of them in the past. Speaking of the very first writers who described the Tupinambá of coastal Brazil, Cristina Pompa notes that "These Indians seemed not to believe in anything, being adverse to the current notions of what it was to be a pagan. At the same time, however, in order to justify evangelization, Tupi culture was presented as bearing, in bas-relief, the possibility of a monotheistic religion." (2003: 41; see also pp. 44-5) For the Europeans, in those days, "It was, in fact, the Devil, the king of lies who falsified and degraded the pure images of faith in order to be able to conquer the soul of Indians." (ibid.: 49) We must not be surprised, therefore, to find contemporary interpreters of *candomblé* stating that, deep down and all things considered, theirs too is a monotheistic religion.

Faced with this, however, it becomes necessary to state that there is no universalistic necessity in the formulation of an absolutely evil figure such as the Sarakatsani Devil that John Campbell described. Olavo Bilac, a Brazilian poet and thinker of the early 20th century, starts his famous essay on the Brazilian Devil by alerting us to that precise fact (1912: 133). Both the monotheistic God and the Devil are functions of a polarization of Good and Evil that is part of the Christian tradition and has always been a source of problems for it. Again, as the various medieval heresies demonstrate, it has always been particularly difficult for Catholicism to contain the theological dangers that would derive from falling into excessive dualism.

As it happens, the evidence we have from most of the religious forms that emerged over the centuries from Brazilian popular religious experience is that they respond to a contrary dynamic. One should note that what is at stake is not the disappearance of an image of evil or of its vehicles. Rather, what we observe in popular Brazil is that the dissolution of the image of God as omnipotent, absolute and immanent accompanies a corresponding change in the image of the Devil. There appears to be no drive towards dualist solutions.

Let us hear what Édison Carneiro has to say concerning *Êxu*, a central figure of the *candomblés* of Bahia:

Exu [...] has been ill understood. His reign is all the crossroads, all the hidden and dangerous places of this world, so it was not easy to find a simile for him in the image of the Christian Devil. [...] the invocation of Êxu by the sorcerers, whenever they wish to make yet one more victim, has helped to give him the character of a evil ôrixá, contrary to man, representing the occult forces of Evil.

As it happens, however, Êxu is not an ôrixá – he is the servant of the ôrixás, an intermediary between men and the ôrixás. If we want something from Xangô, for example, we must *despachar* Êxu [lit. send him off], so that his influence may help us gain that thing more easily. It does not matter the quality of the favour – Êxu will do what we ask for so long as we give him the things he likes: palm oil, goat meat, water or rum, tobacco smoke. If we forget about him, not only will we fail to receive our favour, but he will also unleash all the forces of Evil against us; those forces that, as an intermediary, he holds in his hands. [...] Êxu is like the ambassador of the mortals. His aim is to carry out the wishes of men – good or evil [...] Thus, he can intercede with the ôrixás for evil, quite as much as for good. It depends on who is asking. (1991 [1948]: 68-9)

The long quote seems justified for what the passage reveals of how undevilish this Devil that emerges from colonial Brazil turns out to be. Once again, there is nothing new to the conclusion that, when the referent is no longer a monotheistic, immanent model of divinity but a more polytheistic and less fideistic model, a structural adjustment necessarily occurs concerning the image of the Devil. The conception of the Devil depended on the nature of the conception of the divinity—the two go together. Once Good stops being absolute, Evil does too—so the two alterations occur concomitantly. Evil is no longer something one can keep away, it becomes part of the everyday world and it becomes comprehensible within it.

The problem lies in the difficulty that contemporary authors have in accepting such a notion. A good example emerges from the work of Édison Carneiro himself, perhaps the most noted early ethnographer of *candomblé*. The author spends the whole of four pages trying to refute the idea that Bahian *candomblé* should be seen as polytheistic and idolatrous (1991 [1948]: 22-4). Why would he need to carry out this extensive demonstration, if not because there would be something wrong with *candomblé* if these "accusations", as he calls them, were to apply?

Following on Alfred Gell's suggestion, it seems necessary to deconstruct actively this modernist conception both of idolatry and of polytheism (1998: 115). This dilemmatic condition, the ambiguity or the "syncretism" of these practices, conceptions and customs of Brazilian popular life, is caused by the very prejudices that we impose upon them. According to Carneiro, the cult figures that we find portrayed all over Brazil "do not represent directly the divinities, but the humans that are possessed by them." (1991: 24) He argues that their true representations are the *moradias* (residences) and their insignia. But if we follow, once again, Alfred Gell's opinion, the distinction can only be seen as spurious.

In fact, it is almost immediately denied by Carneiro himself when he is forced to admit that Exú is the exception: "Êxu, however, is not properly speaking a divinity, but their messenger and, in Africa, as the protector of villages, cult houses and homes, it would be natural that he would find a more direct representation than the remaining celestial beings." (ibid.: 24) Now, where would that "naturalness" come from? And why would it be more directly related to Africa than all other aspects of *candomblé*? We are here confronted, once again, with the way in which the deep roots of modernist prejudice undermine self-representations—the so-called "Brazilian dilemma" (DaMatta 1979, Pina Cabral 2007). Conditions are created for a primitivizing othering of self that soon turns against the very subject of the analysis, undermining his or her own self image.

As one reads the literature on these topics, one is repeatedly surprised by the way in which the directionality between polytheism and monotheism—the former necessarily leading to the latter—is implicitly accepted and repeatedly studied, observed and elaborated. The contrary movement, however, would seem to be considered as an impossibility—as going against the movement of history, the necessary history of progress. To pass from monotheism to polytheism: when such a thing happens in history it is always treated as recidivism, a re-emergence of telluric forces insufficiently repressed. How can one agree to pass from "faith" to "superstition"? Such is the puzzle motivating modernist prejudice.

This modernist model of history is so pervasive that the very authors who analyze critically the emergence of a modernist ideology are, in the end, guided by the silences it produces. What is at stake here, therefore, is to contemplate the possibility that Édison Carneiro need not have felt ashamed of polytheism, of idolatry or of the un-dualistic nature of this religion that held him in such lifelong fascination. Faith, and faith in a unique and immanent God, need not be an inexorable future; it might well turn out to be a historical detour like many others, containing quite as many mind traps as any other such detour.

Thus we must turn the direction of our argument around. We have been shown by numerous historians how the Brazilian colonial subjects (Portuguese, Jewish, Amerindian or African) were violently subjugated by a Church and State apparatus in order to ensure that they sustained beliefs (a "faith", in the sense of "to believe in") that they did not necessarily always hold ("to believe that"). But now we must make space to understand how the colonial space, in fact, opened up pockets of relative freedom that allowed those subjects to entertain beliefs of a non-monotheistic nature that, elsewhere, would have been literally unthinkable. Let us not forget that colonial subjects—and slaves in particular—were treated almost as if they were not human and very little effort was spent on humanizing them. Left to their own devices they started thinking in ways that were structurally compatible with the world they lived in: that is, polytheistically and idolatrously. Later still, when slavery came to an end at the end of the 19th century, they were abandoned to their luck in the cities. As Édison Carneiro argues, they constructed there a religion (*candomblé*) that was compatible with their marginal ways of living.

There is an unexpected twist in this process: that is, the realization that the extremes of domination produce margins for the very system of domination (cf. Pina Cabral 1997). In colonial Brazil there were large areas of space that remained unchristianized, bureaucratically ambivalent and administratively marginal. When we read the Inquisition records we are surprised at how deep into the jungle the *capitães-do-mato* (the Inquisition police) managed to reach and how people, sooner or later, ended up having to account for their religious vagaries. But we must also have in mind the other side of the coin: in Brazil it has been possible for many centuries to find spaces of escape from ideological domination that, in Europe and in Portugal in particular, simply never existed.

In short, the tendency for polytheism and idolatry that we register in Brazilian popular religions need not be seen as a form of recidivism, primitivism or collapse into something anterior—recidivistic European "paganism" or the idealized Africa that constantly re-emerges from the accounts of *candomblé* by its learned protectors (Nina Rodrigues originally, Carneiro himself, Roger Bastide, Pierre Verger, etc.). We must experiment with the notion that there is nothing ineluctable or necessary about the notion of a unique God, the notion of "faith" or the rejection of idolatry. Once we realize that such notions are associated to a State and Church apparatus without which they would not be sustainable, we then understand that they may well fade out in spaces of marginality such as colonial and 19th century popular Brazil.

The non-fideistic and non-monotheistic dispositions that emerged in Brazilian popular religion—as practiced in *candomblé*, in *umbanda*, in spiritism, as manifested in the inconstancy of Indians or still in the contemporary tendency for a free and recurrent movement of individuals between different churches and faiths—can now be seen as an acquisition, a historical gain to freedom, something that is better adjusted to these people's daily experience of mobility. This being the case, the presence of the Devil in that daily interchange must also be understood in a different manner.

This does not mean that we must stop thinking of good or evil, of desire and fear, of social enhancement or social destruction; it does not mean either that a figure that personifies the dangers in the world ceases to make sense. All it means is that we need no longer search for a figure (somehow divine or, at least, spiritual) that serves as a counterpoint to the monotheistic faith, countering divine compassion with absolute, irredeemable evil. We must accept that, in such a world, the essences interpenetrate.

One interesting aspect of such an exercise is that it reveals how our interpretations of history are marked by the contrary thesis. This is how Laura de Mello e Souza concludes her work:

Much like the worldview of the European discoverer or the popular religiosity of which it was a part, colonial sorcery was multiple and heterogeneous, constituted basically of two parts that were integrated into one whole: a baseline of magical practices characteristic of primitive cultures (African and indigenous) and another one of the magical practices characteristic of European populations, deeply intermeshed with the secular paganism that pulsated still under the recent and 'imperfect' Christianization. (1993: 375)

This formulation carries a number of submerged presuppositions; let us try to identify some of them. First, the author says "two parts": but, surely, there are at least four parts if we look at it from the point of view of historical anthropology—the Amerindian part, the African part brought by the slaves, the popular European part and Roman Catholic theology, and it is the author herself who distinguishes the latter two. Secondly, she finds a dichotomy between "primitive cultures" and European culture, and there we have to stop again, as anthropologists have long ceased to recognize a category of *primitive* to which any specific characteristic might be associated which would have allowed us to unite against Europeans both the Amerindians (who were themselves of more than one cultural strain) and the Africans (again from two very distinct cultural areas, West Africa and Angola). Thirdly, why would the baseline be European—why would we claim that the element that integrates all of these imports is not Brazil itself but is one of the imports? And finally, why "paganism"? As a matter of fact the author responds to this question by claiming that Christianization in Portugal had been recent and "imperfect"; but can we be really sure of that. Does that statement not itself presume a series of modernist historical presuppositions?

We must remember that a similar debate is still going on in Europe concerning supposed "pagan survivals" (cf. Pina-Cabral 1992) and, indeed, it is to this very debate that Laura Mello e Souza is implicitly referring. Notwithstanding, it seems worthwhile to remember that, at least in Portugal, Christianization occurred at the time the Roman Empire assumed Christianity as its state religion. The Roman Catholic faith, in particular, has been absolutely dominant since the 6th century—when the Swabian kings were converted to Catholicism near Braga by Saint Martin of Dume. And, contrary to what is often thought, it was never pushed aside by the Islamic presence in the Peninsula—neither north of the Mondego River, where Christian hegemony was never challenged, nor south of it, in the lands that the northerners reconquered a few centuries later and where, during the Moorish Period, there remained a strong Mozarabic Christian population. Thus we must conclude that, by the time the Portuguese started their attempt to police the minds of the Brazilians in the 16th century, over a millennium had passed since the onset of Roman Catholicism in Portugal. Surely that is time enough for consolidation of any faith.

What is at stake, however, is hardly the nature of Iberian Catholicism (itself far less monotheistic than the Sarakatsani version of Orthodoxy), but rather how to avoid the secret operation of modernist prejudice in our historical and anthropological reconstructions. It is not enough to withdraw these presuppositions, since the very empirical material on which we rely as historians and anthropologists was collected with such notions in mind and, to top it all, applies to historical circumstances where those very presuppositions were hegemonic.

In short, my proposal is that we should look at the Brazilian Devil not as a *survival* but as an *emergent phenomenon*: something that is specific to the Brazilian context and to the structuring factors that operate in a land where marginality by relation to constituted power is constantly re-emerging. I concur here with arguments by Roger Sansi-Roca and his colleagues concerning the way in which the Lusophone Atlantic can no longer be approached as dilemmatically split in binary fashion between African primordiality and European colonial violence. The argument for a Creole creativity and its historically emergent specificity must finally be taken more seriously by academics outside Brazil (Sanci-Roca 2007).

The "captive" Brazil that Otávio Velho identifies in the figure of the *Besta-Fera* (1995) and the Brazil *pactário*³ that Guimarães Rosa exemplifies in *Grande Sertão: Veredas* (2001 [1956]) come together with Exú and his wife Maria Padilha (Meyer 1993) in such a way as to form a complex that originally might well have been syncretic, but today has long ceased to be so. Recently, the growing number of Pentecostal Evangelicals has undertaken a decided fight against the "demons" that they identify with Brazilian popular religion. Their main liturgical practices surround the exorcism of such Devils. As their popular designation makes clear (they are called literally "believers", *crentes*), Brazilian Pentecostals fight quite as much for monotheism as for fideism. Their struggle is, after all, not very different from that of the Inquisition in the 16th, 17th and 18th centuries, or that which the bourgeois legal apparatus directed against *candomblé* in the 19th and 20th centuries (see Schritzmeyer 2004).

Their common enemy is the same plural religiosity that Brazilian marginality produces and perpetuates and the diffuse notions of good and evil that emerge with it. The police persecution of *candomblés*, in the sinister but puerile ways that Édison Carneiro reports for the 1940s, was also part of the same process of modernist purification. Both that policing and the constant references to aliogenic origins ("pagan", "primitive", "African") manifested by the erudite supporters of *candomblé* are part of the symbolical work that goes into making Brazilian popular religions "syncretic"—when, in fact, historically, they are no less syncretic than most other religious traditions, Islam and Christianity included.

Such idolatrous, non-fideistic and non-monotheistic conceptions worry those who persecute them as much as they excite those who support them. There is good cause for this, as they are deeply counter-hegemonic to the extent that they manage to bypass and short-circuit the dominant theological and legal apparatuses. The presently emerging consumer society and the new service class that is coming into existence in Brazil are as worried about the counter-hegemonic potential of these forms of popular religiosity as were, in their days, the colonial elite and the bourgeois elite. Note, however, that in these new Pentecostal churches there is no question of abandonment of the centrality of the demonic trope; rather, what one sees there is a new negotiation of its meaning.

A plurality of demons

Let us now jump from the Modern Era which moulded Brazil to the turn of the 20th century, when the formulations of Brazilian national identity were finally consolidated into a self-consciously "modernist" discourse. As we do so,

---

3   *Pactário* is a word that refers to someone who has signed a pact with the Devil.

we continue to observe the pervasiveness and pertinence of the demonic trope and the role it plays in discourses of self-identity, both on the part of those who, while believing that the Devil exists, want to put him and her to practical use by means either of seduction or of exorcism, and on the part of those who, while not believing in the Devil's actual existence, see the Eden/Hades polarity as the central interpretative clue to understanding Brazil. The latter idea, after all, lies behind the Devil that emerges from the works of major literary figures such as Olavo Bilac, Guimarães Rosa or Ariano Suassuna. This Devil is also the devil of the *Paulista* modernists, made famous in Oswald de Andrade's famous cry: "Only anthropophagy unites us." (1990[1928]: 47) This is no longer the Catholic Devil of the Modern Era but the sociologized Devil of Modernism.

The "Brazilian cannibal utopia" that emerges in 20th century art, argues Lúcia Nagib, is driven by the founding images of nationality (2006: 98-99). These formulations of identity reflect a sense of dilaceration between the primitive elements and the European conquering ideal. Furthermore, the confrontation with political and ethical failure does not seem to lead to abandonment of the utopian terms, but rather towards a form of dystopianism. In Nagib's words, "The anthropophagous utopia fails miserably in the same way as, in 1960's Brazil, the revolutionary hopes that brought together intellectuals, workers and peasants were dashed to pieces by the military coup." (2006: 110) In the work of these artists and academics, we witness a dystopian disposition towards the two central moments (the time of "discovery" and the time of the "nation").

Thus, like the Inquisitioners' Devil, this modernist Devil of Brazilian 20th century academic and artistic discourse is also an *other*; yet it is no longer an exterior other, a menacingly exotic one. Rather, to adopt Ariano Suassuna's phrase (2007 [1971]), the "divino-diabolical divinities" that operate as the referents of Brazilian contemporary literature and social analysis are essentially internal devils—they are an inextricable factor of the "Brazilian nation", the "Brazilian people". They are marks of the sense of incompleteness that characterizes this national identity: the dilemmatic condition that Roberto DaMatta theorizes in the 1970s.

Nagib's film analysis comes handy again here, exemplifying a far more pervasive process—one that also affects our own anthropological practice in a curious "loop effect" from which the present essay cannot surely be excluded. Speaking of fully contemporary films, such as *Central Brasil*, she argues, "As they speak of a class different from their own, film directors are transformed into guilty ethnographers that search redemption by representing an other in a benevolent and idealized manner." (2006: 72)[4]

---

4   Note that Esther Hamburger has argued that yet more recent films about urban slums (e.g. *Cidade de Deus*) use demonic violence in a new way, attributing to it

The Devil whose *despacho* (sacrificial offering, lit. "to send off") I come across at a crossroads in Maragojipe, for example, does indeed configure an *inversion* of the world in which I live. The pact I sign with him or her opens the doors of my world to unpredictability, disorder. But it must be understood that that very same Devil whom I meet at a crossroads tonight always had already seduced me: I have always been its captive. My world always had within itself the source of that disorder and only exists as a reaction to the potential of its very inversion. The Brazil of modernist anthropophagy, to use Andrade's metaphor again, confronts the interior and recidivist alterity of "savagery" quite as much as the exterior and futuristic alterity of "civilization". But that savagery now is no longer represented by the Indians, having been re-semanticized by the generation of anthropologists like Roberto DaMatta and film directors such as Walter Salles into an urban dystopia—but the dilemmatic nature of the reformulation continues both in academic discourse (cf. Pina-Cabral 2007) and in artistic discourse (cf. Nagib 2006: 70[5]).

The dilemmatic condition is caused by the utopian disposition; that is, by the adherence to the modern programme of "critical purification" (cf. Latour 1994). In the process of distancing itself from both of those referents—that is, in wanting to be another—Brazil and its intellectuals both trust themselves to a phantasmagoria of modernity and attribute to their world a phantasmagorical appearance (the demonic illusion). The diabolical representation, therefore, is a factor of the social, cultural, and economic dependence in which Brazil and its elites have been living during the past two centuries. Otávio Velho calls this dilemmatic condition "our ambiguous social currency" (1995: 162-7).

The contrast between, on the one hand, this dependence (this Third Worldliness) and, on the other hand, the certainty of Brazil's own Europeanness/Westerness is the spring of the dynamics of dilemma. António Cândido starts his master work, the *Introdução à Literatura Brasileira*, with the following sentence: "Brazilian literature is part of the literatures of Western Europe." (2007: 11) I do not doubt the historical validity of the identification for the majority of the writers that he has in mind; I merely want to call attention to the fact that, once one assumes such a posture, the confrontation with the inevitable realization that Brazil is *also* an "other" sets in motion a dilemmatic (diaboli-

---

a new creative twist. It would seem that they alter the previous relation between artist (upper class) and subject (popular) by negotiating with local subjects the making of the actual process of making the film (2007).

5   Concerning *Central Brasil*, the author insightfully argues, "Now naturalized through a documentarist appeal, fiction transforms the central station into the very savage and adverse nature that encompasses the villain named Pedrão, murderer of street kids and member of a gang of traffickers of human organs." (Nagib 2007: 70)

cal) dynamic in the national project. Such a confrontation is important as this literature is the mainstay and one of the main means of formulation of the national project itself.

In the late 19th century, Euclides da Cunha drafted his major work *Os Sertões* as a response to the pain caused in him by the brutality of the confrontation with Brazil's interior diversity—that "tragedy of the clash of cultures," as António Candido called it. The book reflects the violent challenge to the author's identity resulting from his encounter with profound inhumanity. Being a confirmed Republican, Euclides da Cunha considered the religious leader António Conselheiro and his followers a menace to the new political order. Hence he publicly argued in favour of the military campaign to repress the movement. As the events unfolded, however, he was personally confronted with the violent physical destruction and systematic murder by the military of these "others". In the process, these others came to reveal themselves to be "brothers" and the writer was assaulted by deep feelings of co-responsibility that so tortured him that he undertook the task of attempting to make sense of what was at stake. He wrote what remains perhaps the most extraordinary feat of Lusophone anthropological literature: *Os Sertões* (1933 [1902]).

Willi Bolle argues that half a century later, the central problem that Guimarães Rosa addresses in Brazil's most famous novel—*Grande Sertão: Veredas*—is essentially the same (2004: 26-7). For Euclides da Cunha, the dilemma was lived in flesh and blood; Guimarães Rosa, however, wisely transports it to the realm of fiction by means of the demonic trope. However, what he describes through his Brazilian rendering of the Faustian bargain is no less true or ethically challenging.

To this day, Brazil's religious kaleidoscope is integrated by the fear of the Devil. "The Devil," the anthropologist Ronaldo de Almeida tells us, "is the figure of the Christian universe within which are framed all the divinities of other religions. Thus, he becomes paradoxically the articulator of the continuity between the beliefs and of the circulation of people through all that Catholic-Afro-Spiritist-Pentecostal pool of religiousness." (2000: 199) The Devil pervades the tropical utopia and is constantly being evoked by fiction and by the mass culture, not with the terrific moralistic implications that he or she would have in an North American Protestant context, for example, but with an eye to a playful and workaday relationship. This is clearly exemplified in the Bahian public's enthusiastic response to long running plays such as *Vixe Maria: Deus e o Diabo na Bahia*, where Bahian life is described through the gaze of a long-suffering Devil. In such performances we witness the emergence, with almost clinical precision, of the three supposed "defects" which the central character of Ariano Suassuna's novel *Romance d'A Pedra do Reino* attributes to himself: "historical deviation", "obscene deviation" and "demonic derision".

As he puts it, his proneness to laughter "is not a matter of despair: it is only that I constantly see the Damned one in all of her aspects!" (2007: 540) Faced with that vision, he confesses, he had to become truly "*um safado galopeiro e galhofeiro*" ("a riding and deriding bastard" – ibid.: 539). Seriousness and belief dissolve when faced with the aptness of the demonic metaphor to describe such a world. In a similar vein, Olavo Bilac declares at the conclusion of his essay on the Devil, "But let us not waste any more time with this horror! Let us rather laugh a little at the Devil's expense, for whose fault so many people have suffered, cried and died in this world." (1912: 155) The oxymoronic tragedy of the sentence is, I believe, a marvellous manifestation of how the demonic trope comes to condense Brazil's sense of itself as dilemmatic.

A nation of pactários

According to Willi Bolle, Guimarães Rosa's masterwork is centrally integrated by the argument that, like the novel's main character, Riobaldo, Brazil is a nation of *pactários*, that is of people who signed a pact with the Devil. There, the sense of jeopardy is so intense that all possible wellbeing comes to depend on some sort of compromise with the forces of evil that surround one. Willi Bolle's argument in *Grandesertão.br* is convincing but we are still left with the question of knowing what kind of Devil we are talking about. For not all Devils are alike and it makes a difference what sort of Devil is at stake—as becomes apparent by contrast to the Sarakatsani Devil.

As a matter of fact, the Devil presents him/herself in different guises: in the words of Olavo Bilac, "you may be sure that any man imagines the Devil according to their own temperament ..." (1912: 161). The very same perky black dog, written about by Goethe or by Ariano Suassuna (2007: 520), ends up looking like a pack of hounds, becoming plural. The theological context in which this polythetic sequence of images is reflected largely determines its meaning as well as the powers that are attributed to it and, further still, the implications of attempting to put those powers to use. In Brazil itself, the notion shatters into a plurality of representations *Diabo /Demónio /Belzebú /Satanás /Capeta /Sacy / Capóra /Bode-Velho /Besta-Fera /Exú /Maria Padilha/ Pomba-gira /Ogun-Xerokê*, etc. One does, of course, distinguish each one of these, but one also knows for sure that one is talking about the same entity—Édison Carneiro's problems with the relation between Exú and the Devil are a function of his condition as an intellectual, not in any way a reflection of his Bahian subjects' opinion. The range of definitional overlap between all of these demons is considerable, probably as large as the divergence between them. As Donald Davidson might have argued (2004), we are fooled by our common language both if we think that all those demons are the same *and* if we fail to recognize the considerable overlap of similarities. Parts of their common history are alike, others differ. The Devil's plurality is an intrinsic part of his and her essential deviousness.

Capeta or *Bode-Velho*—demonic invocations much in use in the interior drylands (*sertão*)—appear as principles of death, but it has to be acknowledged that such a death is seldom distant from a sardonic restatement of life. Forms of predatory, demonic alliance are inscribed into the very *fantasias galhofeiras* (derisive fantasies) that identify the *sertão*, being redolent with a transgressive kind of sexuality. The demonic dog of Suassuna does not limit himself to provoking laughter in his victims, as in Goethe's *Dr. Faustus*. There is no denying that Suassuna's Paraiban version of the Devil's dog also produces laughter. But, instead of merely wagging his tail, he does it by fouling up the most prim and proper lady of the town ("fucking her", as her senile husband comes to admit).[6]

The demonic sexual bivalence that Laura de Mello e Souza encounters in the sexual fantasies of the Inquisitors—reflected in the confessions they extract under torture—are still present in figures such as the *Exú Duas Cabeças,* the two-headed hermaphrodite version of Exú, that one encounters for sale in Salvador's markets. Thus, in Brazil, we meet up with an explicit discourse and a complex imagistic elaboration of the Devil's sexual ambivalence—which points less towards a gender issue, in the anthropological definition of the term, then towards a discourse on desire and sexuality and the way they pervade everyday relations.

Conclusion

Back at the turn of the 20th century, Olavo Bilac explained to us that there were two polar positions that structure the Devil's plurality in Brazil: "I was speaking to you of the sorcery of the blacks in the *sanzalas*, at the time of captivity. Now note, in the legends of the *sertão*, a tradition of the Shabbat is also to be found." (1912: 150) Indeed, the *Capeta* of the drylands, typified in the figure of the Old Goat (*Bode Velho*), approximates a more dualist world in which the principle of Evil can be identified when faced with God's goodness. In contrast, the coastal *Exú*, bisexual and ambivalent, immanent to all divinities, is far from effecting a clear differentiation with the divinity of the type that John Campbell identified among the Sarakatsani.

Contrary to the Sarakatsani, however, both of the Brazilian Devils have to be approached through some form of compromise. The former, more easily

---

6   In the Globo film version of *A Pedra do Reino* the dog is transmuted into a Devil and the copulation is explicit.

othered, reaches out paradigmatically to the principle of the "pact"; the latter, immanent and less perceptibly external, reaches out syntagmatically to the principle of the "captivity". Between the two extremes and in the superimposition of both, a field of demonic variation is constituted, the main matrix of which is the impossibility of formulating oneself. This referential bipolarity when faced with the impossibility of formulating the lived world is expressed in Brazilian literature through all these processes of fantastic demonic mediation that we have been identifying.

Again—and, as it would seem, contrary to the Greek case—if I stress that, in the Brazilian Devil's sexual ambivalence, the issue of gender is less important than that of actual sexuality, it is because this eroticization is explicitly used both by contemporary literature and by popular culture as a means to formulate a national self-image in which love and violence not only coexist but embrace each other. This embrace between *love* (as in passion, sexual pleasure and the sharing of identity) and *violence* (pain, destruction, death) is properly speaking the adobe that keeps together this dilemmatic Brazil—as so many writers have noted before me. The terms used by Bilac to end his essay point in the same direction. He has recourse to the metaphor of Carnival in order to explain that "the Wisdom of our civilized epoch" no longer fears to walk arm in arm with the Devil, "as it knows he is nothing but an invention" (1912: 165-6). If it were otherwise, Bilac tells us, he would not be able to afford to finish his paper with the following supposition: "Let us, then, imagine that Satan had truly existed, and still exists today." If he did, then clearly he would be responsible for two of the most important inventions of "our era": "the woman's kiss" and "Science"! And so he closes off the essay: "If he is indeed the author of all that is imputed to him, it has to be confessed that men owe him an enormous debt of gratitude." (1912: 168-9)

To close off myself, I return to the wisdom of my lady friend, with which I started this paper; much like Olavo Bilac, she too could see in the Devil a series of salvific elements that are indispensable if we are to live well in this ambiguous and dangerous world ... a world that, to the extent that it is permeated by the Devil, is identical to many other human worlds but which, in the Brazilian case, and unlike the Sarakatsani, is profoundly dilemmatized by an internal polarization that attributes to it a characteristically demonic appearance.

All attempts to exorcise the Devil based on a monotheistic outlook will ultimately reinforce the categories that produce Brazil's dilemmaticity and, thus, reproduce the conditions for the Devil's reappearance. The pervasiveness of the Devil in the form of the various "compromises" that characterize Brazilian popular religion suggests that a documentation of internal altering can only be achieved if the original utopian drive that created their land through "discovery" and "captivity" is set aside in favour of a historicist conception of Brazilian society as an emergnt phenomenon in its own right.

BIBLIOGRAPHY

[Note: all quotations in English of works cited in Portuguese are the author's responsibility].

Adler, Jeremy and Richard Fardon (1999) "An Oriental in the West: The Life of Franz Baermann Steiner" in Jeremy Adler and Richard Fardon (eds), *Franz Baerman Steiner – Selected Writings,* vol. 1, Oxford, Berghahn Books, 16-100.

Almeida, Ronaldo de (2000) "Pombas-Giras, Espíritos, Santos e Outras Devoções" in *Novos Estudos CEBRAP* 57, São Paulo, 2000, 197-9.

Andrade, Oswald de (1990) *A Utopia Antropofágica,* São Paulo, Ed. Globo

Bilac, Olavo (1912) "O Diabo" in *Conferência Literárias,* Rio de Janeiro, F. Alves & Cia, 129-69.

Bolle, Willi (2004) *Grandesertão.br.*, São Paulo, Livr. Duas Cidades/Ed. 34, 2004.

Buarque de Holanda, Sérgio (1996 [1959]) *Visão do Paraíso: os motivos edênicos no descobrimento e colonisação do Brasil,* São Paulo, Brasiliense.

Campbell, John (1964) *Honour, Family and Patronage,* Oxford, Clarendon Press.

Candido, António (2007 [1987/1997]) *Iniciação à Literatura Brasileira,* 5ª ed., Rio de Janeiro, Ouro sobre Azul.

Carneiro, Édison (1991 [1948]) *Candomblés da Bahia.* 9ª edição, Rio de Janeiro, Civilização Brasileira.

Cunha, Euclides da (1933 [1902]) *Os Sertões. (Campanha de Canudos),* 12ª ed., Rio de Janeiro, Azevedo e Cia.

DaMatta, Roberto (1979) *Carnavais, Malandros e Heróis: para um sociologia do dilema brasileiro.* Rio de Janeiro, Zahar Eds.

Davidson, Donald (2004) *Problems of Rationality,* Oxford, Clarendon Press

Derrida, Jacques (1998) *Archive Fever: A Freudian Impression.* Transl. E. Prenowitz, University of Chicago Press.

Freyre, Gilberto (2003 [1933]) *Casa Grande & Sanzala: Formação da família brasileira sob o regime de economia patriarcal.* 47 ed., São Paulo, Global Editora.

Gell, Alfred (1998) "The Distributed Person" in *Art and Agency: An Anthropological Theory,* Oxford, Clarendon Press, 96-153.

Guimarães Rosa, João (2001 [1956]) *Grande Sertão: Veredas.* 19 ed., Rio de Janeiro, Nova Fronteira.

Hamburger, Esther (2007) "Violência e pobreza no cinema brasileiro recente" in *Novos Estudos Cebrap* 78. São Paulo, Julho, 113-30.

Lambert, Malcolm (1998) *The Cathars*, Oxford, Blackwell.
Latour, Bruno (1994 [1991]) *Jamais fomos modernos: ensaio de Antropologia Simétrica*, São Paulo, Editora 34.
Mello e Souza, Laura de (1993) *Inferno Atlântico: demonologia e colonização, secs XVI-XVIII*, São Paulo, Companhia das Letras.
—— (2005 [1986]) *O Diabo e a Terra de Santa Cruz: feitiçaria e religiosidade popular no Brasil colonial*, São Paulo, Companhia das Letras.
Meyer, Merlyse (1993) *Maria Padilha e toda a sua quadrilha: De amante do rei de Castela a pomba-gira de umbanda*, Livr. Duas Cidades, São Paulo.
Nagib, Lúcia (2006) *A utopia no cinema brasileiro*, São Paulo, Cosac & Naify.
Onians, R.B. (1951) *The Origins of European Thought about the Body, the Mind, the Soul, the World, Time and Fate*, Cambridge University Press.
Peristiany, J.G. (ed.) (1966) *Honour and Shame: the Values of Mediterranean Society*, University of Chicago Press.
Pina Cabral, João de (1992) "The Gods of the Gentiles are Demons: the Problem of Pagan Survivals in European Culture" in Kirsten Hastrup (ed.), *Other Histories*, London, Routledge, 45-61.
—— (1997) "The Threshold Diffused: Margins, Hegemonies and Contradictions in Contemporary Anthropology" in Patrick McAllister (ed.), *Culture and the Commonplace: Anthropological Essays in Honour of David Hammond-Tooke*, Johannesburg, Witwatersrand University Press, 31-52.
—— (2007) "A pessoa e o dilema brasileiro: uma perspectiva anticesurista" in *Novos Estudos CEBRAP*, São Paulo, 95-112.
—— and John Campbell (eds) (1992) *Europe Observed*, Oxford, Macmillan/St.Antony's College.
Pompa, Cristina (2003) *Religião como tradução: missionários, Tupi e Tapuia no Brasil colonial*, Bauru, SP, EDUSC.
Ruel, Malcolm (2002 [1982]) "Christians as Believers" in Michael Lambek (ed.), *A Reader in the Anthropology of Religion*, Oxford, Blackwell, 99-113.
Sansi-Roca, Roger (2007), "The Fetish in the Lusophone Atlantic" in Nancy Naro, Roger Sansi-Roca and David H. Treece (eds), *Cultures of the Lusophone Black Atlantic*, New York, Palgrave-Macmillan, 19-39.
Schritzmeyer, Ana Lúcia Pastore (2004), *Sortilégio de saberes: curandeiros e juízes nos tribunais brasileiros (1900-1990)*, São Paulo, IBCCRIM.
Stewart, Charles (1991) *Demons and the Devil: Moral Imagination in Modern Greek Culture*, Princeton University Press.
Suassuna, Ariano (2007 [1971]) *Romance d'A Pedra do Reino e o Príncipe do Sangue do vai-e-volta*, 9 ed. Rio de Janeiro, José Olympio.

Velho, Otávio (1995) *Besta-Fera: Recriação do Mundo*, Rio de Janeiro, Relume/ Dumará.

Vieira, P. António (1959) *Sermões*, Porto, Lello & Irmãos.

13

JOHN CAMPBELL

Michael Llewellyn Smith[1]

John Campbell's career, mainly passed in the surroundings of St Antony's College, Oxford—not exactly cloistered, although the college was founded in a former convent—was set in motion by war service in Greece and the influence of the great anthropologist E.E. Evans-Pritchard. In the early 1950s these two factors led him back to Greece, for the fieldwork among the Sarakatsani, transhumant shepherds of Epirus, which was the foundation of his work as an anthropologist. As he himself admits, contingency played a more than usually strong part in his life.

John Campbell (hereafter John) was born in 1923 in the London borough of Merton, and educated at King's College School Wimbledon, where he excelled (captain of the school, captain of the rugby football 1st XV, in John's words "all those ridiculous things"). He studied the classics, won a county major scholarship in ancient history, and went up to Pembroke College, Cambridge in 1941. Classics seemed irrelevant in the atmosphere of war, and he chose to read economics, a decision later regretted. Having completed part 1 of the economics tripos in two terms, he joined the army. Commissioned as a 2nd Lieutenant in the Middlesex Regiment, and starting from his experience at school in the OTC, he rapidly learned a lot about 4.2 inch mortars and Vickers machine guns, graduating to active service in North Africa and Italy as a mortar specialist.

The desert war was more or less over when John arrived in Algiers. Attached to the Highland Division he landed in Sicily on 10 July 1943 and took part

---

1 As well as John and Sheila Campbell themselves, I am grateful to Julie du Boulay, Michael Gilsenan, Mark Mazower and Harry Shukman for information used in this paper.

in the first phase of the invasion, which ended for him when he was severely wounded in the right leg on 20 July. Evacuated by air to North Africa, he spent two or three months recuperating before returning to his battalion. Transferred to the 5th army of General Mark Clark, the battalion took part in the Anzio landing in January 1944, and in the ensuing months of intense and unpleasant fighting. Later, as a counter mortar officer, he was attached to the 28th British Infantry Brigade as they worked their way up the peninsula beyond Florence. Embarked from Italy for garrison duty in Palestine, he was on his way there in December 1944 when the troubles broke out in Athens between the Communists (ELAS) and General Scobie's allied forces. The 28th British Infantry Brigade was one of the British units sent to Athens. John landed just before Christmas and was therefore present during the most dramatic phase of the fighting, briefly based in Glyfada and later in a former Embassy building on Vasilissis Sophias Avenue, which housed the brigade headquarters. Here for a time he acted as a liaison officer to a division of the newly formed Greek National Guards.

John stayed in Athens until the Varkiza agreement of February 1945 which signalled the end of the fighting. The Brigade remained in Greece as a necessary security force, in Livadeia. He comments that, typically, there was not much to do. To keep occupied, he obtained local leave, and went off with his closest friend Michael Stern in a jeep. They explored much of the Peloponnese, including the Mani. There was a later expedition to Evvia where, by coincidence, on a walk to a monastery south of Limni they passed the buildings of the Anglo-Hellenic Lignite Company at Katounia. It was here that Philip Sherrard, who was then serving in the army in Italy and whom John had not yet met, was eventually to establish his estate. This extended period of exploration in southern Greece, where the two young men were struck by the harsh conditions in the countryside, was a major factor in John's later return to Greece as a research student.

John flew home to England on leave prior to going to the Far East for a further tour of duty. But at that stage the atom bombs were dropped on Nagasaki and Hiroshima and Japan surrendered. John called at the War Office to discover what his next employment might be. His interlocutor looked at his file and said, "I see you have a rather good academic record: would you like to go back to university?" As a member of the notional category of "people of national importance", he thus escaped the convention "first in first out" and returned to Pembroke College for the Michaelmas term 1945, to resume the economics tripos, though increasingly disenchanted with the subject. By Christmas he fell ill with what was thought to be pneumonia. He missed the next term's work. Tuberculosis was diagnosed, and John spent a year in the Brompton hospital, a "useless existence" mitigated only by reading books. At that stage of medical knowledge, the only treatment was to put the patient to bed and enforce idleness, ensuring that the lungs were not exercised. Sometimes this resulted in a cure, sometimes not, in which case the patient died.

In John's case, when no cure ensued he was sent to a sanatorium at Montana Vermala near Crans in the mountains of Switzerland. Here he met his future wife Sheila Methven, who had also contracted TB after a brief career in the South African Women's Army. Meeting Sheila was a life-changing experience. The relationship blossomed, and was continued by correspondence after they had both left Switzerland.

After eight or nine months in the Swiss mountains, John appeared to be improving. In 1948 he took ship for Melbourne, to carry on the treatment at his father's home in Australia. Sheila, back in South Africa, more or less cured, came from Natal University to visit him in Australia. She brought with her books from her university courses, including significantly one on social anthropology.

Medical advances in the treatment of tuberculosis, notably the discovery of streptomycin, enabled his doctors to operate on John. In early 1951, his left lung was removed by pneumonectomy. This led to a more or less complete cure, opening up the prospect of a return to university in England. He returned via Cape Town, meeting Sheila and her family, and persuaded her to break off her studies at Natal University. The two established themselves at Cambridge in Michaelmas term 1951, and just before Christmas that year they were married.

By now, some five years after leaving the army, John felt that he had moved beyond the conventional in the form of the economics tripos and must try something else. An interest in anthropology began in Australia when he looked at the materials which Sheila had brought out from her university. It was a further coincidence that Sheila was connected by marriage to Professor Evans-Pritchard ("E-P"), the foremost anthropologist of his generation, who established his reputation through his fieldwork among the Nuer of the Sudan.[2] Evans-Pritchard happened to be visiting his relatives in South Africa when John arrived in Durban. Talking with him about his experiences in Sudan, Ethiopia and Libya made a deep impression.

Overcoming a certain amount of institutional resistance, John therefore renounced economics and embarked on part 2 of the Cambridge anthropology and archaeology tripos. Having completed this in two years, with sufficient distinction to win a grant for doctoral research, he faced the question: where?

---

2 Sheila's uncle Jack Stanley had married Joyce, daughter of the South African politician and diplomat George Heaton Nicholls (1876-1959). Evans-Pritchard married Heaton Nicholls's other daughter Ioma.

John has described in an essay, "Fieldwork among the Sarakatsani, 1954-55", how he came to do fieldwork in Greece.[3] The anthropology tripos at Cambridge was heavily biased towards primitive societies. Students had to read every available monograph on African, South American and Indian societies. Standing on the shoulders of established ethnographers was not an attractive prospect. Recollection of Greece in the war, desperately poor and in some ways primitive, suggested another option. It was ground unexplored by anthropologists. Meyer Fortes, the chairman of the Cambridge anthropology department, made it clear that if he selected Greece for fieldwork he would have to "paddle his own canoe." John consulted S.J. Papastavrou, who taught modern Greek at Cambridge, and the ancient historian Nicholas Hammond, then fellow of Clare College and an expert on northern Greece from his war service with SOE. Both gave useful advice. Evans-Pritchard, who paid a visit to Cambridge at about this time, encouraged him to come to Oxford, which offered the prospect of supervision by the Greek anthropologist John Peristiany.[4]

John and Sheila moved to Oxford in 1953 with, for John, the double aim of working with Peristiany and joining Evans-Pritchard's institute. He spent a year at the Institute of Social Anthropology, reading widely in the anthropology of semi-literate societies, studying the history of Greece, and reading whatever little he could find on the sociology of Greece. He also joined an undergraduate course studying modern Greek, and had conversational practice with the wife of the poet and scholar Constantine Trypanis.

For his fieldwork John chose the Zagori area in Epirus. The Zagorochoria is the mountainous area north of Ioannina in northwestern Greece, running up towards the border with Albania. This was not one of the parts of Greece which John had visited during the war, but it had been suggested by Hammond and Papastavrou. It was a poor region of mountain villages, inhabited in the summer months by transhumant shepherds. These shepherd communities, the Sarakatsani, lived in a state of mutual hostility but at the same time tense interdependence with the villagers.

---

3   John Campbell, "Fieldwork among the Sarakatsani, 1954-55", in *Europe Observed*, ed, João de Pina-Cabral and John Campbell, Macmillan in association with St Antony's College, Oxford, 1992, pp 148-66.

4   John G. Peristiany (1911-88) was senior lecturer in social anthropology, Oxford, 1949-63; United Nations professor of Social Science, Athens, 1960-78. His fieldwork was on the pastoralists of East Africa. Later he concentrated on the anthropology of the Mediterranean. As first Director of the Social Sciences Centre at Athens, he played a large part in encouraging and steering the growth of the social sciences in Greece in the 1960s and 1970s. He served as Ambassador of Cyprus in France.

John's original intention had been to study one or more of these villages. The historical interest of the confederation of 46 villages of the district in the Ottoman period had led him him to the area. But after three months he became increasingly uncertain about the village as an object of study: subject to recent social dislocation and depopulation during the civil war, it was not the "viable, relatively homogeneous community which the anthropological literature encouraged [him] to believe would be a profitable object for anthropological research".[5]

John's chapter about his fieldwork is essential reading for those who wish to understand the conditions under which he carried out the work, the intellectual path which led him to the Zagorochoria, and more widely the way in which anthropologists go about their business. He writes about how he came to work among the Sarakatsani, about the conditions of work and the means of transcending barriers to understanding, and also about how politics affected his work. The most important feature of the chapter for our purposes is the description of the role of "the anthropologist's wife". Sheila's contribution was vital both in introducing John to the Sarakatsani and in exploring and enabling him to study the role of women and girls in the Sarakatsan communities.

John and Sheila were aware that families of Sarakatsan transhumant shepherds lived above the village in their characteristic circular huts of dried mud and grass thatch. He wrote, "Their relations with villagers were uneasy. Our own contacts with them had not gone beyond formal greetings when one day in the heat of summer a young shepherd-boy returning from school had stopped at the village spring to drink, and was there set upon by larger village boys who took the chance of easy sport to bully him. At this point the anthropologist's wife entered indignantly to rescue the victim."[6]

This incident led to an invitation to visit a Sarakatsan encampment and the relationship prospered, leading to an invitation to accompany a family and their flocks down to the plains of Thesprotia for the winter.[7] The Campbells acquired their own hut. The decision to join and study the Sarakatsani, which gave John anxious thought, was encouraged by Evans-Pritchard, who perhaps saw in the Sarakatsani, as did John, a field of study relatively accessible to someone trained on African monographs. The result was his pioneering study of the social structure and value system of the Sarakatsani, *Honour, Family and*

---

5 Campbell, op. cit., pp. 151-2.
6 Ibid., pp. 152.
7 This annual migration of transhumant shepherds with their flocks used to be accomplished on foot, though shepherds usually now use trucks to transport their sheep. The migration (of Vlach rather than Sarakatsan shepherds) is well portrayed in Tim Salmon's film *Dhiava: Autumn Journey* (Cirrus Films, 1997).

Patronage. He was the first social anthropologist to work in Greece, closely followed by Ernestine Friedl.

John describes the pluses and minuses of fieldwork in this new environment. On the minus side was the defensiveness of the Sarakatsani, their hostility to virtually everyone who was not kin. The converse however was also true, that once accepted by certain families, the anthropologist and his wife were treated with respect and affection and came to occupy a special role close to that of confidant in their respective male and female spheres. Another advantage was the willingness, indeed eagerness, of Sarakatsani to expound on matters of genealogy. But the biggest plus (contrary to Evans-Pritchard's firm conviction that spouses should not accompany their husbands in fieldwork) was the presence of Sheila.

"The idealisation of my wife Sheila presented few problems. She was generous, openhearted, and modest. It was noted that her blouse was always buttoned at the neck and wrists. At weddings they took pride in drawing attention to her skill in the ring dances. Only the enemies of our friends put it about that she was shameless and showed her ankles."[8]

The idealized figure of the anthropologist's wife was able to break through barriers which would have been insurmountable for a man, in talking to women of all ages. This was not achieved simply by virtue of being a woman, though that was a necessary condition. Sheila's qualities of openness and good-hearted curiosity opened the door. The building of their own hut was a decisive step, bringing a steady stream of women visitors to visit Sheila. Once this relationship of trust was established, John found that provided he observed a discreet position in the background he could participate in the talk. Entry into the universe of women as well as of men, with the sympathetic intuition enjoined by Evans-Pritchard (who told John "What we want you to do at this stage is to tell us what they think and what they value"), was one of the foundations of *Honour, Family and Patronage*.

Politics and suspicion intruded on the fieldwork, inevitably at a time when tensions between Greece and Britain were rising over Cyprus. The Zagori area, militarily sensitive, lying near the frontier with Albania, was in a military zone for which special permits were required. It was naturally assumed by Greeks that this young couple, pursuing a course of research which must have been largely incomprehensible to them, were up to no good. There was talk of espionage, of reporting on possible landing grounds for parachutists. For some time John and Sheila managed to hold their position, with the help of their patron Panayiotis Kanellopoulos, then Minister of Defence in

---

8   Campbell, op. cit., pp. 154-5.

the government of Marshal Papagos.⁹ But the death of Papagos, resulting in the elevation of Constantine Karamanlis to the position of Prime Minister, and the temporary sidelining of Kanellopoulos quickly led to action to remove John and Sheila from Epirus. They took refuge for a time at the British School at Athens, an institution more geared to archaeologists than anthropologists, but nevertheless a welcome refuge. It provided intellectual credentials and respectability, and enabled John to widen his circle of friends in Athens while manoeuvring to get back into the field, which he eventually achieved. He described the School as a "home from home".[10]

Back in Oxford in 1956, John wrote up his fieldwork notes, completed his thesis, and gained his doctorate. The next career move was a product of chance. While in Greece he had met Philip Sherrard, poet and scholar of the intellectual and spiritual world of the Greeks.[11] Sherrard, who was at this point doing research at St Antony's College, Oxford, resigned his research fellowship there in order to return to Greece to be Assistant Director of the British School at Athens. The two people who mattered most at the still comparatively young college, Bill Deakin (the Warden)[12] and the historian James

---

9   Panayiotis Kanellopoulos (1902-86) the most distinguished of Greece's politician-intellectuals of the 20th century. Author of many books including *History of European Thought*. Prime Minister briefly in 1945, and again briefly in 1967, being deposed by the military junta which took power in April that year.

10 See John Campbell's thoughts about the British School at Athens in Reneé Hirschon, "'Home from Home'; the Role of the BSA in Social Anthropological Fieldwork", unpublished paper to appear in a forthcoming BSA volume, *Scholars, Archives, Travels: the Contribution of the British School at Athens to Byzantine and Modern Greek Studies,* ed. Paschalis Kitromilides, Michael Llewellyn Smith and Eleni Galligas.

11 Philip Sherrard (1922-95). Among his best known works are: *The Marble Threshing Floor: Studies in Modern Greek Poetry,* London 1956; *The Greek East and the Latin West,* Oxford 1959; *Athos, the Mountain of Silence,* Oxford 1960; *George Seferis, Collected Poems 1924-1955,* tr. Edmund Keeley and Philip Sherrard, Princeton 1967; and numerous other translations from Greek poets and from sacred texts.

12 F.W. Deakin (1913-2005), historian, author and first Warden of St Antony's College, Oxford; as research assistant before the war he helped Churchill write his biography of Marlborough. During the war Deakin worked for SOE on Balkan questions, and was parachuted into Yugoslavia to report on the resistance (his report led to the transfer of British support from Mihailovic's Cetniks to Tito's Partisans). He became the first Warden of the newly established St Antony's College in 1950, and was largely responsible for choosing the first Fellows and students, and for the development of the college as a centre for international studies. He retired from the wardenship in 1968, and moved to the south of France. Author of *The Brutal Friendship,* 1962, on Hitler and Mussolini; and *The Embattled Mountain,* 1971, an account of his experiences in

Joll,[13] liked Sherrard and his work and did not wish to see the Greek connection severed. Sherrard suggested to them that John, albeit an anthropologist, would be the right man to maintain it. (In John's reconstruction of the scene, under interrogation by Deakin and Joll, Philip Sherrard "had to admit that I was an anthropologist—however, he said, I was very interested in history".) John was duly appointed to fill the remaining term of Sherrard's fellowship.

One further period in Athens followed. John Peristiany, John's former supervisor, had taken leave of absence from Oxford in order to become the first Director of the Greek Social Sciences Centre (EKKE) in Athens, a position and an institute supported by UNESCO. In 1962 he returned to Oxford for six months to decide on his long term future, and John replaced him temporarily in Athens. He recalls the people at the Centre, which was attached to the Greek Ministry of Coordination, as a heterogeneous group of Greeks and foreigners from different disciplines collected together by Peristiany. John's six months at the Centre were clearly, among other things, a lesson in the workings of Greek bureaucracy. They were also an introduction to the intriguing character of Andreas Papandreou, then Director of the Centre for Economic Research with which the Social Sciences Centre collaborated on the first *Social and Economic Atlas of Greece*. John remembers convivial discussions with Papandreou on the nature of Greek political institutions, "about which he had few illusions and which in his years of power he did little to reform", a neat summary of Andreas' mixture of intelligence and cynicism.[14]

Looking back, John concluded that Peristiani had completed the first stage of his creative work at the Centre, gathering a nucleus of social scientists, embarking on research projects, inviting foreign scholars, starting a library, letting it be known in academic and governmental circles that the Centre existed. It was poised to take forward its development with the organization of international anthropological conferences on Mediterranean cultures, and with new research projects on urbanization, education, rural development, ethnic minorities: in sum, despite the seven-year gap caused by the military regime of 1967-74, it made an important contribution to the development of academic

---

    Yugoslavia during the war.

13   James Bysse Joll (1918-74), historian. He worked in SOE during the war. After three years as Fellow of New College, he became Fellow and Subwarden of the new St Antony's College, and was a major influence on its formation and development. Among his books are *Intellectuals in Politics; The Anarchists; Europe since 1870*.

14   John Campbell, "The Social Sciences Centre, Athens, 1962", in *Koinonikes Epistemes kai Protoporia stin Ellada 1950-1967*, ed. Ioanna Lambiri-Dimaki, Gutenberg and Athens: EKKE, 2003, pp. 431-5.

life and public policy in Greece today. For John, these months were both a contribution to this development and a further education in "Greek reality".

John's succession to Sherrard's fellowship was the start of a career-long connection with St Antony's. John and his work had the full support of Warden Deakin, but that did not at first bring with it security of tenure. He got by on a succession of appointments as a research fellow. The publication in 1964 of *Honour, Family and Patronage,* to favourable comment, did much for his status and reputation.[15] In 1967 he was elected an Official Fellow of the College, joining the governing body. The first of a succession of British and Greek doctoral students came to John for supervision, in the anthropology of Mediterranean societies, and increasingly as time passed in the history of Greece.

There was a logic about the switch to history, which in any case never excluded anthropology. From his childhood, fed on G.A. Henty's novels, John had been interested in history. His intellectual godfather was Evans-Pritchard, who disagreed with the view that anthropology was a natural science and stressed its relationship to history, as a branch of human knowledge distinct from the functionalism which was in fashion at the time.

However, John's appointment to a university lectureship in modern Balkan history, which followed, proved unsatisfactory. For several years he lectured to undergraduates in subjects that failed either to coincide with his own main research interests or to match the students' needs for their exams. Apart from some aspects of the Eastern Question, there was little in his portfolio that was relevant to their degree courses in modern history. By 1972 John felt sufficiently secure financially to give up the university lectureship and subsist on the stipend from his college fellowship.

Honour, Family and Patronage was followed in 1968 by *Modern Greece,* a collaboration by John Campbell and Philip Sherrard, published by Ernest Benn in the series "Nations of the Modern World".[16] It is the best such general introduction I know to Greek history, society and culture. (It is interesting that another excellent general introduction to Greece was written by two Greek scholars, John Koliopoulos and Thanos Veremis, one of whom was John's doctoral student and both of whom were much influenced by him. It is dedicated by the two authors to John, "a mentor and friend to both authors".)[17] *Modern*

---

15 J.K. Campbell, *Honour, Family and Patronage: a Study of Institutions and Moral Values in a Greek Mountain Community,* Oxford 1964.

16 John Campbell and Philip Sherrard, *Modern Greece,* London: Ernest Benn, 1968.

17 John S. Koliopoulos and Thanos M. Veremis, *Greece: the Modern Sequel,* London: Hurst, 2002. Veremis was John's student. There is also a longer Greek edition of the book.

Greece contains a chapter about the dictator Ioannis Metaxas, one of the more interesting figures in the history of Greece in the first half of the 20th century, which is the fruit of an abortive essay in biography, when John was given access by Metaxas' daughter to his papers in Athens.[18] More recently, when he gave the Christopher lecture at Harvard in 1990 (fifty years after the Italian attack on Greece) John returned to his interest in Metaxas. Other distinctions included the Sir John Myres lecture at Oxford in 1976, later published as a paper entitled "The Greek Hero".[19] And in the year 2000 John received an honorary doctorate from the University of Thessaloniki.

As a college man, first from his house in Winchester Road, later from Boars Hill, John served as a member of the governing body, and held the main offices of Senior Tutor, tutor for admissions, and for two years Sub-Warden. For many years he was a member of the Investment committee, a task requiring a shrewd financial head and a capacity for enjoyment of lunches in city boardrooms. One of his closest friends in the college was Harry Shukman, who had rooms in Winchester Road next to John's for a period of nearly thirty years. The college fellow whose work perhaps influenced him most was Theodore Zeldin, the historian of France and of happiness.[20] Of the wardens of the college with whom John served, he found Raymond Carr[21] the most stimulating, original and amusing—in the words of one fellow, "always ready to laugh at his own and others' cock-ups". While John discharged his college duties with impeccable loyalty, his attitude to the college as an institution, as to all other institutions of authority, was sceptical, amused, even to a degree anarchic. This made him a very good source of talk about college life, within the limits of discretion imposed by membership of the governing body. Like others who knew the college in its early days, he regrets some of the changes, inevitable as they may have been: the passing of Warden Deakin's generously cavalier attitude to money when it came to supporting Fellows' research; the shift from

---

18   A photographer and former senior figure in Metaxas' youth movement EON, whom John got to know in Katounia, Evvia, introduced him to Metaxas's daughter, who gave him access to the papers and introduced him to some of Metaxas's former collaborators. The project foundered when they both realized that it would not be possible for him to write the sort of biography which she envisaged.

19   J.K. Campbell, "The Greek Hero", in *Honor and Grace in Anthropology,* ed. J.G. Peristiany and Julian Pitt-Rivers, Cambridge 1992, pp. 129-49.

20   Theodore Zeldin, at various times Fellow of St Antony's College, Senior Tutor and Dean. Author of the two-volume Oxford history of France, 1848-1945, and other books about France and happiness.

21   Raymond Carr, historian of Spain, Warden of St Antony's College, 1968-87.

research fellows, who were the majority in the early days, to faculty lecturers with teaching responsibilities.

The aspect of John's university career that deserves most emphasis is his role as teacher and supervisor of a whole generation of doctoral students of anthropology and history who have gone on to make their mark in the academic worlds of Britain, Greece and the United States. They add up to an impressive total of some forty postgraduates. Anthropologists came to John because of his reputation and his ground-breaking book. Historians had less to go on. But the history faculty of the university would not accept postgraduate students unless they had an appropriate supervisor. For those interested in Greece, John became that person. His students included the historians Helen Angelomatis-Tsougarakis, Basil C. Gounaris, Gelina Harlaftis, Elizabeth Kontogeorgi and Thanos Veremis from Greece; Mark Mazower and myself from Britain; and the anthropologists Julie du Boulay, Michael Herzfeld, Renée Hirschon, Roger Just and Charles Stewart.

Talking to John's former students, it is not easy to pin down particular methods which marked him out. They agree on his informed and sympathetic interest, his preference for clear English over jargon. Mark Mazower recalls how when he arrived and visited John in his rooms, to talk about what he might work on, John said vaguely, "Someone has just dumped those in my office. You might take a look." They were the box files of the Ionian Bank Archives, and put Mark on the trail of his dissertation. "He had a knack like that."

Julie du Boulay wrote to me that "the rest of us are just padding along in his footprints". He was alert both to the practical aspects of ethnography and to a great range of symbolic and religious ideas. His greatest quality was his sensitivity to the entirety of the lives of the people. In *Honour, Family and Patronage* he threw out ideas from "the texture of Sarakatsan thinking" which provided a store for other anthropologists to develop. He did not arrive with preconceived ideas which then dictated what he found. He was thus able to render the complexity of their thought with simplicity and directness.

For Julie, the same qualities informed his role as supervisor. Rigorous himself in anthropological method, he was tolerant of weakness in his students. His amused probing (not quite the same as scepticism, I think) comes out in a exchange reported by Julie, who said that in the old days villagers used to see visions and dream dreams. When John queried the accuracy of this, she said that they would see things like the Panaghia (the Virgin Mary) sitting on a rock:

JKC: But the examiner would say that they thought they saw the Panaghia sitting on a rock but what they really saw was a candle flickering.

JduB: But the villagers would say that the examiners thought they saw a candle flickering but what they really saw was the Panaghia sitting on a rock.

JKC: Ah, but the Panaghia isn't in the the examiners' world view.

Thus for anthropologists, John's own fieldwork was a model. For historians, the insights provided by the anthropologist into social values and relations, notably patronage, proved fruitful both for his students, and more widely among the community of historians. George Mavrogordatos, a leading historian of modern Greece, is a notable example.

A writer and teacher can be seen as a point at which various influences converge, and from which in turn influences radiate outwards, through readers and pupils. The influences John exerted on and through his students have been traced by the anthropologist Peter Loizos.[22] They extended more widely than the Greek world, affecting scholars such as Albert Hourani and, through him, a generation of students of the Middle East. One of these, Michael Gilsenan, writes that "those of us who were not going to work in East Africa or the Southern Sudan or some of the more "classic" areas for Oxford anthropologists were hugely excited by this new monograph which seemed pioneering in so many ways, not least its sense of moving anthropology into Europe from the margins. Albert [Hourani], of course, had studied it closely. I took it as in some sense of the term a model of what might be done..."[23]

Probably the most pervading influence on John was that of Evans-Pritchard, through his writing style and his humane view that anthropology is allied to history as part of the story of human beings. Jargon in any context, and the sterile side of functionalism, were always alien; clarity, human empathy and elegance of style and cogency of argument important. His Cambridge supervisor Emrys Peters was also unsympathetic to functionalism. The work of Julian Pitt-Rivers on Andalusia was important in suggesting a manner of approach to the subject at a time when there was really no model to follow for what he proposed. Other influences include the works of Emile Durkheim; R.G. Collingwood's *The Idea of History*; R.B. Onions' *The Origins of European Thought*; C.M. Woodhouse's classic study of the war in Greece, *Apple of Discord*; and John's colleague Theodore Zeldin's *History of France*.

A close friend whose influence was of a different sort was Philip Sherrard, with whom John collaborated on *Modern Greece*. No doubt the influence went as much in the other direction. The two men were contemporaries, with differ-

---

22   Peter Loizos, "Anthropologists and Historians, in Greece and the Christian Mediterranean, with particular reference to the influence of John Campbell", in IV International Congress of History, *Historiography of Modern and Contemporary Greece 1833-2002*, ed. Paschalis M. Kitromilides and Triantaphyllos E. Sklavenitis, Athens 2004, vol. 1, pp. 307-17.

23   Professor Michael Gilsenan, New York University, personal communication to the author.

ent interests and different casts of mind: Sherrard a poet who believed deeply in the traditions of the Eastern Orthodox Church, a man capable of profoundly influencing younger seekers after the truth, by no means unworldly in his own life; Campbell of a sceptical frame of mind, probably far from subscribing to Sherrard's beliefs, but ready to learn from him about aspects of the Greek experience outside his own field, and to appreciate his insight into the immaterial world which was so much a part of what John had studied in the Sarakatsani. The collaboration was ideal, Sherrard contributing chapters on literature and religion, Campbell some two-thirds of the book, and the two working together productively on the first chapter. Though a frequent visitor with his family to Katounia, and although the two families were close friends, John never bought into the complex of houses there.

Another close professional relationship and friendship has been that with Richard Clogg, who because of the circumstances which led to his leaving King's College, London was available to join St Antony's as Associate Fellow after John retired in 1990, and to carry on his historical work there, being elected to the governing body in 1995. As the College's official history remarks, "It can be argued that, as the result of the efforts of Campbell and Clogg, Oxford has become one of only two centres of modern Greek historical studies in Britain, Kings College, London, being the other."[24]

More important than any other influence, in John's life and work, has been his wife Sheila Campbell. It was she who opened up the world of the Sarakatsani for him; who "shared the fieldwork in physical and political conditions which were often unpleasant, and who first won the confidence of a secretive people".[25]

---

24   C.S. Nicholls, *The History of St Antony's College Oxford, 1950-2000,* Macmillan Press in association with St Antony's College, 2000, p. 71.

25   Campbell, *Honour, Family and Patronage,* p. vii.

BIBLIOGRAPHY

Campbell, J.K. (1964) *Honour, Family and Patronage: a Study of Institutions and Moral Values in a Greek Mountain Community*, Oxford: OUP.

—— (1992) "Fieldwork among the Sarakatsani, 1954-55", in *Europe Observed*, ed. João de Pina-Cabral and John Campbell, Macmillan in association with St Antony,s College, Oxford, 148-66.

—— and Philip Sherrard (1968) *Modern Greece*, London: Ernest Benn.

—— (1992) "The Greek Hero", in *Honor and Grace in Anthropology*, ed. J.G. Peristiany and Julian Pitt-Rivers, Cambridge: CUP, 1992, 129-49.

—— (2003) "The Social Sciences Centre, Athens, 1962", in *Koinonikes Epistemes kai Protoporia stin Ellada 1950-1967*, ed. Ioanna Lambiri-Dimaki, Gutenberg and Athens: EKKE, 431-5.

—— (1972) "The Greek Civil War", in *The International Regulation of Civil Wars*, ed. Evan Luard, London: Thames and Hudson, 1972, 37-64.

Loizos, Peter (2004) "Anthropologists and Historians, in Greece and the Christian Mediterranean, with particular reference to the influence of John Campbell", in IV International Congress of History, *Historiography of Modern and Contemporary Greece 1833-2002*, ed. Paschalis M Kitromilides and Triantaphyllos E. Sklavenitis, Athens, vol. 1, 307-17.

Nicholls, C.S. (2000) *The History of St Antony's College Oxford, 1950-2000*, Macmillan in association with St Antony's College.

AUTUMNAL REFRAIN

by Haris Vlavianos

For John Campbell

When the last leaves have fallen
we'll return at last to our familiar, intimate place,
to this cherished sanctuary
that our fatigued body has left unfulfilled
for the necessities of an inevitable knowledge.

It is difficult, almost impossible,
even to choose the adjective
that would lend some meaning
to this bare coldness,
this causeless grief,
that spreads gradually, steadily,
eroding your life's most inner recesses.
A simply, natural gesture
might be the first step,
the beginning of a new attempt.
If not now, not today,
tomorrow without fail.

Lack of imagination?
That too will have to be invented, naturally;
and the stage will be set
as the instructions on the paper demand.
The stone house must be kept erect.
The arch in the front room
(your precious, priceless past) especially this.

And the old lintel with the mermaid.
And the fig tree in the garden, and the oleanders,
and the dry stonewall, all must remain.
All.
That the ruin, the rift, the absence may be revealed.
That the strife, the fall, the work may be appraised.

The autumnal wind
that gave these words their body,
fiercely effacing their metaphysical gleam,
knows all too well the secret they conceal.
As do you
who stoop to get a dry leaf from your doorstep.
The leaf of reality.
The exquisite poem of the genuine.

[Translated from the Greek by the author and Mina Karavanta].

INDEX

Acton, Lord: 131
Adam: 210 220 228
Aegean Islands: 14 19 47 74-5 191
Aegean Sea: 3 5 13-4 16 19 20 32 70 98
Africa: 147 235 240-4 255-6 259
Aigina: 190
Albania: 46 132-3 258 260
Aleppo: 17
Alexander the Great: 109
Alexandria: 11 12 78
Alfonsín, Raul: 141
Algiers: 255
"Alkis": 177
Almeida, Ronaldo de: 247
Alonistaina: 52
Ambeli: 172 175-6 209-10 222-3 227
American Broadcasting Corporation (ABC): 141
Amerindians: 235 241-2
Amouliani (Halkidiki): 173
Amyna, Dimokratiki: 142
Andalusia: 266
Andrade, Oswald de: 234 245-6
Andros: 76
Anglo-Hellenic Lignite Company: 256
Angola: 242
Anzio Landing: 256
Apeiranthos: 101 102
Apple of Dischord: 266
Archbishop of Crete: 75
Arensberg, Conrad: 151
Argaki: 172 173 176
Argentina: 141
Argokoili: 89-93 96-7 103-4
Argyros, Athanasios: 117
Arianism: 237
Armatoloi: 114

Armée d'Orient: 117
Aschenbrenner, : 173
Asia Minor: 14 71 74 102 110 117 123 173 204
Athens College: 139
Athens University: 104 139
Athens: 56 60 63-4 102 115 117 124-5 169-70 190 256 261-2 264
Athos, Mount: 98
Australia: 169 182 257
Austria: 19 72 75 82
Ayios Ioannis tou Tourkou [Tinos]: 72
Ayios Nikolaos: 70 76 78 80 83
Azov: 11

Bahia: 235 239-40 247 248
Balkan Wars: 116 118-9
Balkans: 200
Barbary States: 9 17 31
Barcelona: 6 7 9
Barros, João de: 233
Bastide, Roger: 241
Bavaria: 83 90
Belgium: 131
Benn, Ernest: 263
Besta-Fera: 244
Bey, Halil: 75
Bilac, Olavo: 238 245 248-9
Bitolja [Monastir]: 116 120 121
Black Sea: 5 8 11-4 20
Bolle, Willi: 247-8
Bonaparte, Napoleon: 6 8
Bouboulina, Laskarina: 46 49 60 62
Bourdieu, Pierre: 153 154 179
Braga: 243
Brazil: 231-51
British Infantry Brigade: 256

271

British School (Athens): 261
Bulgaria: 109-12 114-5 119-23 125
Burkhardt, Jakob: 131

Cadiz: 6 7 9
Cambridge University: see University of Cambridge
Campbell, John K.: 70 121-2 147-58 160-5 169 172 174 189 193 195 204 210 220-3 225 227-8 231-2 238 249 255-67 269
Campbell, Sheila: 257-61 267
Canada: 169 182
Cândido, António: 246 247
Cape Town: 257
Capodistrias, Ioannis: 52 90 101
Carneiro, Édison: 239-41 244 248
Carr, Raymond: 264
Catharism: 237
Catholicism: 69-72 74 76-9 82 83 85 93 94 99 100-1 237-9 242-3 245
Centre for Economic Research (Athens): 262
Centre Union Party (EDIN): 138 140
Chios: 47 57 58 74-5 85 98
Chlomoutsi (Fortress): 55
Chora: 97 100-1
Christ: see Jesus Christ
Christmas: 224
Civil War, Greek: 122-4 139 146 180
Clare College, Cambridge: 258
Clark, General Mark: 256
Clogg, Richard: 267
Cold War: 141
Collaro, Bishop: 70 77 78 82
Collingwood, R.G.: 266
Communist Balkan Federation: 117
Communist Democratic Army: 122
Conselheiro, António: 247
Constantine the Great: 92
Constantine, Crown Prince: 115
Constantine, Saint: 105
Constantinople: 57 75-6 78 84 98
Continental Blockade: 13
Continental System: 8
Cook, Captain James: 104-5
Corfu: 133
Corinth: 51 102
Counter-Reformation: 237
Cowan, Jane K.: 159 163-4 173 192

Creole: 243
Crete: 47 75 99 110 114 117-8 121 157 162 195 204
Cunha, Euclides da: 247
Cyclades: 70 73-5 81 83 99
Cyprus: 47 172 176 181 195 260

DaMatta, Roberto: 245-6
Danglis, Panagiotis: 115
David, Pierre: 82
Davidson, Donald: 249
Deakin, William: 261-4
Dellios, Ioannis: 117
Demertzis, Konstantinos: 117
Demetrius, Saint: 224
Denmark 6
Derrida, Jacques: 237
Devil: 231-2 234 235-9 242-50
Dormition of the Mother of God: 211 224
Douglas, Mary: 150 193
Dr. Faustus: 249
Dragoumis, Ion: 111 117
Dragoumis, Stephanos: 111 116-7
Droysen, Johann Gustav: 104
Dubisch, Jill: 173 175-6
Durban: 257
Durkheim, Emile: 266

Easter: 211 220 224 226
Eden: 234-6 245
Edessa: 120
Egypt: 6 53 56 62 81
Elias, Prophet: 224
Ellinika Chronika: 52
Embros: 110
England: see Great Britain
Epidavros: 48, 132
Epirus: 117 118 189 255 258
Etaireia Makedonikon Spoudon: 121
Etaireia, Philomousos: 64
Ethiopia: 257
Ethniki Etaireia: 110
Eurocommunist Party: 142
Europe: 4 8 11 13 16 28 58 60 139 140 147 151 154 158 165 176 182-3 210 235 237 241-3 266
European Community (EC): 141
European Union (EU): 191
Eusebia: 235

INDEX

Evans-Pritchard, E.E.: 147-8 151-2 154-5 157-8 162-4 255 257-60 263 266
Eve: 210
Evgenios II, Patriarch: 75
Evia: 172, 256
Exaltation of the Cross: 211
Exoburgo: 85
Êxu: 239 240 244 248-9

Fabvier, General Charles Nicholas: 63
Falatadhos: 69 82-3
Faubion, James: 185
Filiki Etaireia: 78-9
Finlay, George: 130
Florence: 256
Fortes, Meyer: 258
France: 2 6 8 16 19 53 62-3 72 77-8 82 94 133 203 264
French Revolution: 11
Freyre, Gilberto: 236
Friedl, Ernestine: 194 197-8 260

Galaxidi: 14
Gandhi, Indira: 141
Gastouni: 61
Gell, Alfred: 240
Genoa: 4-6 8-14 18
Georgantopouloi Family: 78 81 83
Georgantopoulos, Antonios: 78
Georgantopoulos, Fransiskos: 78 84
Georgantopoulos, Ioannis: 78
Georgantopoulos, Konstantinos: 79-81
George, Saint: 224
Germany: 203
Giddens, Anthony: 153
Gilsenan, Michael: 266
Glauber, Rocha: 234
Glyfada: 256
God and the Devil in the Land of the Sun: 234
God: 210 214 218-20 222 224 226 237-9 241
Goethe, Johann Wolfgang. von: 248-9
Gounaris, Basil C.: 265
Gouras, General Asimina: 62
Grande Sertão: Veredas: 244
Great Britain: 1 6 8 19 55 62 72 105 256 260 265
Great Lent: 211
Greco-Turkish War (1919-22): 129

Greek Communist Party: 117 137 139
Greek National Guards: 256
Greek People's Liberation Army (ELAS): 122 256
Greek Social Sciences Centre (EKKE): 262
Greek War of Independence: 20 45-7 49 51 59 61 70 80 83 94 101 129
Gregorios, Patriarch: 75
Grivas, General Theodorakis: 49-50
Guatemala: 99
Gulf of Corinth: 15
Gulf of Volos: 14
Gulf War (1990-1): 141
Gyparis, Pavlos: 118

Hades: 234-6 245
Hadzirados: 76
Hammond, Nicholas: 258
Hapsburg Empire: 4
Harlaftis, Gelina: 265
Harvard University: 139 264
Hatzi (Crete): 174
Hawaii: 104-5
Hell: 238
Henty, G.A.: 263
Hermes: 85
Herzfeld, Michael: 190 192-4 197 200 265
Highland Division: 255
Hiroshima: 256
Hirschon, Renée: 154 157 173 175-6 190-1 193 195 197-200 228 265
History of France: 266
HMS Cambrian: 74
Holanda, Sérgio Buarque de: 234
Holland: 6
Holy Friday: 228
Holy Mysteries: 212
Holy Thursday: 221 223 228
Holy Week: 228
Homer: 133
Honour, Family, and Patronage: 147 150 152-5 158 159 161 163 189 231 259-60 263 265
Hourani, Albert: 266
Hydra: 14 16 48 73 75-7 79 81 82

Iberian Peninsula: 7 243
Ileia: 55

273

Iliad: 162
Ilinden: 110
India: 141
Indicopleustes, Cosmas: 98
Inglezou, Altana Grylinou: 52
Inquisition: 233 235 237 241 244 245 249
Institute of Social Anthropology: 258
Internal Macedonian Revolutionary Organisation (IMRO): 113
Introdução à Literatura Brasileira: 246
Ioannina: 258
Ionia: 1 14 19 29 54-6 169
Ionian Bank Archives: 265
Ionian Sea: 3 15-6
Iosif of Rogai, Bishop: 58
Iraq: 141
Isaiah, Prophet: 228
Islam: 53 57 243-4
Istanbul: 5 12-3 20 72
Italy: 3 4 8 255-6
Iviron: 98

Jackson, Andrew: 139
Japan: 192 196 256
Jefferson, Thomas: 139
Jenkins, Romily: 130
Jerusalem: 8 19
Jesuits: 236-7
Jesus Christ: 91-2 210-9 222 224-7 233
Jews: 114 235 238 241
John the Baptist, Saint: 92
Joll, James: 261-2
Just, Roger: 265

Kagkadis, Iakovos: 81
Kagkadis, Stamatelos: 80-1 84
Kagkadis, Stamatios: 84
Kairi, Evanthia: 64
Kalamos: 56
Kalapothakis, Dimitrios: 110-1 115 116
Kalavryta: 55
Kallergis, Dimitrios: 51 116
Kallergis, Sophia (née Rentis): 51
Kalo: 176
Kalymnos: 81 181
Kanellopoulos, Panayiotis: 260 261
Kapodistrias, Ioannis: 48 85
Kapudan Pasha: 75-6 81 101
Karaiskakis, Georgios: 50 54

Karamanlis, Constantine: 137-8 142 261
Karatzas, Ioannis: 50
Karpathos: 190
Karpofora (Messenia): 173
Kasomoulis, Nikolaos: 52
Kasos: 14 81
Katechakis, Georgios: 118
Katomeri: 169-70 172 180-1
Katounia: 256 267
Kavala: 119
Kavaranta, Mina: 270
Kaynarca, Küçük: 18
King George II: 115 119
King Otto: 71 85 90 93 95 102-3
King's College School Wimbledon: 255
King's College, London: 267
Kirtsoglou, Elisabeth: 185
Kokkinia: 190 195 198 204 228
Kolbe, Al.: 52
Kolettis, Ioannis: 54
Koliopoulos, John: 263
Kolokotronis, Eleni (née Bouboulina): 49-50
Kolokotronis, Gennaios: 50-51
Kolokotronis, Kollinos: 50
Kolokotronis, Panos: 49-50
Kolokotronis, Photeini (née Tzavelas): 50
Kolokotronis, Theodoros: 49-50 54 57
Kolonaki: 185 190
Kontogeorgi, Elizabeth: 265
Koppel, Ted: 141
Koraes, Adamantios: 133
Koronos: 90-2 96 101 103
Kroushevo: 121
Kydonies (Ayavalik): 56
Kydonies: 57

Laikon Komma: 117
Lamb of God: 215
Land of the Holy Cross: 234
Laskaris, Vassilis: 101
Latour, Bruno: 246
Leach, Edmund: 150 163
Leros: 81
Lesbos: 14
Leukada: 169
Levant: 3-5 8-9 14 30-1 57 82
Lévi-Strauss, Claude: 163
Liberal Party: 117 120 123

INDEX

Libya: 257
Limni: 256
Livadeia: 256
Livadha: 48 69 82-3
Livorno: 6-12 15 18
Locke, John: 140
Loizos, Peter: 153 172-3 175-6 266
London Conference: 94
London: 255
Louis XVIII, King: 77
Loutra: 77
Luke, Saint: 93 104

Macedonia: 47 56 109-25 191
Macedonian Scientific Institute: 121
Madrid, Miguel de la: 141
Maggioros, Ioannis (Doumbrogiannis): 92-3 96
Makedoniki Enosis: 120
Makedonikon Komitaton: 110
Makedonomachoi: 109-10 115-6 120 122
Makris, Eupraxia (née Razi-Kotsikas): 51
Makronisi: 180
Makrygiannis, Ioannis: 51 55
Malaby, Thomas: 157 159 163
Malaga: 6-7 9
Malaysia: 199
Malta: 3-4 6-9 14-5 18-9
Mani: 50 61-2 256
Manolas, Christodoulos: 91-2
Mansolas, Drosos: 81
Mantzarakis, Evangelos: 77 79 81
Marengo: 8
Marina, Saint: 91-2
Markis, Dimitrios: 51
Maro: 185
Marri Baluchi: 159
Marseilles: 4 6-10
Martin of Dume, Saint: 243
Mary: see Virgin Mary
Maurer, Professor Georg von: 93 95 104
Mauromichalis, Kyriakoulis: 61
Mauss, Marcel: 163 192-3
Mavrikion (Peloponnesos): 176
Mavrogordatos, George: 266
Mavrokordatos, Aikaterina: 50
Mavrokordatos, Alexandros: 50
Mavromatis, Gerasimos: 92 96
Mavromichalis, Georgios: 51
Mavromichalis, Kyriakoulis: 116

Mavromihalis, Konstantinos: 50
Mavroyeni, Manto: 46 51-2 59-60 62
Mavroyeni, Stefanos: 83
Mavroyeni, Georgios: 83-4
Maya: 99-100
Mediterranean Sea: 3-5 7 9 11 13-4 20 71 82 147 202 262-3
Mega Spilaion (Monastery): 55
Meganisi: 169 173 177
Mehmet Ali: 81
Melas, Pavlos: 110-11
Melbourne: 257
Merton: 255
Mesi: 72
Messolongi: 14, 51-2 56-8 60
Metaxas, Ioannis: 119 121 139 264
Metaxas, Konstantinos: 72-3
Mexico: 141
Meyer, Johan Jacob: 52
Miaoulis, Admiral Andreas: 79-80
Middle East: 200 266
Middlesex Regiment: 255
Milos: 101
Ministry of Religion (Greece): 52-3
Minnesota: 139
Modern Greece: 263-4 266
Modis, Georgios: 122
Moldavia: 78
Montana Vermala: 257
Moraites: 57
More, Thomas: 234
Morea: 49 55 63 75-6
Mother of God: see Virgin Mary
Mourouzis, Phanariote Dimitrios 16
Mouzelis, Nicos: 143
Muslims: 1 23 25 33-4 72 77 94 111 116-7 119
Muzzulù: 69
Mykonos: 14 53 62 73 76
Myres, Sir John: 264
Mytilini: 190 197

Nafplion: 76 79
Nagasaki: 256
Nagib, Lúcia: 234 245-6
Naousa: 57
Napoleonic Wars: 6 8 14
Natal University: 257
National Church of Greece: 83-4

National Organisation 'Pavlos Melas': 110 118-9
"Nations of the Modern World": 263
Nauplio: 50 56-7 59 60 62
Nautis, Kyriaki: 59
Nautis, Michail: 59
Navariko: 61
Navarino: 82
Naxos: 73 76 81 83-4 89-95 97-105
Nea Moni: 98
Needham, Rodney: 147
Nena: 185
New Deal: 139
New Democracy: 138 142 144
New World: 234-5
New York Greek Committee: 71
Nicaea: 98
Nikitaras, Angelina (née Nikitas Stamatelopoulos): 62
Nikitopoulis, Nikolaos: 64
"Nikos": 170 172 177
Noronha, Fernando: 234
North Atlantic Treaty Organisation (NATO): 141
Northern Sporades: 56
Notaras, Ioannis: 51
Notaras, Panagiotis: 51
Nuer: 148 152
Nyerere, Julius: 141

Odessa: 11-2 75 78
Odyssey: 133
Orthodox Church: 69-72 77-80 83-5 90 93-5 97 100-3 132-3 152 154 209 215 219 224 227-9 232 267
Os Sertões: 247
Ottoman Empire: 1-8 10-3 15-8 45-6 49 52-3 55-8 60 63-4 69 70-8 81 83-5 94 101 110 112-3 115 132 200 259
Oxford University: 147 151 155 157 255 258 261-2 264 267

Padilha, Maria: 244
Paine, Robert: 158-60 162 163
Pakistan: 159
Palaskas, Christos: 54
Palestine: 256
Palme, Olaf: 141
Panagia Argokoiliotissa: 89 92 97
Panagia Khrisopigis: 98

Panagia Portaitissa: 98
Panagia Theotokos: 103
Panagia: see Virgin Mary
Panhellenic Socialist Movement (PASOK): 138-46
Papaflessas (née George Flessas): 50 55
Papagos, Marshall: 261
Papandreou, George: 145
Papandreou, Andreas: 137-46 262
Paparrigopoulos, Constantine: 132-3
Papastavrou, S.J.: 258
Pataxiarchis, Efthymios: 156
Pappas, Takis: 143
Paraskevi, Saint: 224
Paros: 73-4 91 96
Pasha, Ibrahim: 55 62
Pasha, Kioutachi: 62-3
Patras: 63
Paulucci, Admiral: 82
Paximades Family: 78-9 81 83
Paximades, Fransiskos: 75 79-81
Peiramatiko: 144
Peloponnese: 14 85 111 121
Pembroke College, Cambridge: 255-6
Pentecost: 211
Pentecostal Evangelicals: 244
Pepelasis, Adamantios: 142
Peristiany, J.G.: 154 194-5 231 258 262
Peters, Emrys: 266
Phanariot: 26 47 50 63 78-9 83
Philiki Etaireia: 59
Pina-Cabral, João de: 232 235 241 243 246
Piraeus: 173 190
Pitt-Rivers, Julian: 266
Plato: 234
Polyavaros: 62
Pompa, Cristina: 235 238
Populist Party: 117-20 123
Poros: 52
Portugal: 233 241 243
Prussia: 19 52
Psara: 14 47 56-8 72 76 81
Puckler-Muskau, Prince Hermann Ludwig Heinrich von: 85

Radcliffe-Brown, Alfred: 155 162
Ragusa: 3 4 8
Ranke, Leopold von: 104
Raybaud, Maxime: 73 75

INDEX

Razi-Kotsikas, Samos: 51
Rentis, Theocharis: 51
Republic: 234
Rhodes: 190
Richia (Peloponnese): 177
Rodrigues, Nina: 241
Romance d'A Pedra do Reino: 248
Romania: 154
Romano, Ruggiero: 3 5
Romans: 132 237 243
Roosevelt, Franklin Delano: 139
Rosa, Guimarães: 244-5 247 248
Roumeli: 57 85
Royalist Party: 121
Ruel, Malcolm: 238
Russia: 11 16 18-20 75
Russo-Ottoman Wars: 6 12 18-9

Sachtouris, Admiral: 84
Sahlins, Marshall: 104-5
Saint Basil's Day: 218
Sakelariou, Rita: 142
Sakhas, Manouil: 92 96
Salamina: 56 63
Salles, Walter: 246
Salonica: 4
Sami: 158
Samos: 76 118-9
Sansi-Roca, Roger: 243
Santorini: 14 76-7 80 100
Sarakatsani: 147-50 152 154 156 158 161 164 172 174 189 195 204-5 210 220-7 231-2 236 238 243 248-50 255 258-60 265 267
Savvaina, Staurianna: 61
Scobie, General Ronald: 256
Searle, John: 197
Second Coalition: 8
Selim III: 3 16 17 20
Serbia: 120
Serres: 117
Sfakia: 81
Shakespeare, William: 129
Sherrard, Philip: 256 261-3 266-7
Shukman, Harry: 264
Sicily: 4 255
Simitis, Costas: 138 143 145
Siphnos: 98
Sisinis, Georgios: 61
Skopelos: 14

Slav-Macedonian National Front: 122
Slavs: 110 112 119-23 125 132-3
Smyrna: 4 59 69 77 82 102
Social and Economic Atlas of Greece: 262
Sofiko: 51
Sohos (Macedonia): 173
Sophia, Saint: 98
Souliote/Souli: 50 61
South Africa: 169 182 257
South African Women's Army: 257
Souza, Laura de Mello e: 233-5 237 242-3 249
Soviet Union: 141
Spadaro, Michel: 72 77
Spain: 4 6 8
Spartochori: 169 170 174-8 180 182
Special Operations Executive (SOE): 258
Spetses: 14 46 49 72 81
Spiridon, Emmanuel: 74 77-9
St. Anthony's College, Oxford: 255 261 263 267
Stasa: 185
Statistical Yearbook of Greece: 175
Sterea Ellada: 61
Stern, Michael: 256
Stevenson, Adlai: 139
Stewart, Charles: 153 232 265
Stornaris, Nikolaos: 52
Suassuna, Ariano: 245 248-9
Sublime Porte: 16 50
Sudan: 257 266
Swabia: 243
Swan, Charles: 71
Sweden: 6 141
Switzerland: 257
Sylivos, Bishop Gavriil: 70-1 73 75 79-80 83-5 95-6 99
Syria: 72
Syros: 56 63-4 73-6 78 82 85 96

Taganrog: 11-2
Tanzania: 141
Terra da Santa Cruz: 233
The Devil and the Land of the Holy Cross: 233
The Fall: 210 220 228
The Idea of History: 266
The Origins of European Thought: 266
The Sanusi of Cyrenaica: 148
Theodore, Saint: 224

Theotokis, Georgios: 115-6
Thesaly: 14
Thesprotia: 259
Thessaloniki: 109-10 112 118 121 123
Thessaly: 47
Thomas, Keith: 237
Thrace: 47 60
Tinos: 14 69-77 79-85 89 93-5 99-100 175
Toynbee, Arnold: 129-30
Transfiguration: 211
Trieste: 6-7 9 78
Trikkala: 51
Trikorpha: 61
Trikoupis, Spyridion, 50-1 111
Tripolis: 79
Tripolitsa: 53 61
Trypanis, Constantine: 258
Tsontos, Georgios: 121
Tunisia: 73
Tupinambá: 238
Turkey: see Ottoman Empire
Tuscany: 4
Twelve Gospels of the Passion: 228
Tzavelas, Kitsos: 50
Tzochatzopoulos, Akis: 145

Under the Bo Tree: 155
Union for the Democratic Centre: 137-8
United Kingdom (UK): 203
United Nations Educational, Scientific and Cultural Organization (UNESCO): 262
United Nations Relief and Rehabilitation Administration (UNRRA): 123
United States of America (USA): 58 60 131 139-41 169 182 203 234 265
University of Cambridge: 255 257-8 266
University of Thessaloniki: 264
Utopia: 234

Valença: 233

Valtetsi: 61
Varkiza Agreement: 256
Varnakiotis, Andreas: 54
Varvakio: 144
Vasos, Eleni: 62
Vasos, General Mavrovouniotis: 62
Vathy: 169-70
Vatican: 71 82
Velho, Otávio: 244 246
Venice 3-7 9 19 45 71 101 133
Venizelos: 116-9
Veremis, Thanos: 263 265
Verga: 62
Verger, Pierre: 241
Vespucci, Americo: 234
Vieira, António Father: 237
Virgin Mary: 70 75 80 83-5 89-93 99 103-4 210-1 213 215 217 222 224 265
Visvizis, Domna: 60
Vixe Maria: Deus e o Diabo no Bahia: 247
Vlachs: 46 114 120 132 133
Voskopoulos, Tolis: 142
Vothroi: 92 96 102 103

War of Candia: 94
Woodhouse, C.M.: 266
World War II: 125

Yalman, Nur: 155
Yerania: 173 175-6
Young Turk Revolt: 115
Ypsilantis, Demetrios: 51-2 74 79

Zacharia, Konstantina: 61-2
Zagori: 221 258 260
Zagorochoria: 258-9
Zaimis: 50
Zeldin, Theodore: 264 266
Zinkeisen, Johann Wilhelm: 104